MY SPACE

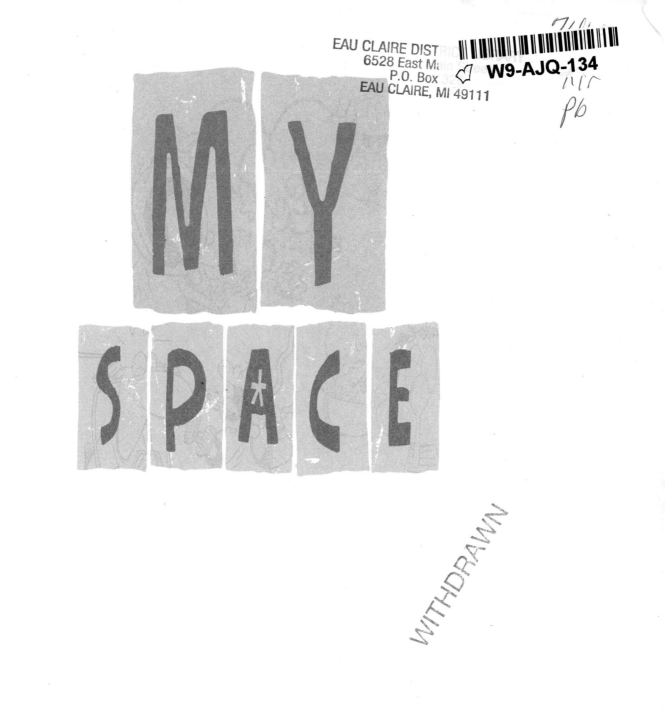

Other *Baby Blues*® Books from Andrews McMeel Publishing

Guess Who Didn't Take a Nap?
I Thought Labor Ended When the Baby Was Born
We Are Experiencing Parental Difficulties . . . Please Stand By
Night of the Living Dad
I Saw Elvis in My Ultrasound
One More and We're Outnumbered!
Check, Please . . .
threats, bribes & videotape
If I'm a Stay-at-Home Mom, Why Am I Always in the Car?
Lift and Separate
I Shouldn't Have to Scream More Than Once!
Motherhood Is Not for Wimps
Baby Blues®: Unplugged
Dad to the Bone
Never a Dry Moment
Two Plus One Is Enough
Playdate: Category 5
Our Server Is Down
Something Chocolate This Way Comes
Briefcase Full of Baby Blues®
Night Shift
The Day Phonics Kicked In

Treasuries

The Super-Absorbent Biodegradable Family-Size Baby Blues®
Baby Blues®: Ten Years and Still in Diapers
Butt-Naked Baby Blues®
Wall-to-Wall Baby Blues®
Driving Under the Influence of Children
Framed!
X-Treme Parenting

Baby Blues
Scrapbook 24 by
**Rick Kirkman &
Jerry Scott**

MY
SPACE

**Andrews McMeel
Publishing, LLC**

Kansas City

Baby Blues® is syndicated internationally by King Features Syndicate, Inc. For information, write King Features Syndicate, Inc., 300 West Fifty-Seventh Street, New York, New York 10019.

My Space copyright © 2009 by Baby Blues Partnership. All rights reserved. Printed in the United States of America. No part of this book may be used or reproduced in any manner whatsoever without written permission except in the case of reprints in the context of reviews. For information, write Andrews McMeel Publishing, LLC, an Andrews McMeel Universal company, 1130 Walnut Street, Kansas City, Missouri 64106.

09 10 11 12 13 RR2 10 9 8 7 6 5 4 3 2 1

ISBN-13: 978-0-7407-8089-9
ISBN-10: 0-7407-8089-1

Library of Congress Catalog Card Number: 2008940075

www.andrewsmcmeel.com

Find *Baby Blues*® on the Web at
www.babyblues.com.

———— **ATTENTION: SCHOOLS AND BUSINESSES** ————

Andrews McMeel books are available at quantity discounts with bulk purchase for educational, business, or sales promotional use. For information, please write to: Special Sales Department, Andrews McMeel Publishing, LLC, 1130 Walnut Street, Kansas City, Missouri 64106.

To Dr. Gail Hertz, for your friendship, your inspiration, your grace, and your humor. Thank you.

—J.S.

For Taylor—Congratulations on your master's!
For Maddie—Congratulations on your B.A.!
With love, pride, and admiration.

—Mom & Dad

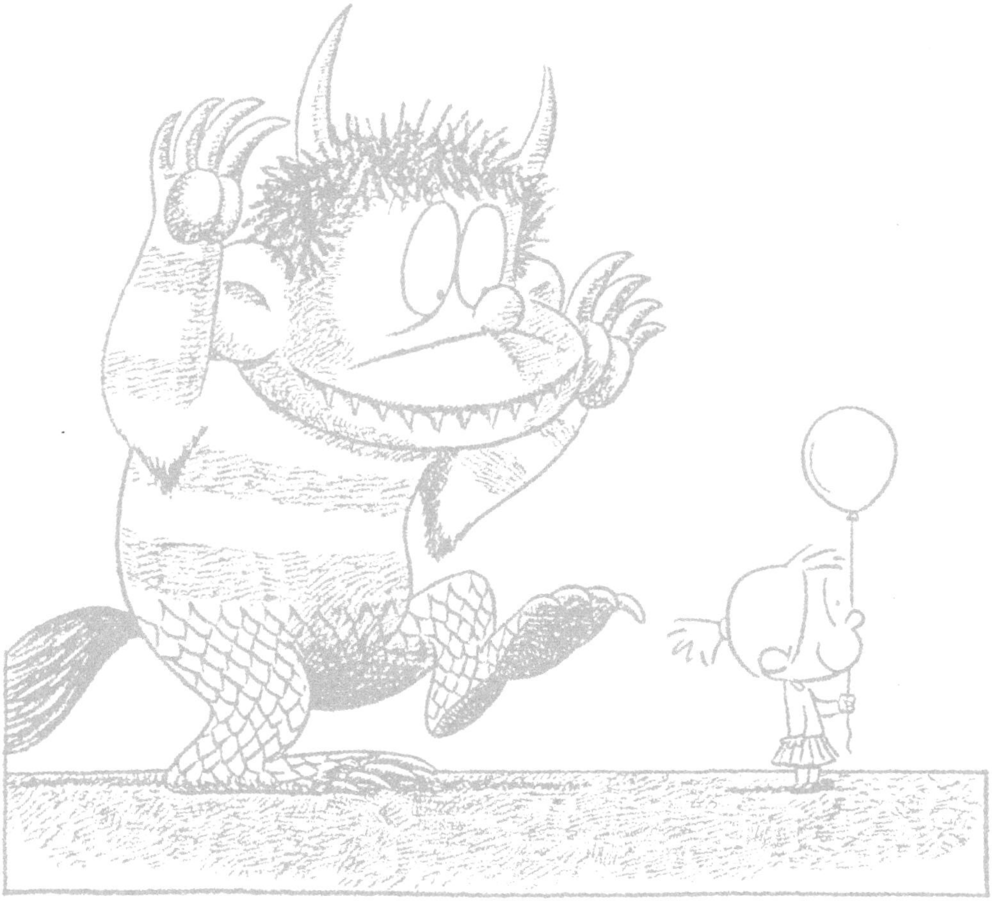

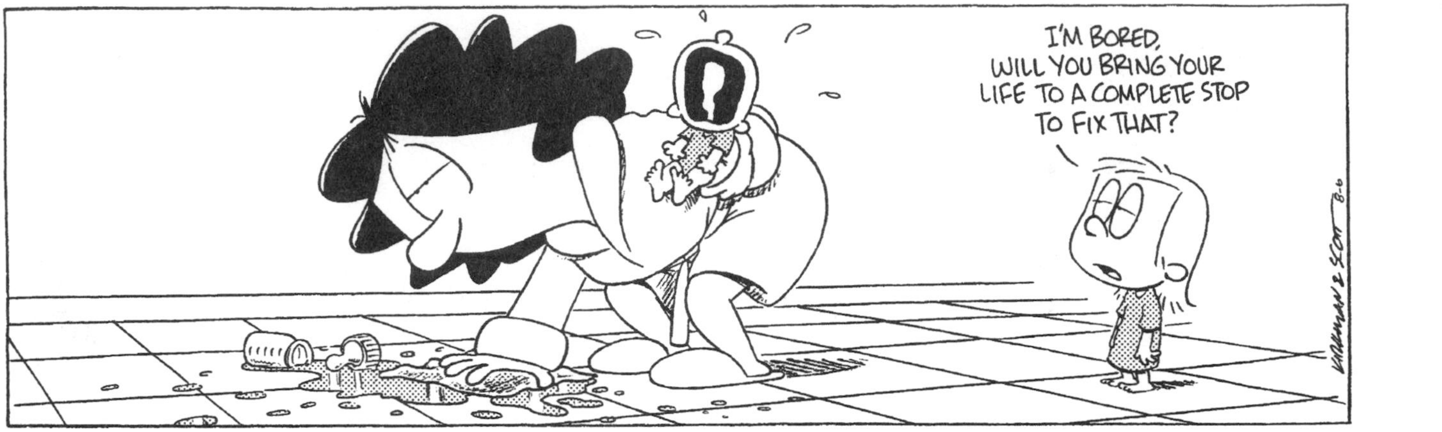
I'M BORED, WILL YOU BRING YOUR LIFE TO A COMPLETE STOP TO FIX THAT?

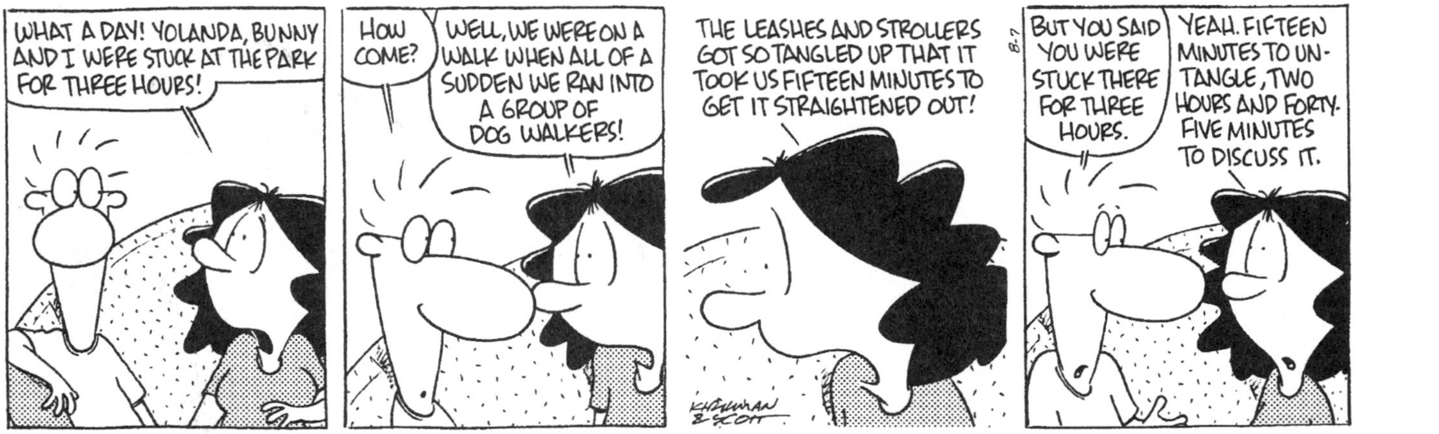
WHAT A DAY! YOLANDA, BUNNY AND I WERE STUCK AT THE PARK FOR THREE HOURS!
HOW COME?
WELL, WE WERE ON A WALK WHEN ALL OF A SUDDEN WE RAN INTO A GROUP OF DOG WALKERS!
THE LEASHES AND STROLLERS GOT SO TANGLED UP THAT IT TOOK US FIFTEEN MINUTES TO GET IT STRAIGHTENED OUT!
BUT YOU SAID YOU WERE STUCK THERE FOR THREE HOURS.
YEAH. FIFTEEN MINUTES TO UN-TANGLE, TWO HOURS AND FORTY-FIVE MINUTES TO DISCUSS IT.

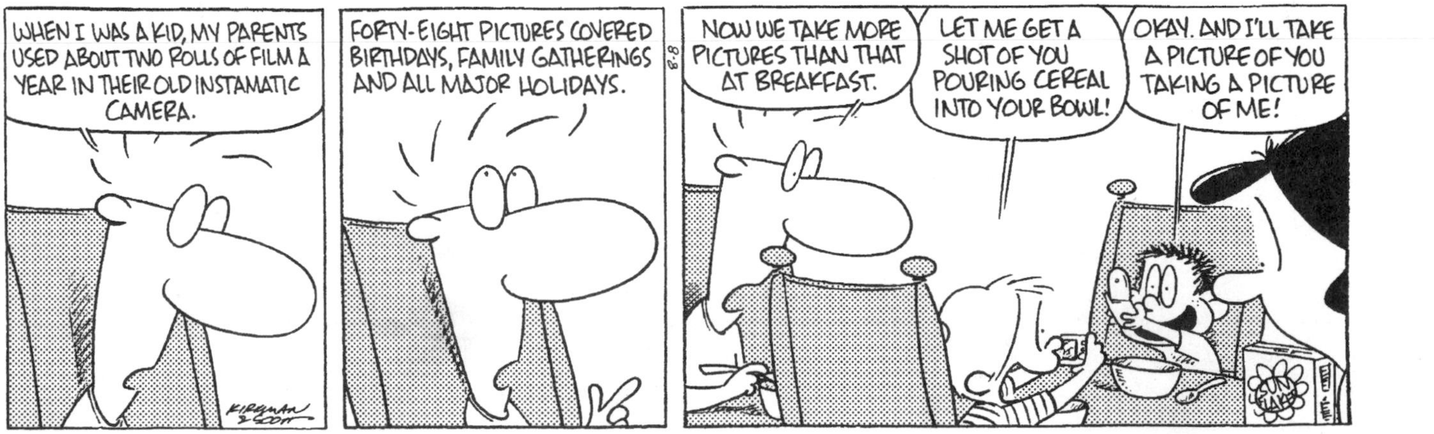
WHEN I WAS A KID, MY PARENTS USED ABOUT TWO ROLLS OF FILM A YEAR IN THEIR OLD INSTAMATIC CAMERA.
FORTY-EIGHT PICTURES COVERED BIRTHDAYS, FAMILY GATHERINGS AND ALL MAJOR HOLIDAYS.
NOW WE TAKE MORE PICTURES THAN THAT AT BREAKFAST.
LET ME GET A SHOT OF YOU POURING CEREAL INTO YOUR BOWL!
OKAY. AND I'LL TAKE A PICTURE OF YOU TAKING A PICTURE OF ME!

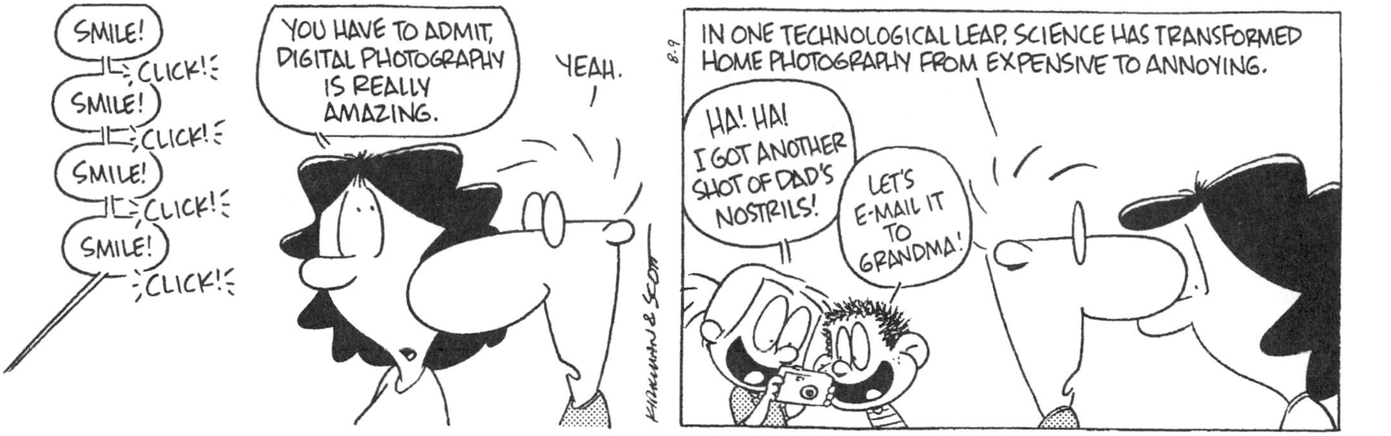
SMILE!
CLICK!
SMILE!
CLICK!
SMILE!
CLICK!
SMILE!
CLICK!
YOU HAVE TO ADMIT, DIGITAL PHOTOGRAPHY IS REALLY AMAZING.
YEAH.
IN ONE TECHNOLOGICAL LEAP, SCIENCE HAS TRANSFORMED HOME PHOTOGRAPHY FROM EXPENSIVE TO ANNOYING.
HA! HA! I GOT ANOTHER SHOT OF DAD'S NOSTRILS!
LET'S E-MAIL IT TO GRANDMA!
KIRKMAN & SCOTT

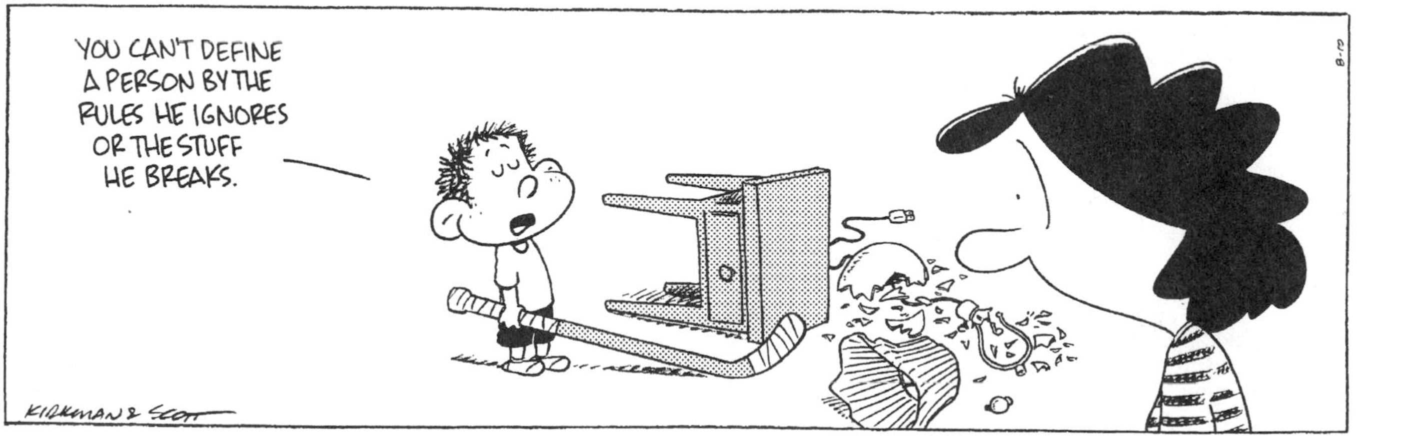
YOU CAN'T DEFINE A PERSON BY THE RULES HE IGNORES OR THE STUFF HE BREAKS.
KIRKMAN & SCOTT

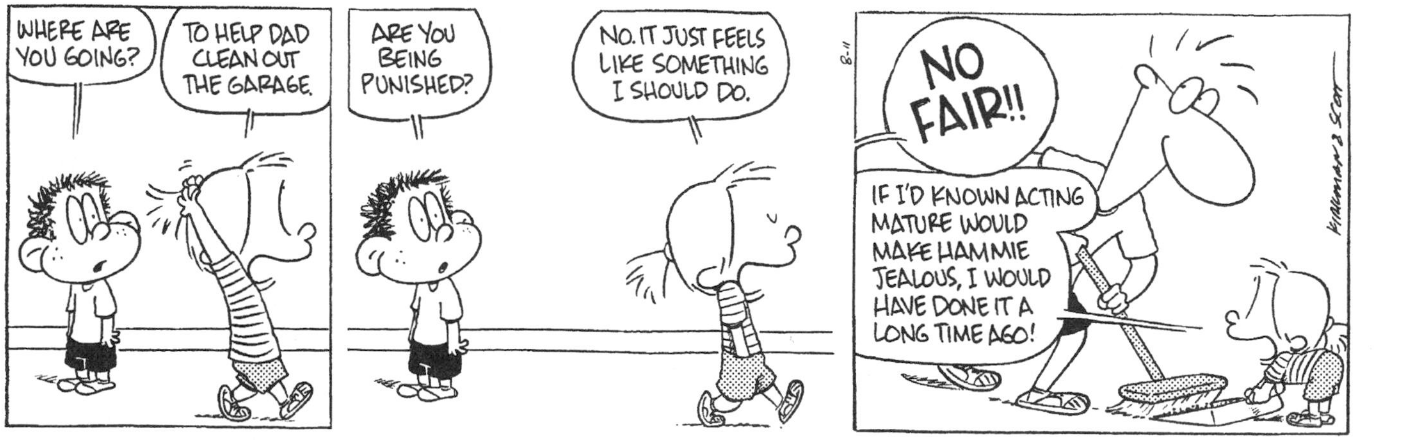
WHERE ARE YOU GOING?
TO HELP DAD CLEAN OUT THE GARAGE.
ARE YOU BEING PUNISHED?
NO. IT JUST FEELS LIKE SOMETHING I SHOULD DO.
NO FAIR!!
IF I'D KNOWN ACTING MATURE WOULD MAKE HAMMIE JEALOUS, I WOULD HAVE DONE IT A LONG TIME AGO!
KIRKMAN & SCOTT

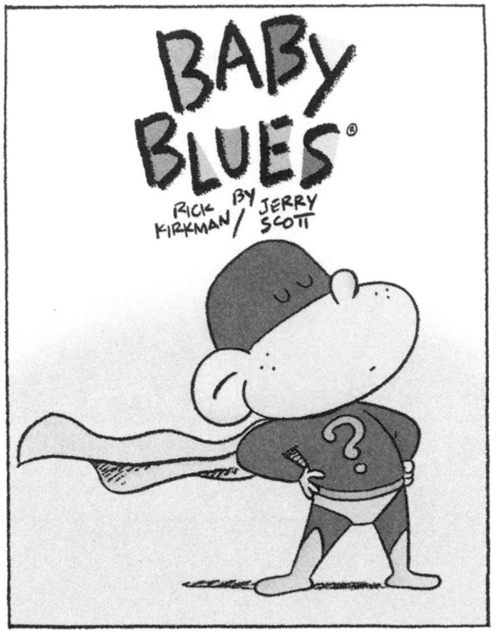
BABY BLUES®
BY RICK KIRKMAN / JERRY SCOTT

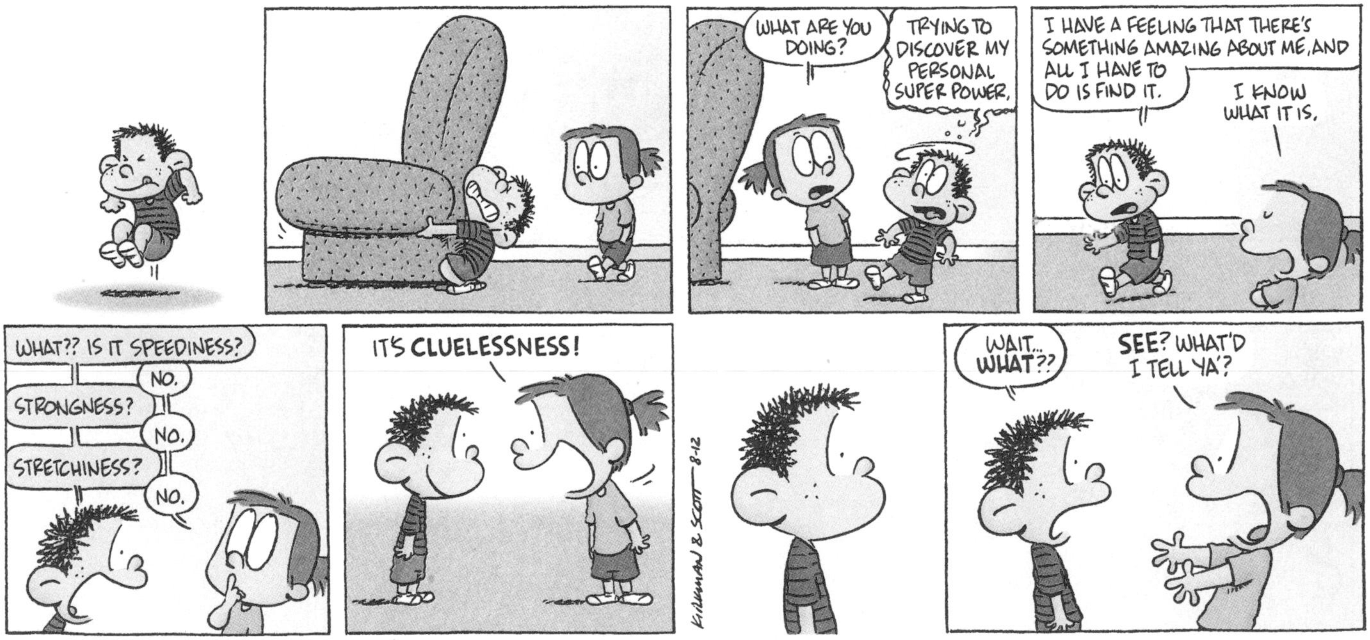
WHAT ARE YOU DOING?
TRYING TO DISCOVER MY PERSONAL SUPER POWER.
I HAVE A FEELING THAT THERE'S SOMETHING AMAZING ABOUT ME, AND ALL I HAVE TO DO IS FIND IT.
I KNOW WHAT IT IS.
WHAT?? IS IT SPEEDINESS?
NO.
STRONGNESS?
NO.
STRETCHINESS?
NO.
IT'S CLUELESSNESS!
KIRKMAN & SCOTT 8-12
WAIT... WHAT??
SEE? WHAT'D I TELL YA'?

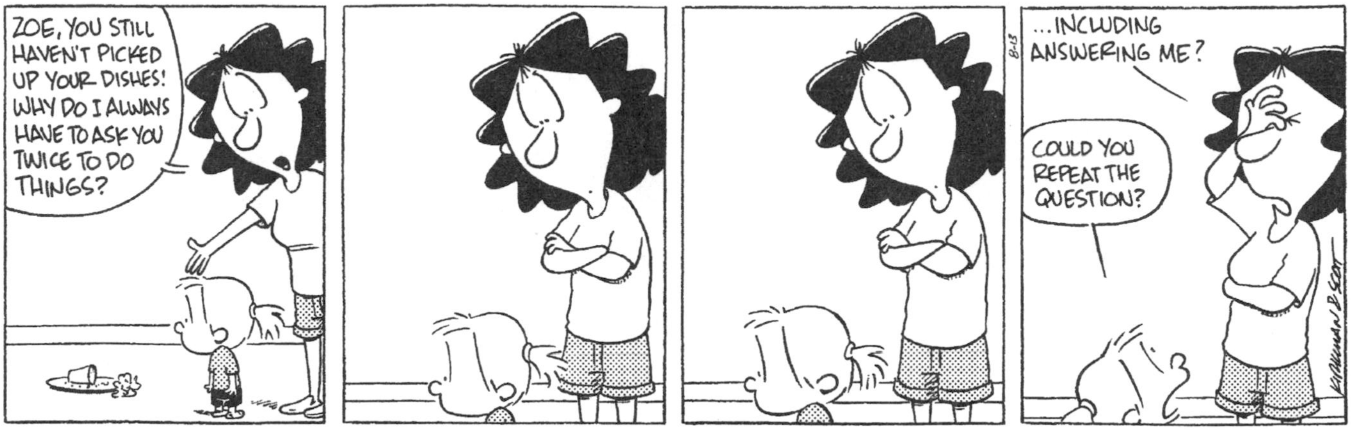
ZOE, YOU STILL HAVEN'T PICKED UP YOUR DISHES! WHY DO I ALWAYS HAVE TO ASK YOU TWICE TO DO THINGS?
COULD YOU REPEAT THE QUESTION?
...INCLUDING ANSWERING ME?
KIRKMAN & SCOTT

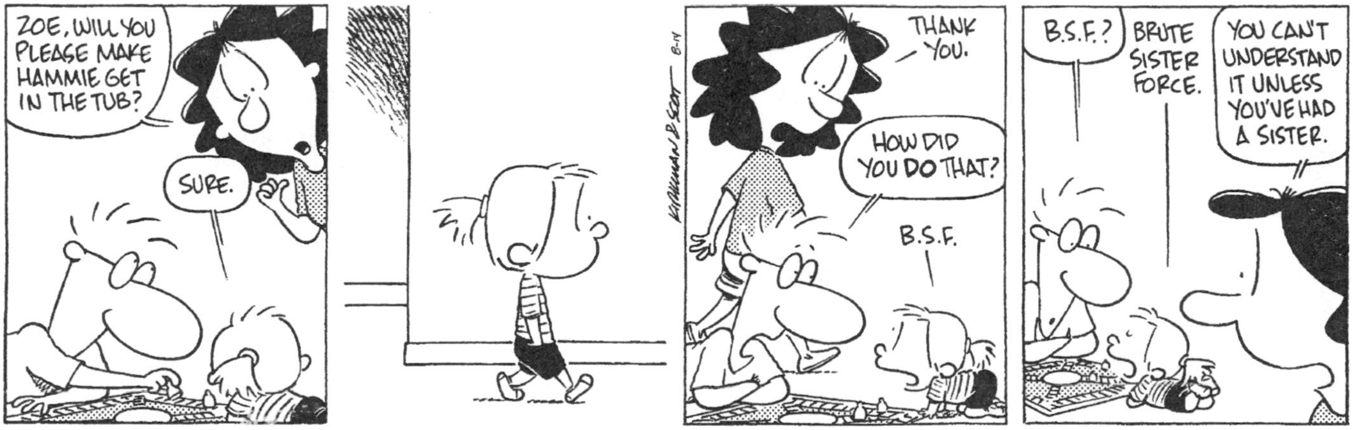
ZOE, WILL YOU PLEASE MAKE HAMMIE GET IN THE TUB?
SURE.
KIRKMAN & SCOTT
THANK YOU.
HOW DID YOU DO THAT?
B.S.F.
B.S.F.?
BRUTE SISTER FORCE.
YOU CAN'T UNDERSTAND IT UNLESS YOU'VE HAD A SISTER.

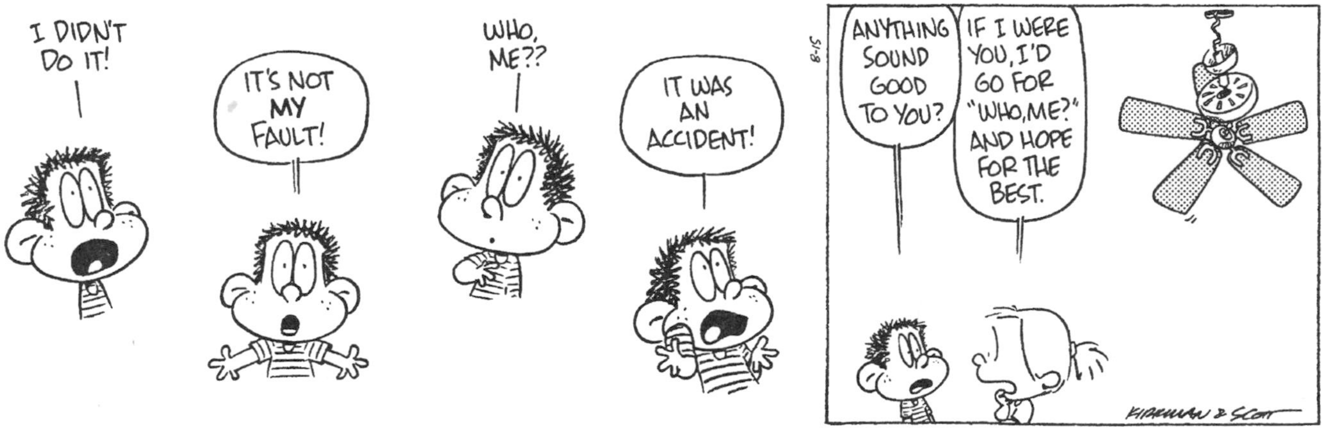
I DIDN'T DO IT!
IT'S NOT MY FAULT!
WHO, ME??
IT WAS AN ACCIDENT!
ANYTHING SOUND GOOD TO YOU?
IF I WERE YOU, I'D GO FOR "WHO, ME?" AND HOPE FOR THE BEST.
KIRKMAN & SCOTT

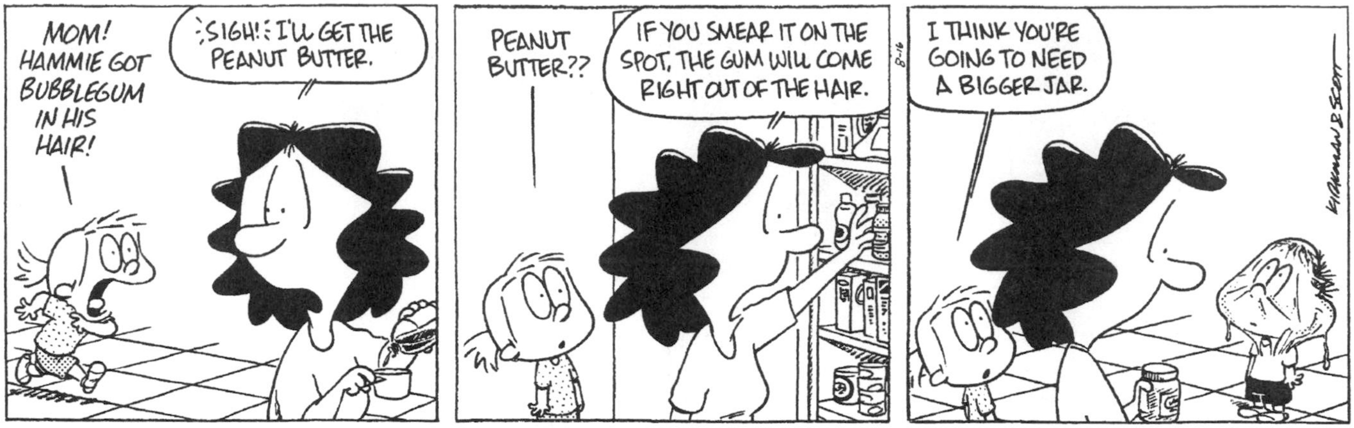
MOM! HAMMIE GOT BUBBLEGUM IN HIS HAIR!
:SIGH!: I'LL GET THE PEANUT BUTTER.
PEANUT BUTTER??
IF YOU SMEAR IT ON THE SPOT, THE GUM WILL COME RIGHT OUT OF THE HAIR.
I THINK YOU'RE GOING TO NEED A BIGGER JAR.

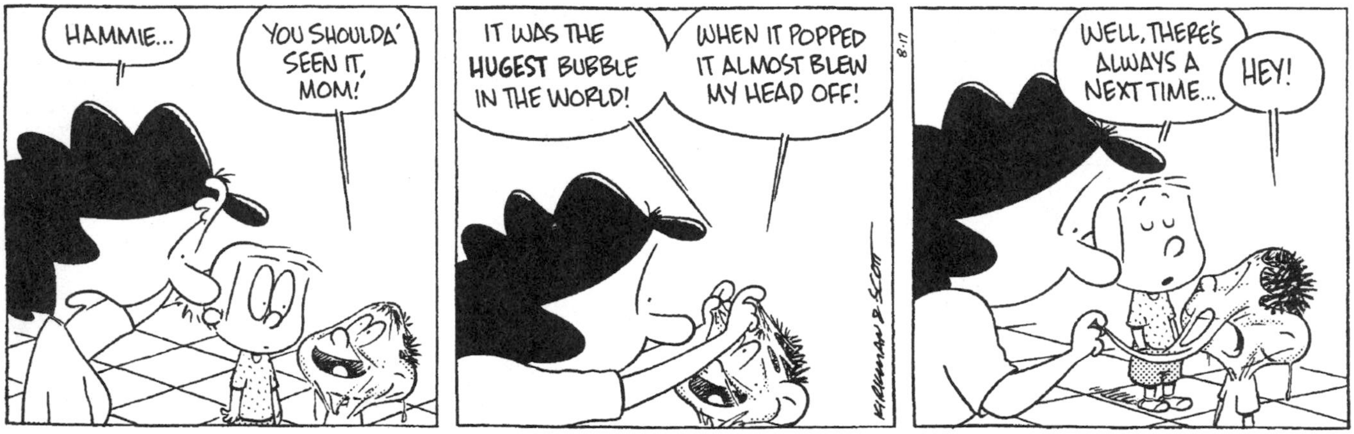
HAMMIE...
YOU SHOULDA' SEEN IT, MOM!
IT WAS THE **HUGEST** BUBBLE IN THE WORLD!
WHEN IT POPPED IT ALMOST BLEW MY HEAD OFF!
WELL, THERE'S ALWAYS A NEXT TIME...
HEY!

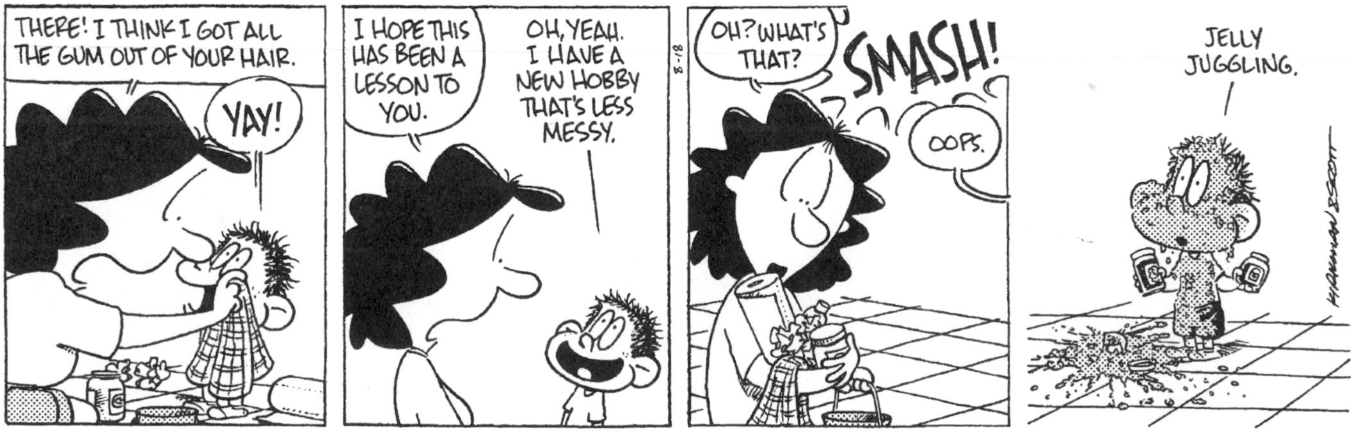
THERE! I THINK I GOT ALL THE GUM OUT OF YOUR HAIR.
YAY!
I HOPE THIS HAS BEEN A LESSON TO YOU.
OH, YEAH. I HAVE A NEW HOBBY THAT'S LESS MESSY.
OH? WHAT'S THAT?
SMASH!
OOPS.
JELLY JUGGLING.

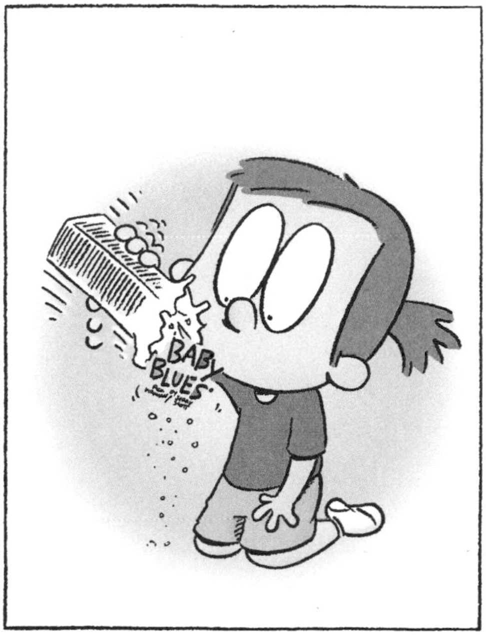
BABY BLUES

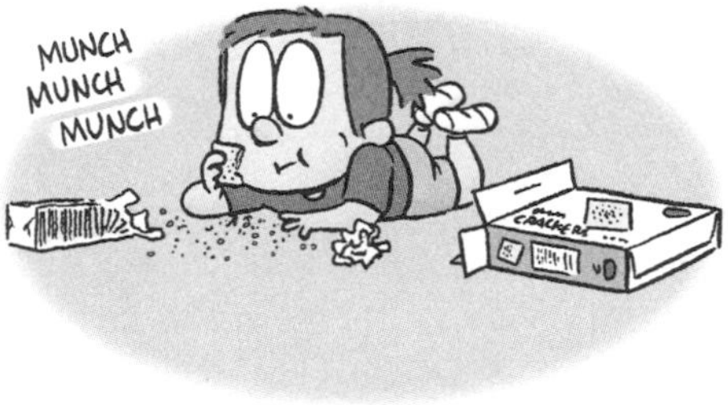
MUNCH
MUNCH
MUNCH

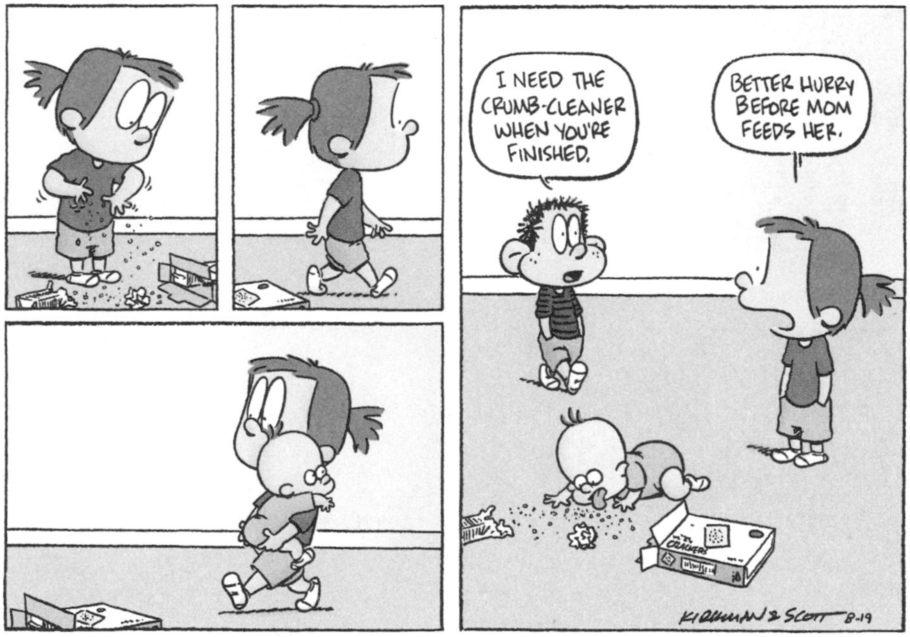
I NEED THE CRUMB-CLEANER WHEN YOU'RE FINISHED.
BETTER HURRY BEFORE MOM FEEDS HER.
KIRKMAN & SCOTT 8-19

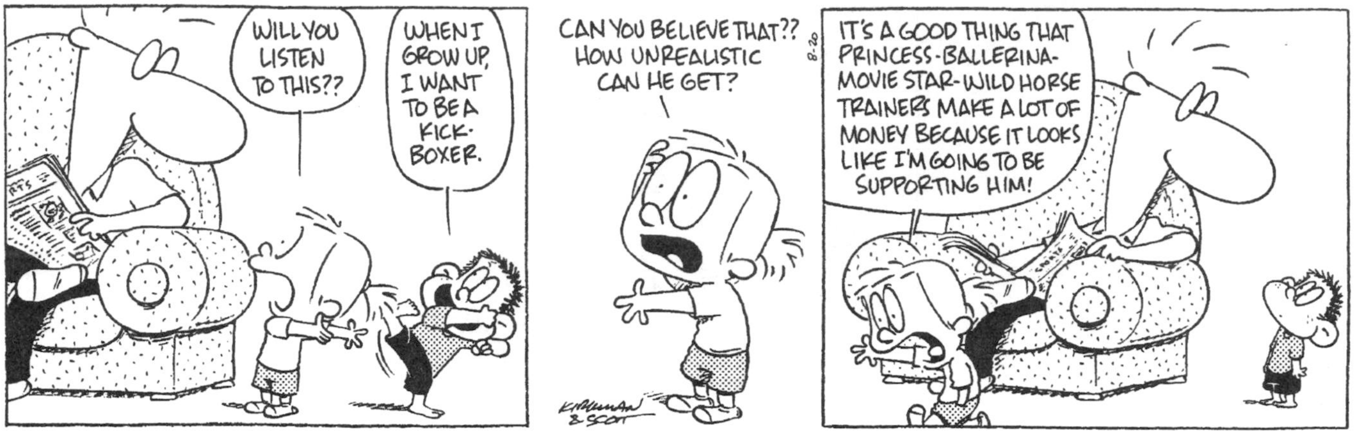
WILL YOU LISTEN TO THIS??
WHEN I GROW UP, I WANT TO BE A KICK-BOXER.
CAN YOU BELIEVE THAT?? HOW UNREALISTIC CAN HE GET?
IT'S A GOOD THING THAT PRINCESS-BALLERINA-MOVIE STAR-WILD HORSE TRAINERS MAKE A LOT OF MONEY BECAUSE IT LOOKS LIKE I'M GOING TO BE SUPPORTING HIM!
KIRKMAN & SCOTT
8-20

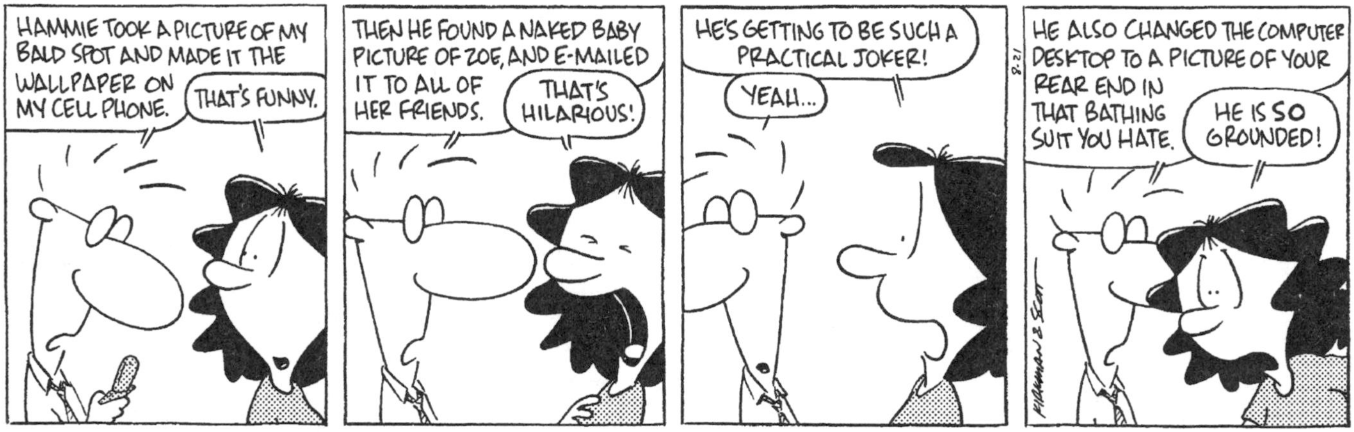
HAMMIE TOOK A PICTURE OF MY BALD SPOT AND MADE IT THE WALLPAPER ON MY CELL PHONE.
THAT'S FUNNY.
THEN HE FOUND A NAKED BABY PICTURE OF ZOE, AND E-MAILED IT TO ALL OF HER FRIENDS.
THAT'S HILARIOUS!
HE'S GETTING TO BE SUCH A PRACTICAL JOKER!
YEAH...
HE ALSO CHANGED THE COMPUTER DESKTOP TO A PICTURE OF YOUR REAR END IN THAT BATHING SUIT YOU HATE.
HE IS SO GROUNDED!
8-21
KIRKMAN & SCOTT

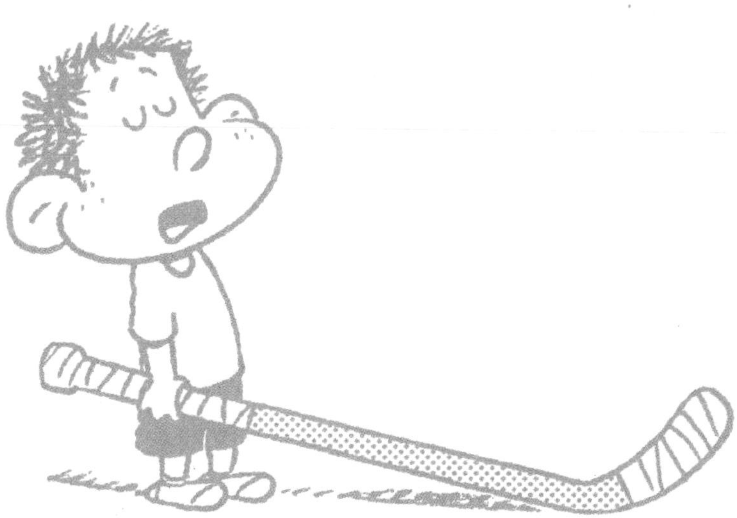

Patient Parenting Tip #406

Keep kids off guard with random acts of generosity.

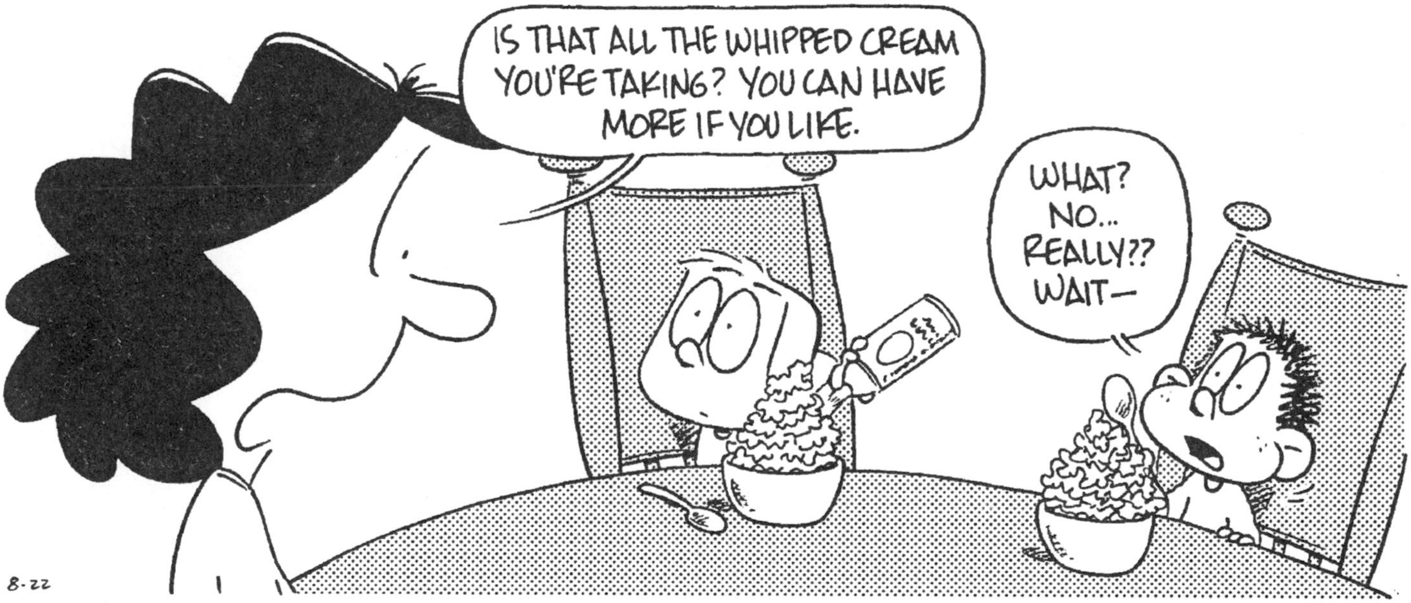
IS THAT ALL THE WHIPPED CREAM YOU'RE TAKING? YOU CAN HAVE MORE IF YOU LIKE.
WHAT? NO... REALLY?? WAIT—
8-22

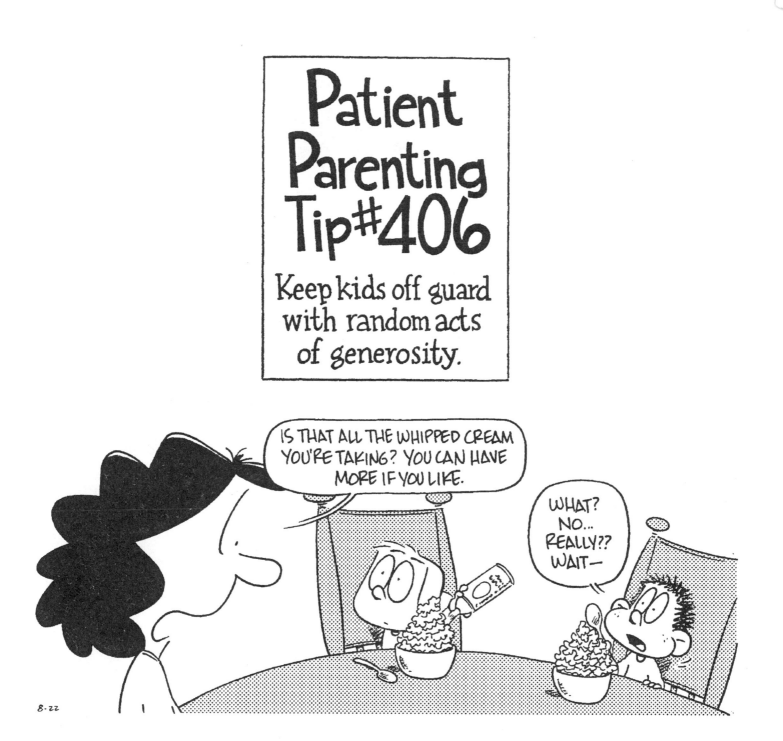

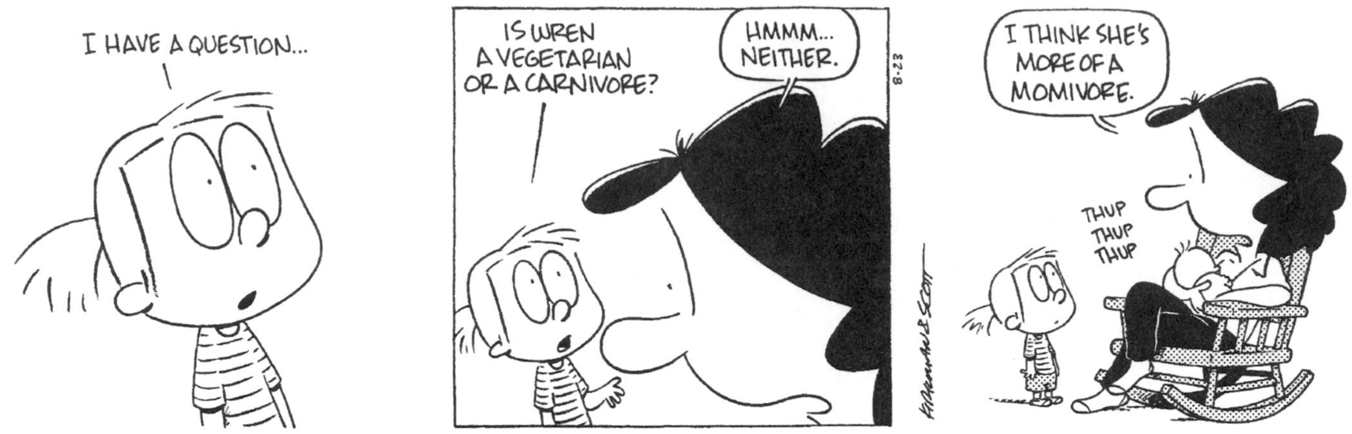
I HAVE A QUESTION...
IS WREN A VEGETARIAN OR A CARNIVORE?
HMMM... NEITHER.
I THINK SHE'S MORE OF A MOMIVORE.
THUP THUP THUP

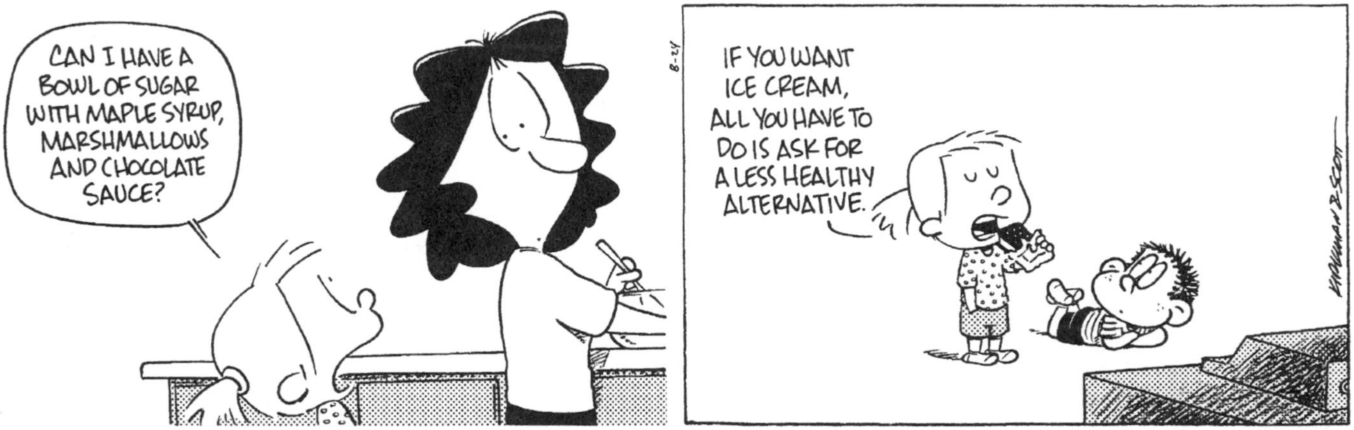
CAN I HAVE A BOWL OF SUGAR WITH MAPLE SYRUP, MARSHMALLOWS AND CHOCOLATE SAUCE?
IF YOU WANT ICE CREAM, ALL YOU HAVE TO DO IS ASK FOR A LESS HEALTHY ALTERNATIVE.

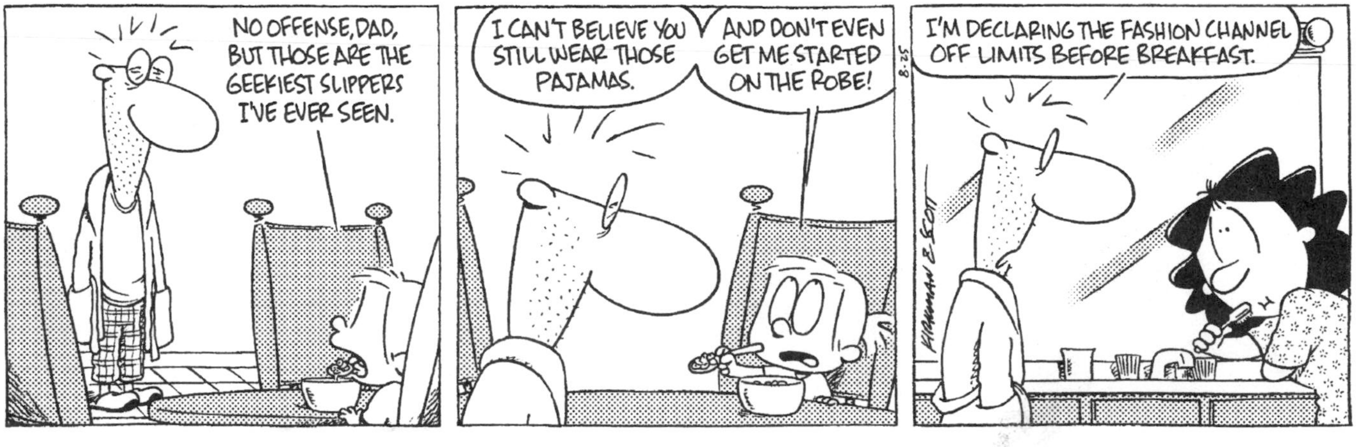
NO OFFENSE, DAD, BUT THOSE ARE THE GEEKIEST SLIPPERS I'VE EVER SEEN.
I CAN'T BELIEVE YOU STILL WEAR THOSE PAJAMAS.
AND DON'T EVEN GET ME STARTED ON THE ROBE!
I'M DECLARING THE FASHION CHANNEL OFF LIMITS BEFORE BREAKFAST.

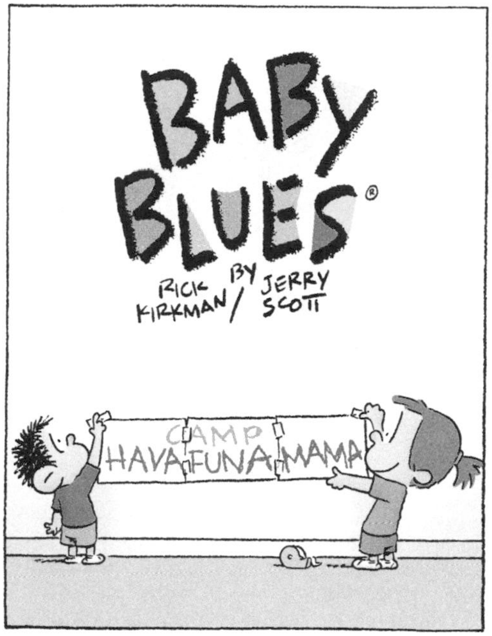
BABY BLUES®
BY RICK KIRKMAN / JERRY SCOTT
CAMP HAVA FUNA MAMA

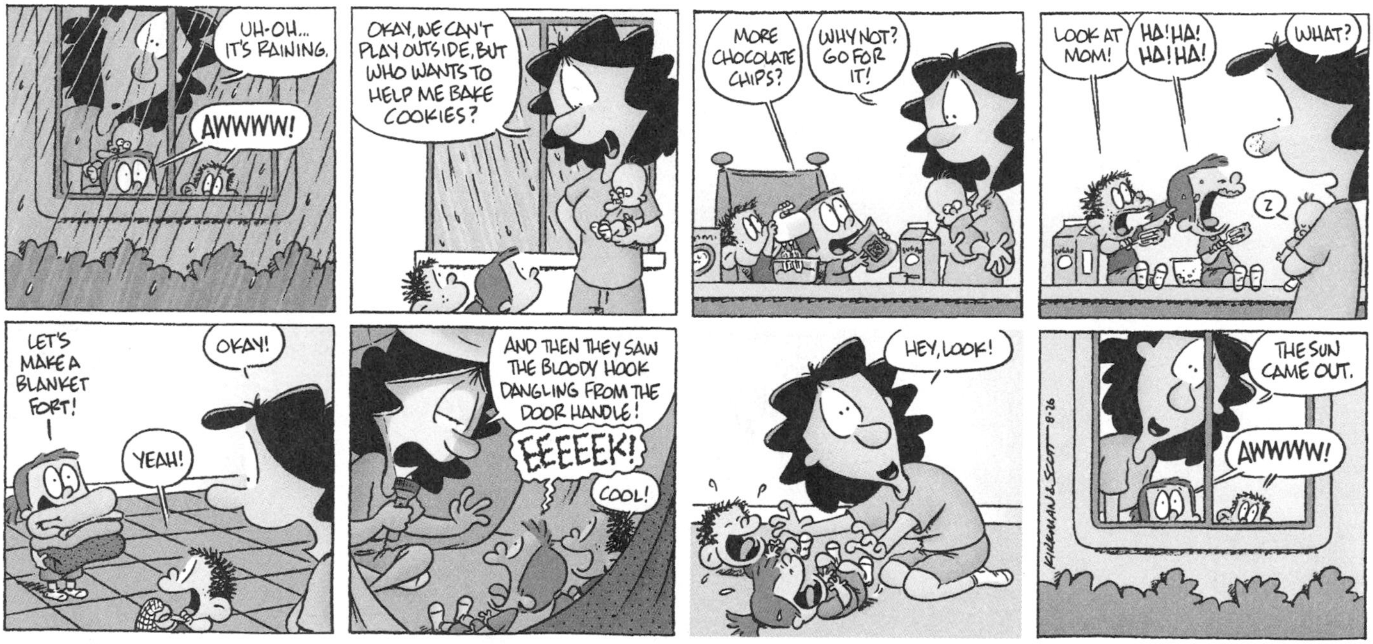
UH-OH... IT'S RAINING.
AWWWW!
OKAY, WE CAN'T PLAY OUTSIDE, BUT WHO WANTS TO HELP ME BAKE COOKIES?
MORE CHOCOLATE CHIPS?
WHY NOT? GO FOR IT!
LOOK AT MOM!
HA! HA! HA! HA!
WHAT?
LET'S MAKE A BLANKET FORT!
OKAY!
YEAH!
AND THEN THEY SAW THE BLOODY HOOK DANGLING FROM THE DOOR HANDLE!
EEEEEK!
COOL!
HEY, LOOK!
KIRKMAN & SCOTT
THE SUN CAME OUT.
AWWWW!

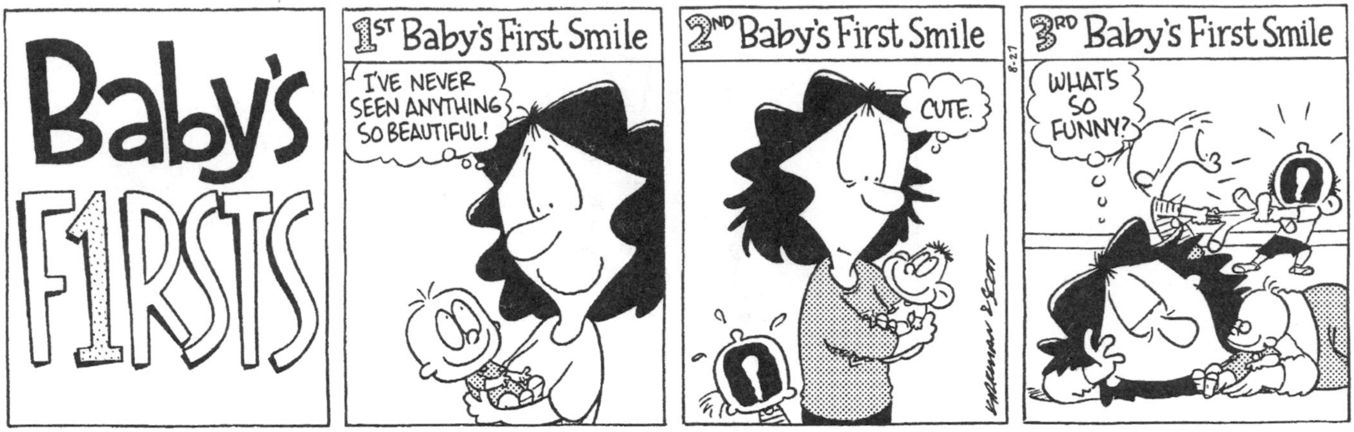
Baby's F1RSTS
1ST Baby's First Smile
I'VE NEVER SEEN ANYTHING SO BEAUTIFUL!
2ND Baby's First Smile
CUTE.
8-27
3RD Baby's First Smile
WHAT'S SO FUNNY?

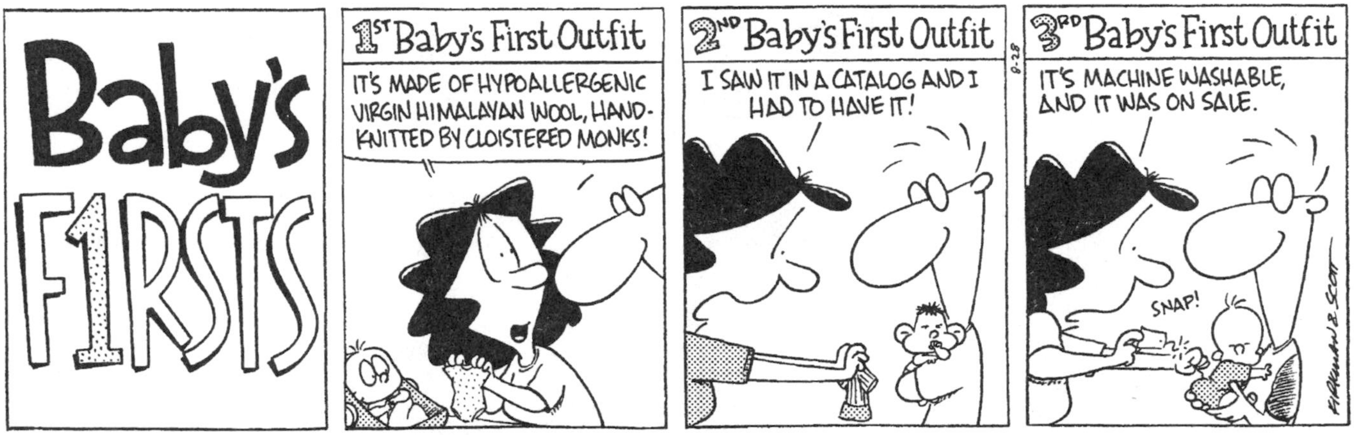
Baby's F1RSTS
1ST Baby's First Outfit
IT'S MADE OF HYPOALLERGENIC VIRGIN HIMALAYAN WOOL, HAND-KNITTED BY CLOISTERED MONKS!
2ND Baby's First Outfit
8-28
I SAW IT IN A CATALOG AND I HAD TO HAVE IT!
3RD Baby's First Outfit
IT'S MACHINE WASHABLE, AND IT WAS ON SALE.
SNAP!

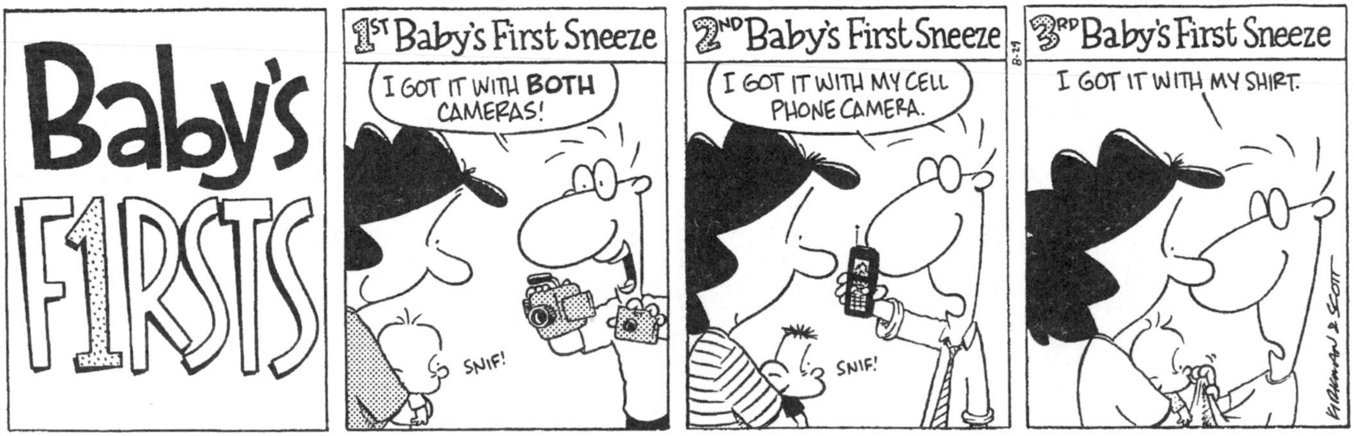
Baby's F1RSTS
1ST Baby's First Sneeze
I GOT IT WITH BOTH CAMERAS!
SNIF!
2ND Baby's First Sneeze
8-29
I GOT IT WITH MY CELL PHONE CAMERA.
SNIF!
3RD Baby's First Sneeze
I GOT IT WITH MY SHIRT.

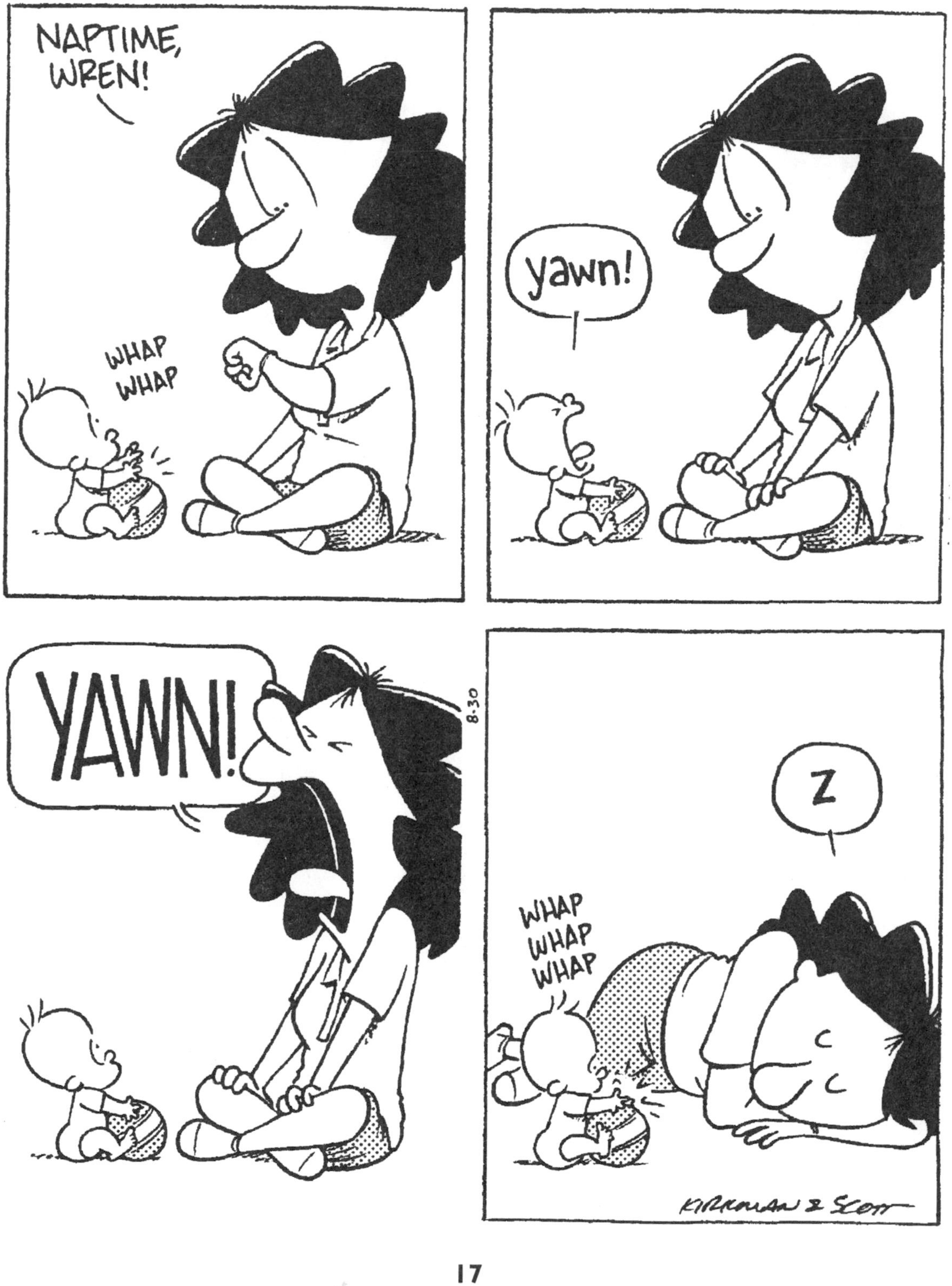
NAPTIME, WREN!
WHAP WHAP
yawn!
YAWN!
8-30
Z
WHAP WHAP WHAP
KIRKMAN & SCOTT

8-31
WHEN LIFE GIVES YOU LEMONS...
!
Z
KIRKMAN & SCOTT

GNAW
GNAW
GNAW
WAP!
WAP!
WAP!
9-1
YOUR SERVE.
FORFEIT.
KIRKMAN & SCOTT

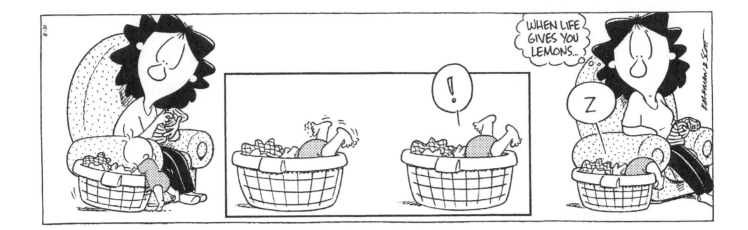

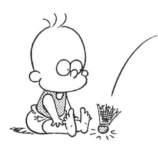

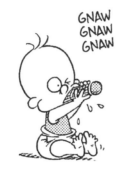

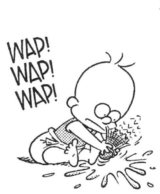

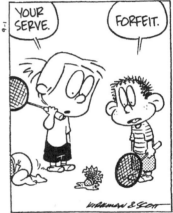

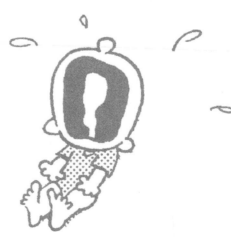

BABY BLUES®
BY RICK KIRKMAN / JERRY SCOTT

HI MOM. HI DAD. WHAT'S FOR LUNCH?
GRILLED CHEESE AND HOT DOGS.
WILL YOU USE THE FAKE CHEESE? IT MELTS SO MUCH BETTER THAN THE REAL STUFF!
YEAH. AND IT TASTES ABOUT A MILLION TIMES BETTER, TOO.
AND I LIKE THOSE FAKE HOT DOGS.
OH, YEAH! THESE ARE GOOD!
FOR DESSERT CAN WE HAVE SOME OF THAT FAKE WHIPPED CREAM YOU BOUGHT?
YUM!
IF YOU USED PAPER PLATES, YOU'D BE FOUR-FOR-FOUR.
FINE! RUB IT IN, WHY DON'T YOU?
KIRKMAN & SCOTT

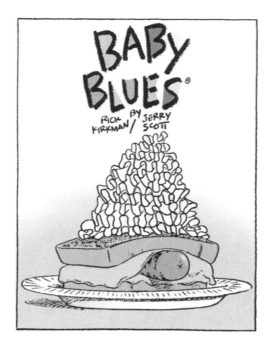

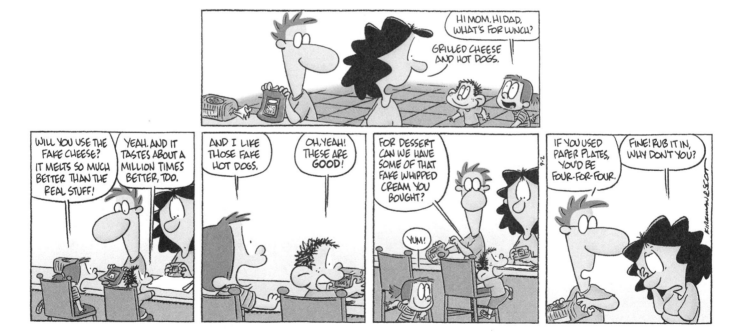

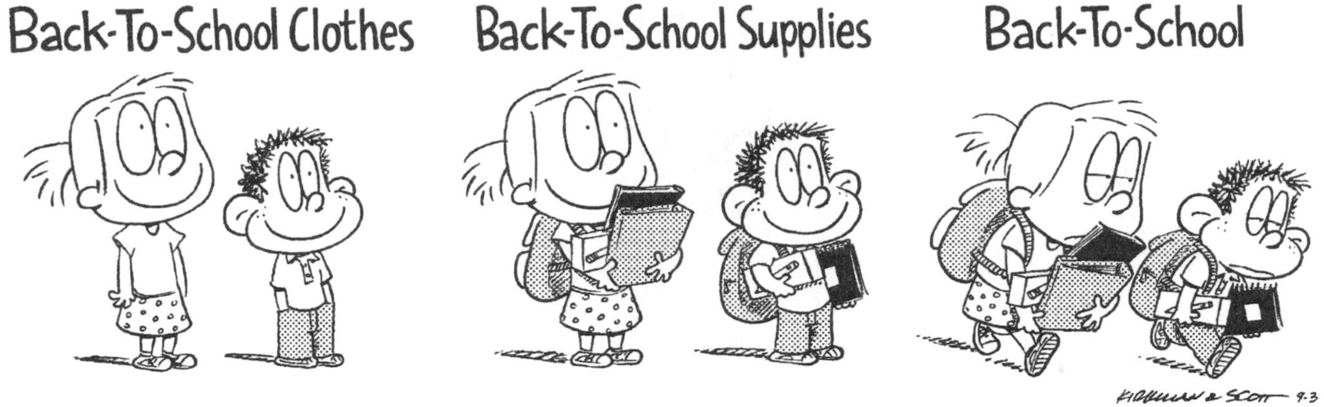
Back-To-School Clothes
Back-To-School Supplies
Back-To-School
KIRKMAN & SCOTT 9-3

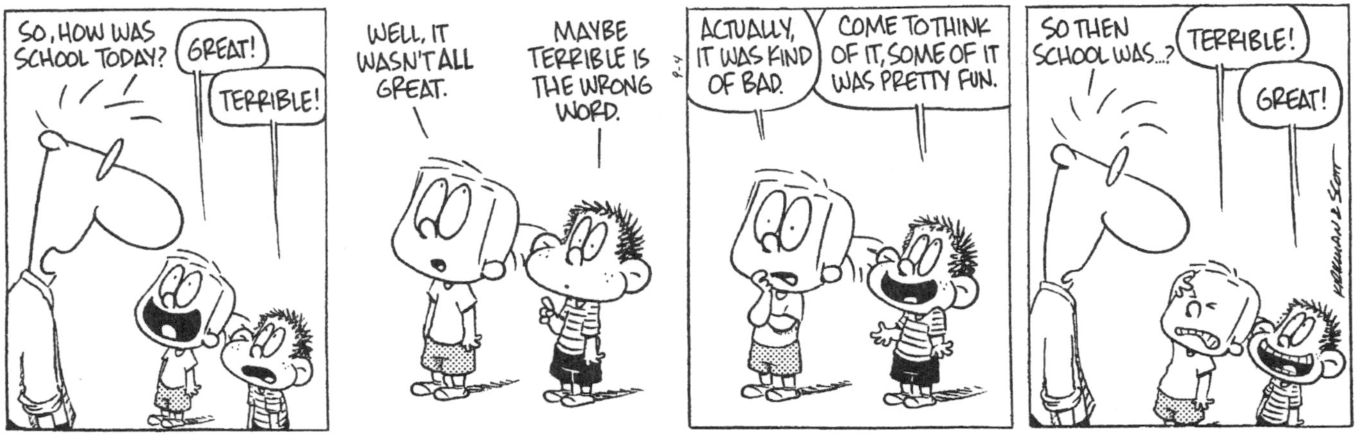
SO, HOW WAS SCHOOL TODAY?
GREAT!
TERRIBLE!
WELL, IT WASN'T ALL GREAT.
MAYBE TERRIBLE IS THE WRONG WORD.
ACTUALLY, IT WAS KIND OF BAD.
COME TO THINK OF IT, SOME OF IT WAS PRETTY FUN.
SO THEN SCHOOL WAS...?
TERRIBLE!
GREAT!
KIRKMAN & SCOTT

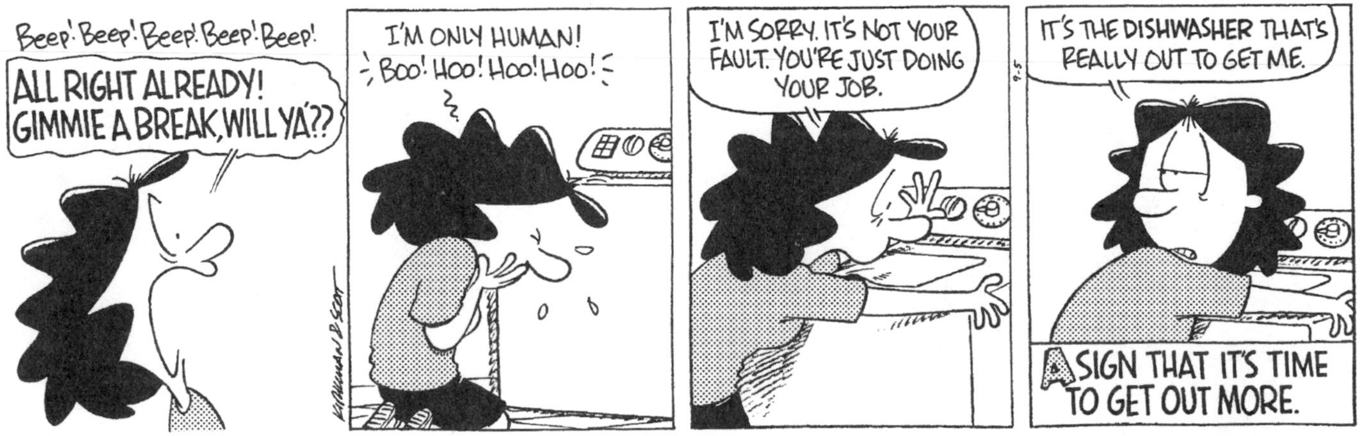
Beep! Beep! Beep! Beep! Beep!
ALL RIGHT ALREADY! GIMMIE A BREAK, WILL YA'??
I'M ONLY HUMAN!
Boo! Hoo! Hoo! Hoo!
I'M SORRY. IT'S NOT YOUR FAULT. YOU'RE JUST DOING YOUR JOB.
IT'S THE DISHWASHER THAT'S REALLY OUT TO GET ME.
A SIGN THAT IT'S TIME TO GET OUT MORE.
KIRKMAN & SCOTT

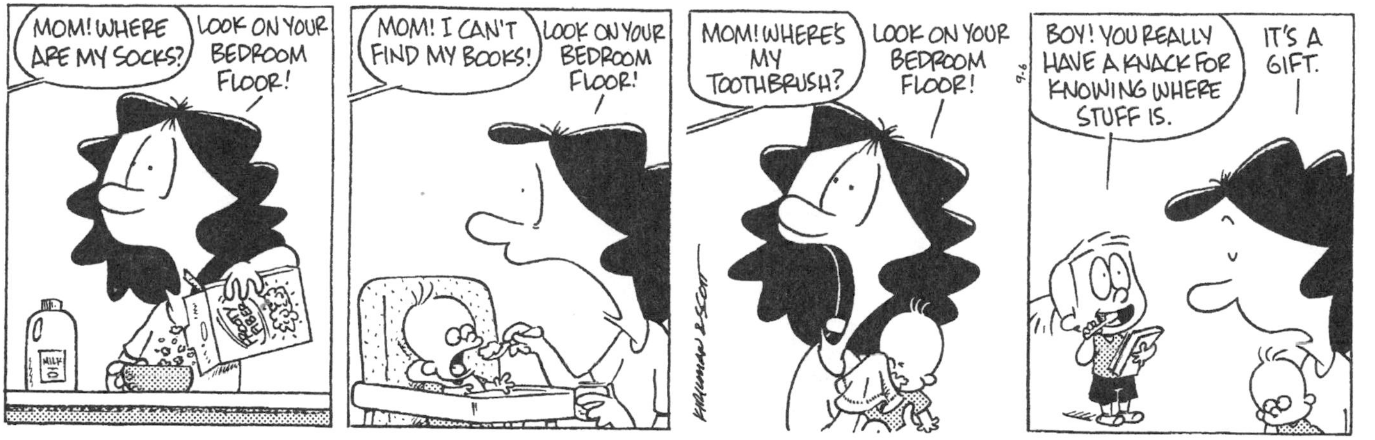
MOM! WHERE ARE MY SOCKS?
LOOK ON YOUR BEDROOM FLOOR!
MOM! I CAN'T FIND MY BOOKS!
LOOK ON YOUR BEDROOM FLOOR!
MOM! WHERE'S MY TOOTHBRUSH?
LOOK ON YOUR BEDROOM FLOOR!
BOY! YOU REALLY HAVE A KNACK FOR KNOWING WHERE STUFF IS.
IT'S A GIFT.

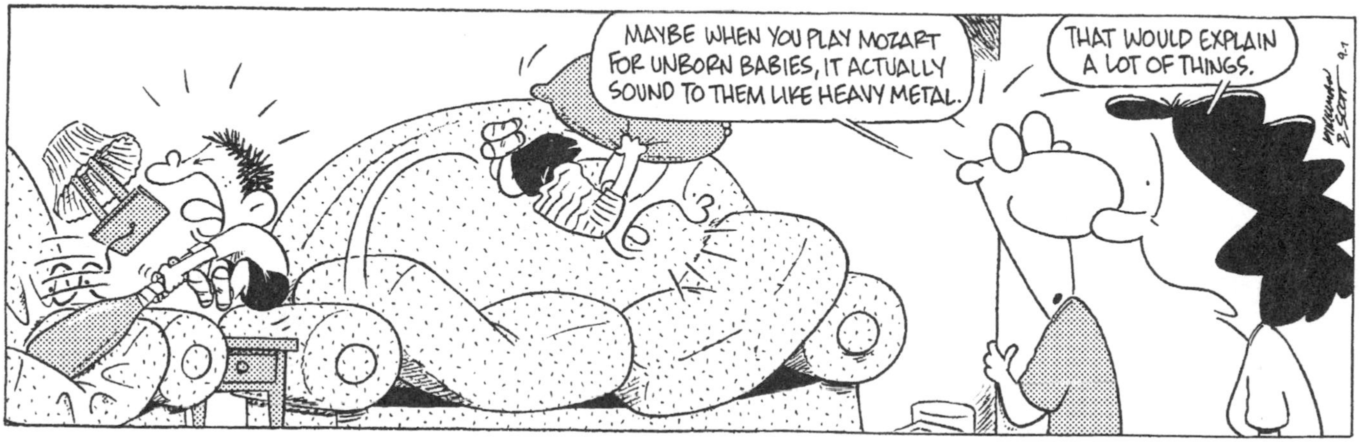
MAYBE WHEN YOU PLAY MOZART FOR UNBORN BABIES, IT ACTUALLY SOUND TO THEM LIKE HEAVY METAL.
THAT WOULD EXPLAIN A LOT OF THINGS.

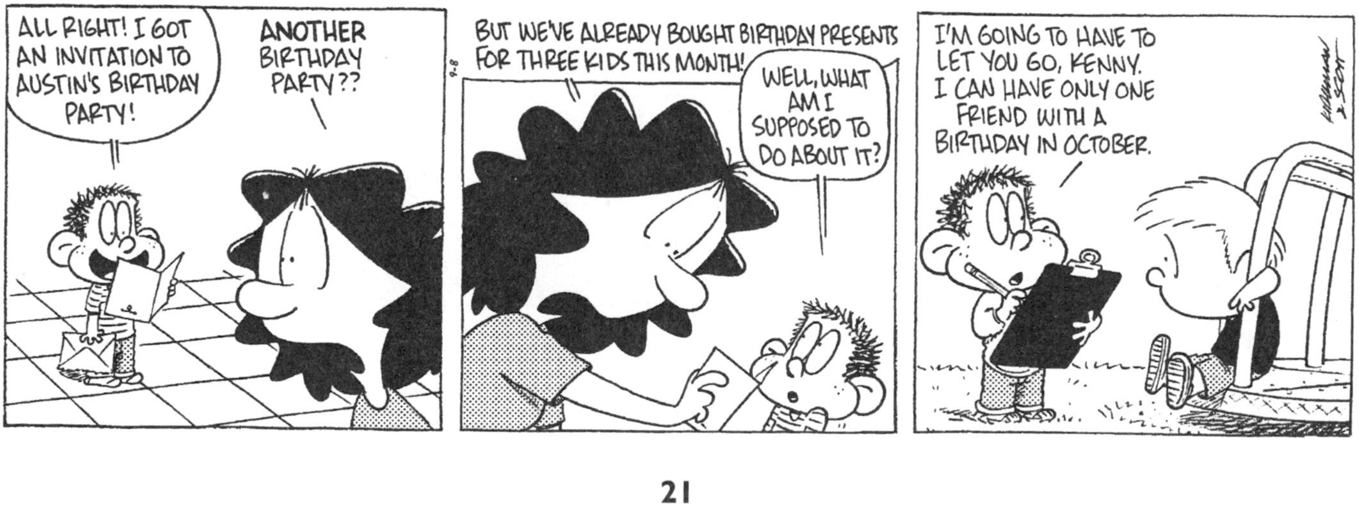
ALL RIGHT! I GOT AN INVITATION TO AUSTIN'S BIRTHDAY PARTY!
ANOTHER BIRTHDAY PARTY??
BUT WE'VE ALREADY BOUGHT BIRTHDAY PRESENTS FOR THREE KIDS THIS MONTH!
WELL, WHAT AM I SUPPOSED TO DO ABOUT IT?
I'M GOING TO HAVE TO LET YOU GO, KENNY. I CAN HAVE ONLY ONE FRIEND WITH A BIRTHDAY IN OCTOBER.

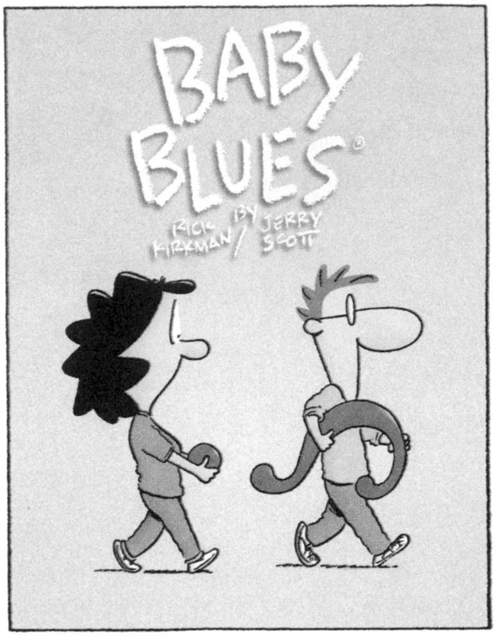
BABY BLUES®
BY RICK KIRKMAN / JERRY SCOTT

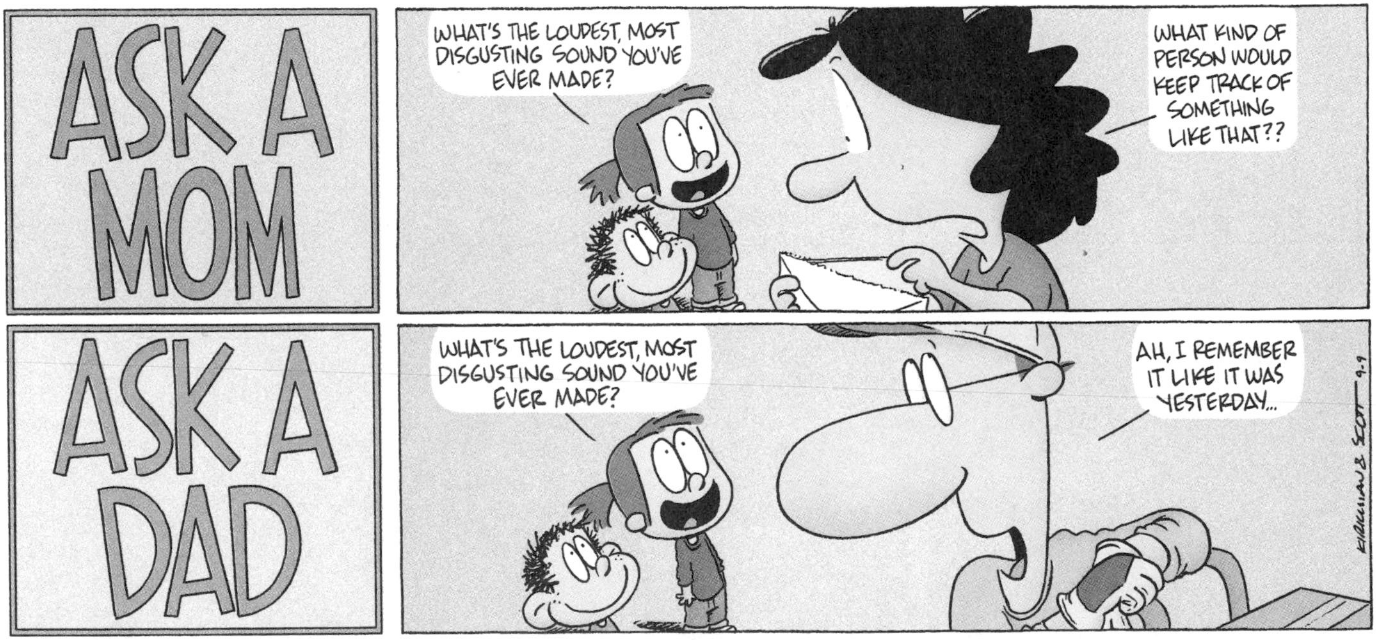
ASK A MOM
WHAT'S THE LOUDEST, MOST DISGUSTING SOUND YOU'VE EVER MADE?
WHAT KIND OF PERSON WOULD KEEP TRACK OF SOMETHING LIKE THAT??
ASK A DAD
WHAT'S THE LOUDEST, MOST DISGUSTING SOUND YOU'VE EVER MADE?
AH, I REMEMBER IT LIKE IT WAS YESTERDAY...

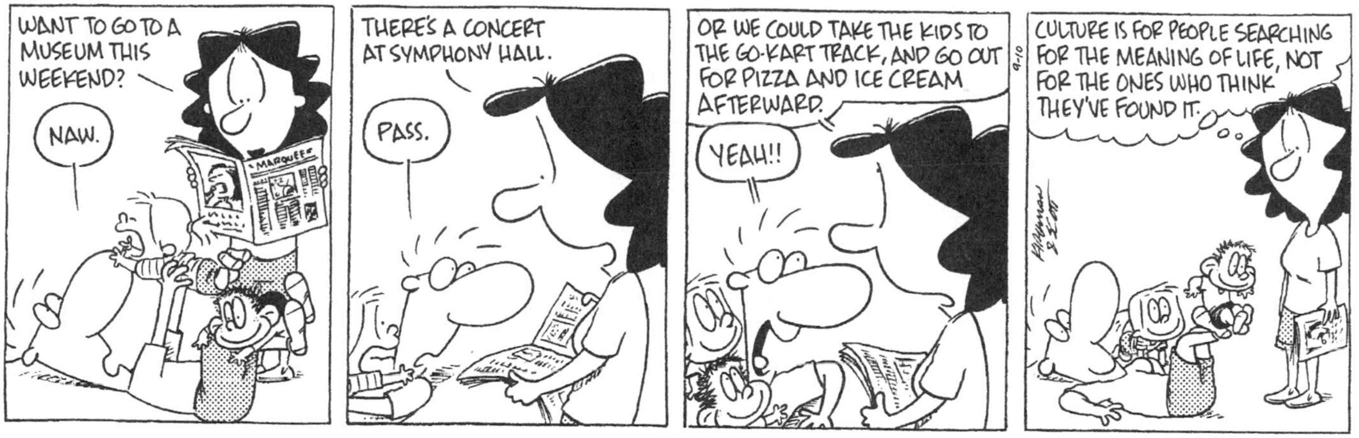
WANT TO GO TO A MUSEUM THIS WEEKEND?
NAW.
THERE'S A CONCERT AT SYMPHONY HALL.
PASS.
OR WE COULD TAKE THE KIDS TO THE GO-KART TRACK, AND GO OUT FOR PIZZA AND ICE CREAM AFTERWARD.
YEAH!!
CULTURE IS FOR PEOPLE SEARCHING FOR THE MEANING OF LIFE, NOT FOR THE ONES WHO THINK THEY'VE FOUND IT.

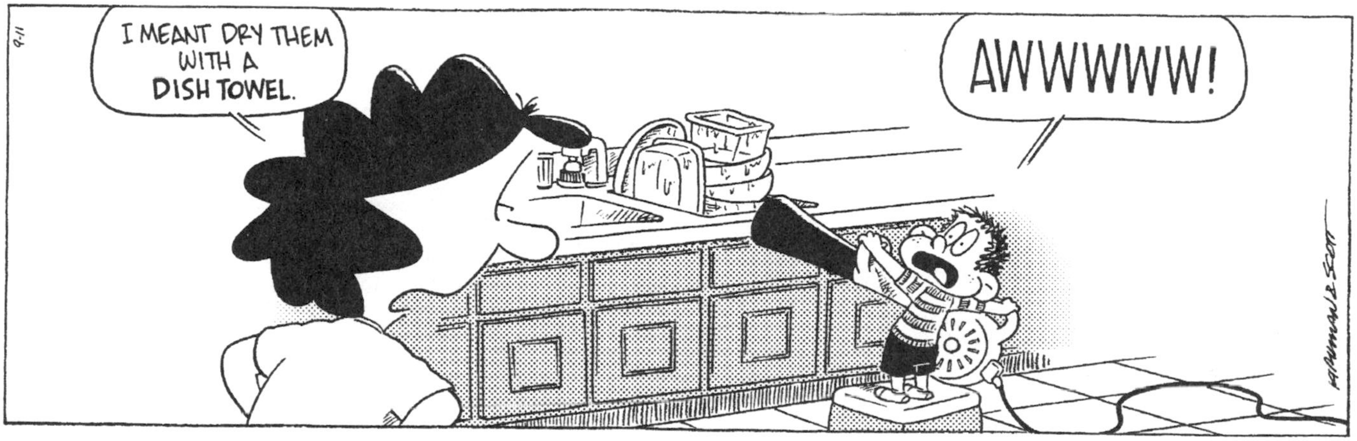
I MEANT DRY THEM WITH A DISH TOWEL.
AWWWWW!

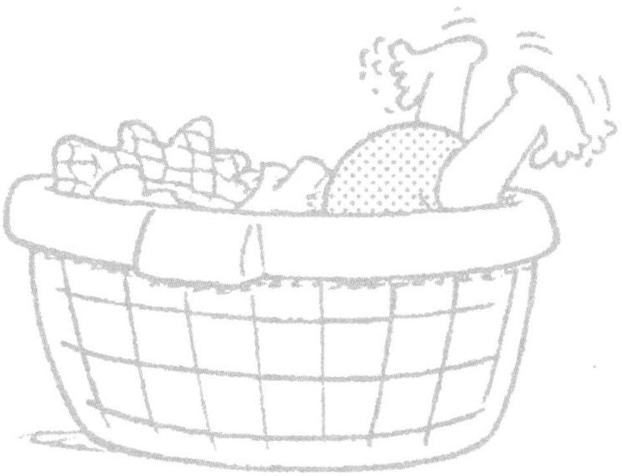

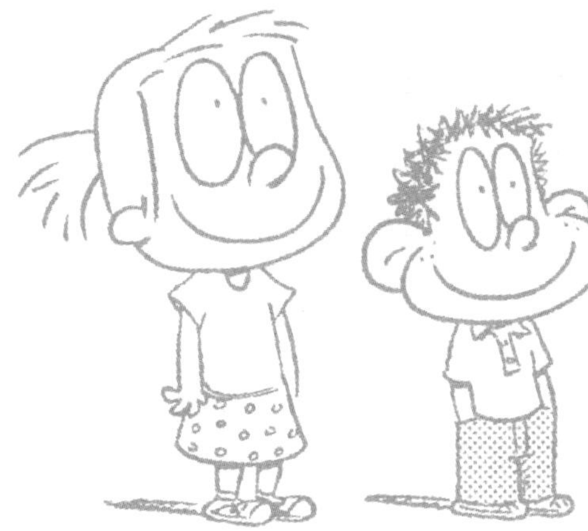

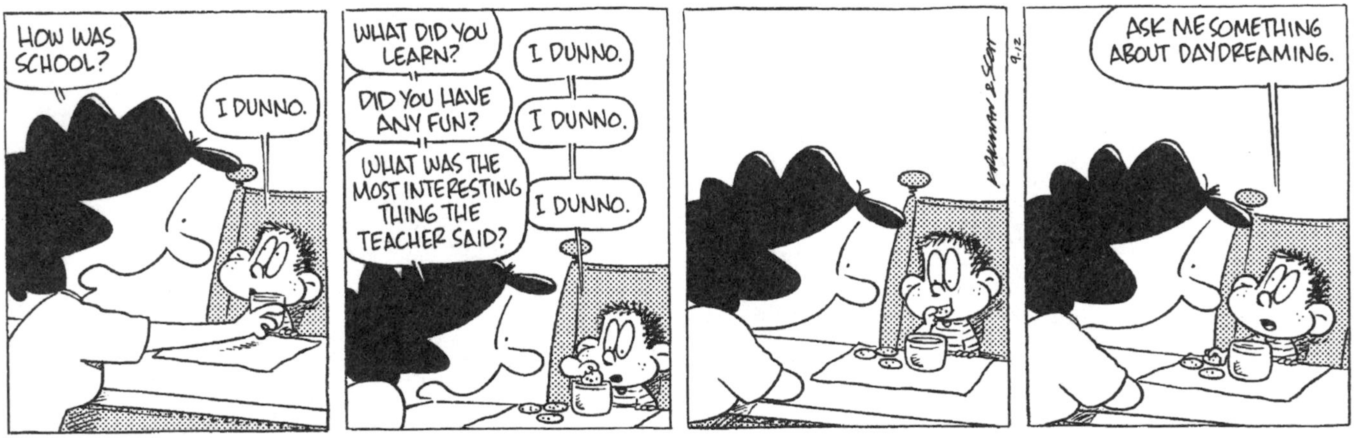

HOW WAS SCHOOL?
I DUNNO.
WHAT DID YOU LEARN?
I DUNNO.
DID YOU HAVE ANY FUN?
I DUNNO.
WHAT WAS THE MOST INTERESTING THING THE TEACHER SAID?
I DUNNO.
ASK ME SOMETHING ABOUT DAYDREAMING.

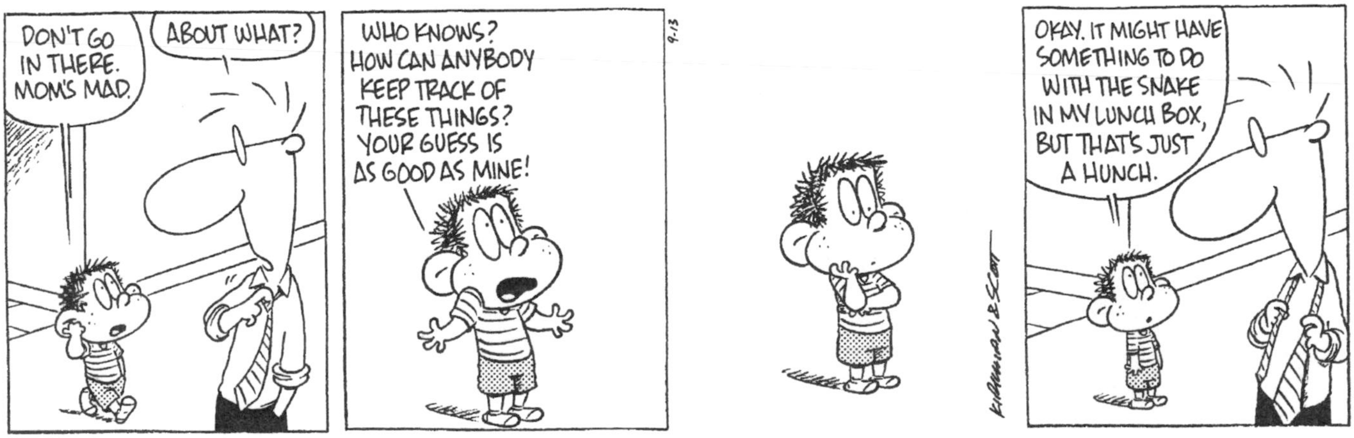

DON'T GO IN THERE. MOM'S MAD.
ABOUT WHAT?
WHO KNOWS? HOW CAN ANYBODY KEEP TRACK OF THESE THINGS? YOUR GUESS IS AS GOOD AS MINE!
OKAY. IT MIGHT HAVE SOMETHING TO DO WITH THE SNAKE IN MY LUNCH BOX, BUT THAT'S JUST A HUNCH.

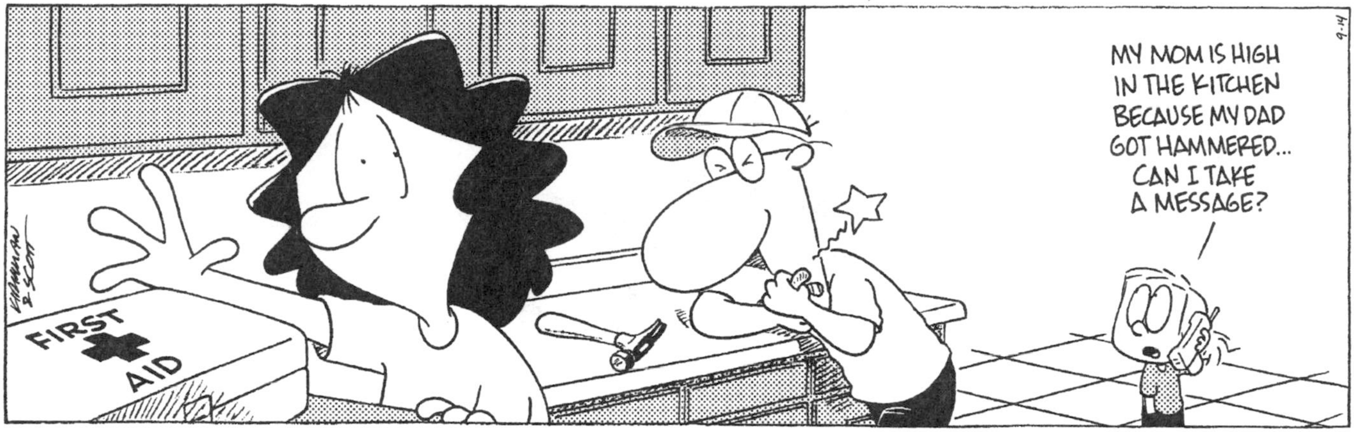
FIRST AID
MY MOM IS HIGH IN THE KITCHEN BECAUSE MY DAD GOT HAMMERED... CAN I TAKE A MESSAGE?

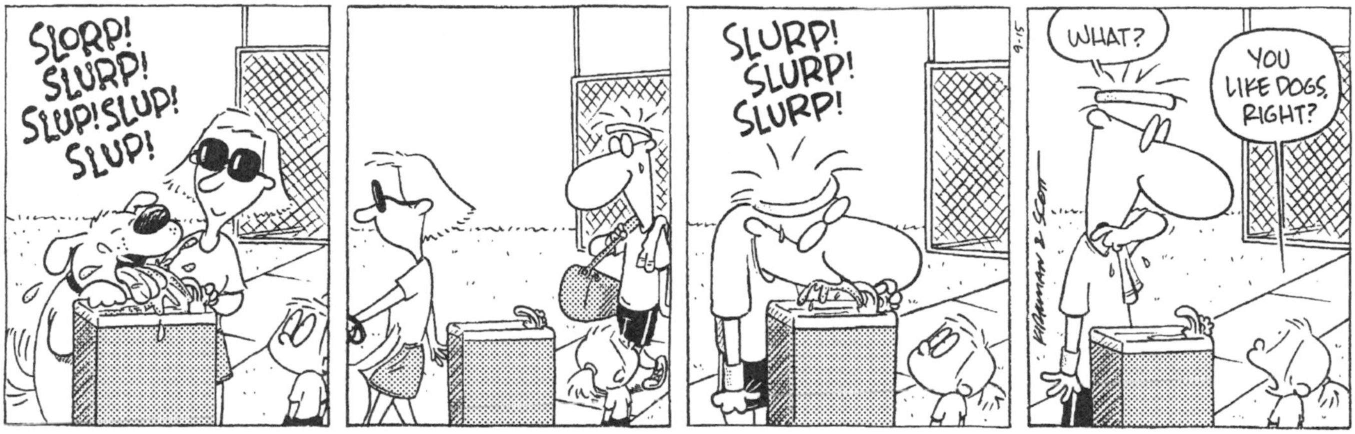
SLORP! SLURP! SLUP! SLUP! SLUP!
SLURP! SLURP! SLURP!
WHAT?
YOU LIKE DOGS, RIGHT?

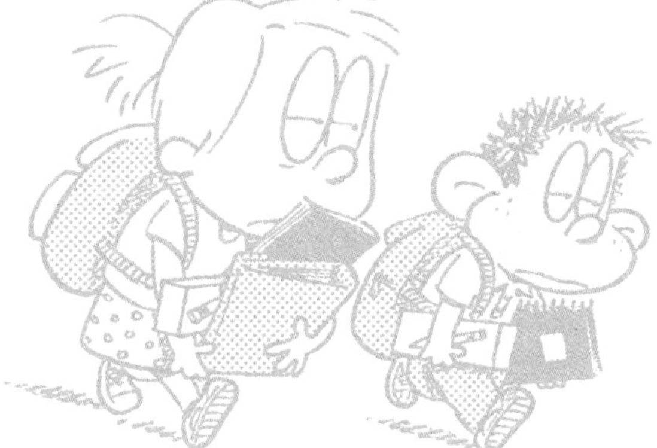

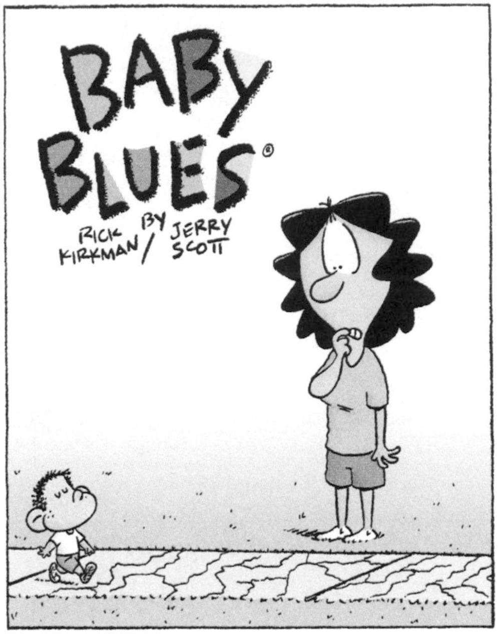
BABY BLUES®
BY RICK KIRKMAN / JERRY SCOTT

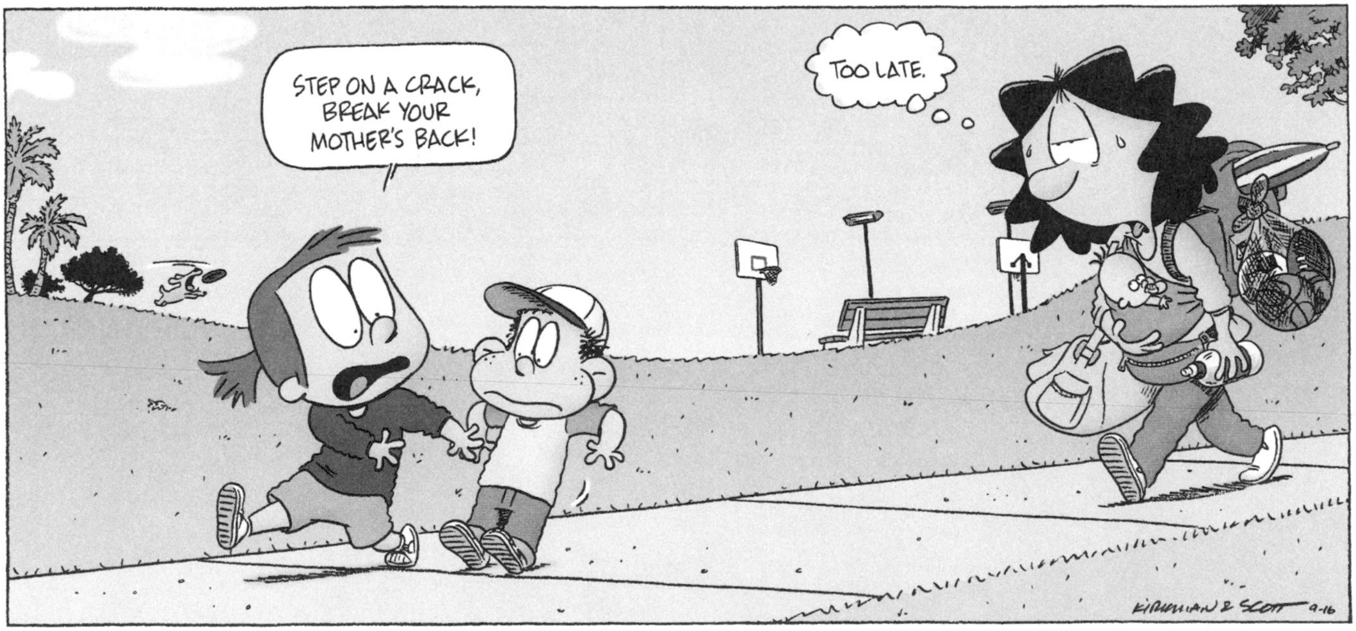
STEP ON A CRACK, BREAK YOUR MOTHER'S BACK!
TOO LATE.
KIRKMAN & SCOTT 9-16

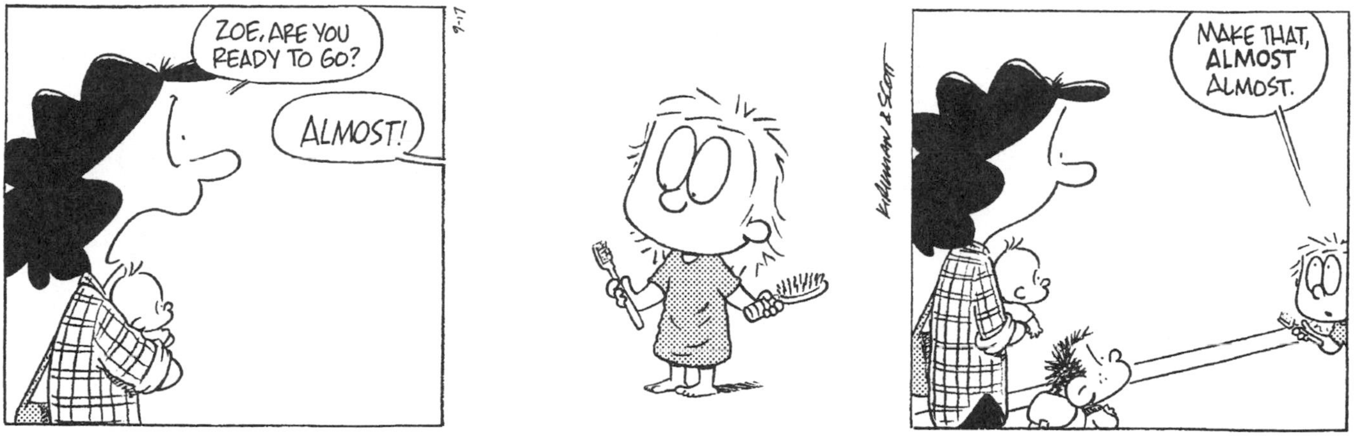
ZOE, ARE YOU READY TO GO?
ALMOST!
MAKE THAT, **ALMOST** ALMOST.

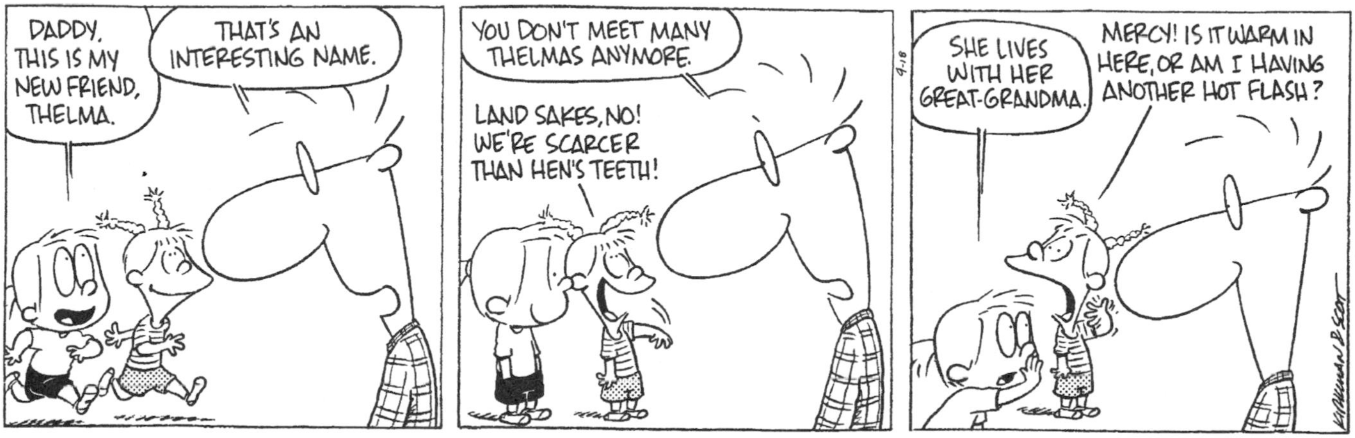
DADDY, THIS IS MY NEW FRIEND, THELMA.
THAT'S AN INTERESTING NAME.
YOU DON'T MEET MANY THELMAS ANYMORE.
LAND SAKES, NO! WE'RE SCARCER THAN HEN'S TEETH!
SHE LIVES WITH HER GREAT-GRANDMA.
MERCY! IS IT WARM IN HERE, OR AM I HAVING ANOTHER HOT FLASH?

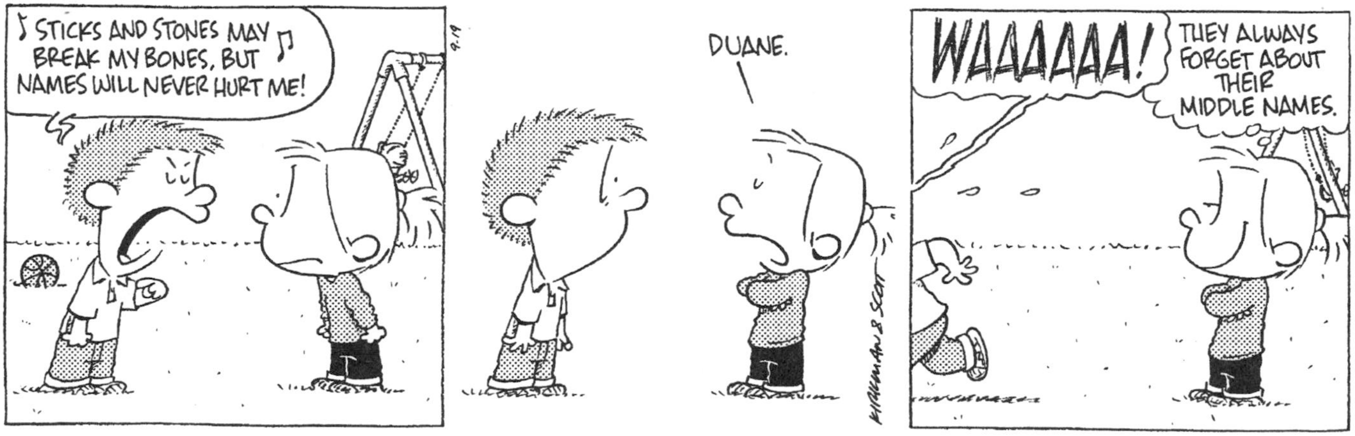
♪ STICKS AND STONES MAY BREAK MY BONES, BUT NAMES WILL NEVER HURT ME! ♫
DUANE.
WAAAAAA!
THEY ALWAYS FORGET ABOUT THEIR MIDDLE NAMES.

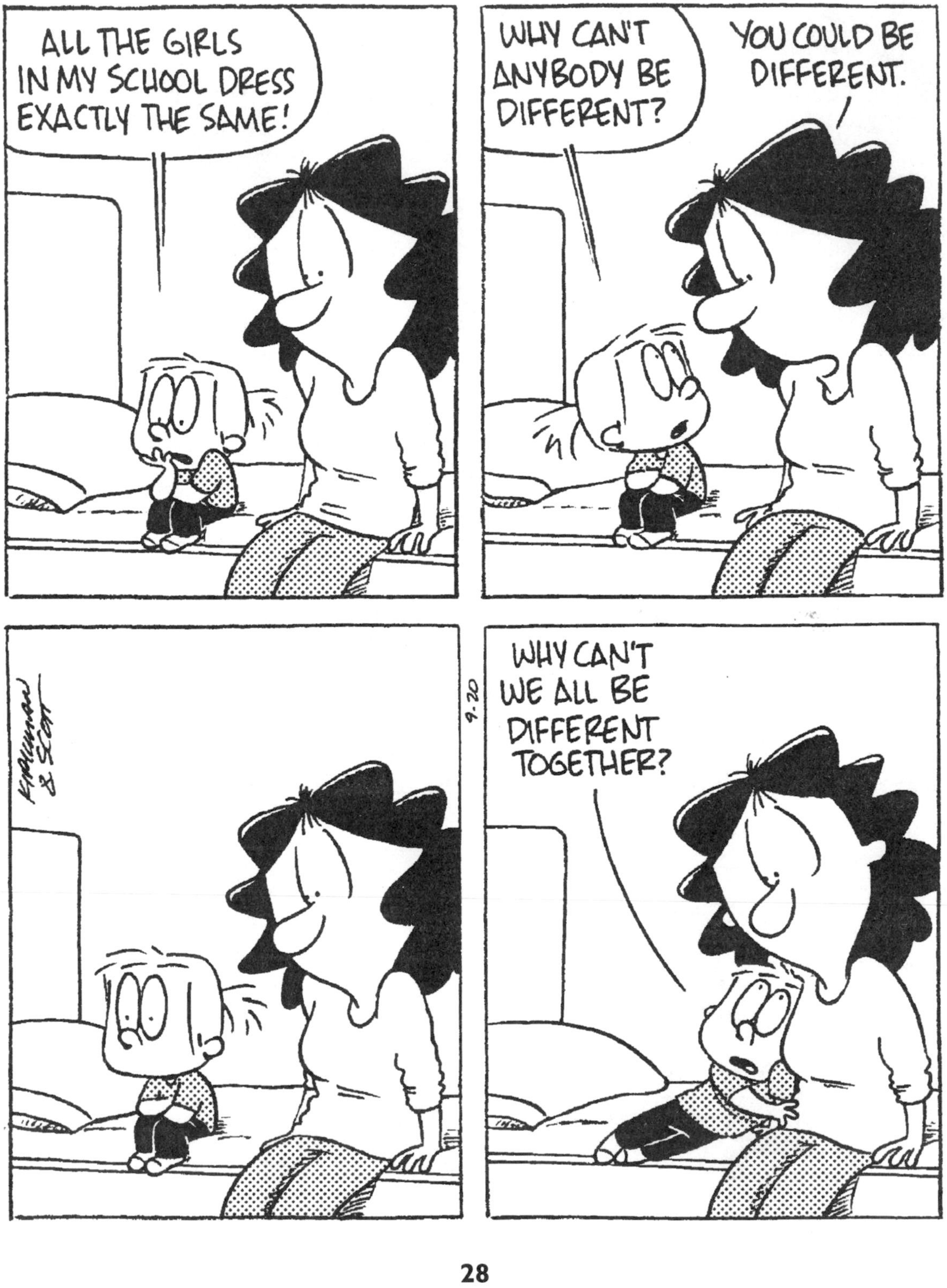
ALL THE GIRLS IN MY SCHOOL DRESS EXACTLY THE SAME!
WHY CAN'T ANYBODY BE DIFFERENT?
YOU COULD BE DIFFERENT.
WHY CAN'T WE ALL BE DIFFERENT TOGETHER?
9.20

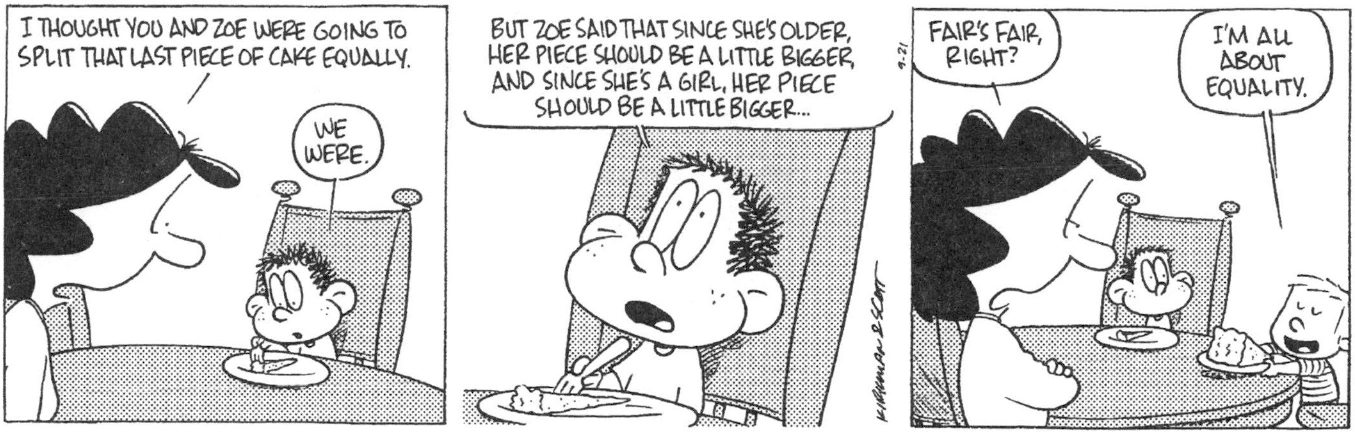
I THOUGHT YOU AND ZOE WERE GOING TO SPLIT THAT LAST PIECE OF CAKE EQUALLY.
WE WERE.
BUT ZOE SAID THAT SINCE SHE'S OLDER, HER PIECE SHOULD BE A LITTLE BIGGER, AND SINCE SHE'S A GIRL, HER PIECE SHOULD BE A LITTLE BIGGER...
FAIR'S FAIR, RIGHT?
I'M ALL ABOUT EQUALITY.

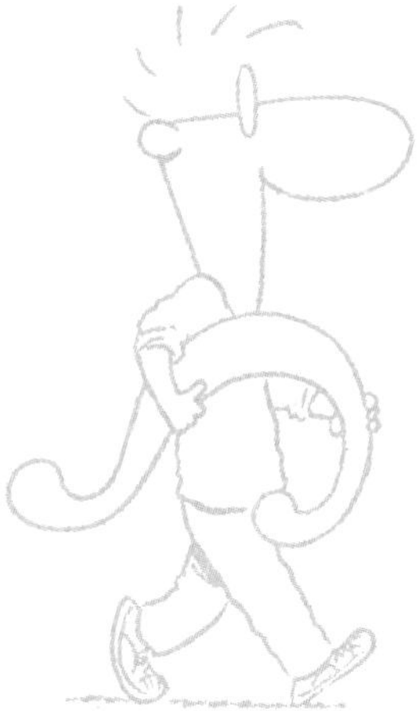

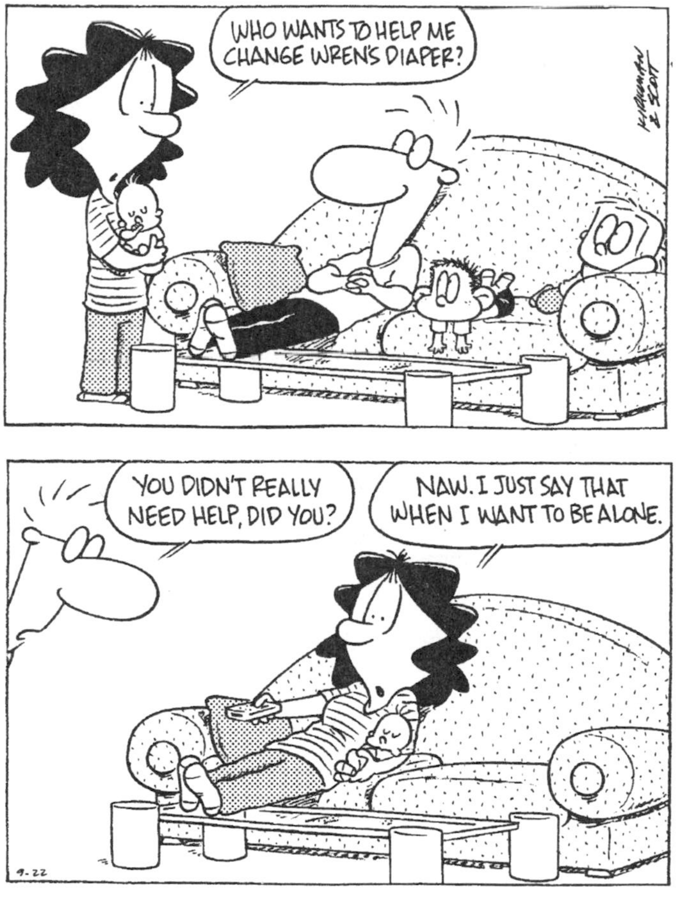
WHO WANTS TO HELP ME CHANGE WREN'S DIAPER?
YOU DIDN'T REALLY NEED HELP, DID YOU?
NAW. I JUST SAY THAT WHEN I WANT TO BE ALONE.

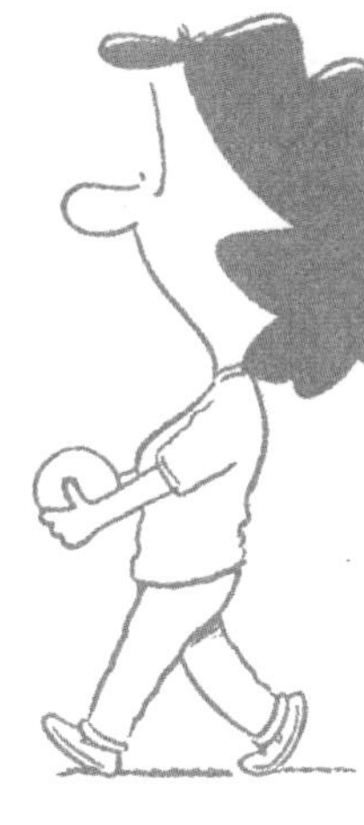

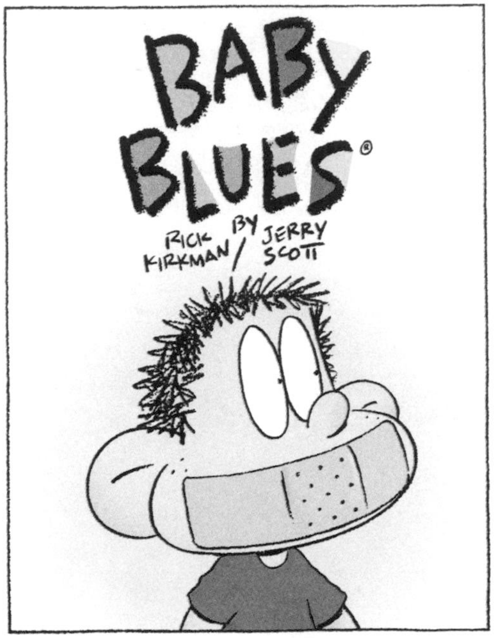
BABY BLUES®
BY
RICK KIRKMAN / JERRY SCOTT

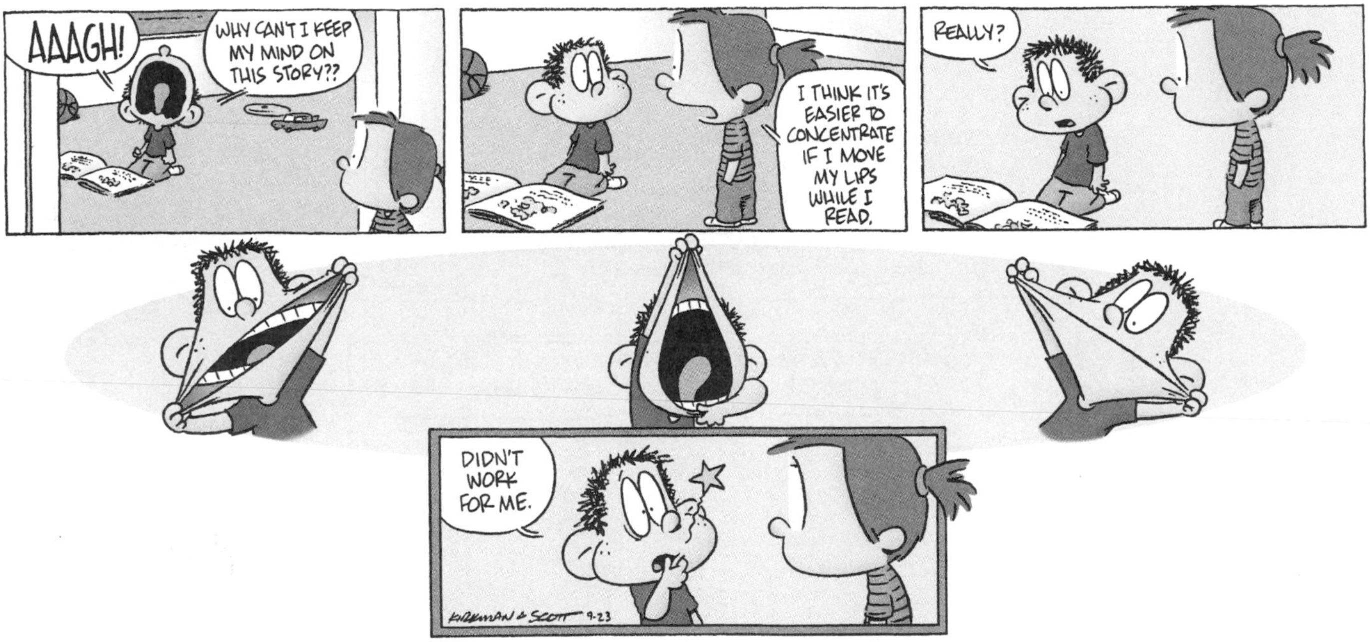
AAAGH!
WHY CAN'T I KEEP MY MIND ON THIS STORY??
I THINK IT'S EASIER TO CONCENTRATE IF I MOVE MY LIPS WHILE I READ.
REALLY?
DIDN'T WORK FOR ME.
KIRKMAN & SCOTT 9-23

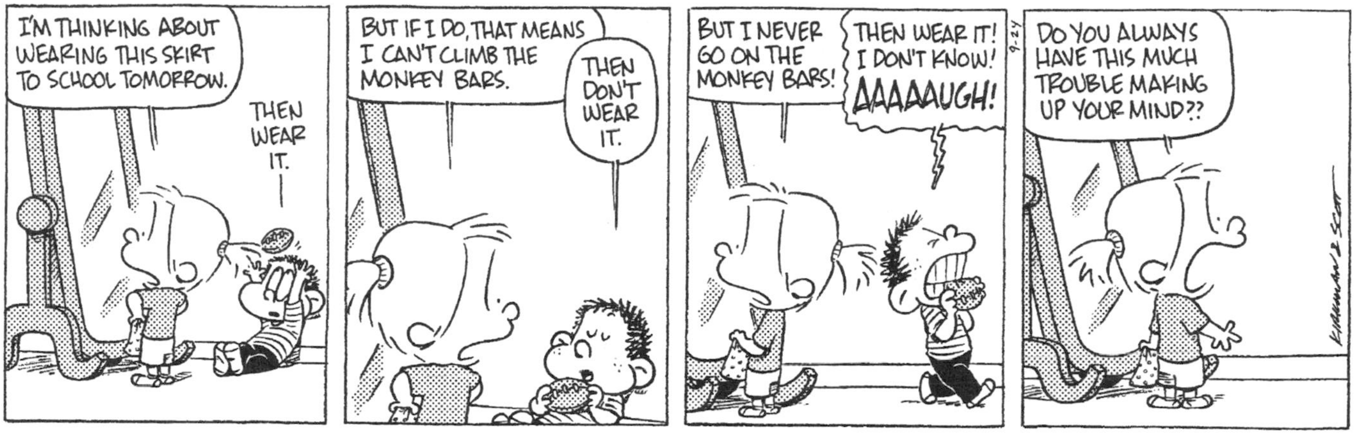
I'M THINKING ABOUT WEARING THIS SKIRT TO SCHOOL TOMORROW.
THEN WEAR IT.
BUT IF I DO, THAT MEANS I CAN'T CLIMB THE MONKEY BARS.
THEN DON'T WEAR IT.
BUT I NEVER GO ON THE MONKEY BARS!
THEN WEAR IT! I DON'T KNOW! AAAAAUGH!
DO YOU ALWAYS HAVE THIS MUCH TROUBLE MAKING UP YOUR MIND??

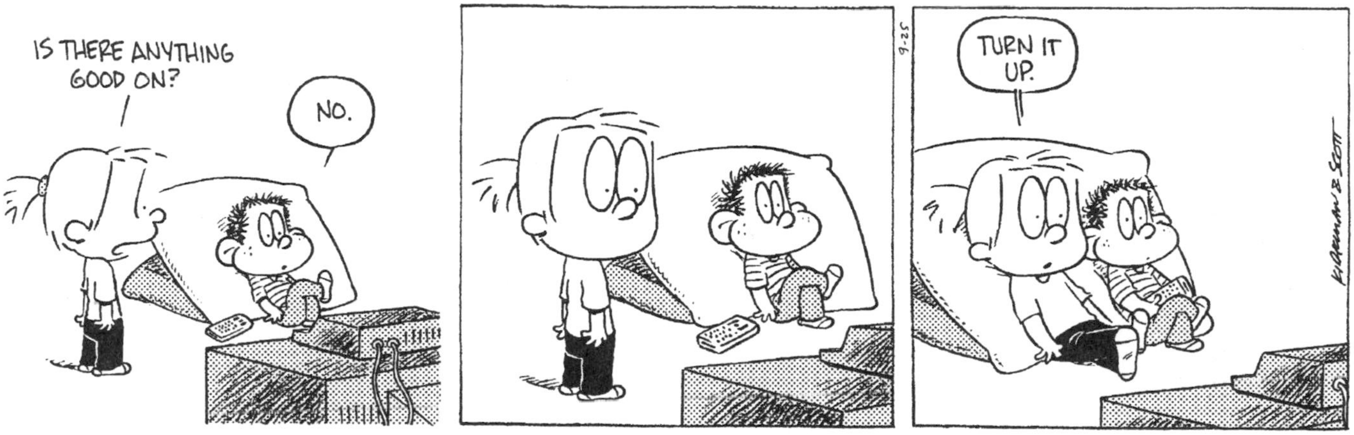
IS THERE ANYTHING GOOD ON?
NO.
TURN IT UP.

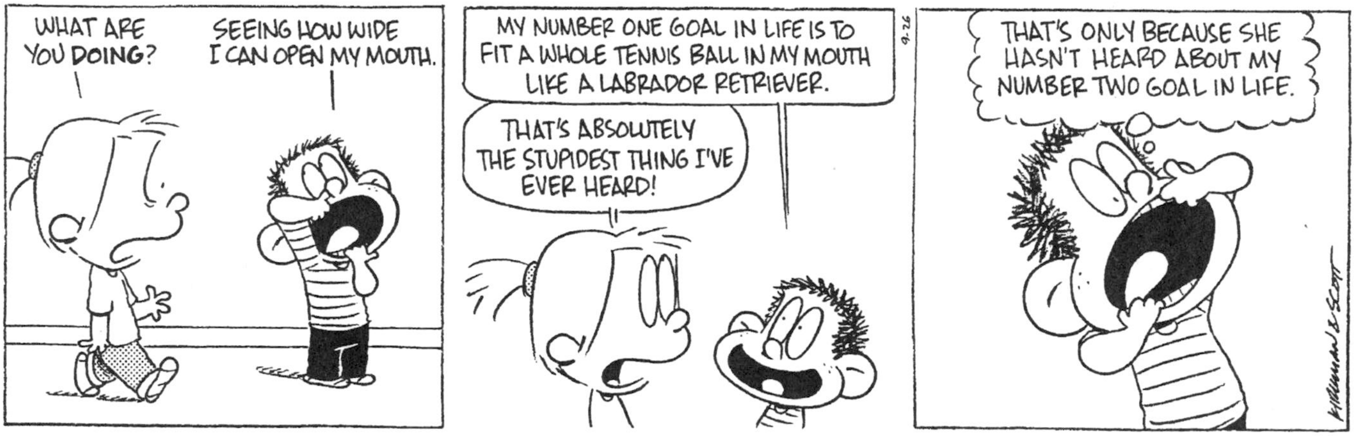
WHAT ARE YOU **DOING**?
SEEING HOW WIDE I CAN OPEN MY MOUTH.
MY NUMBER ONE GOAL IN LIFE IS TO FIT A WHOLE TENNIS BALL IN MY MOUTH LIKE A LABRADOR RETRIEVER.
THAT'S ABSOLUTELY THE STUPIDEST THING I'VE EVER HEARD!
THAT'S ONLY BECAUSE SHE HASN'T HEARD ABOUT MY NUMBER TWO GOAL IN LIFE.

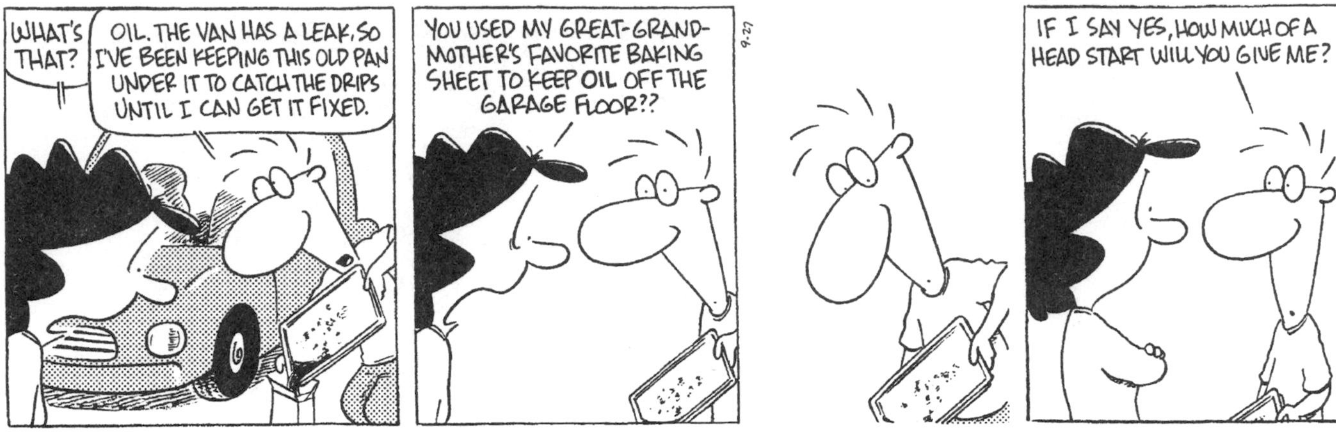
WHAT'S THAT?
OIL. THE VAN HAS A LEAK, SO I'VE BEEN KEEPING THIS OLD PAN UNDER IT TO CATCH THE DRIPS UNTIL I CAN GET IT FIXED.
YOU USED MY GREAT-GRANDMOTHER'S FAVORITE BAKING SHEET TO KEEP **OIL** OFF THE GARAGE FLOOR??
IF I SAY YES, HOW MUCH OF A HEAD START WILL YOU GIVE ME?

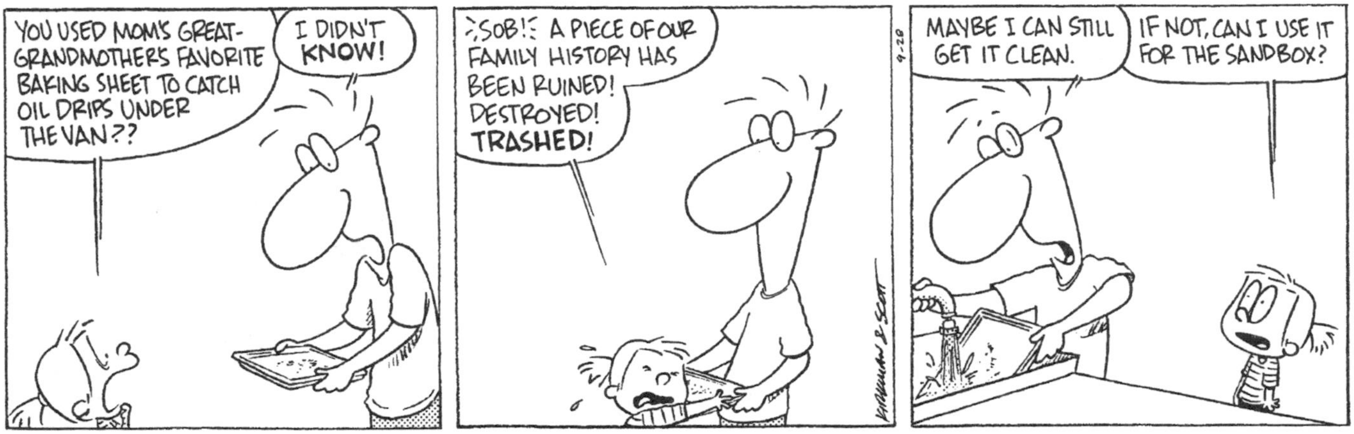
YOU USED MOM'S GREAT-GRANDMOTHER'S FAVORITE BAKING SHEET TO CATCH OIL DRIPS UNDER THE VAN??
I DIDN'T **KNOW**!
SOB! A PIECE OF OUR FAMILY HISTORY HAS BEEN RUINED! DESTROYED! **TRASHED!**
MAYBE I CAN STILL GET IT CLEAN.
IF NOT, CAN I USE IT FOR THE SANDBOX?

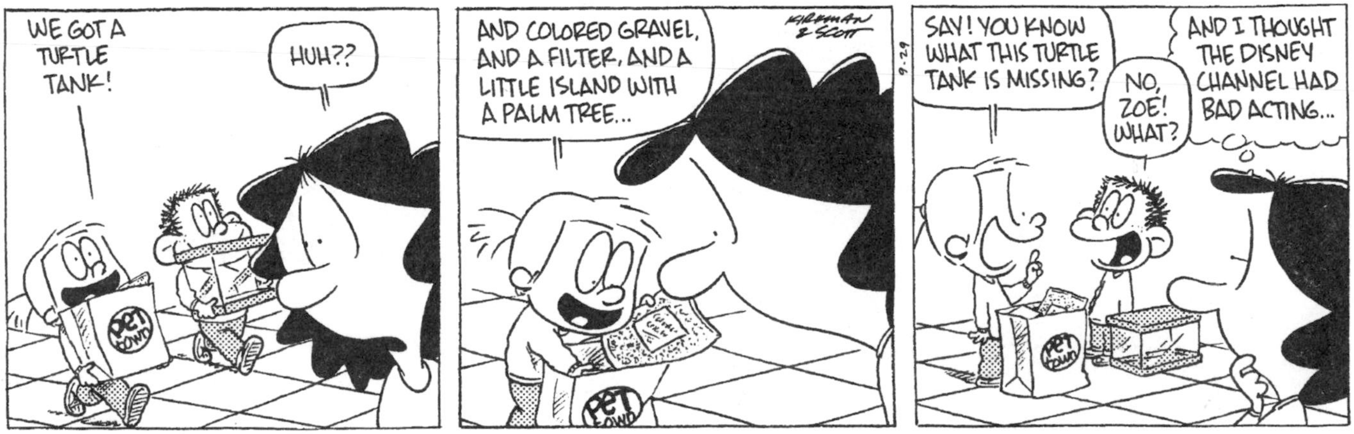
WE GOT A TURTLE TANK!
HUH??
PET TOWN
AND COLORED GRAVEL, AND A FILTER, AND A LITTLE ISLAND WITH A PALM TREE...
SAY! YOU KNOW WHAT THIS TURTLE TANK IS MISSING?
NO, ZOE! WHAT?
AND I THOUGHT THE DISNEY CHANNEL HAD BAD ACTING...

BABY BLUES®

GRRR...
HOW MANY TIMES HAVE YOU TOLD ME NOT TO TAKE MY PENS APART?
JUST LOOK AT ME! WHAT WAS I **THINKING**?
YOU TOLD ME SO!
YOU TOLD ME SO!
YOU TOLD ME SO!
WHEN ZOE'S RESPONSI-BILITY GENE KICKS IN, IT KICKS IN **HARD**.
IF ANYBODY CALLS, I'LL GET BACK TO THEM AFTER I'VE FINISHED GROUNDING MYSELF!
9-30 KIRKMAN & SCOTT

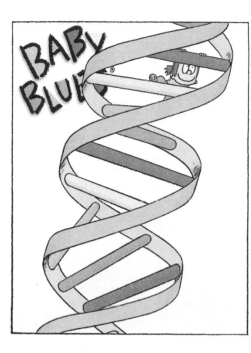

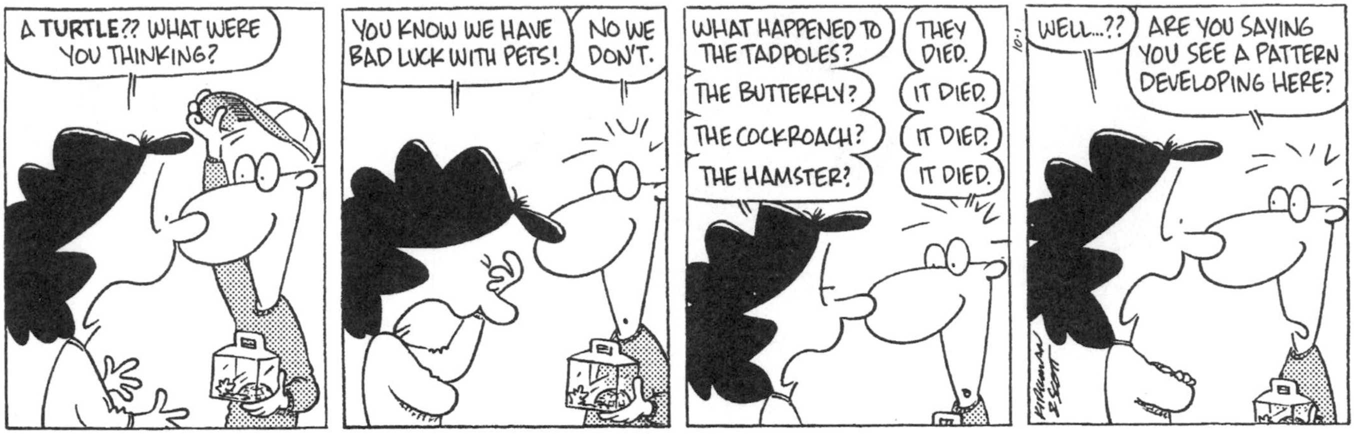
A TURTLE?? WHAT WERE YOU THINKING?
YOU KNOW WE HAVE BAD LUCK WITH PETS!
NO WE DON'T.
WHAT HAPPENED TO THE TADPOLES?
THEY DIED.
THE BUTTERFLY?
IT DIED.
THE COCKROACH?
IT DIED.
THE HAMSTER?
IT DIED.
WELL...??
ARE YOU SAYING YOU SEE A PATTERN DEVELOPING HERE?

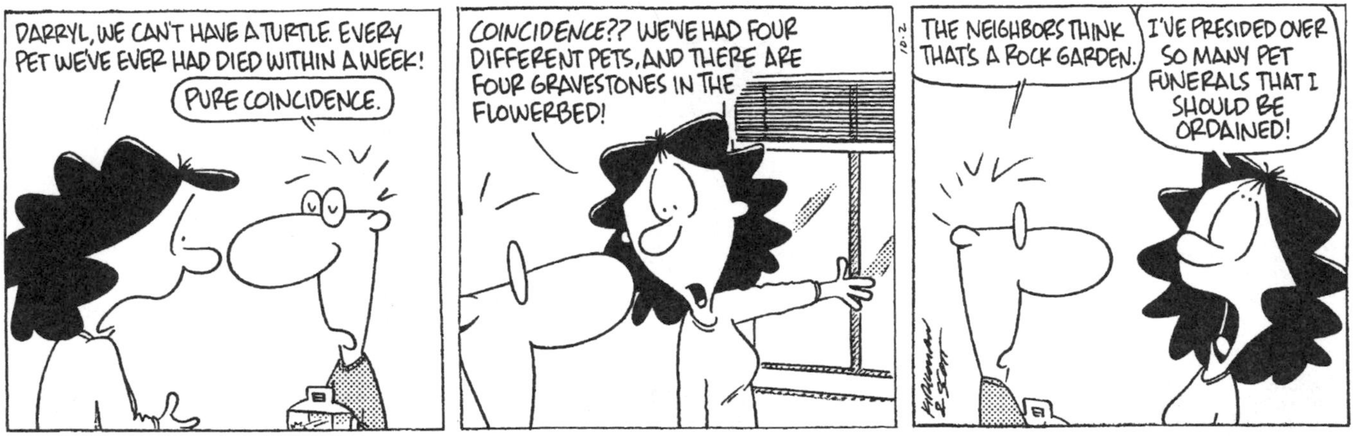
DARRYL, WE CAN'T HAVE A TURTLE. EVERY PET WE'VE EVER HAD DIED WITHIN A WEEK!
PURE COINCIDENCE.
COINCIDENCE?? WE'VE HAD FOUR DIFFERENT PETS, AND THERE ARE FOUR GRAVESTONES IN THE FLOWERBED!
THE NEIGHBORS THINK THAT'S A ROCK GARDEN.
I'VE PRESIDED OVER SO MANY PET FUNERALS THAT I SHOULD BE ORDAINED!

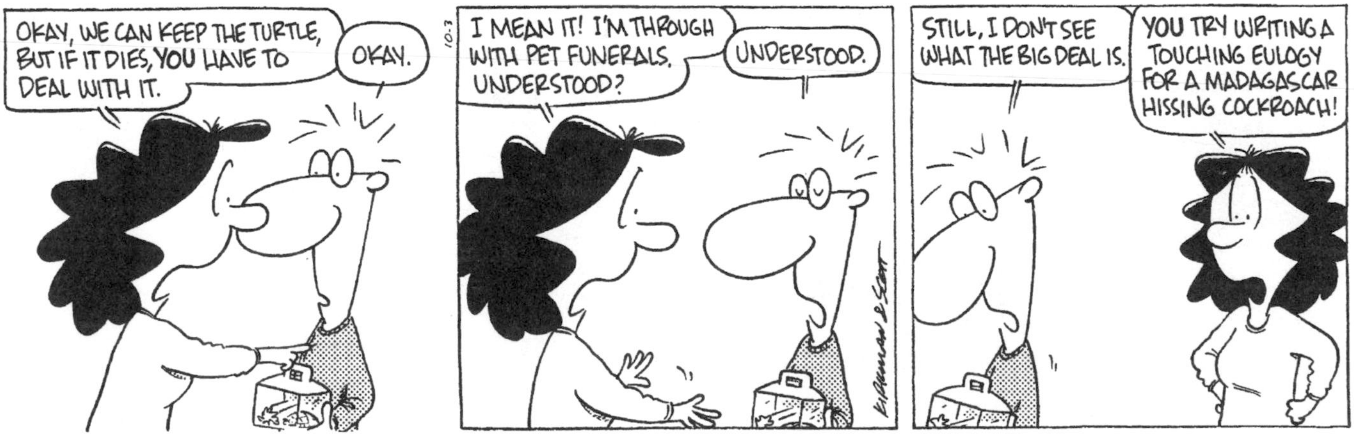
OKAY, WE CAN KEEP THE TURTLE, BUT IF IT DIES, YOU HAVE TO DEAL WITH IT.
OKAY.
I MEAN IT! I'M THROUGH WITH PET FUNERALS. UNDERSTOOD?
UNDERSTOOD.
STILL, I DON'T SEE WHAT THE BIG DEAL IS.
YOU TRY WRITING A TOUCHING EULOGY FOR A MADAGASCAR HISSING COCKROACH!

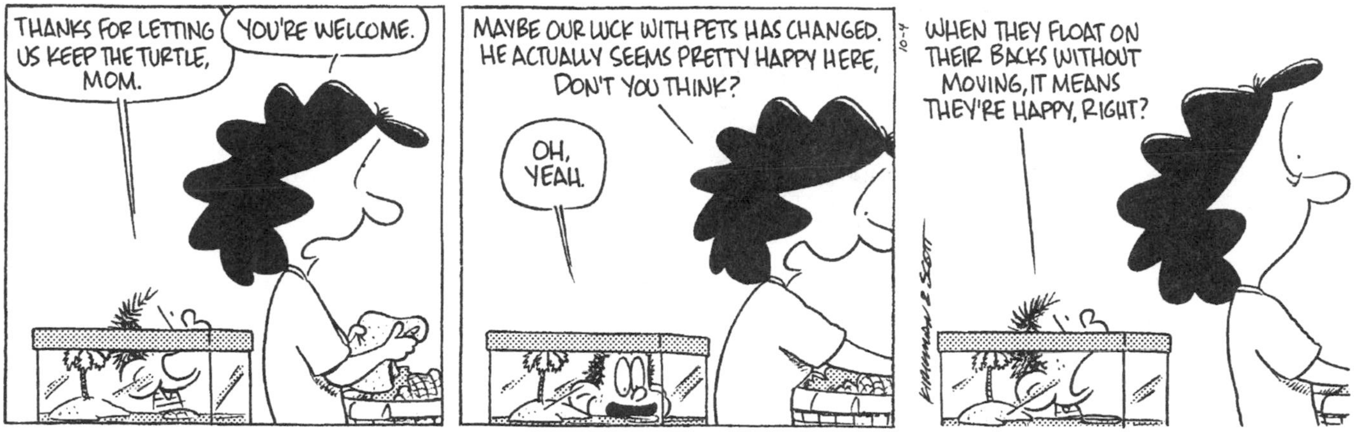
THANKS FOR LETTING US KEEP THE TURTLE, MOM.
YOU'RE WELCOME.
MAYBE OUR LUCK WITH PETS HAS CHANGED. HE ACTUALLY SEEMS PRETTY HAPPY HERE, DON'T YOU THINK?
OH, YEAH.
WHEN THEY FLOAT ON THEIR BACKS WITHOUT MOVING, IT MEANS THEY'RE HAPPY, RIGHT?

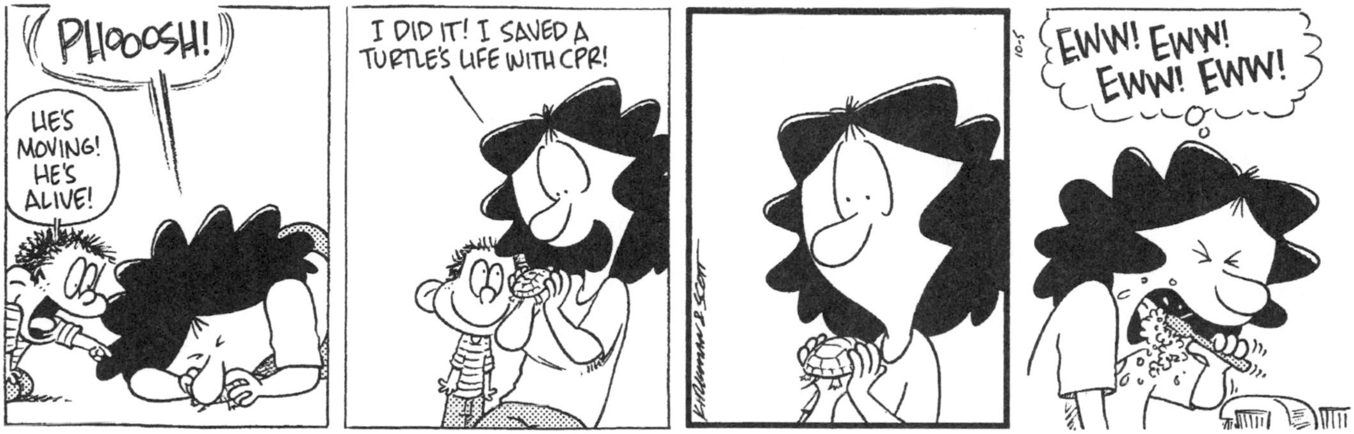
PHOOOSH!
HE'S MOVING! HE'S ALIVE!
I DID IT! I SAVED A TURTLE'S LIFE WITH CPR!
EWW! EWW! EWW! EWW!

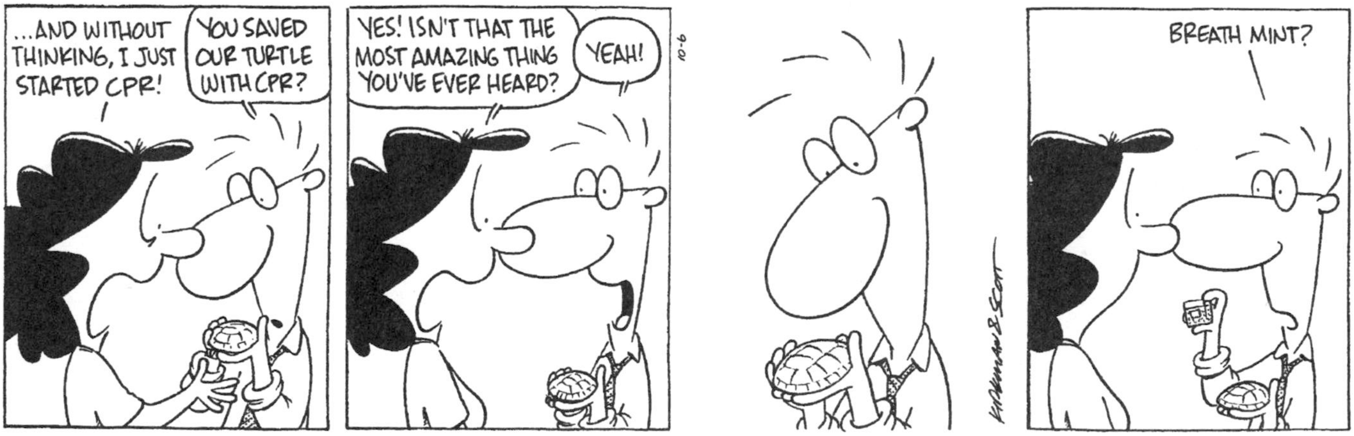
...AND WITHOUT THINKING, I JUST STARTED CPR!
YOU SAVED OUR TURTLE WITH CPR?
YES! ISN'T THAT THE MOST AMAZING THING YOU'VE EVER HEARD?
YEAH!
BREATH MINT?

BABY BLUES®
BY RICK KIRKMAN / JERRY SCOTT
US MAIL
COME ON YOU GUYS! WE'RE GOING TO BE LATE FOR SCHOOL!
BUT I DON'T HAVE MY SHOES ON!
YOU CAN PUT YOUR SHOES ON IN THE CAR! MOVE IT!
WHAT ABOUT BREAKFAST?
YOU CAN EAT AFTER YOU PUT YOUR SHOES ON. GO!
WHILE YOU'RE AT IT, YOU CAN BUTTON YOUR SHIRTS, COMB YOUR HAIR AND FINISH YOUR HOMEWORK IN THERE, TOO!
SLAM!
IF THIS VAN HAD A BATHROOM, YOU AND I COULD JUST LIVE IN THE VAN!
YEAH!
DON'T GIVE ME ANY IDEAS...
10-7 KIRKMAN & SCOTT

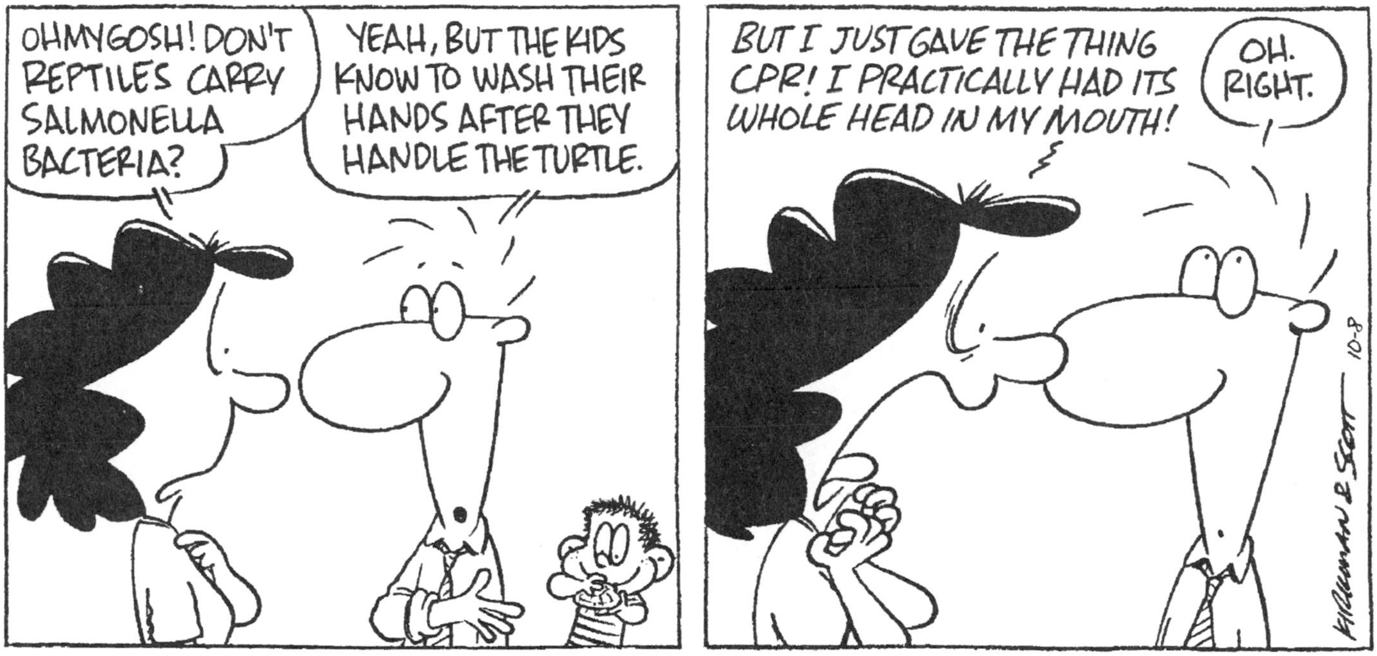
OHMYGOSH! DON'T REPTILES CARRY SALMONELLA BACTERIA?
YEAH, BUT THE KIDS KNOW TO WASH THEIR HANDS AFTER THEY HANDLE THE TURTLE.
BUT I JUST GAVE THE THING CPR! I PRACTICALLY HAD ITS WHOLE HEAD IN MY MOUTH!
OH. RIGHT.
10-8
KIRKMAN & SCOTT

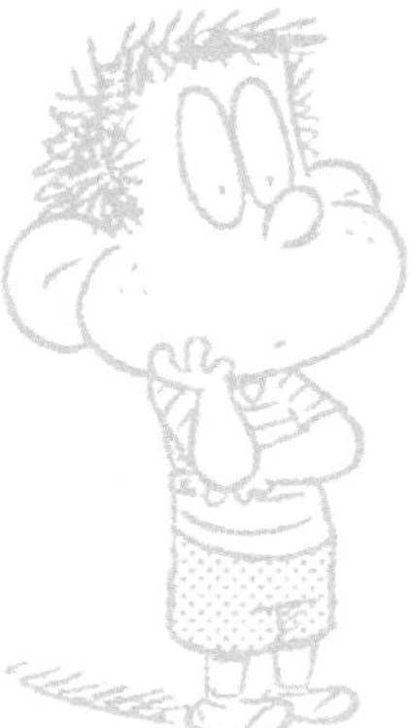

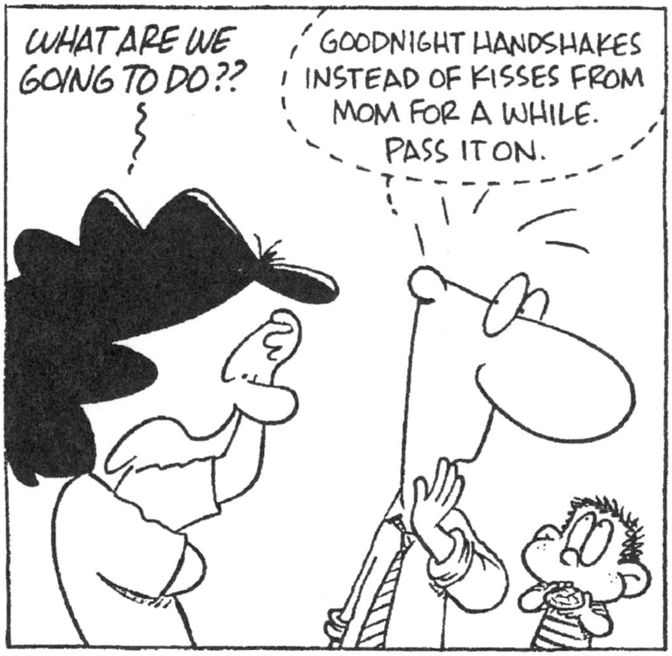
WHAT ARE WE GOING TO DO??
GOODNIGHT HANDSHAKES INSTEAD OF KISSES FROM MOM FOR A WHILE. PASS IT ON.

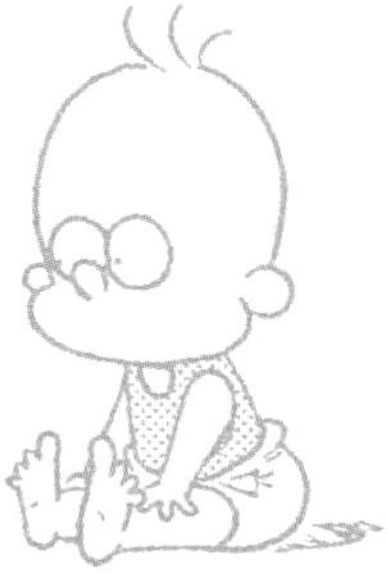

HERE IT IS...
MOST PEOPLE INFECTED WITH SALMONELLA DEVELOP DIARRHEA, FEVER AND ABDOMINAL CRAMPS FOUR TO SIX HOURS AFTER INFECTION.
THE ILLNESS USUALLY LASTS FOUR TO SEVEN DAYS AND MOST PEOPLE RECOVER WITHOUT TREATMENT.
10-9
THAT DOESN'T SEEM TOO BAD.
RECOVER?? I'M A MOTHER! I DON'T HAVE TIME TO RECOVER!!

IT'S BEEN OVER SIX HOURS SINCE YOU GAVE THE TURTLE CPR, AND SO FAR YOU DON'T SHOW ANY SIGNS OF HAVING SALMONELLA.
MAYBE YOU HAVE A STRONG IMMUNE SYSTEM.
MAYBE OUR TURTLE WASN'T SHEDDING THE BACTERIA.
10-10
...OR MAYBE IT'S THE ELEVEN BOTTLES OF MOUTHWASH YOU'VE GONE THROUGH.
BLEAH! TURTLE LIPS!!

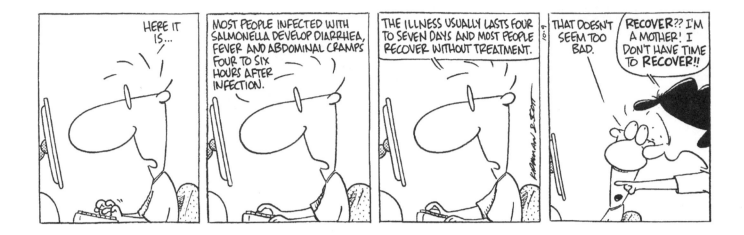

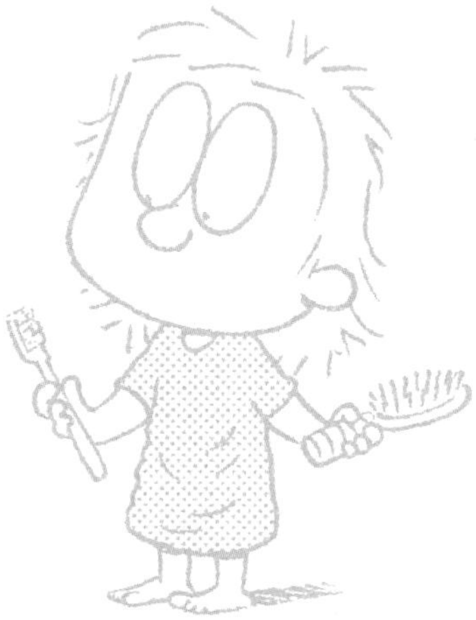

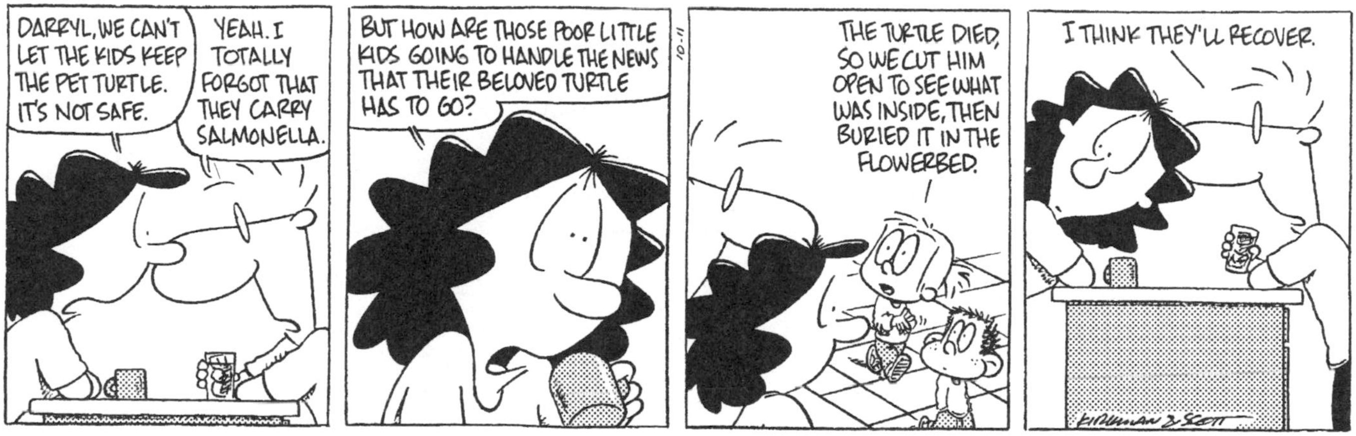
DARRYL, WE CAN'T LET THE KIDS KEEP THE PET TURTLE. IT'S NOT SAFE.
YEAH. I TOTALLY FORGOT THAT THEY CARRY SALMONELLA.
BUT HOW ARE THOSE POOR LITTLE KIDS GOING TO HANDLE THE NEWS THAT THEIR BELOVED TURTLE HAS TO GO?
10-11
THE TURTLE DIED, SO WE CUT HIM OPEN TO SEE WHAT WAS INSIDE, THEN BURIED IT IN THE FLOWERBED.
I THINK THEY'LL RECOVER.
KIRKMAN & SCOTT

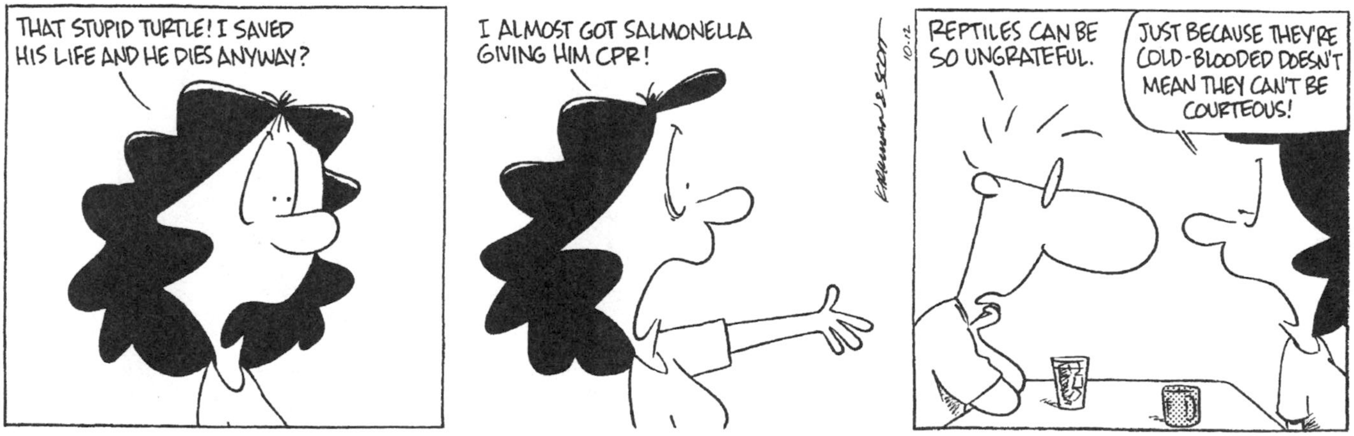
THAT STUPID TURTLE! I SAVED HIS LIFE AND HE DIES ANYWAY?
I ALMOST GOT SALMONELLA GIVING HIM CPR!
KIRKMAN & SCOTT
10-12
REPTILES CAN BE SO UNGRATEFUL.
JUST BECAUSE THEY'RE COLD-BLOODED DOESN'T MEAN THEY CAN'T BE COURTEOUS!

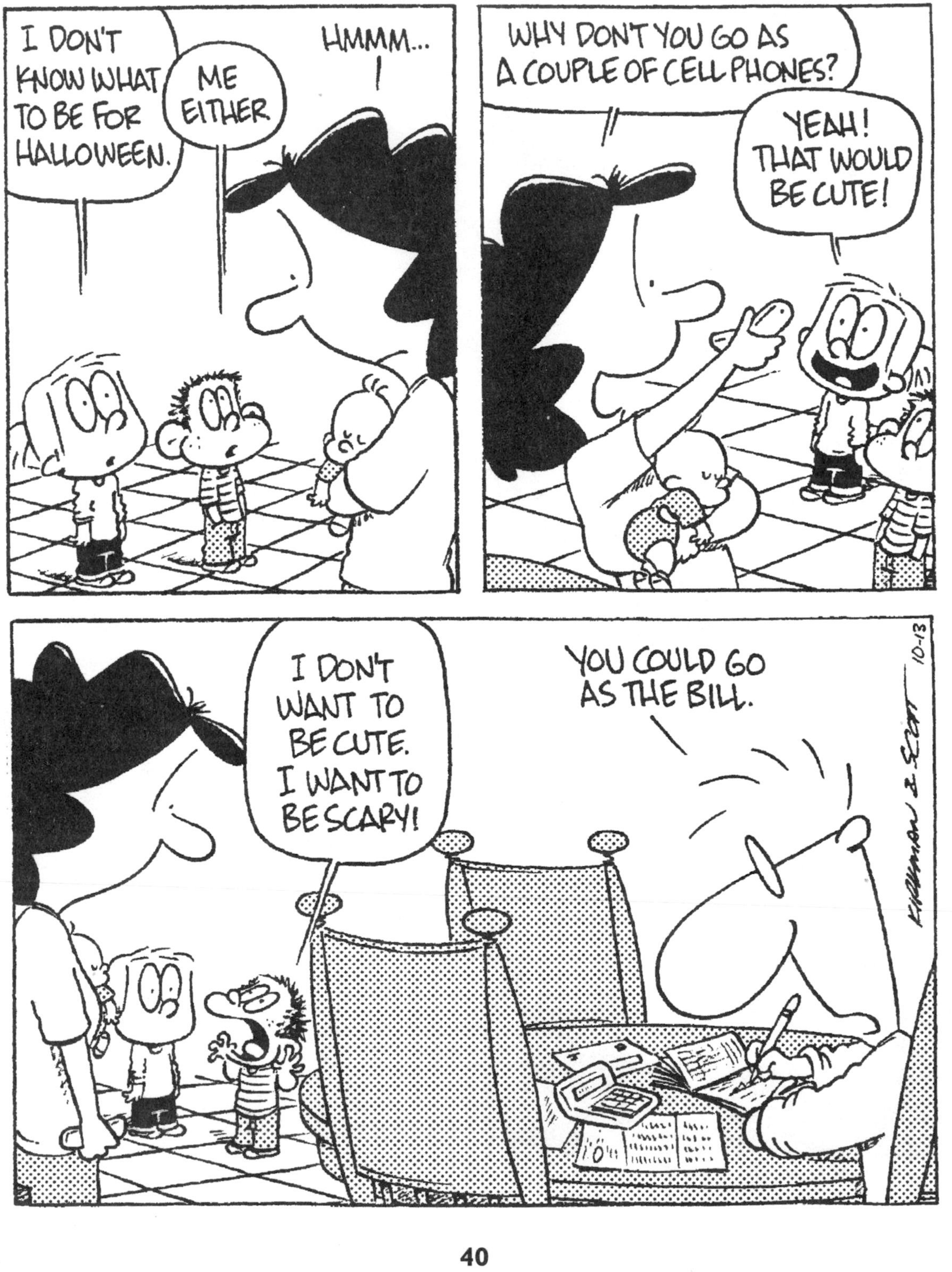

I DON'T KNOW WHAT TO BE FOR HALLOWEEN.
ME EITHER.
HMMM...
WHY DON'T YOU GO AS A COUPLE OF CELL PHONES?
YEAH! THAT WOULD BE CUTE!
I DON'T WANT TO BE CUTE. I WANT TO BE SCARY!
YOU COULD GO AS THE BILL.
KIRKMAN & SCOTT
10-13

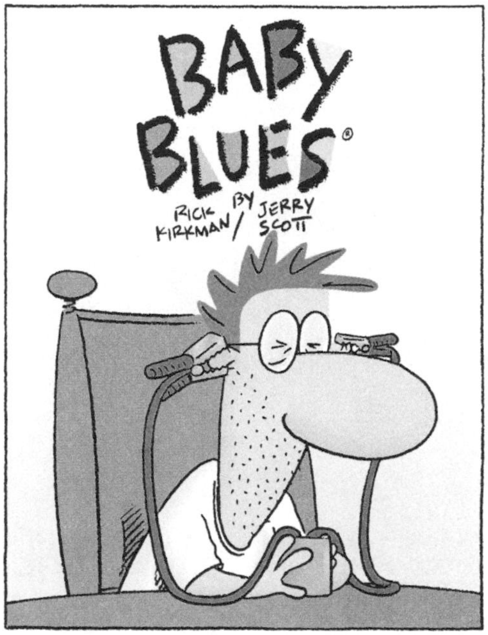
BABY BLUES®
BY RICK KIRKMAN / JERRY SCOTT

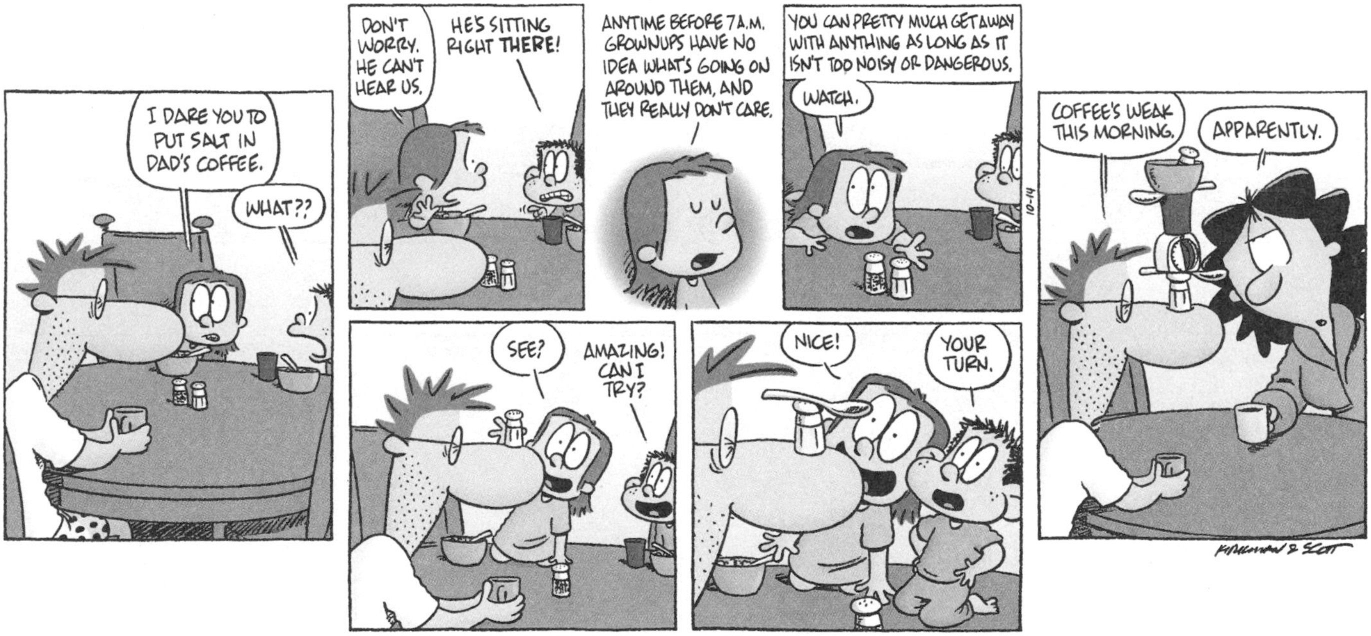
I DARE YOU TO PUT SALT IN DAD'S COFFEE.
WHAT??
DON'T WORRY. HE CAN'T HEAR US.
HE'S SITTING RIGHT THERE!
ANYTIME BEFORE 7 A.M. GROWNUPS HAVE NO IDEA WHAT'S GOING ON AROUND THEM, AND THEY REALLY DON'T CARE.
YOU CAN PRETTY MUCH GET AWAY WITH ANYTHING AS LONG AS IT ISN'T TOO NOISY OR DANGEROUS.
WATCH.
10-14
SEE?
AMAZING! CAN I TRY?
NICE!
YOUR TURN.
COFFEE'S WEAK THIS MORNING.
APPARENTLY.
KIRKMAN & SCOTT

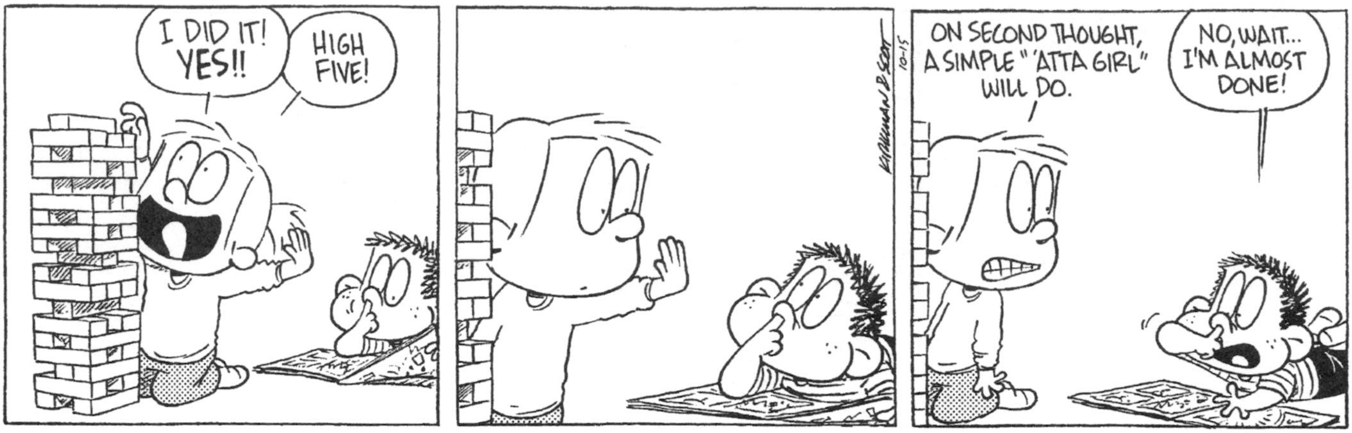
I DID IT! YES!!
HIGH FIVE!
ON SECOND THOUGHT, A SIMPLE "'ATTA GIRL" WILL DO.
NO, WAIT... I'M ALMOST DONE!

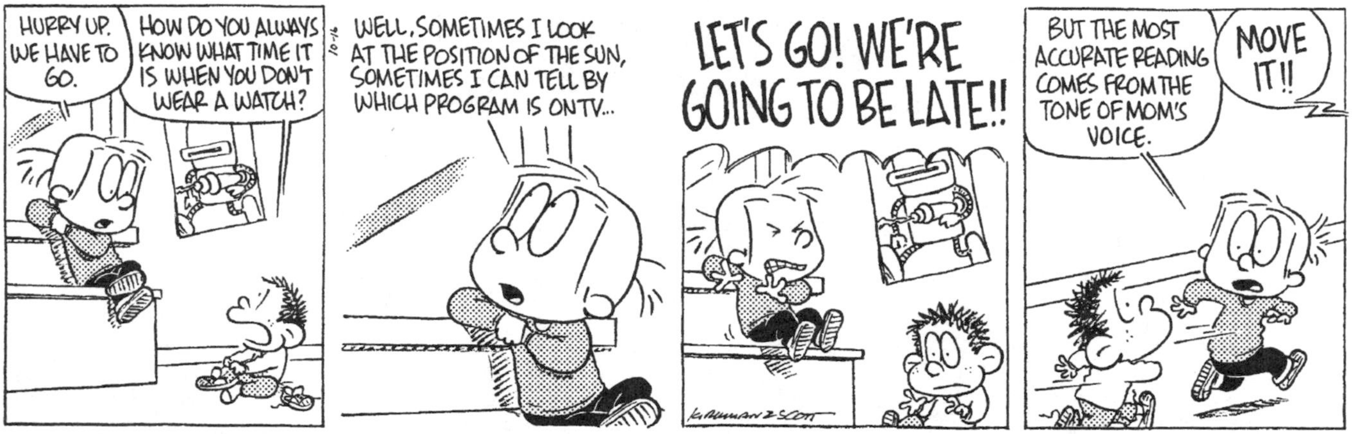
HURRY UP. WE HAVE TO GO.
HOW DO YOU ALWAYS KNOW WHAT TIME IT IS WHEN YOU DON'T WEAR A WATCH?
WELL, SOMETIMES I LOOK AT THE POSITION OF THE SUN, SOMETIMES I CAN TELL BY WHICH PROGRAM IS ON TV...
LET'S GO! WE'RE GOING TO BE LATE!!
BUT THE MOST ACCURATE READING COMES FROM THE TONE OF MOM'S VOICE.
MOVE IT!!

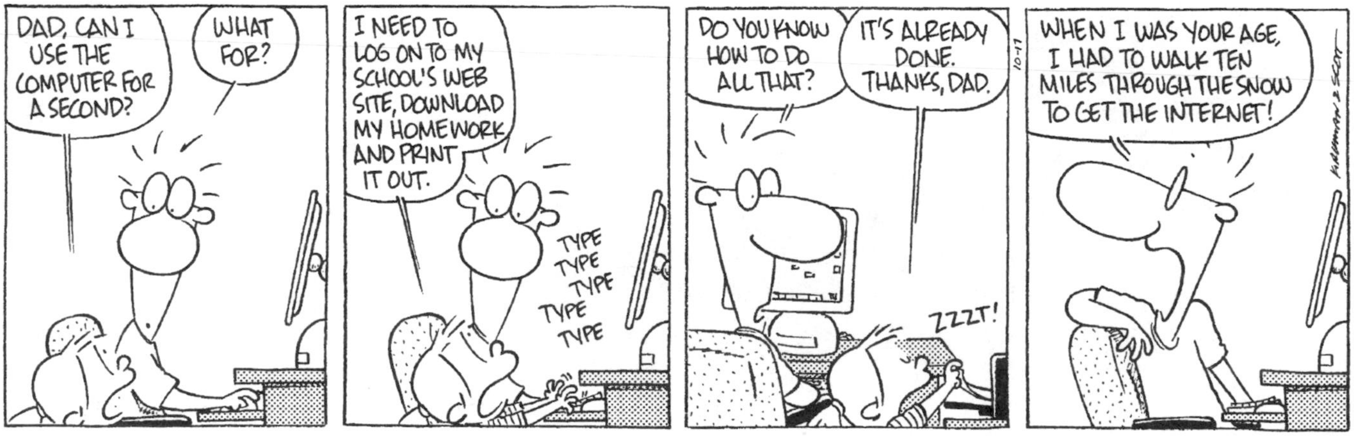
DAD, CAN I USE THE COMPUTER FOR A SECOND?
WHAT FOR?
I NEED TO LOG ON TO MY SCHOOL'S WEB SITE, DOWNLOAD MY HOMEWORK AND PRINT IT OUT.
TYPE TYPE TYPE TYPE TYPE
DO YOU KNOW HOW TO DO ALL THAT?
IT'S ALREADY DONE. THANKS, DAD.
ZZZT!
WHEN I WAS YOUR AGE, I HAD TO WALK TEN MILES THROUGH THE SNOW TO GET THE INTERNET!

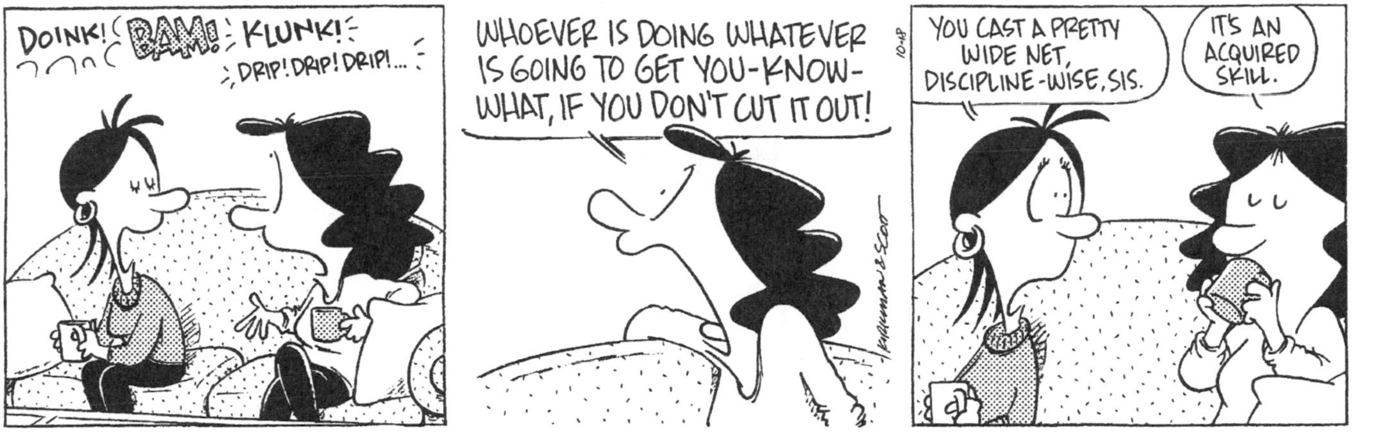
DOINK! BAM! KLUNK!
DRIP! DRIP! DRIP!...
WHOEVER IS DOING WHATEVER IS GOING TO GET YOU-KNOW-WHAT, IF YOU DON'T CUT IT OUT!
YOU CAST A PRETTY WIDE NET, DISCIPLINE-WISE, SIS.
IT'S AN ACQUIRED SKILL.

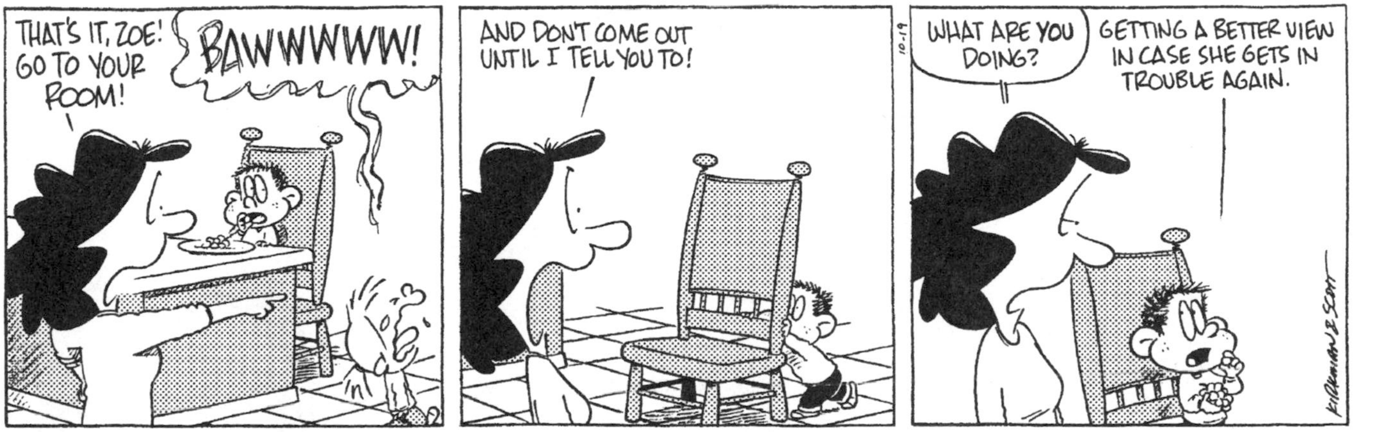
THAT'S IT, ZOE! GO TO YOUR ROOM!
BAWWWWW!
AND DON'T COME OUT UNTIL I TELL YOU TO!
WHAT ARE YOU DOING?
GETTING A BETTER VIEW IN CASE SHE GETS IN TROUBLE AGAIN.

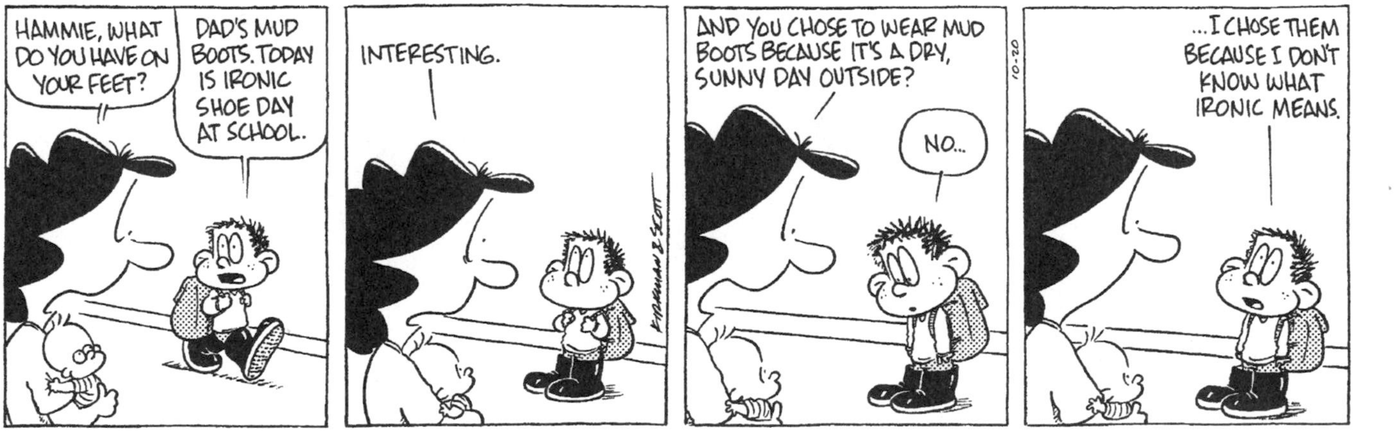
HAMMIE, WHAT DO YOU HAVE ON YOUR FEET?
DAD'S MUD BOOTS. TODAY IS IRONIC SHOE DAY AT SCHOOL.
INTERESTING.
AND YOU CHOSE TO WEAR MUD BOOTS BECAUSE IT'S A DRY, SUNNY DAY OUTSIDE?
NO...
...I CHOSE THEM BECAUSE I DON'T KNOW WHAT IRONIC MEANS.

BABY BLUES®
BY RICK KIRKMAN / JERRY SCOTT

DID HAMMIE TELL YOU THAT HE WAS GOING ROCK CLIMBING?
WHAT??
ARE YOU SERIOUS?
YEAH. HE TOOK ROPE, GLOVES... EVERYTHING!
HE DOESN'T KNOW ANYTHING ABOUT ROCK CLIMBING! HE'LL KILL HIMSELF!
THAT'S WHAT I TOLD HIM.
WE HAVE TO FIND HIM BEFORE HE GETS HURT!
HE WENT TOWARD THE VACANT LOT! HURRY!!
I CAN'T LOOK! IS HE OKAY?
THIS LOOKED SO MUCH COOLER ON TV.
10-21 KIRKMAN & SCOTT

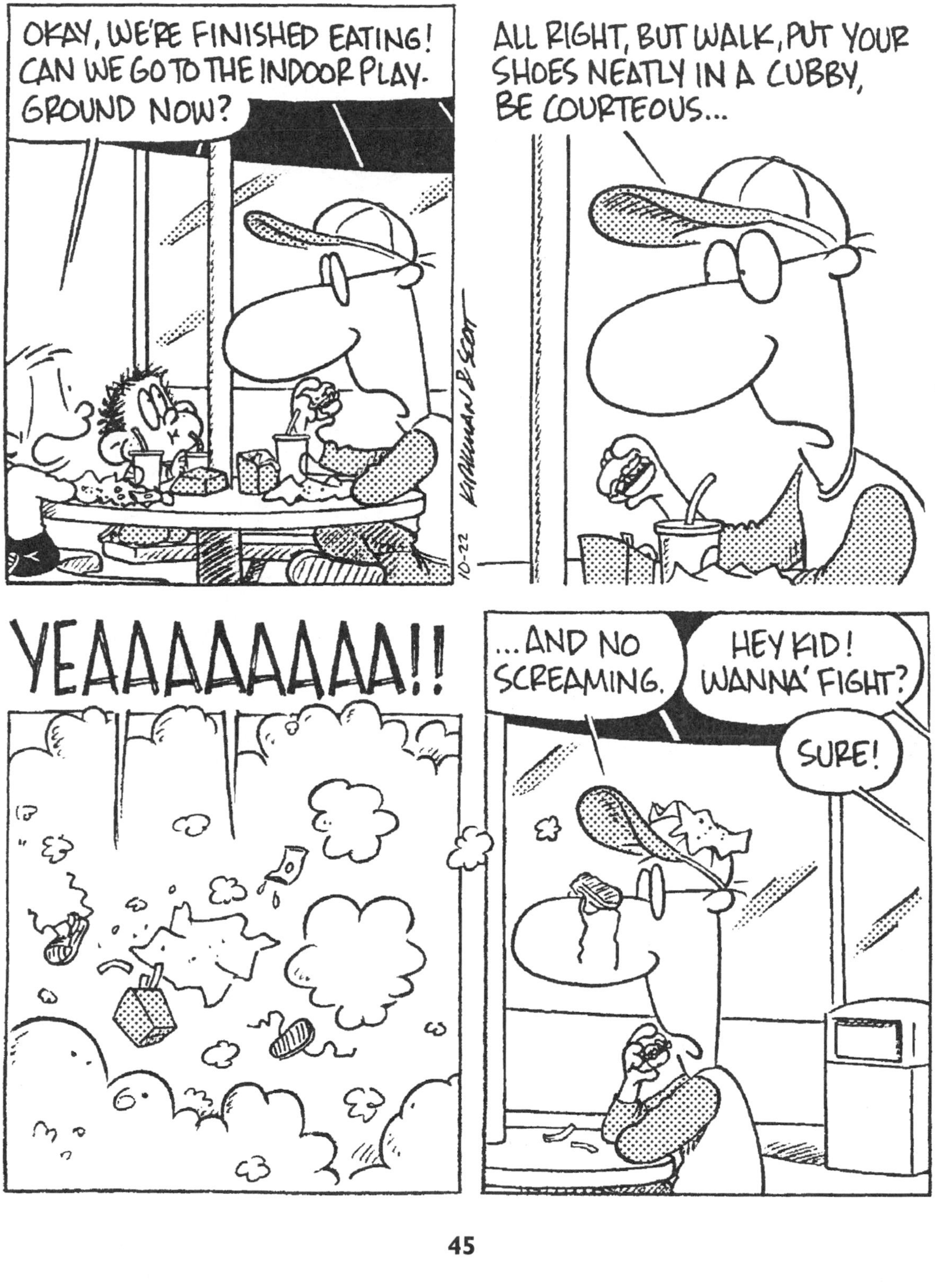
OKAY, WE'RE FINISHED EATING! CAN WE GO TO THE INDOOR PLAY-GROUND NOW?
KIRKMAN & SCOTT
10-22
ALL RIGHT, BUT WALK, PUT YOUR SHOES NEATLY IN A CUBBY, BE COURTEOUS...
YEAAAAAAAAA!!
...AND NO SCREAMING.
HEY KID! WANNA' FIGHT?
SURE!

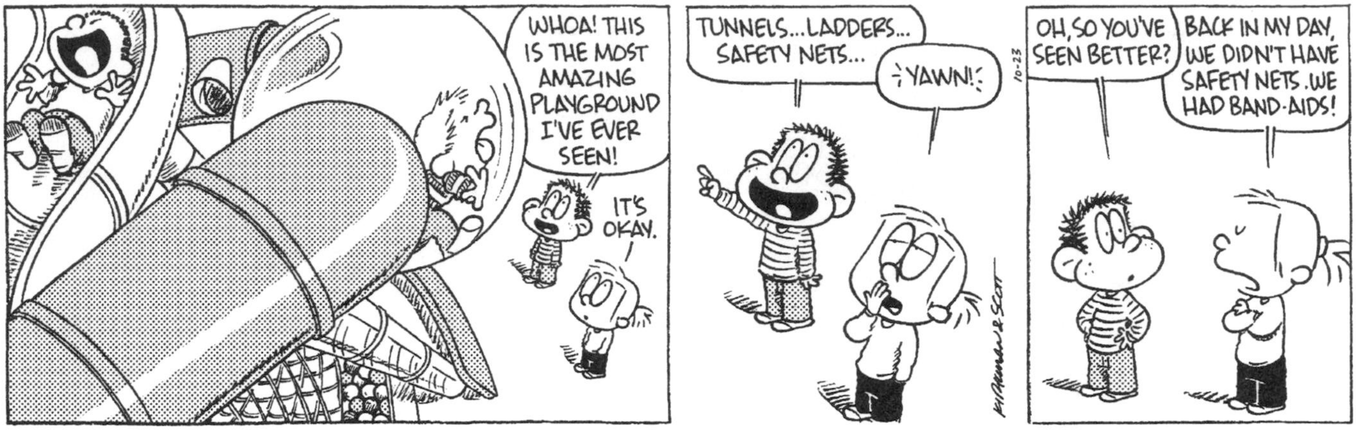
WHOA! THIS IS THE MOST AMAZING PLAYGROUND I'VE EVER SEEN!
IT'S OKAY.
TUNNELS...LADDERS... SAFETY NETS...
YAWN!
10-23
OH, SO YOU'VE SEEN BETTER?
BACK IN MY DAY, WE DIDN'T HAVE SAFETY NETS. WE HAD BAND-AIDS!

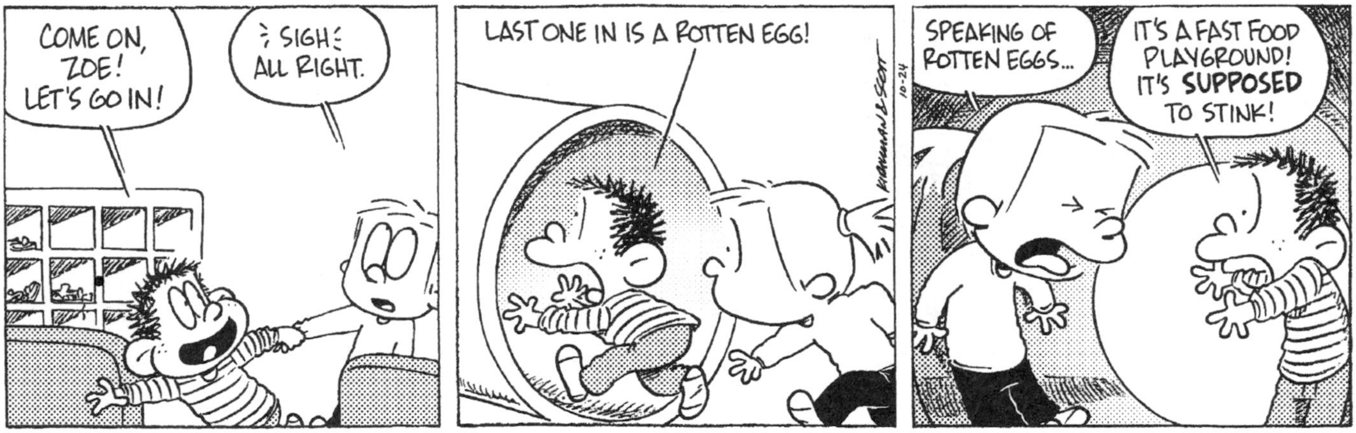
COME ON, ZOE! LET'S GO IN!
SIGH ALL RIGHT.
LAST ONE IN IS A ROTTEN EGG!
10-24
SPEAKING OF ROTTEN EGGS...
IT'S A FAST FOOD PLAYGROUND! IT'S **SUPPOSED** TO STINK!

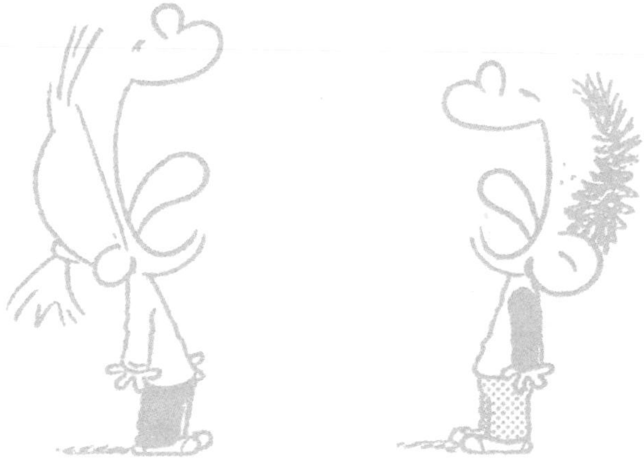

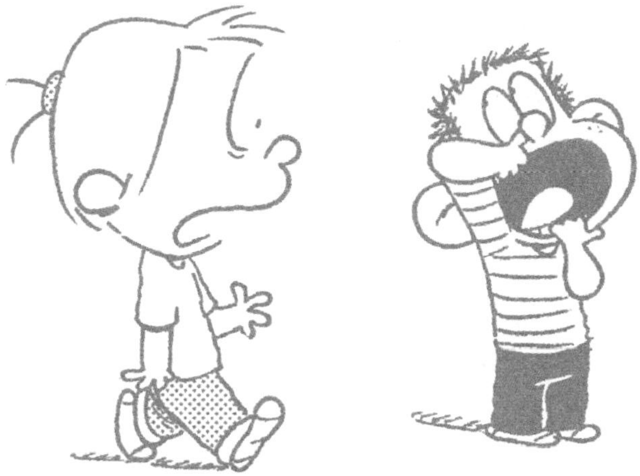

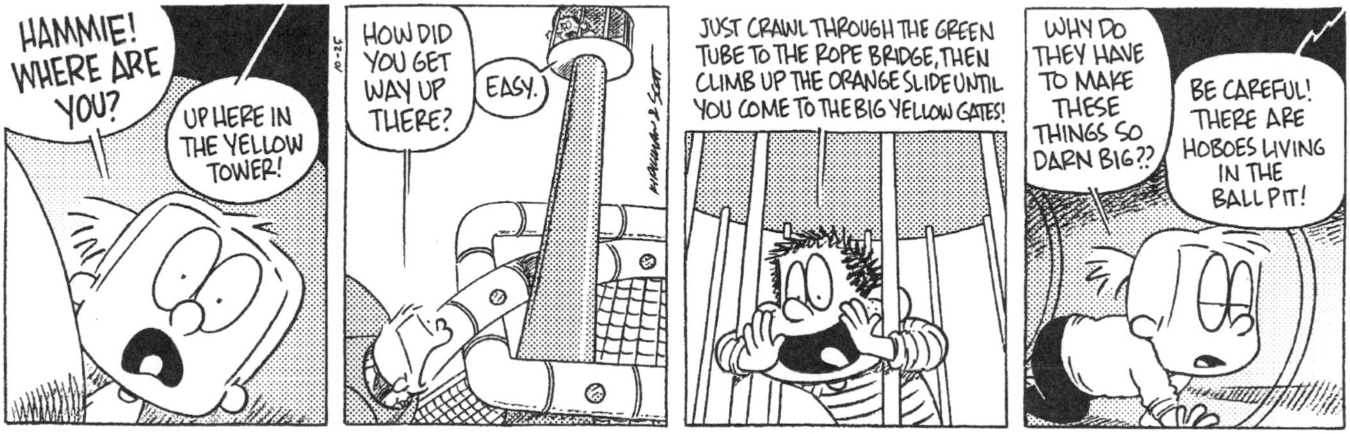

HAMMIE! WHERE ARE YOU?
UP HERE IN THE YELLOW TOWER!
HOW DID YOU GET WAY UP THERE?
EASY.
JUST CRAWL THROUGH THE GREEN TUBE TO THE ROPE BRIDGE, THEN CLIMB UP THE ORANGE SLIDE UNTIL YOU COME TO THE BIG YELLOW GATES!
WHY DO THEY HAVE TO MAKE THESE THINGS SO DARN BIG??
BE CAREFUL! THERE ARE HOBOES LIVING IN THE BALL PIT!

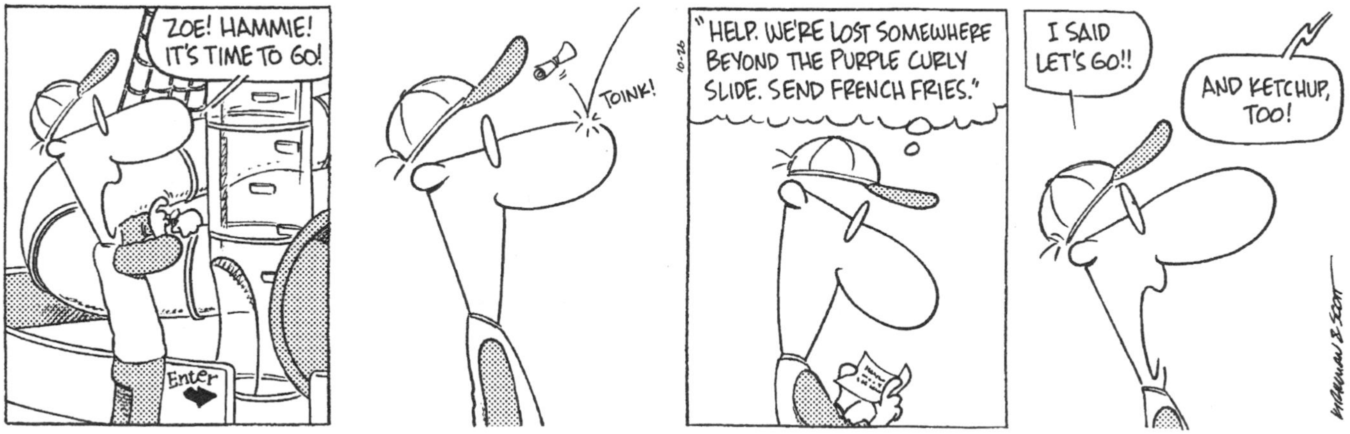

ZOE! HAMMIE! IT'S TIME TO GO!
Enter
TOINK!
"HELP. WE'RE LOST SOMEWHERE BEYOND THE PURPLE CURLY SLIDE. SEND FRENCH FRIES."
I SAID LET'S GO!!
AND KETCHUP, TOO!

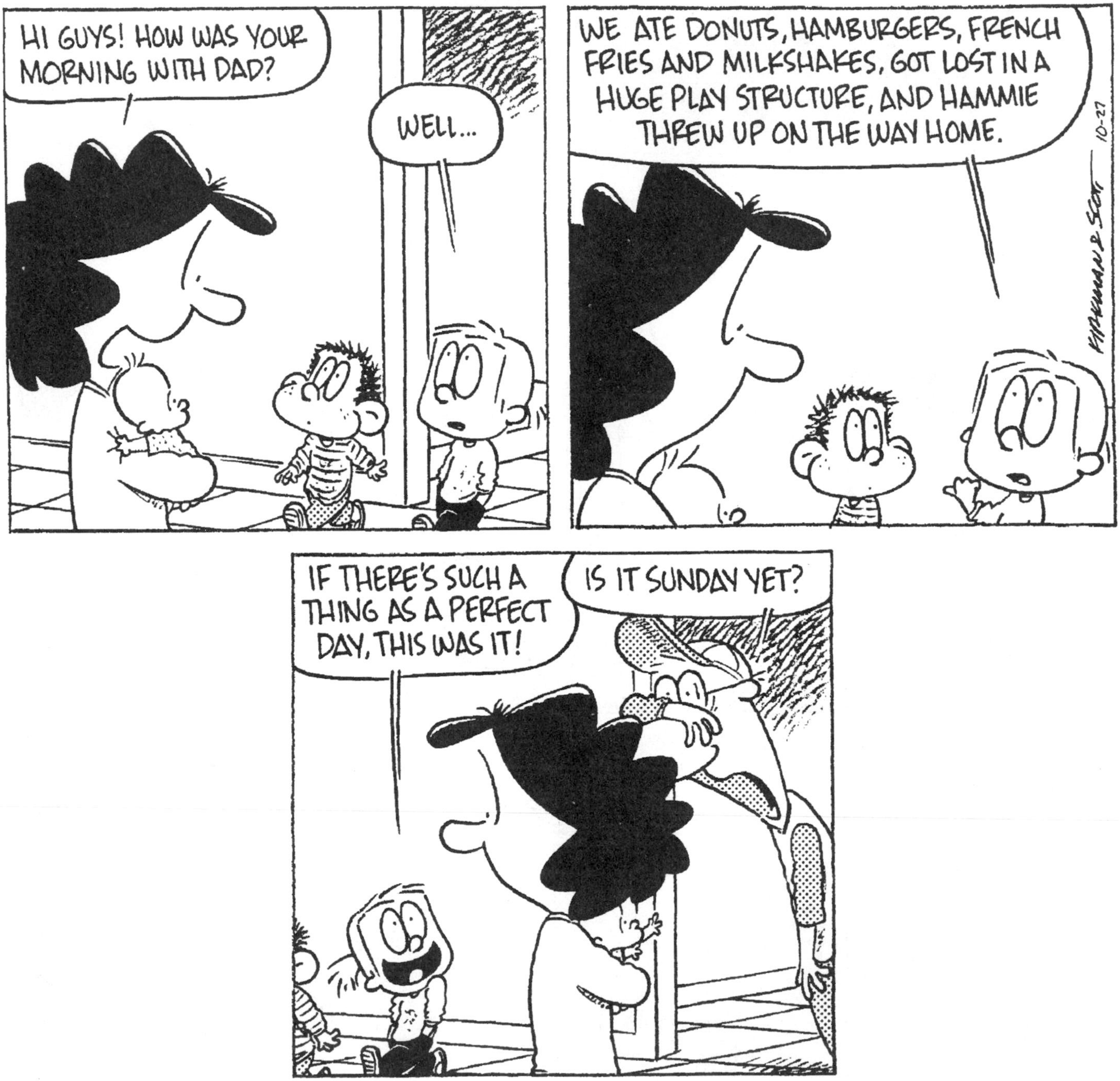
HI GUYS! HOW WAS YOUR MORNING WITH DAD?
WELL...
WE ATE DONUTS, HAMBURGERS, FRENCH FRIES AND MILKSHAKES, GOT LOST IN A HUGE PLAY STRUCTURE, AND HAMMIE THREW UP ON THE WAY HOME.
10-27
KIRKMAN & SCOTT
IF THERE'S SUCH A THING AS A PERFECT DAY, THIS WAS IT!
IS IT SUNDAY YET?

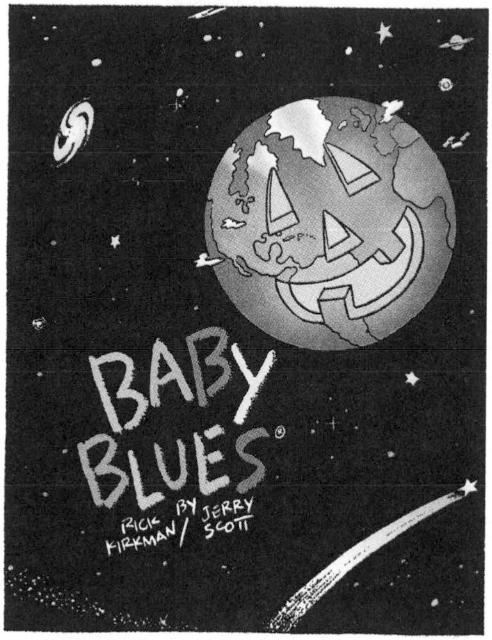
BABY BLUES®
BY RICK KIRKMAN / JERRY SCOTT

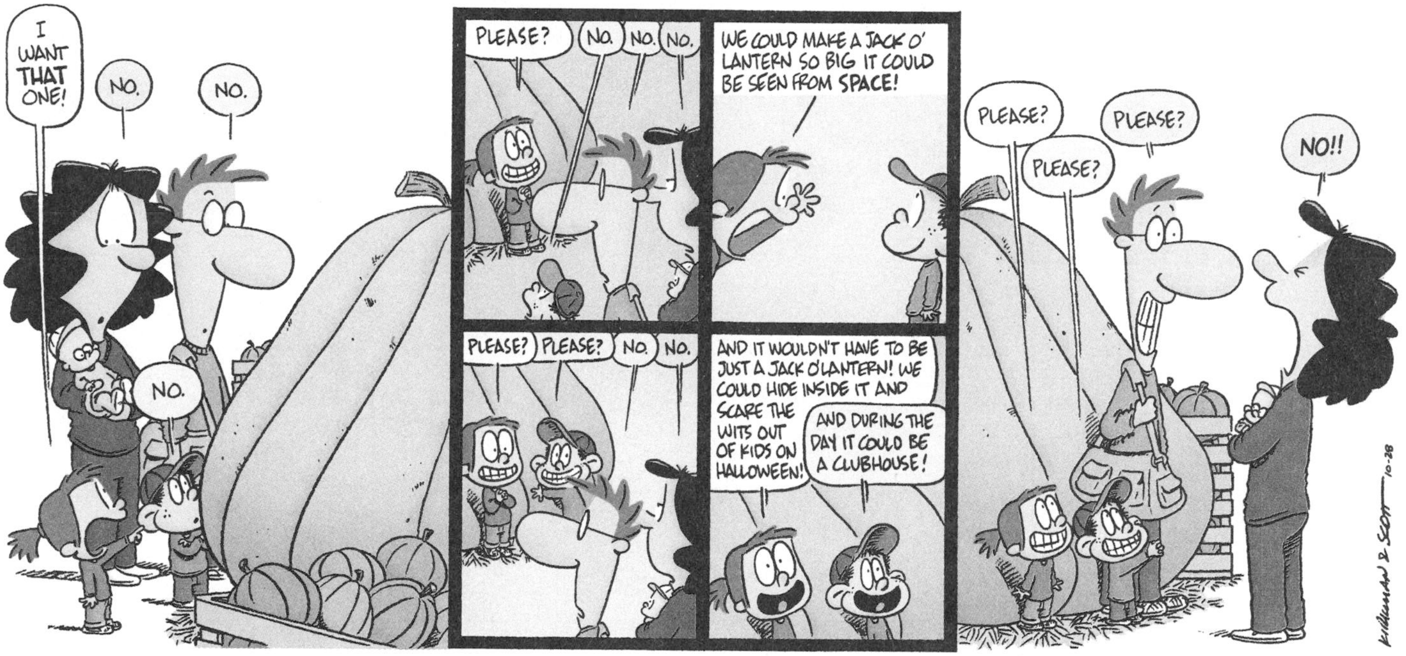
I WANT THAT ONE!
NO.
NO.
NO.
PLEASE?
NO.
NO.
NO.
WE COULD MAKE A JACK O' LANTERN SO BIG IT COULD BE SEEN FROM SPACE!
PLEASE?
PLEASE?
NO.
NO.
AND IT WOULDN'T HAVE TO BE JUST A JACK O'LANTERN! WE COULD HIDE INSIDE IT AND SCARE THE WITS OUT OF KIDS ON HALLOWEEN!
AND DURING THE DAY IT COULD BE A CLUBHOUSE!
PLEASE?
PLEASE?
PLEASE?
NO!!
KIRKMAN & SCOTT
10-28

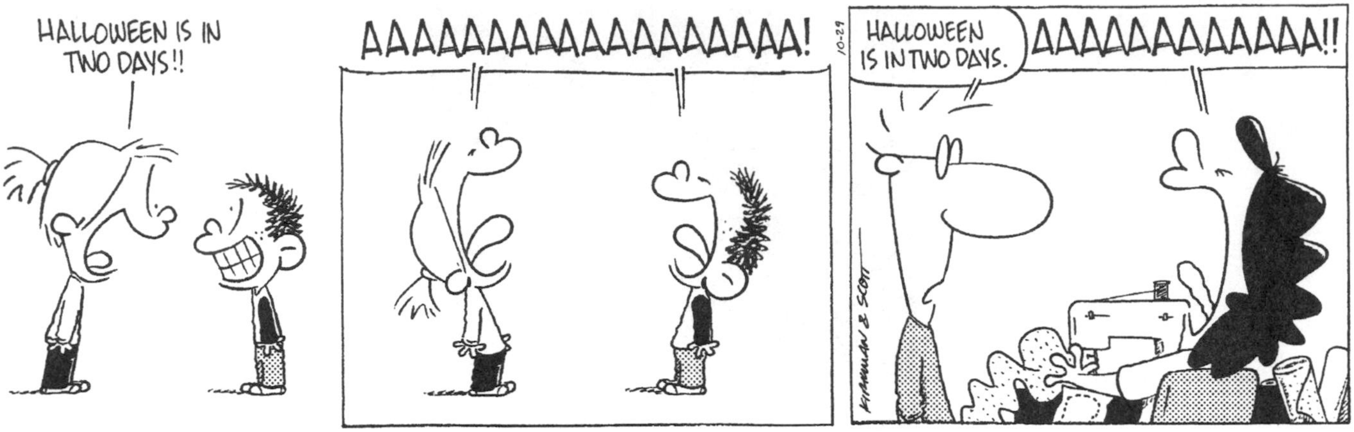
HALLOWEEN IS IN TWO DAYS!!
AAAAAAAAAAAAAAAAAA!
10-29
HALLOWEEN IS IN TWO DAYS.
AAAAAAAAAAAA!!
KIRKMAN & SCOTT

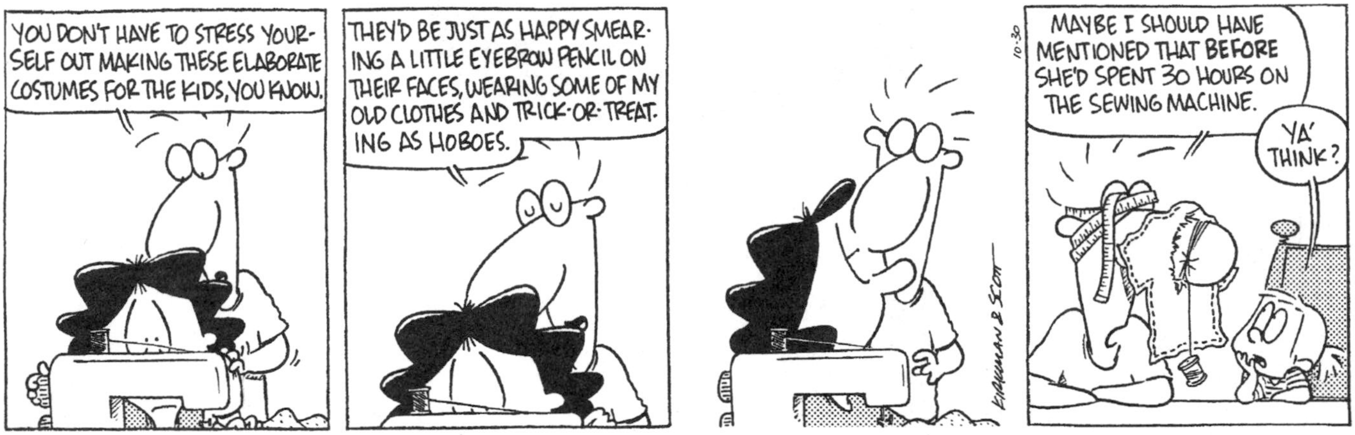
YOU DON'T HAVE TO STRESS YOURSELF OUT MAKING THESE ELABORATE COSTUMES FOR THE KIDS, YOU KNOW.
THEY'D BE JUST AS HAPPY SMEARING A LITTLE EYEBROW PENCIL ON THEIR FACES, WEARING SOME OF MY OLD CLOTHES AND TRICK-OR-TREATING AS HOBOES.
KIRKMAN & SCOTT
10-30
MAYBE I SHOULD HAVE MENTIONED THAT BEFORE SHE'D SPENT 30 HOURS ON THE SEWING MACHINE.
YA' THINK?

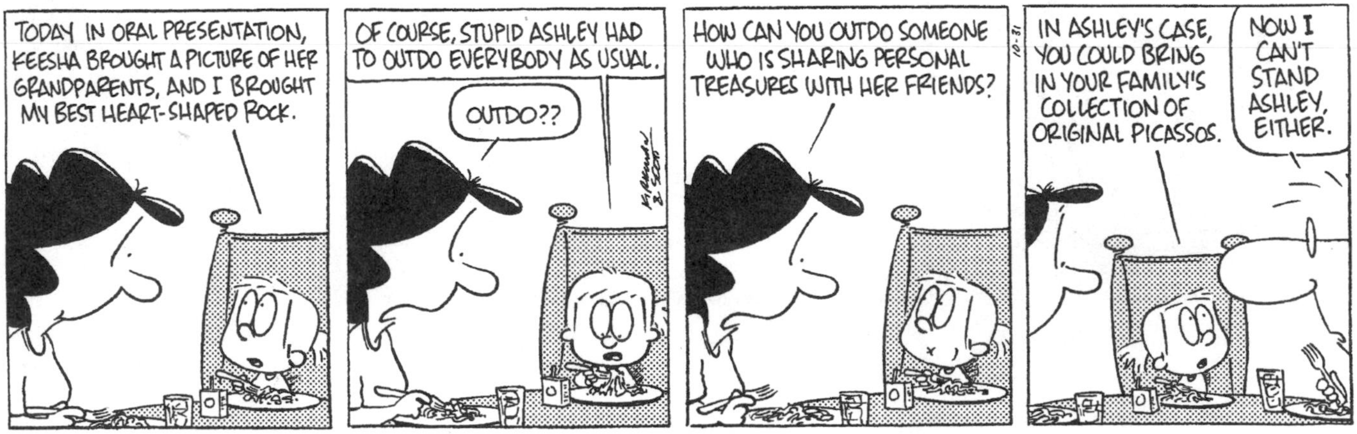
TODAY IN ORAL PRESENTATION, KEESHA BROUGHT A PICTURE OF HER GRANDPARENTS, AND I BROUGHT MY BEST HEART-SHAPED ROCK.
OF COURSE, STUPID ASHLEY HAD TO OUTDO EVERYBODY AS USUAL.
OUTDO??
KIRKMAN & SCOTT
HOW CAN YOU OUTDO SOMEONE WHO IS SHARING PERSONAL TREASURES WITH HER FRIENDS?
10-31
IN ASHLEY'S CASE, YOU COULD BRING IN YOUR FAMILY'S COLLECTION OF ORIGINAL PICASSOS.
NOW I CAN'T STAND ASHLEY, EITHER.

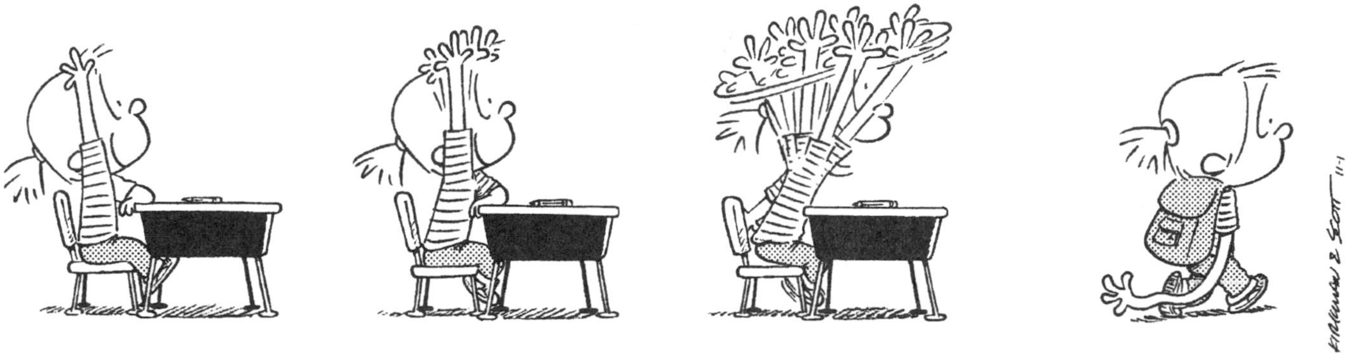

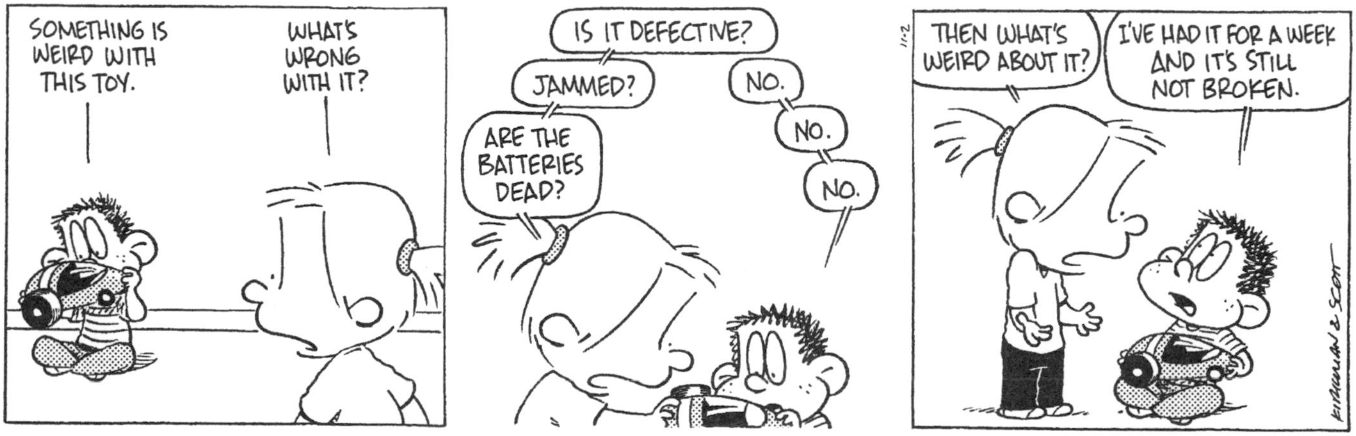
SOMETHING IS WEIRD WITH THIS TOY.
WHAT'S WRONG WITH IT?
IS IT DEFECTIVE?
NO.
JAMMED?
NO.
ARE THE BATTERIES DEAD?
NO.
THEN WHAT'S WEIRD ABOUT IT?
I'VE HAD IT FOR A WEEK AND IT'S STILL NOT BROKEN.

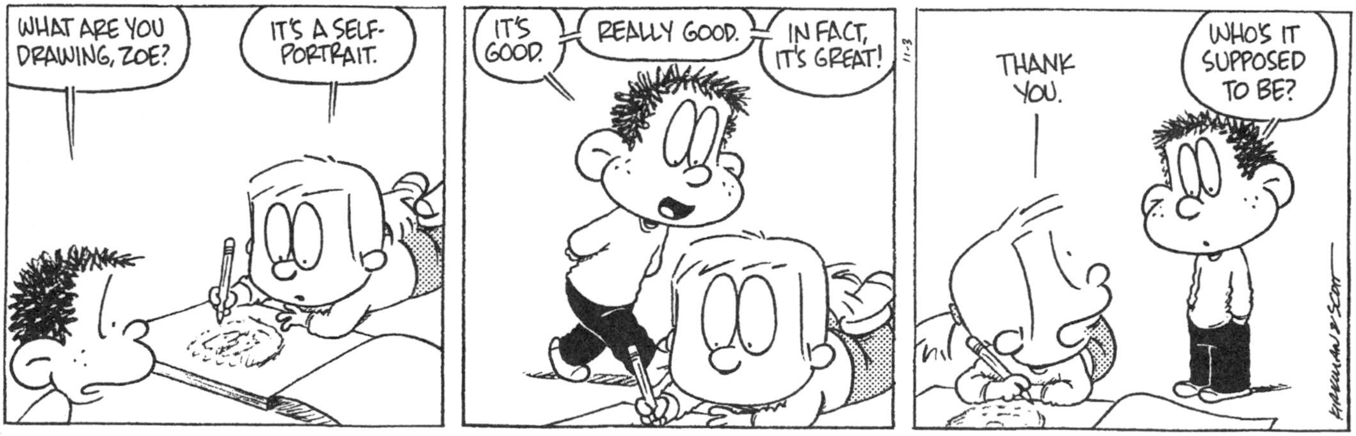
WHAT ARE YOU DRAWING, ZOE?
IT'S A SELF-PORTRAIT.
IT'S GOOD.
REALLY GOOD.
IN FACT, IT'S GREAT!
THANK YOU.
WHO'S IT SUPPOSED TO BE?

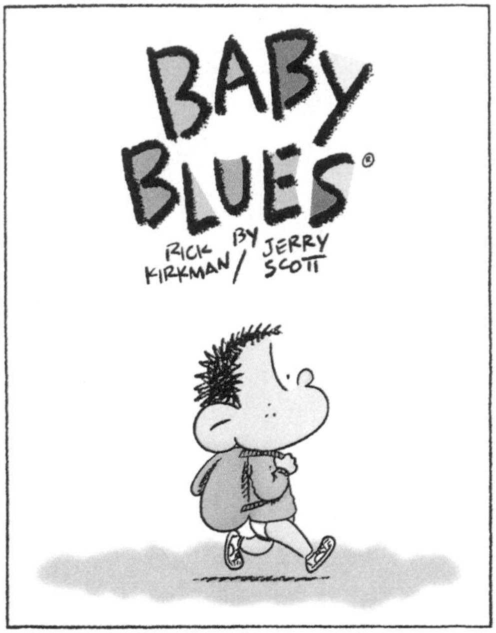
BABY BLUES®
BY RICK KIRKMAN / JERRY SCOTT

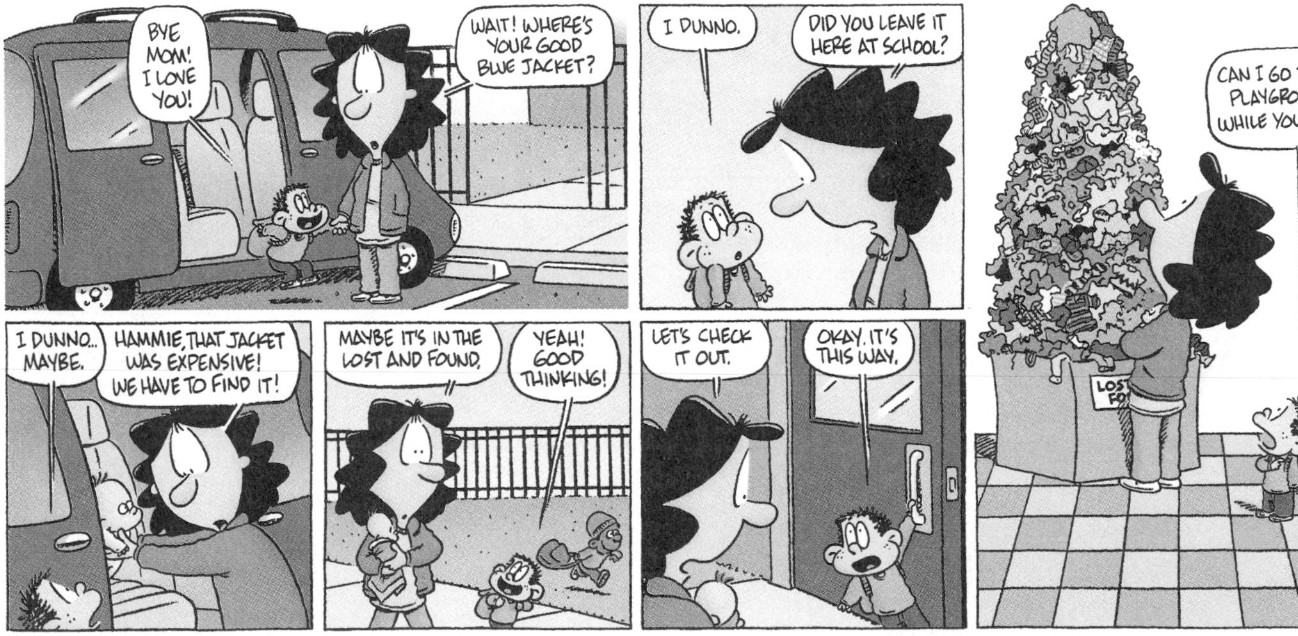
BYE MOM! I LOVE YOU!
WAIT! WHERE'S YOUR GOOD BLUE JACKET?
I DUNNO.
DID YOU LEAVE IT HERE AT SCHOOL?
I DUNNO... MAYBE.
HAMMIE, THAT JACKET WAS EXPENSIVE! WE HAVE TO FIND IT!
MAYBE IT'S IN THE LOST AND FOUND.
YEAH! GOOD THINKING!
LET'S CHECK IT OUT.
OKAY. IT'S THIS WAY.
CAN I GO TO THE PLAYGROUND WHILE YOU LOOK?
KIRKMAN & SCOTT 11-4

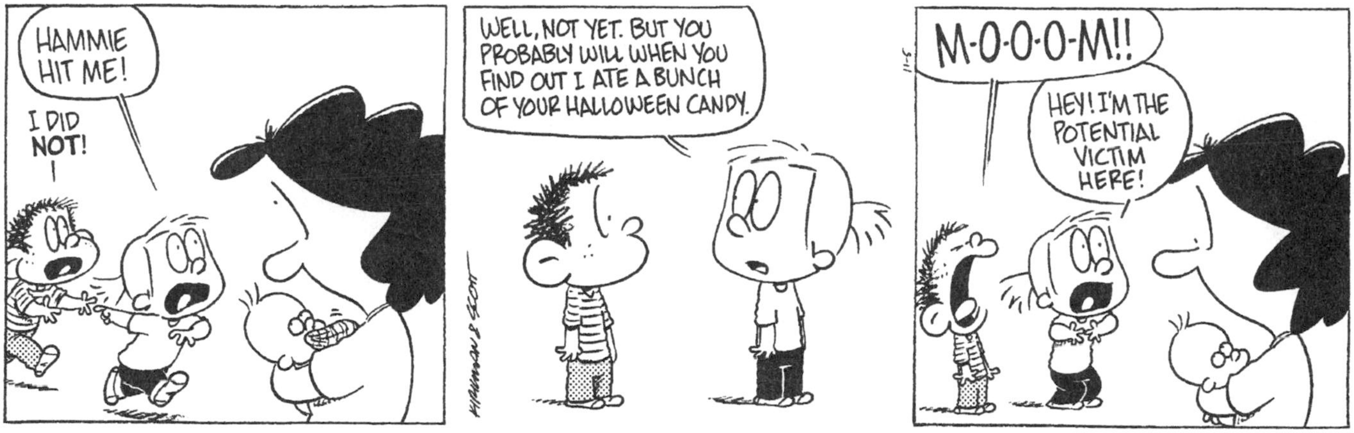
HAMMIE HIT ME!
I DID **NOT**!
WELL, NOT YET. BUT YOU PROBABLY WILL WHEN YOU FIND OUT I ATE A BUNCH OF YOUR HALLOWEEN CANDY.
M-O-O-O-M!!
HEY! I'M THE POTENTIAL VICTIM HERE!

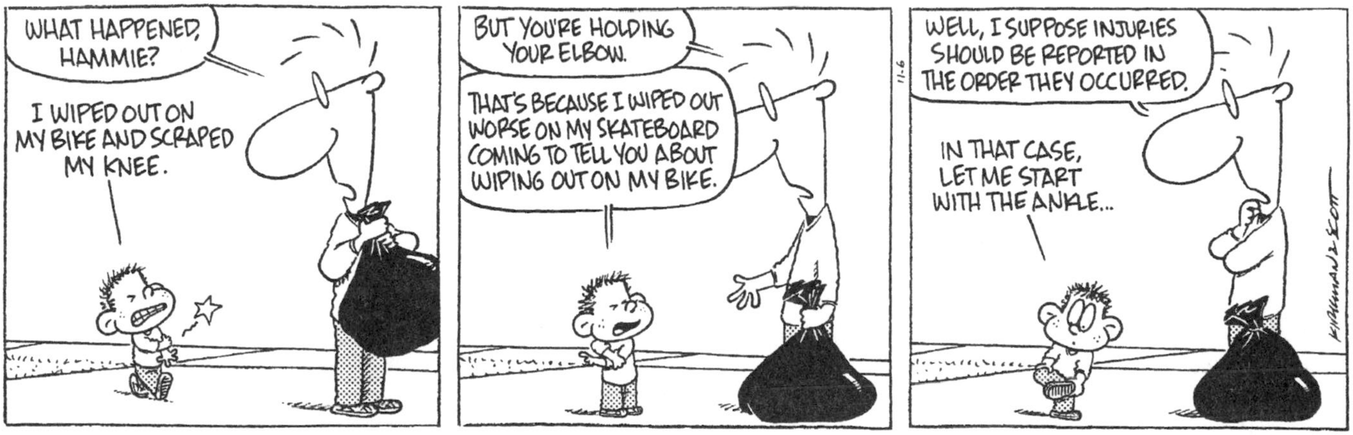
WHAT HAPPENED, HAMMIE?
I WIPED OUT ON MY BIKE AND SCRAPED MY KNEE.
BUT YOU'RE HOLDING YOUR ELBOW.
THAT'S BECAUSE I WIPED OUT WORSE ON MY SKATEBOARD COMING TO TELL YOU ABOUT WIPING OUT ON MY BIKE.
WELL, I SUPPOSE INJURIES SHOULD BE REPORTED IN THE ORDER THEY OCCURRED.
IN THAT CASE, LET ME START WITH THE ANKLE...

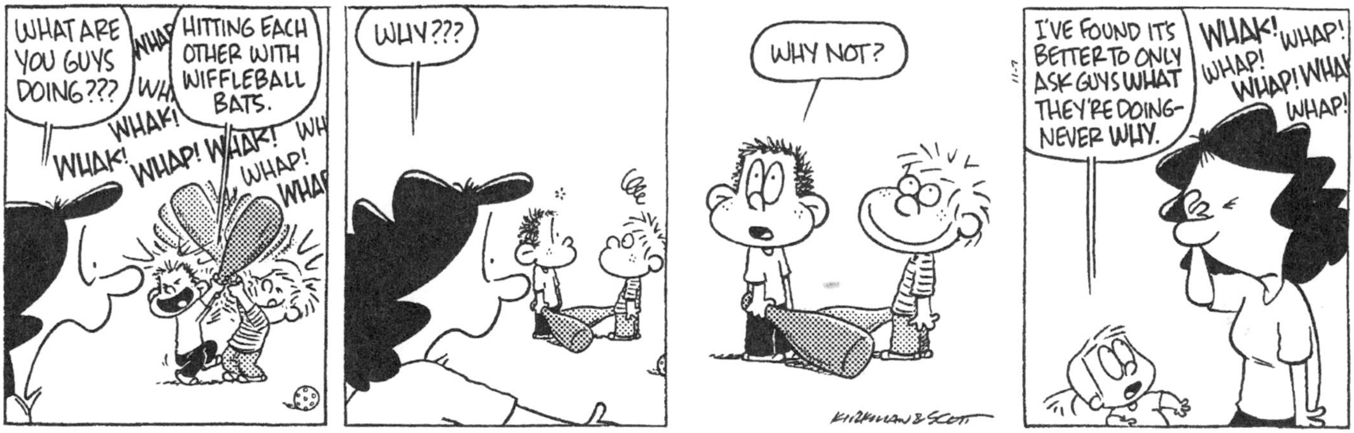
WHAT ARE YOU GUYS DOING???
HITTING EACH OTHER WITH WIFFLEBALL BATS.
WHAK! WHAP! WHAK! WHAP!
WHY???
WHY NOT?
I'VE FOUND IT'S BETTER TO ONLY ASK GUYS **WHAT** THEY'RE DOING-NEVER **WHY**.
WHAK! WHAP! WHAP! WHAP! WHAP!

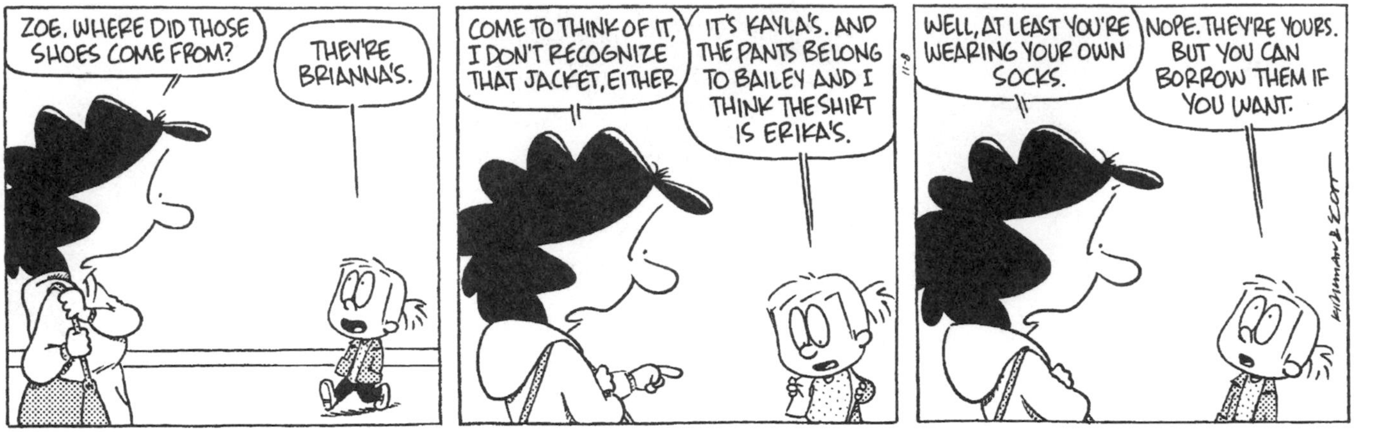
ZOE, WHERE DID THOSE SHOES COME FROM?
THEY'RE BRIANNA'S.
COME TO THINK OF IT, I DON'T RECOGNIZE THAT JACKET, EITHER.
IT'S KAYLA'S. AND THE PANTS BELONG TO BAILEY AND I THINK THE SHIRT IS ERIKA'S.
11-8
WELL, AT LEAST YOU'RE WEARING YOUR OWN SOCKS.
NOPE. THEY'RE YOURS. BUT YOU CAN BORROW THEM IF YOU WANT.
KIRKMAN & SCOTT

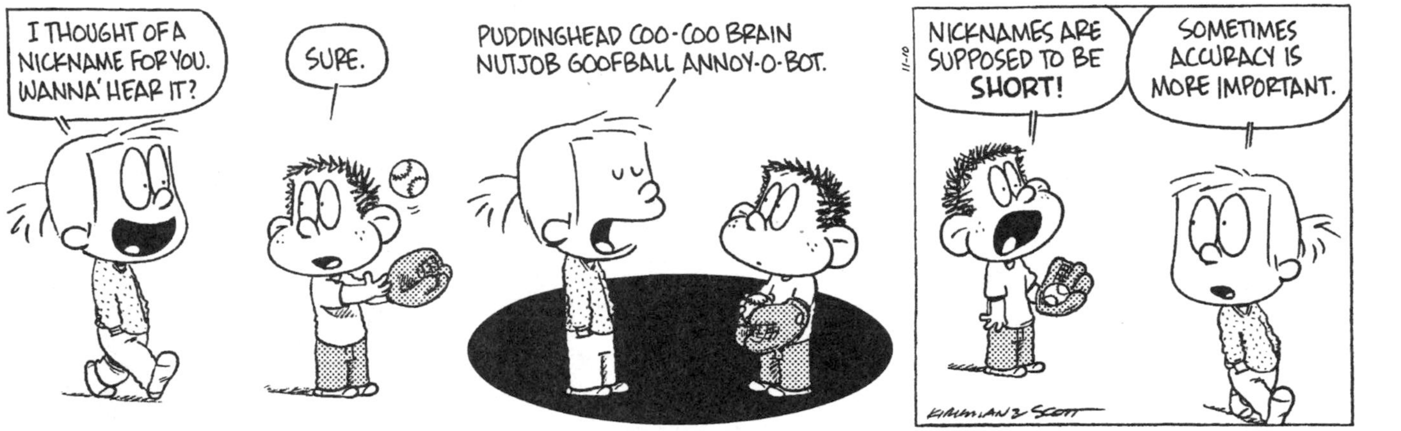
I THOUGHT OF A NICKNAME FOR YOU. WANNA' HEAR IT?
SURE.
PUDDINGHEAD COO-COO BRAIN NUTJOB GOOFBALL ANNOY-O-BOT.
11-10
NICKNAMES ARE SUPPOSED TO BE **SHORT!**
SOMETIMES ACCURACY IS MORE IMPORTANT.
KIRKMAN & SCOTT

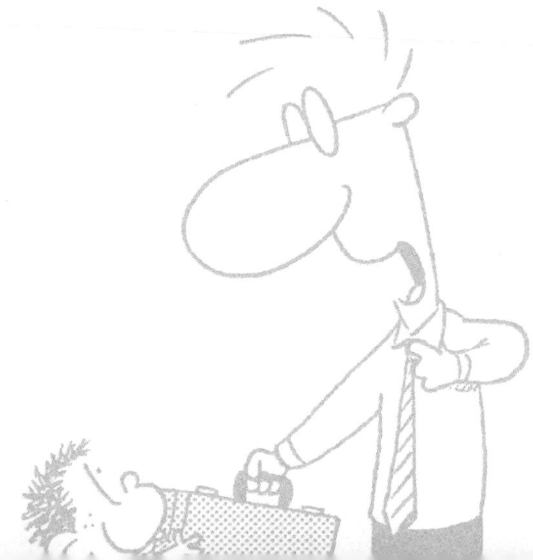

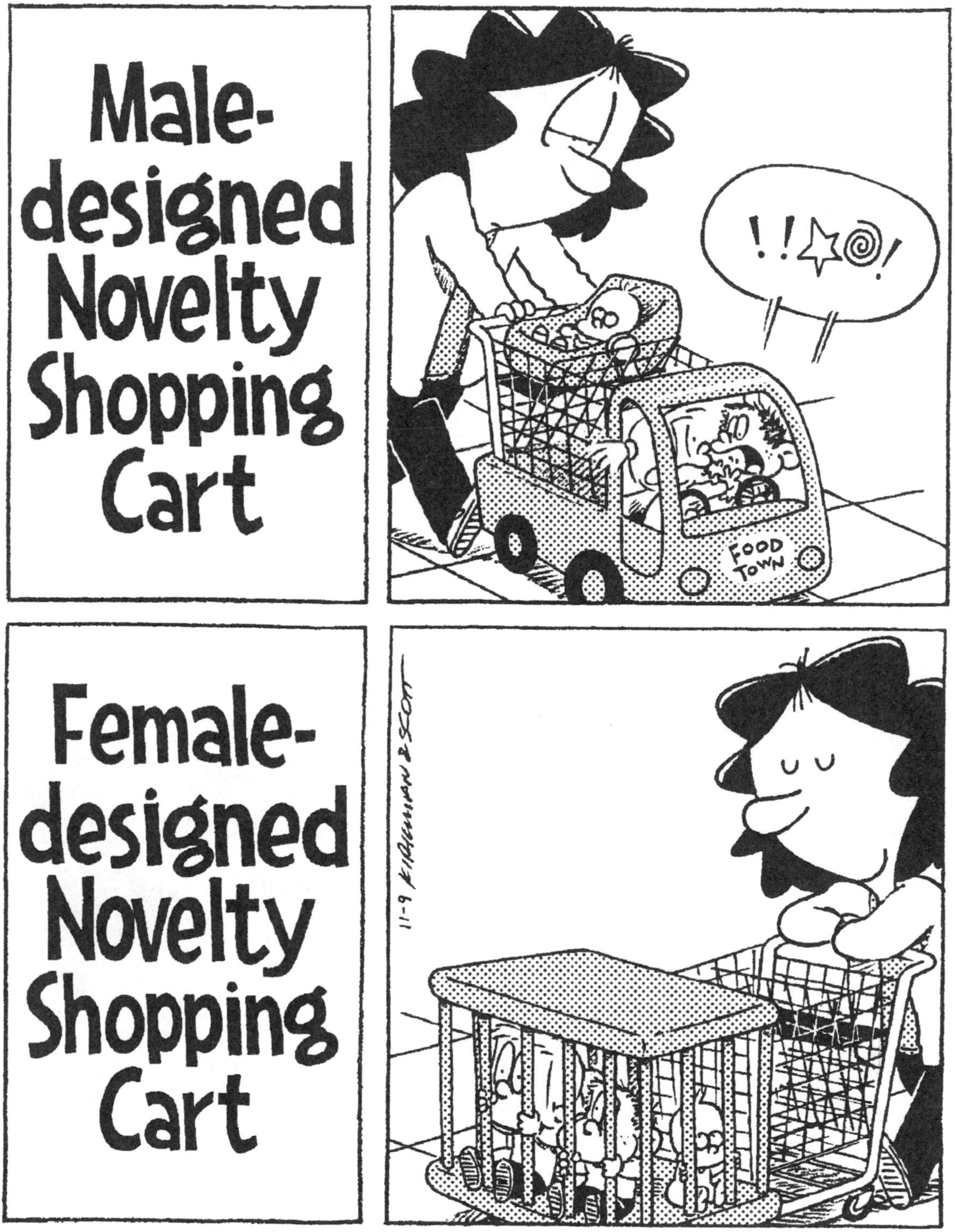
Male-designed Novelty Shopping Cart
FOOD TOWN
Female-designed Novelty Shopping Cart
11-9 KIRKMAN & SCOTT

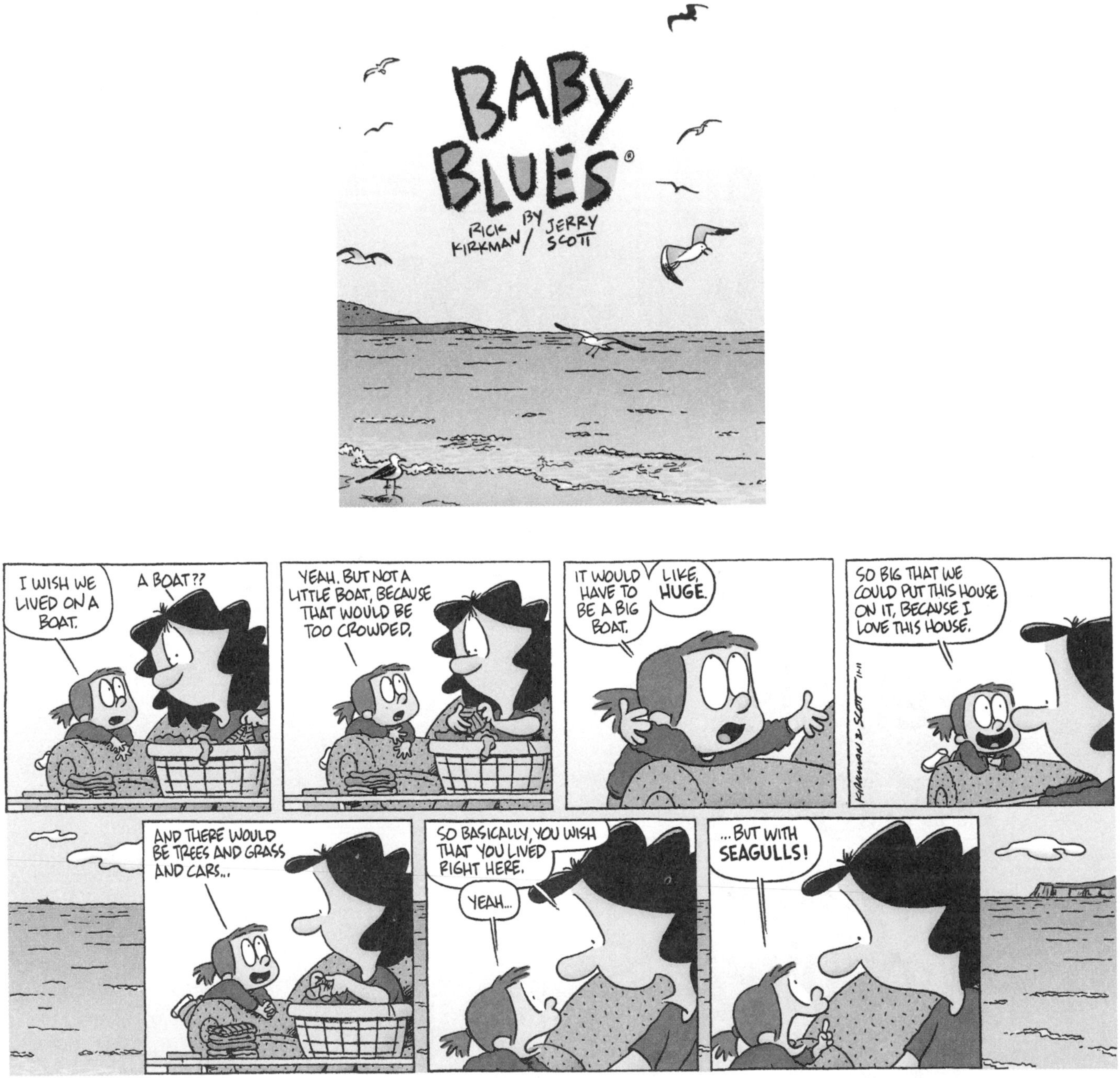
BABY BLUES®
RICK KIRKMAN / BY / JERRY SCOTT
I WISH WE LIVED ON A BOAT.
A BOAT??
YEAH. BUT NOT A LITTLE BOAT, BECAUSE THAT WOULD BE TOO CROWDED.
IT WOULD HAVE TO BE A BIG BOAT.
LIKE, HUGE.
SO BIG THAT WE COULD PUT THIS HOUSE ON IT, BECAUSE I LOVE THIS HOUSE.
KIRKMAN & SCOTT
AND THERE WOULD BE TREES AND GRASS AND CARS...
SO BASICALLY, YOU WISH THAT YOU LIVED RIGHT HERE.
YEAH...
...BUT WITH SEAGULLS!

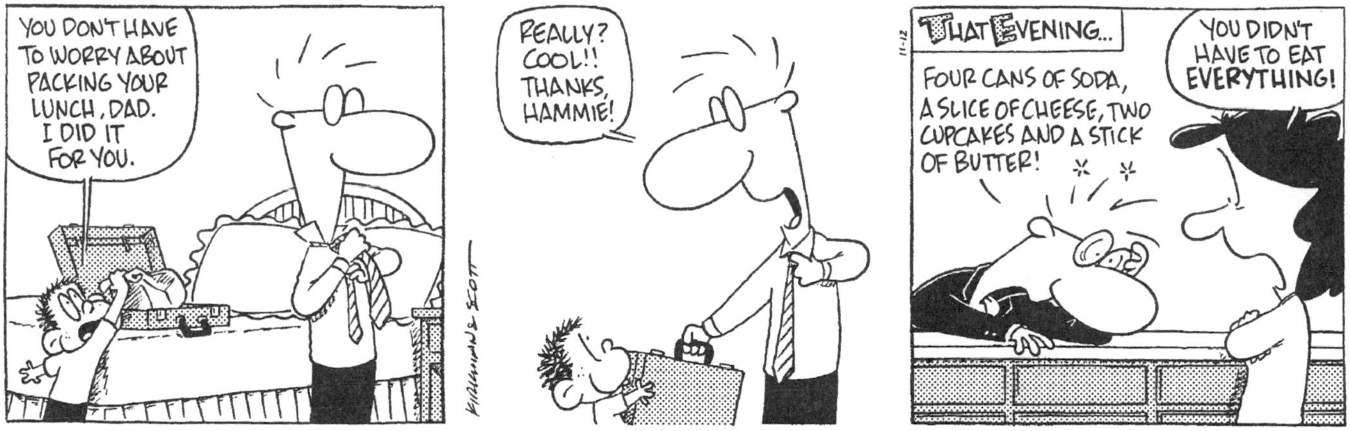
YOU DON'T HAVE TO WORRY ABOUT PACKING YOUR LUNCH, DAD. I DID IT FOR YOU.
REALLY? COOL!! THANKS, HAMMIE!
THAT EVENING...
FOUR CANS OF SODA, A SLICE OF CHEESE, TWO CUPCAKES AND A STICK OF BUTTER!
YOU DIDN'T HAVE TO EAT EVERYTHING!

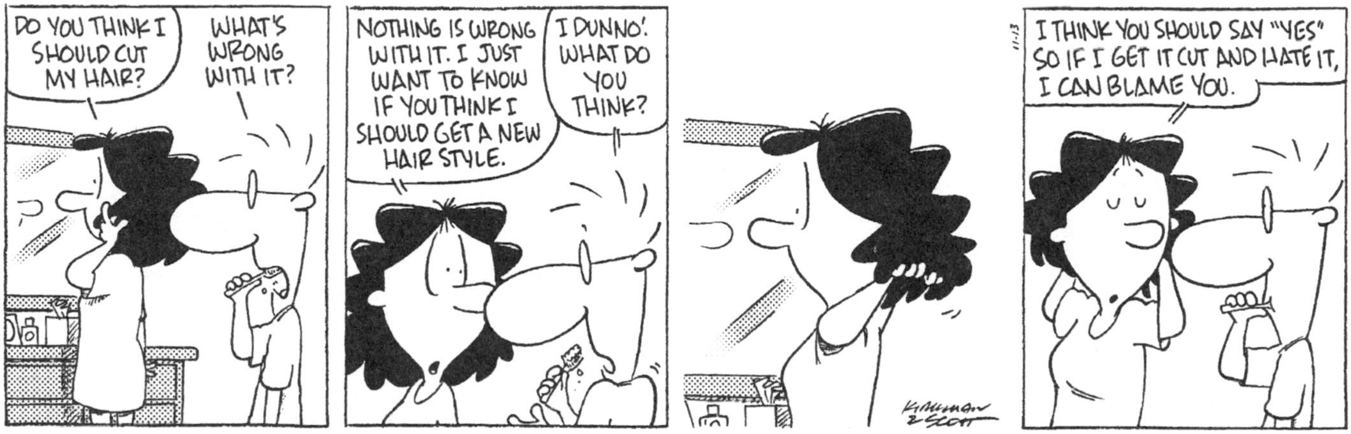
DO YOU THINK I SHOULD CUT MY HAIR?
WHAT'S WRONG WITH IT?
NOTHING IS WRONG WITH IT. I JUST WANT TO KNOW IF YOU THINK I SHOULD GET A NEW HAIR STYLE.
I DUNNO! WHAT DO YOU THINK?
I THINK YOU SHOULD SAY "YES" SO IF I GET IT CUT AND HATE IT, I CAN BLAME YOU.

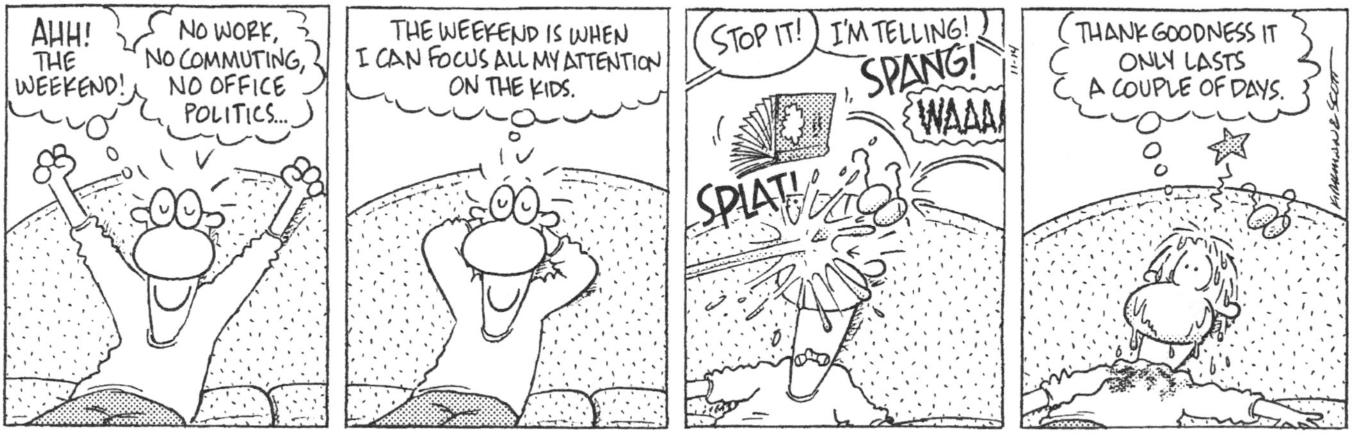
AHH! THE WEEKEND!
NO WORK, NO COMMUTING, NO OFFICE POLITICS...
THE WEEKEND IS WHEN I CAN FOCUS ALL MY ATTENTION ON THE KIDS.
STOP IT!
I'M TELLING!
SPANG!
WAAAA
SPLAT!
THANK GOODNESS IT ONLY LASTS A COUPLE OF DAYS.

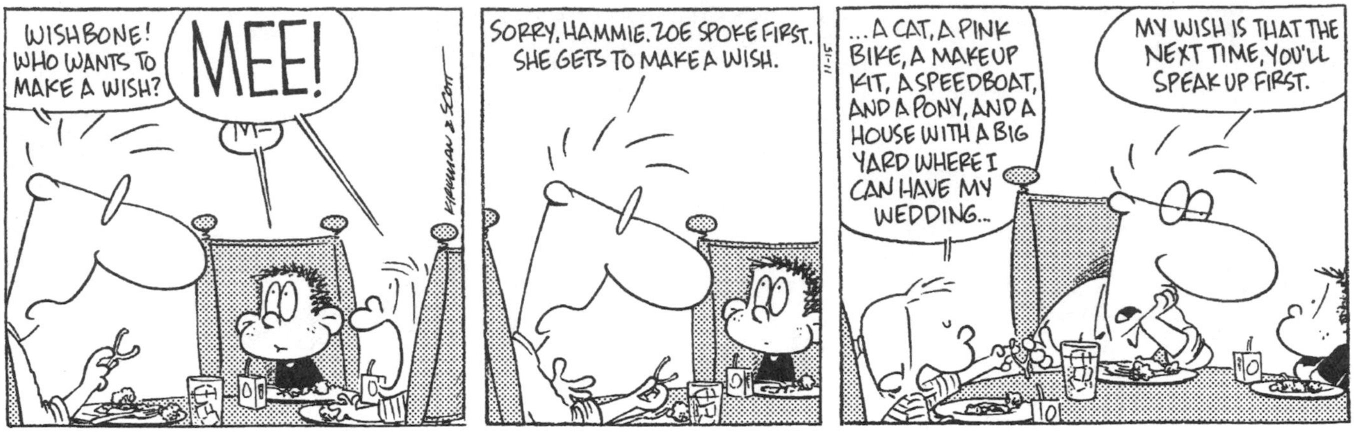
WISHBONE! WHO WANTS TO MAKE A WISH?
M—
MEE!
SORRY, HAMMIE. ZOE SPOKE FIRST. SHE GETS TO MAKE A WISH.
... A CAT, A PINK BIKE, A MAKEUP KIT, A SPEEDBOAT, AND A PONY, AND A HOUSE WITH A BIG YARD WHERE I CAN HAVE MY WEDDING...
MY WISH IS THAT THE NEXT TIME, YOU'LL SPEAK UP FIRST.

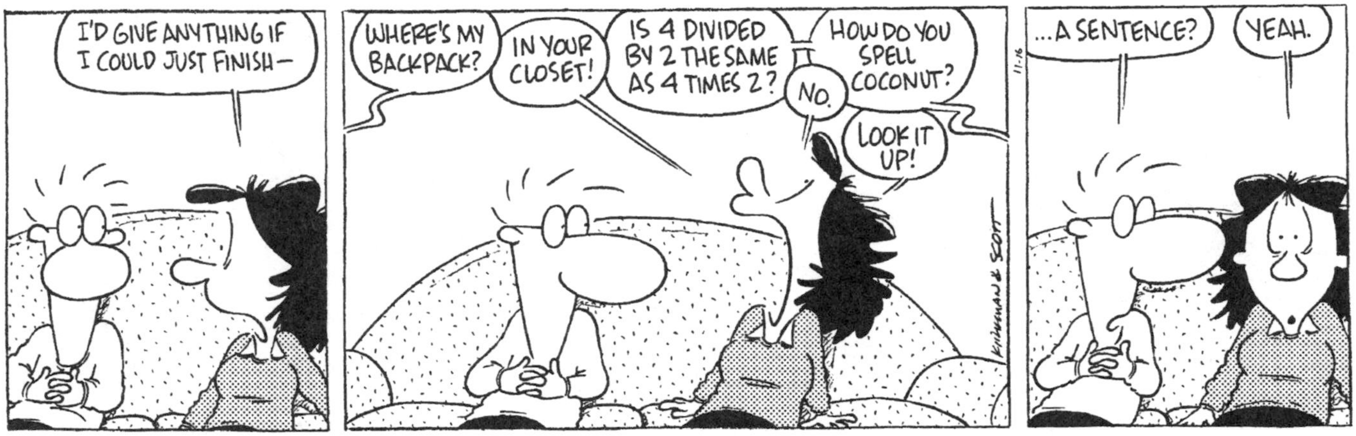
I'D GIVE ANYTHING IF I COULD JUST FINISH—
WHERE'S MY BACKPACK?
IN YOUR CLOSET!
IS 4 DIVIDED BY 2 THE SAME AS 4 TIMES 2?
NO.
HOW DO YOU SPELL COCONUT?
LOOK IT UP!
... A SENTENCE?
YEAH.

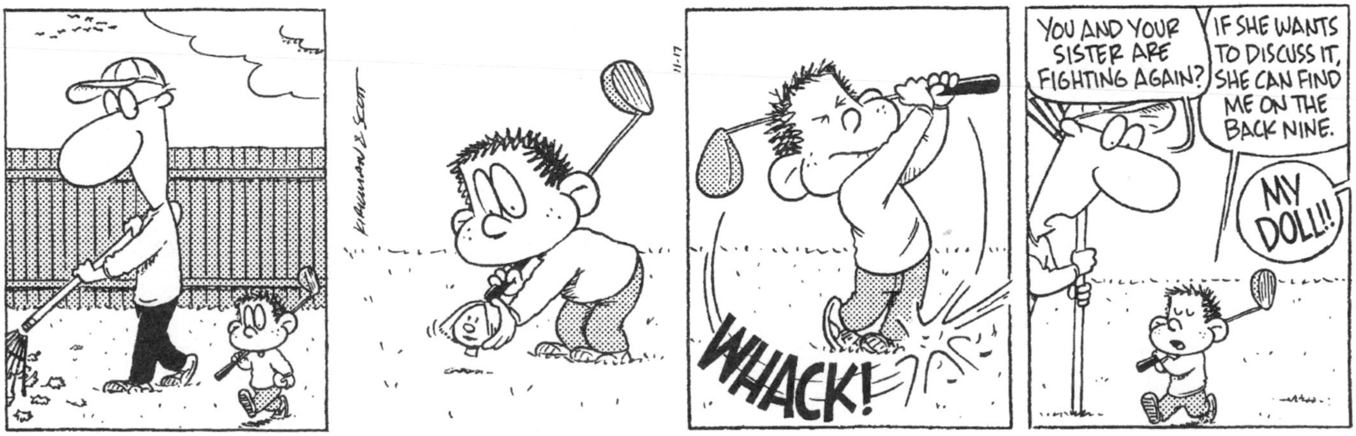
WHACK!
YOU AND YOUR SISTER ARE FIGHTING AGAIN?
IF SHE WANTS TO DISCUSS IT, SHE CAN FIND ME ON THE BACK NINE.
MY DOLL!!

BABY BLUES®
by
Rick Kirkman
Jerry Scott

HI WREN! WOULD YOU LIKE ME TO READ TO YOU?
SURE YOU WOULD!
11-18
WOW! LOOK AT ALL THESE GREAT BOOKS WE HAVE TO CHOOSE FROM!
THERE'S SNOW WHITE AND THE SEVEN DUMB BROTHERS... ONE FISH, TWO FISH, RED FISH, DUMB BROTHER FISH...
WE HAVE WHERE THE WILD THINGS AND THE DUMB BROTHERS ARE... DUMB BROTHER, DUMB BROTHER, WHAT DO YOU SEE?... THE VERY HUNGRY DUMB BROTHER...
WHY DON'T WE START WITH A CLASSIC, HAROLD AND THE PURPLE DUMB BROTHER...
MOM! THEY'RE GANGING UP ON ME AGAIN!
KIRKMAN & SCOTT

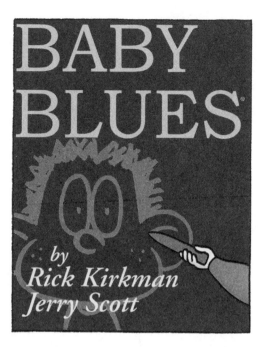

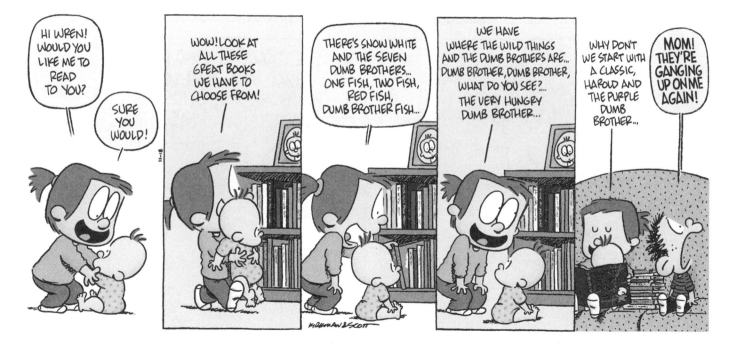

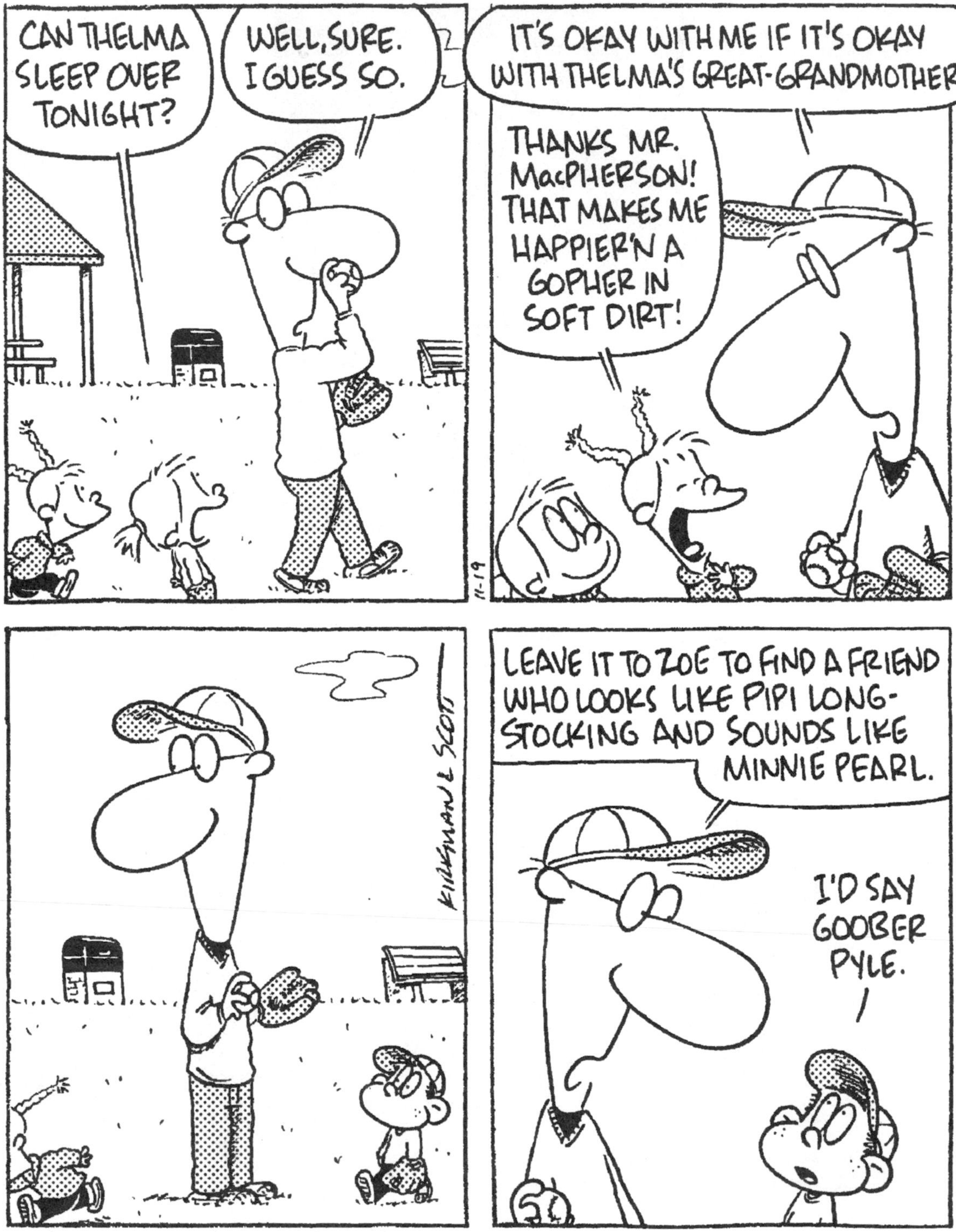
CAN THELMA SLEEP OVER TONIGHT?
WELL, SURE. I GUESS SO.
IT'S OKAY WITH ME IF IT'S OKAY WITH THELMA'S GREAT-GRANDMOTHER.
THANKS MR. MacPHERSON! THAT MAKES ME HAPPIER'N A GOPHER IN SOFT DIRT!
11-19
KIRKMAN & SCOTT
LEAVE IT TO ZOE TO FIND A FRIEND WHO LOOKS LIKE PIPI LONG-STOCKING AND SOUNDS LIKE MINNIE PEARL.
I'D SAY GOOBER PYLE.

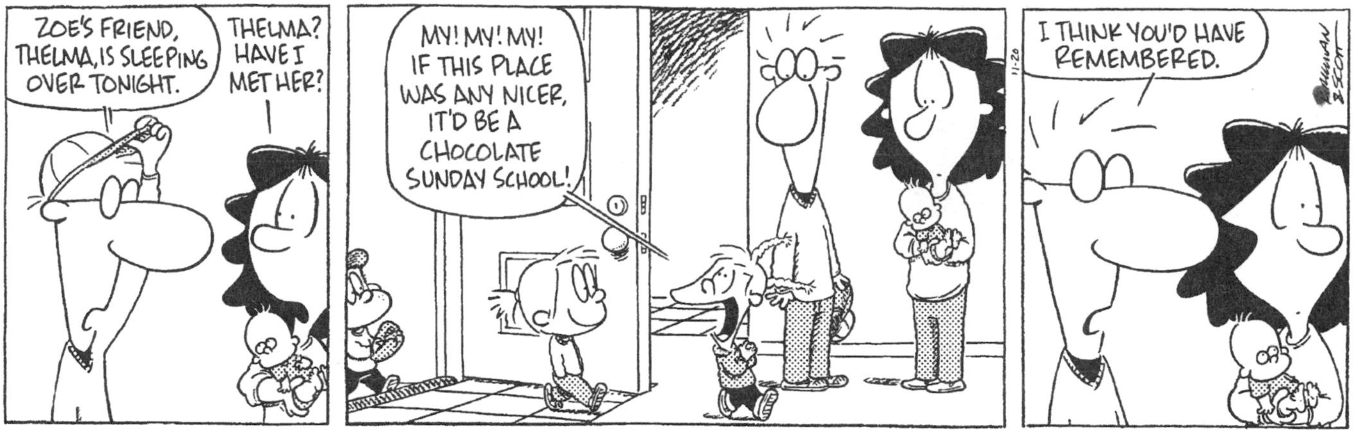
ZOE'S FRIEND, THELMA, IS SLEEPING OVER TONIGHT.
THELMA? HAVE I MET HER?
MY! MY! MY! IF THIS PLACE WAS ANY NICER, IT'D BE A CHOCOLATE SUNDAY SCHOOL!
I THINK YOU'D HAVE REMEMBERED.

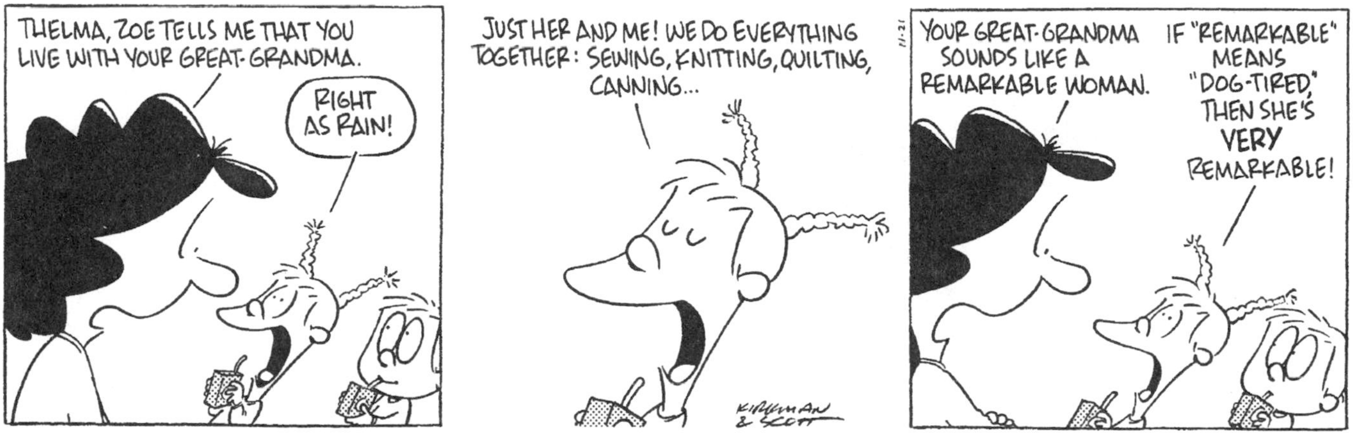
THELMA, ZOE TELLS ME THAT YOU LIVE WITH YOUR GREAT-GRANDMA.
RIGHT AS RAIN!
JUST HER AND ME! WE DO EVERYTHING TOGETHER: SEWING, KNITTING, QUILTING, CANNING...
YOUR GREAT-GRANDMA SOUNDS LIKE A REMARKABLE WOMAN.
IF "REMARKABLE" MEANS "DOG-TIRED," THEN SHE'S **VERY** REMARKABLE!

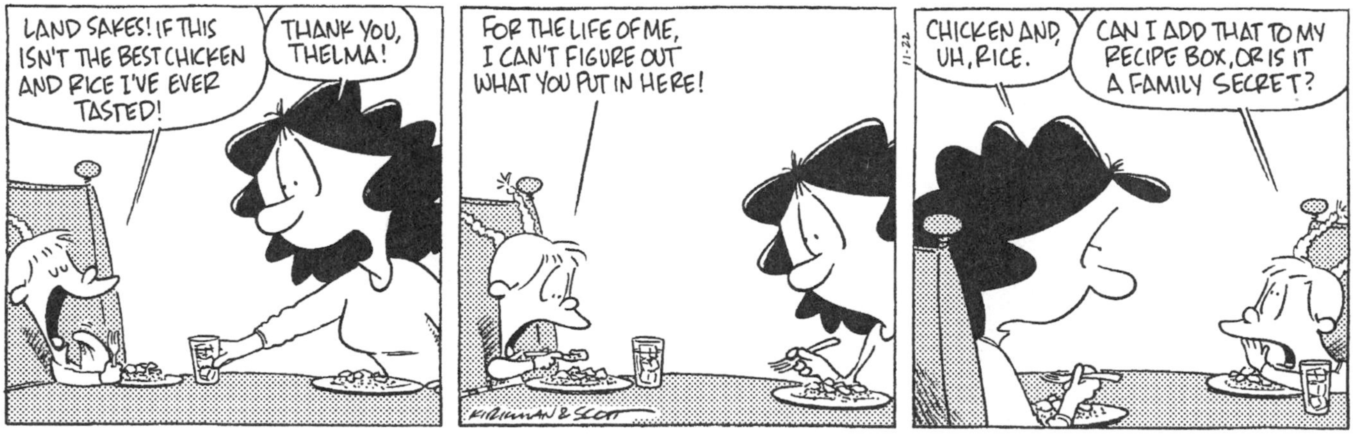
LAND SAKES! IF THIS ISN'T THE BEST CHICKEN AND RICE I'VE EVER TASTED!
THANK YOU, THELMA!
FOR THE LIFE OF ME, I CAN'T FIGURE OUT WHAT YOU PUT IN HERE!
CHICKEN AND, UH, RICE.
CAN I ADD THAT TO MY RECIPE BOX, OR IS IT A FAMILY SECRET?

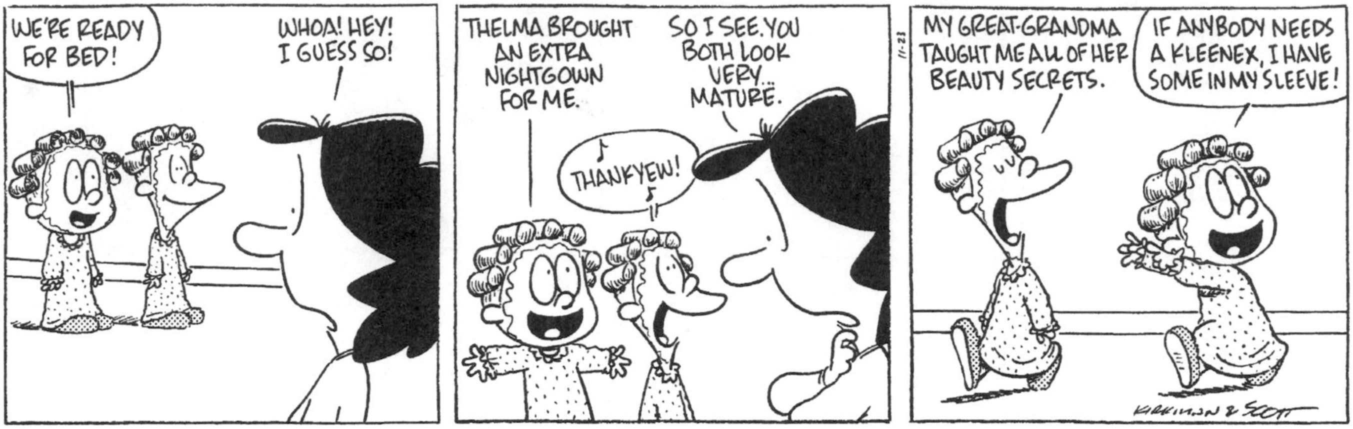
WE'RE READY FOR BED!
WHOA! HEY! I GUESS SO!
THELMA BROUGHT AN EXTRA NIGHTGOWN FOR ME.
THANKYEW!
SO I SEE. YOU BOTH LOOK VERY... MATURE.
11-23
MY GREAT-GRANDMA TAUGHT ME ALL OF HER BEAUTY SECRETS.
IF ANYBODY NEEDS A KLEENEX, I HAVE SOME IN MY SLEEVE!
KIRKMAN & SCOTT

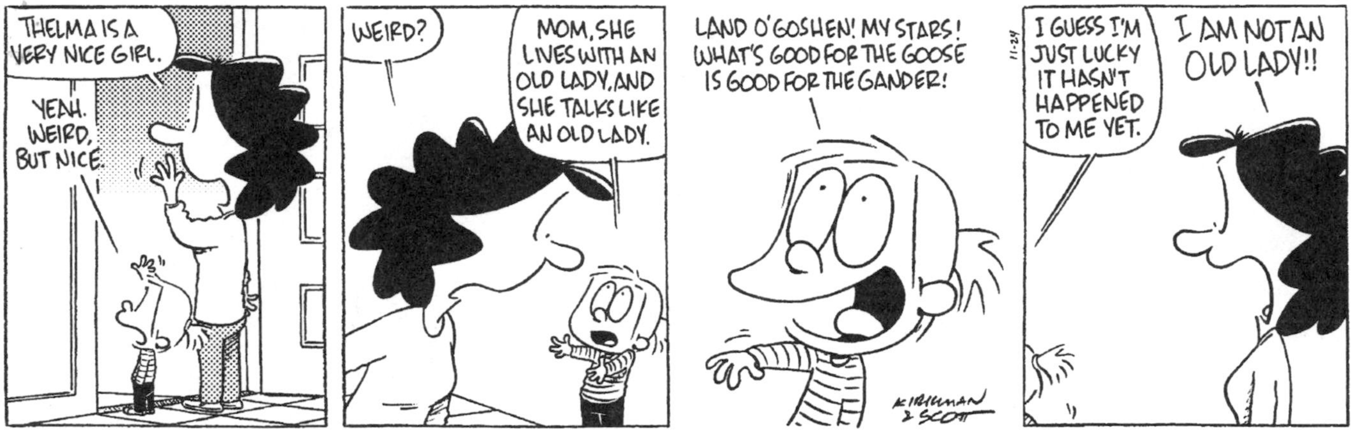
THELMA IS A VERY NICE GIRL.
YEAH. WEIRD, BUT NICE.
WEIRD?
MOM, SHE LIVES WITH AN OLD LADY, AND SHE TALKS LIKE AN OLD LADY.
LAND O'GOSHEN! MY STARS! WHAT'S GOOD FOR THE GOOSE IS GOOD FOR THE GANDER!
KIRKMAN & SCOTT
11-24
I GUESS I'M JUST LUCKY IT HASN'T HAPPENED TO ME YET.
I AM NOT AN OLD LADY!!

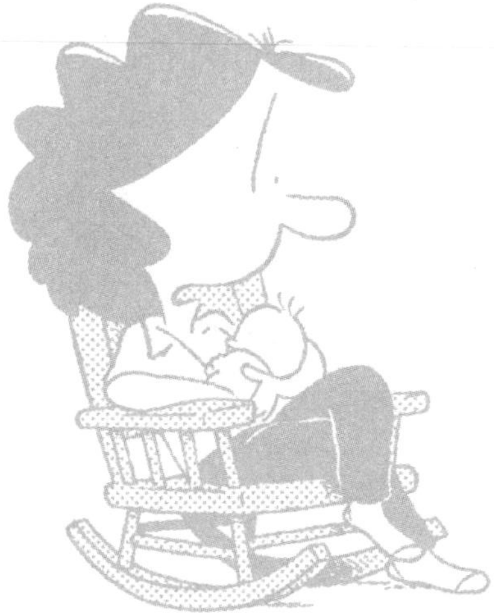

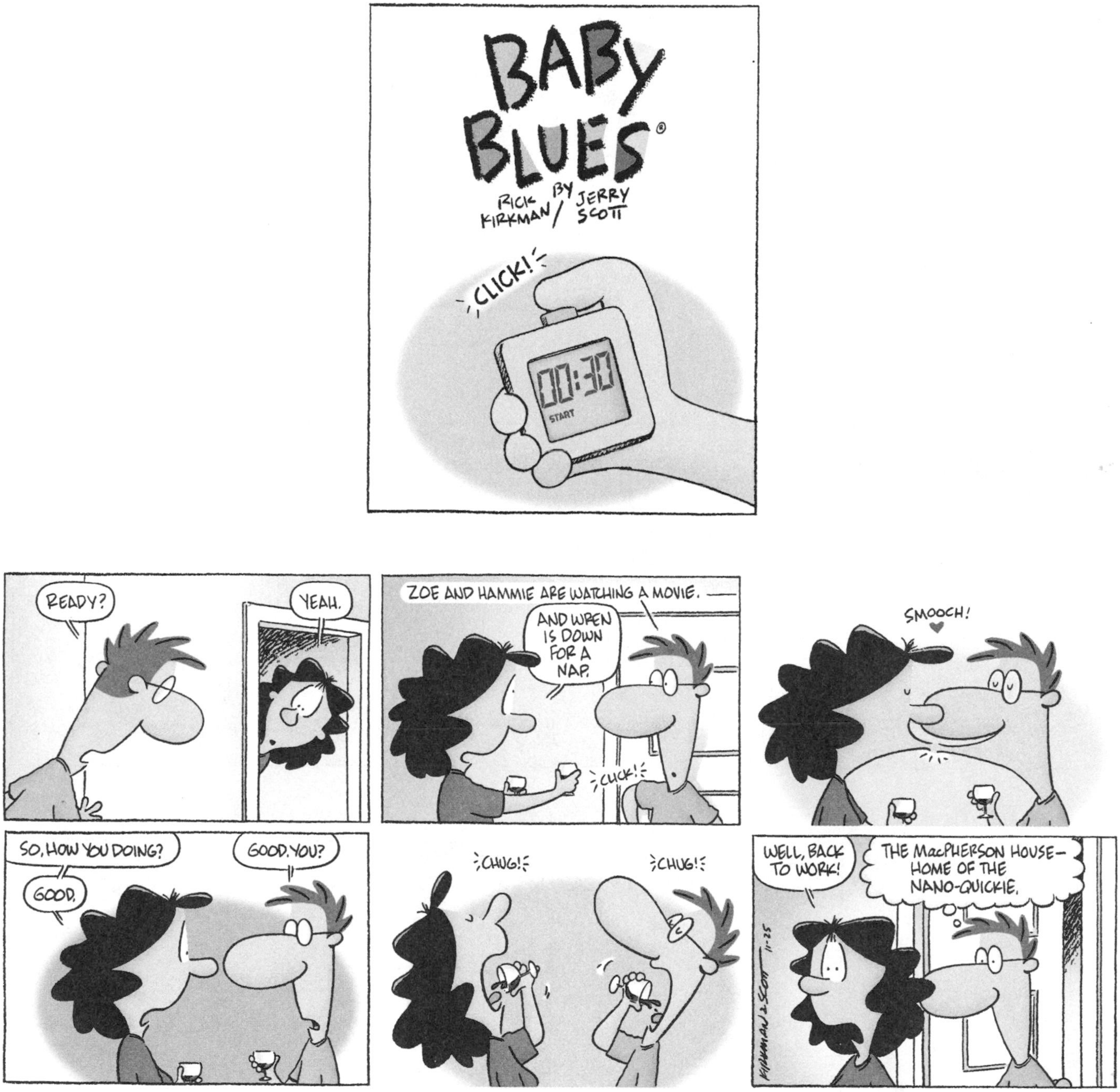
BABY BLUES®
BY RICK KIRKMAN / JERRY SCOTT
CLICK!
00:30
START
READY?
YEAH.
ZOE AND HAMMIE ARE WATCHING A MOVIE.
AND WREN IS DOWN FOR A NAP.
CLICK!
SMOOCH!
SO, HOW YOU DOING?
GOOD.
GOOD. YOU?
CHUG!
CHUG!
WELL, BACK TO WORK!
THE MacPHERSON HOUSE–HOME OF THE NANO-QUICKIE.

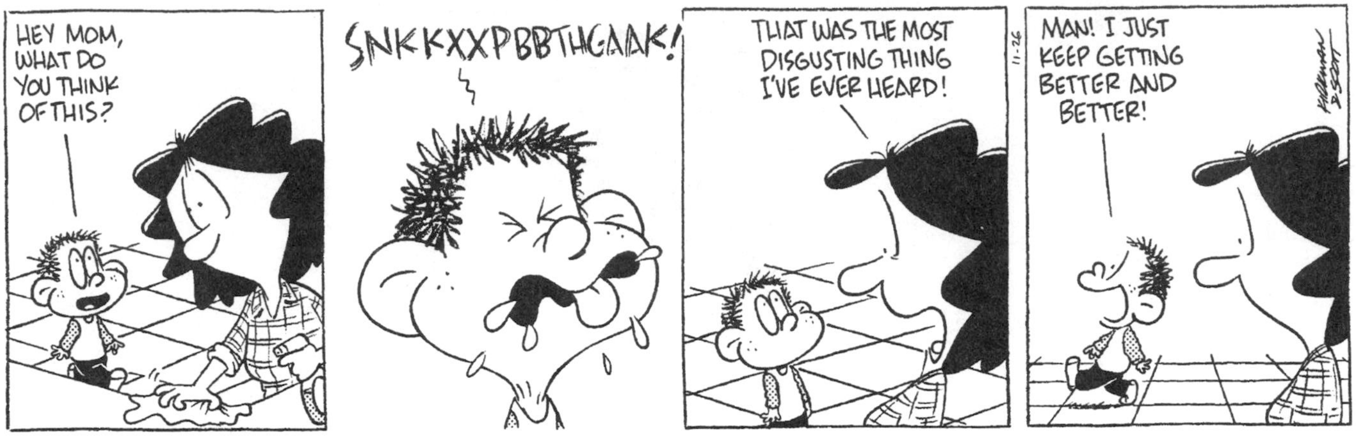
HEY MOM, WHAT DO YOU THINK OF THIS?
SNKKXXPBBTHGAAK!
THAT WAS THE MOST DISGUSTING THING I'VE EVER HEARD!
11-26
MAN! I JUST KEEP GETTING BETTER AND BETTER!

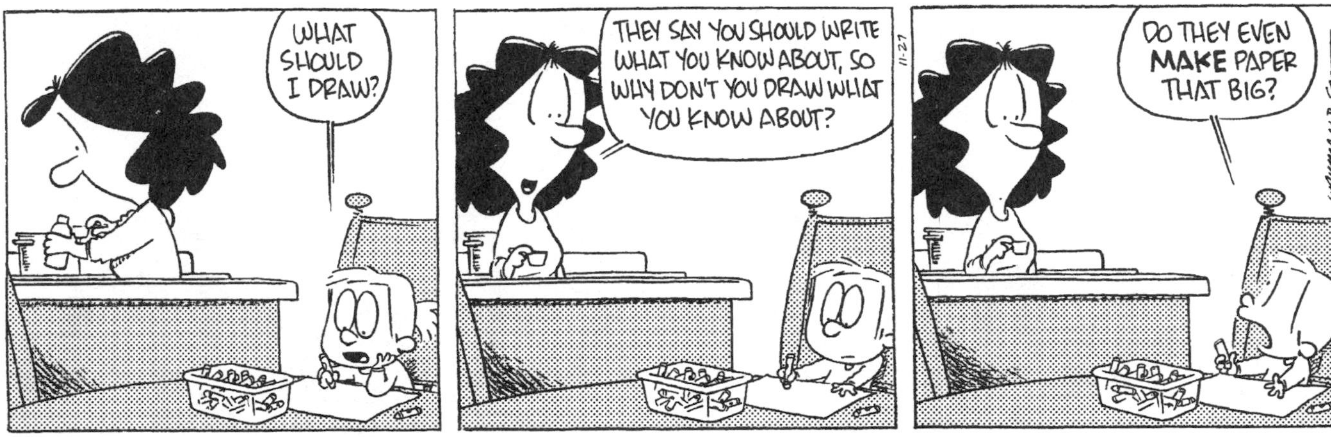
WHAT SHOULD I DRAW?
THEY SAY YOU SHOULD WRITE WHAT YOU KNOW ABOUT, SO WHY DON'T YOU DRAW WHAT YOU KNOW ABOUT?
11-27
DO THEY EVEN **MAKE** PAPER THAT BIG?

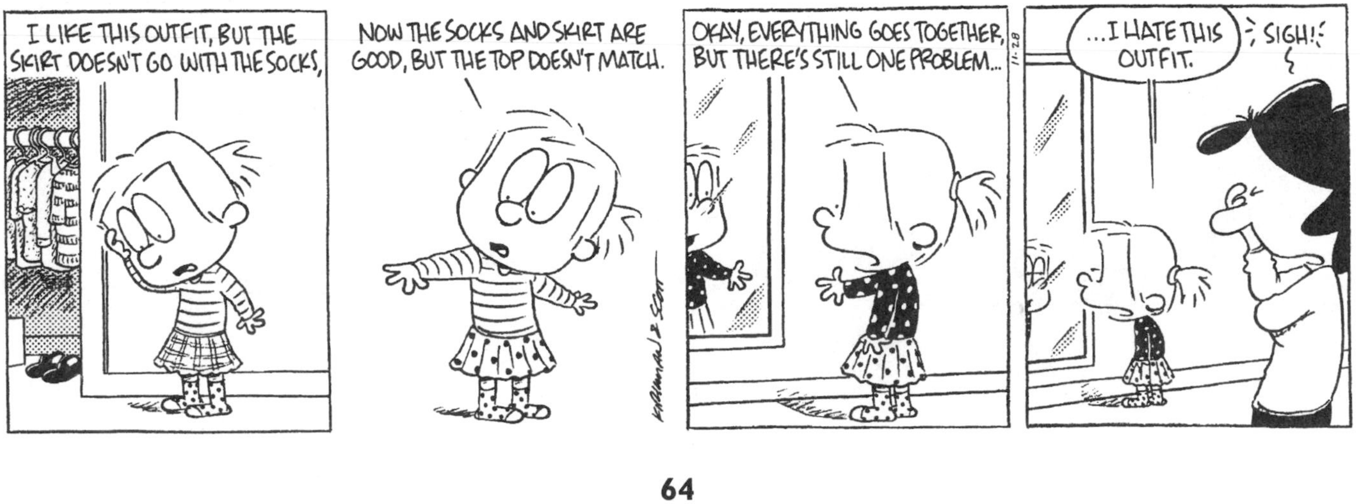
I LIKE THIS OUTFIT, BUT THE SKIRT DOESN'T GO WITH THE SOCKS,
NOW THE SOCKS AND SKIRT ARE GOOD, BUT THE TOP DOESN'T MATCH.
OKAY, EVERYTHING GOES TOGETHER, BUT THERE'S STILL ONE PROBLEM...
11-28
...I HATE THIS OUTFIT.
SIGH!

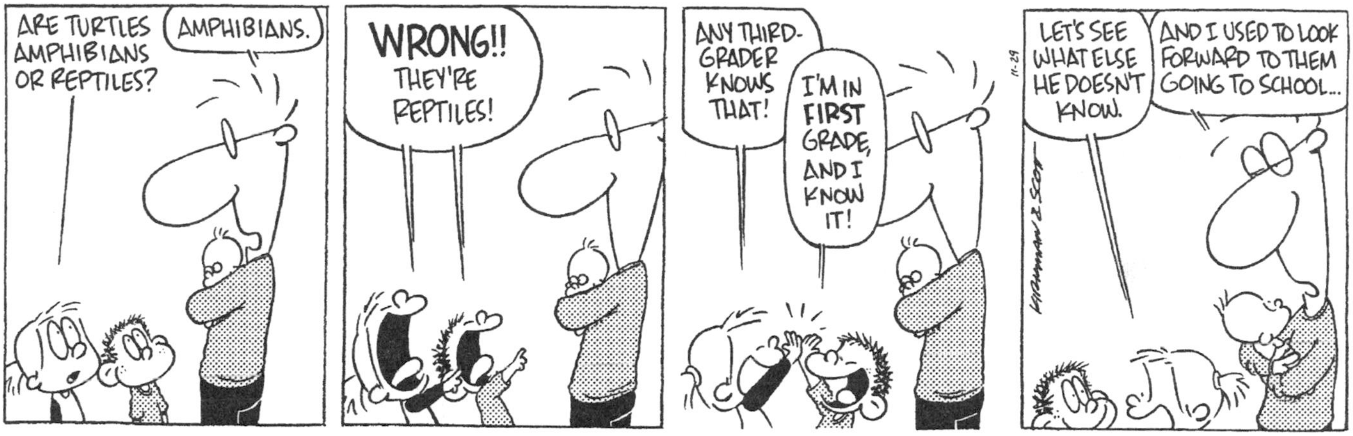
ARE TURTLES AMPHIBIANS OR REPTILES?
AMPHIBIANS.
WRONG!! THEY'RE REPTILES!
ANY THIRD-GRADER KNOWS THAT!
I'M IN FIRST GRADE, AND I KNOW IT!
LET'S SEE WHAT ELSE HE DOESN'T KNOW.
AND I USED TO LOOK FORWARD TO THEM GOING TO SCHOOL...

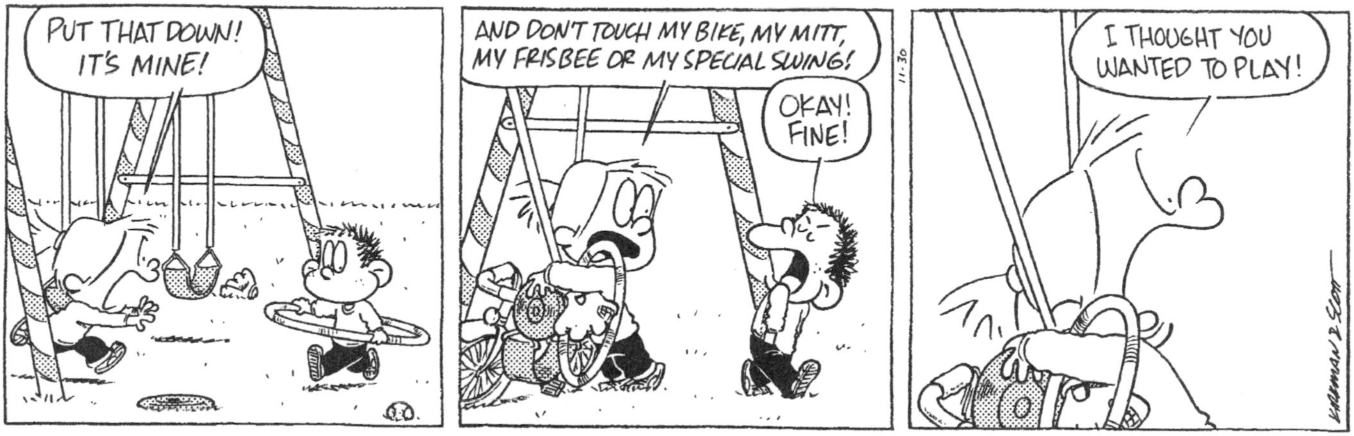
PUT THAT DOWN! IT'S MINE!
AND DON'T TOUCH MY BIKE, MY MITT, MY FRISBEE OR MY SPECIAL SWING!
OKAY! FINE!
I THOUGHT YOU WANTED TO PLAY!

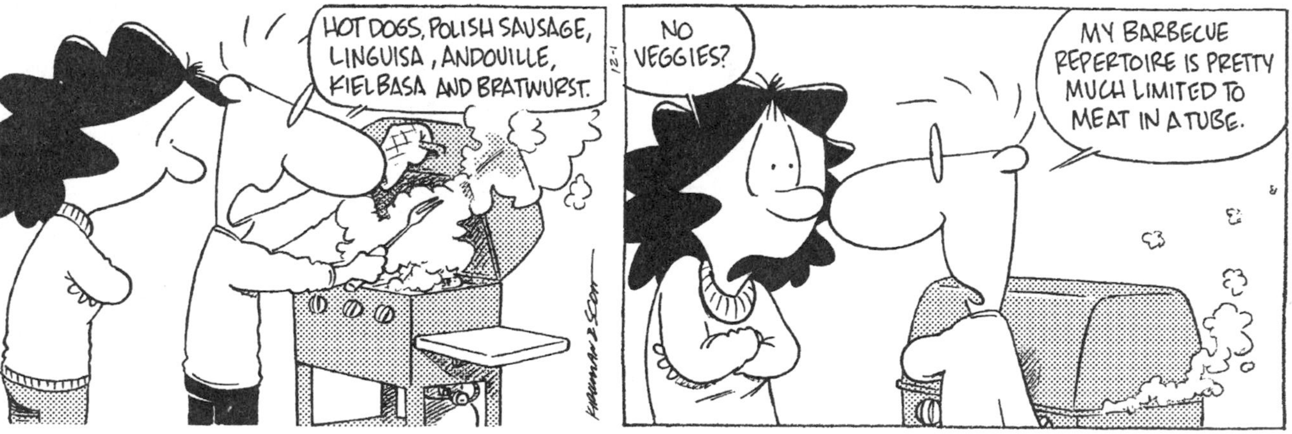
HOT DOGS, POLISH SAUSAGE, LINGUISA, ANDOUILLE, KIELBASA AND BRATWURST.
NO VEGGIES?
MY BARBECUE REPERTOIRE IS PRETTY MUCH LIMITED TO MEAT IN A TUBE.

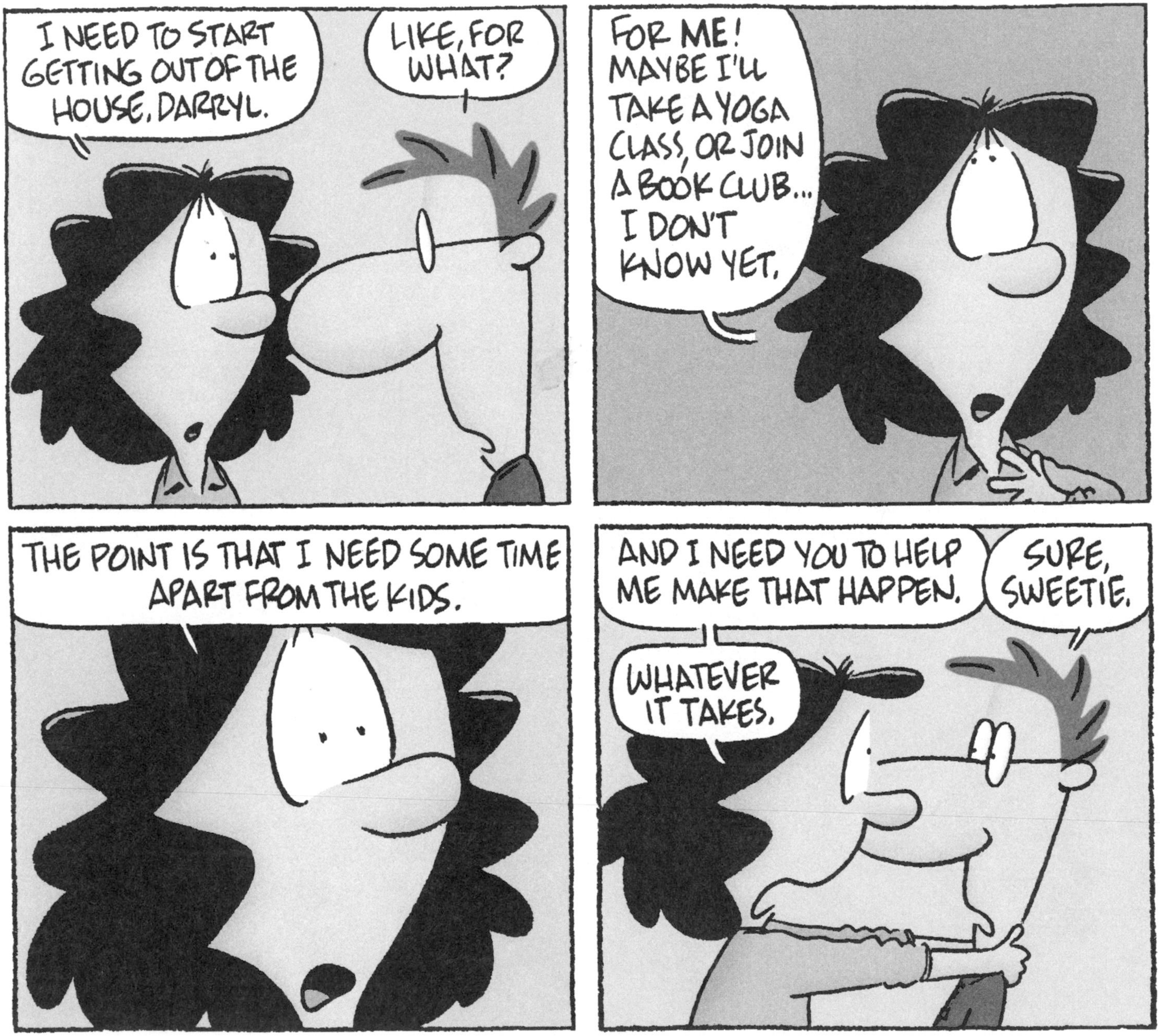
I NEED TO START GETTING OUT OF THE HOUSE, DARRYL.
LIKE, FOR WHAT?
FOR ME! MAYBE I'LL TAKE A YOGA CLASS, OR JOIN A BOOK CLUB... I DON'T KNOW YET.
THE POINT IS THAT I NEED SOME TIME APART FROM THE KIDS.
AND I NEED YOU TO HELP ME MAKE THAT HAPPEN.
SURE, SWEETIE.
WHATEVER IT TAKES.

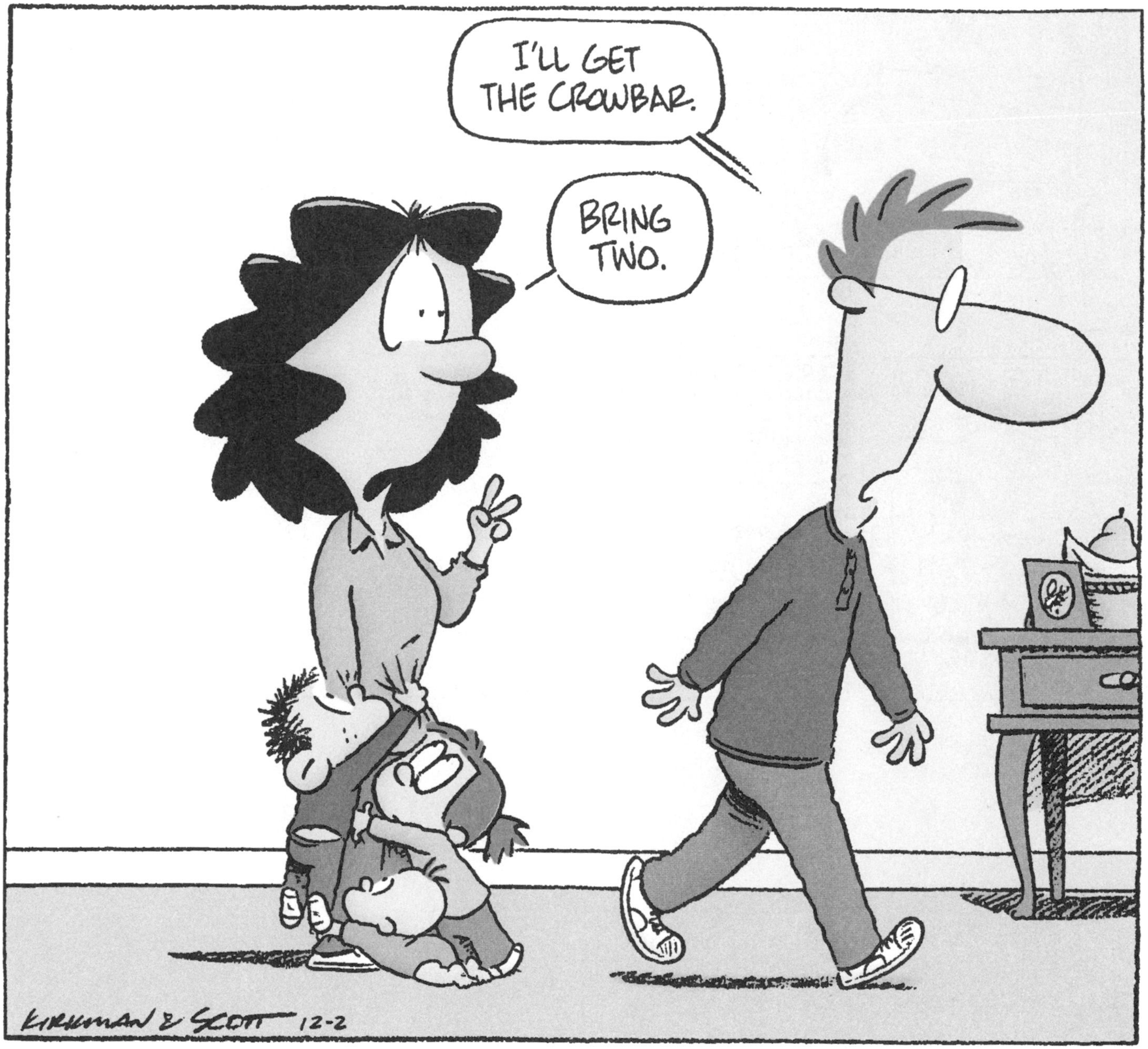
I'LL GET THE CROWBAR.
BRING TWO.
KIRKMAN & SCOTT 12-2

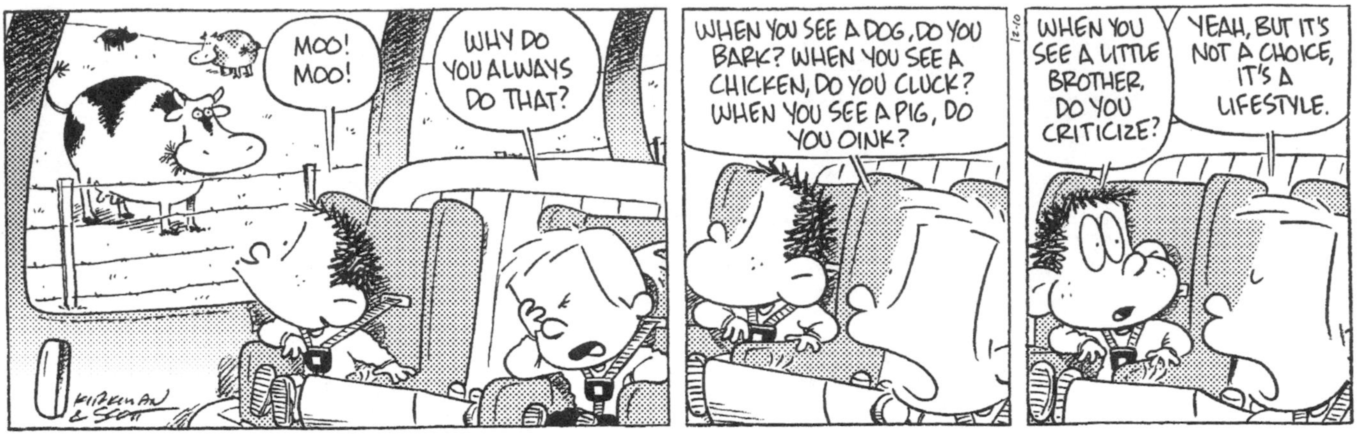
MOO! MOO!
WHY DO YOU ALWAYS DO THAT?
WHEN YOU SEE A DOG, DO YOU BARK? WHEN YOU SEE A CHICKEN, DO YOU CLUCK? WHEN YOU SEE A PIG, DO YOU OINK?
WHEN YOU SEE A LITTLE BROTHER, DO YOU CRITICIZE?
YEAH, BUT IT'S NOT A CHOICE, IT'S A LIFESTYLE.

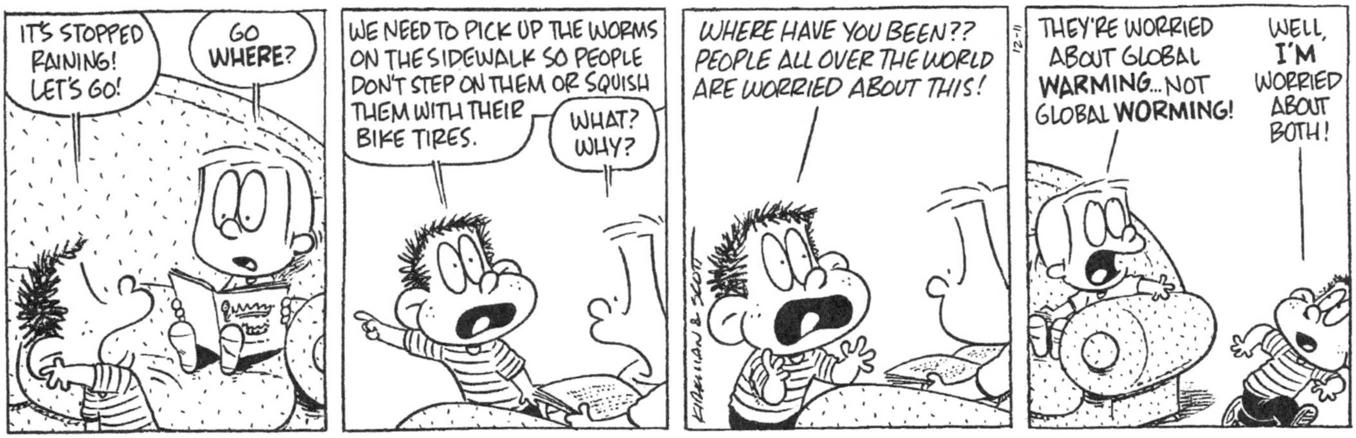
IT'S STOPPED RAINING! LET'S GO!
GO **WHERE**?
WE NEED TO PICK UP THE WORMS ON THE SIDEWALK SO PEOPLE DON'T STEP ON THEM OR SQUISH THEM WITH THEIR BIKE TIRES.
WHAT? WHY?
WHERE HAVE YOU BEEN?? PEOPLE ALL OVER THE WORLD ARE WORRIED ABOUT THIS!
THEY'RE WORRIED ABOUT GLOBAL **WARMING**... NOT GLOBAL **WORMING**!
WELL, **I'M** WORRIED ABOUT BOTH!

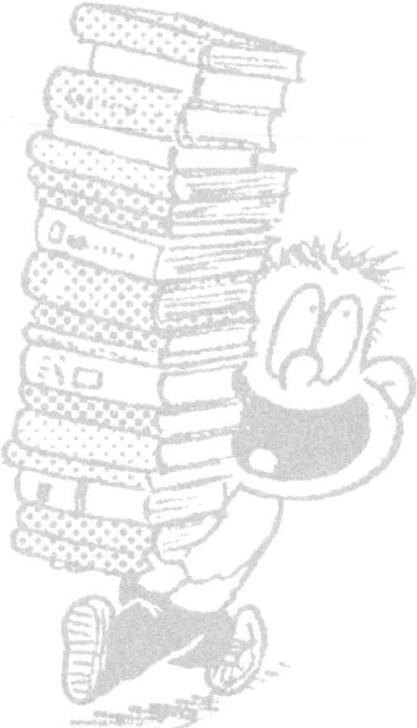

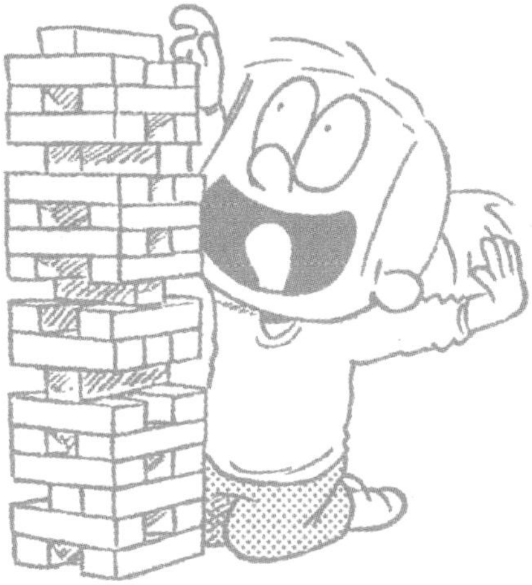

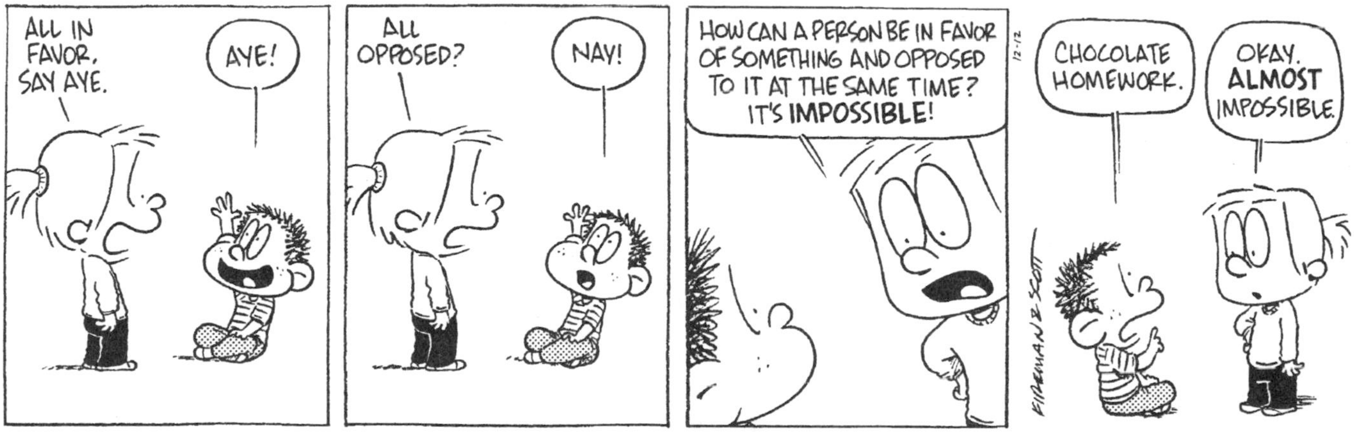
ALL IN FAVOR, SAY AYE.
AYE!
ALL OPPOSED?
NAY!
HOW CAN A PERSON BE IN FAVOR OF SOMETHING AND OPPOSED TO IT AT THE SAME TIME? IT'S **IMPOSSIBLE**!
CHOCOLATE HOMEWORK.
OKAY. **ALMOST** IMPOSSIBLE.

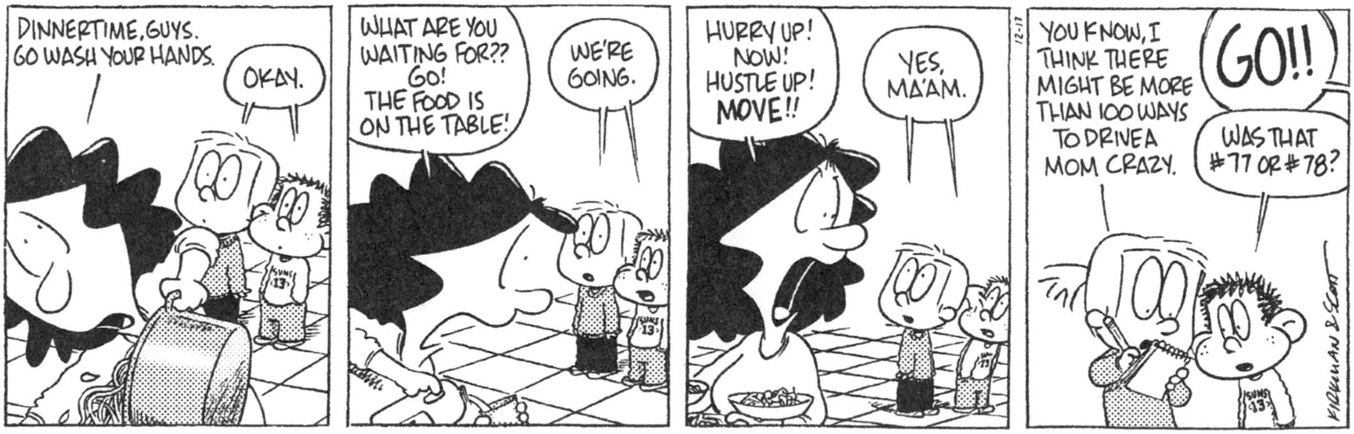
DINNERTIME, GUYS. GO WASH YOUR HANDS.
OKAY.
WHAT ARE YOU WAITING FOR?? GO! THE FOOD IS ON THE TABLE!
WE'RE GOING.
HURRY UP! NOW! HUSTLE UP! **MOVE**!!
YES, MA'AM.
YOU KNOW, I THINK THERE MIGHT BE MORE THAN 100 WAYS TO DRIVE A MOM CRAZY.
GO!!
WAS THAT #77 OR #78?

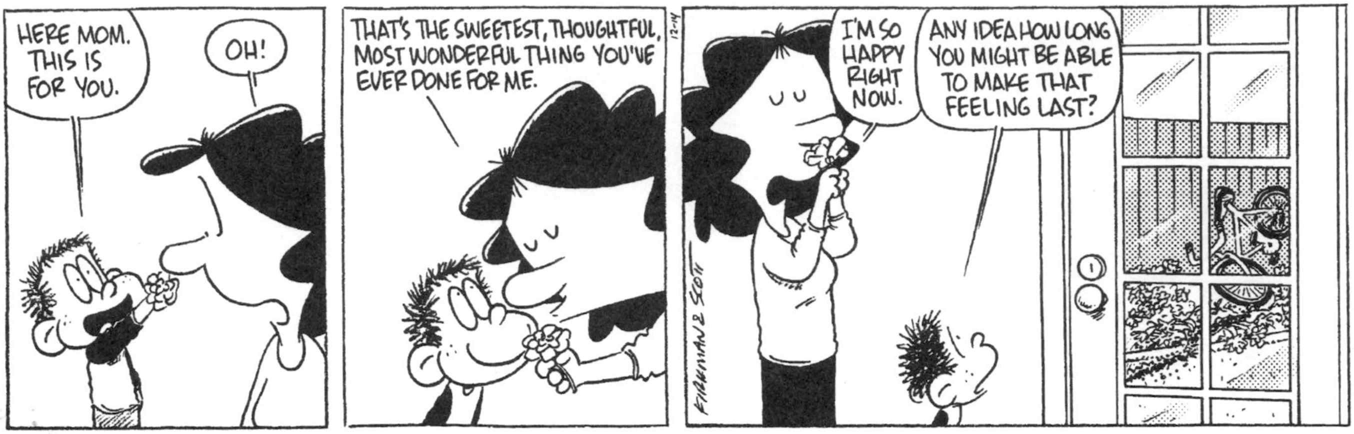
HERE MOM. THIS IS FOR YOU.
OH!
THAT'S THE SWEETEST, THOUGHTFUL, MOST WONDERFUL THING YOU'VE EVER DONE FOR ME.
12-14
I'M SO HAPPY RIGHT NOW.
ANY IDEA HOW LONG YOU MIGHT BE ABLE TO MAKE THAT FEELING LAST?
KIRKMAN & SCOTT

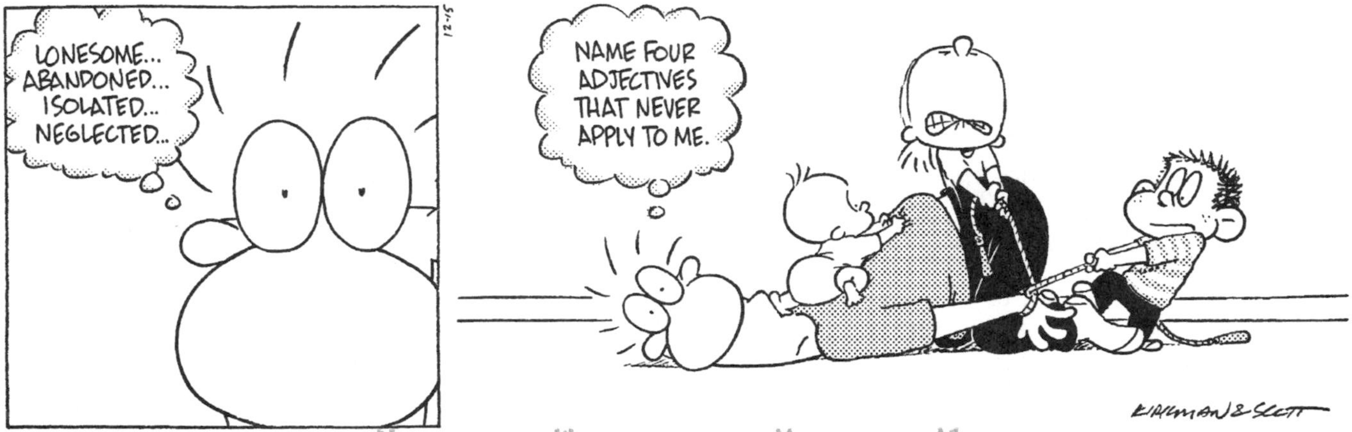
12-15
LONESOME... ABANDONED... ISOLATED... NEGLECTED...
NAME FOUR ADJECTIVES THAT NEVER APPLY TO ME.
KIRKMAN & SCOTT

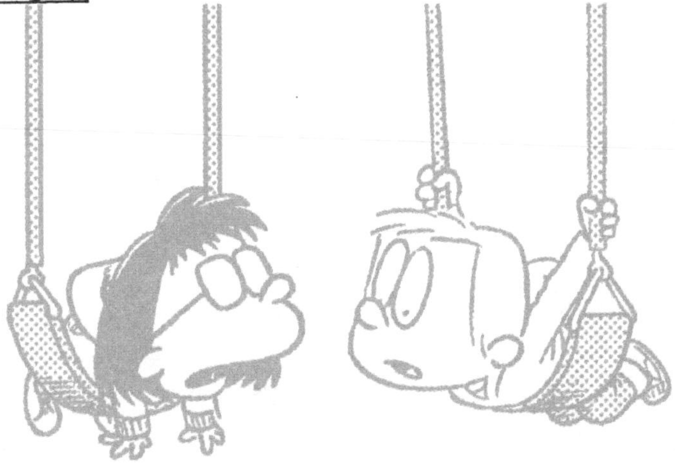

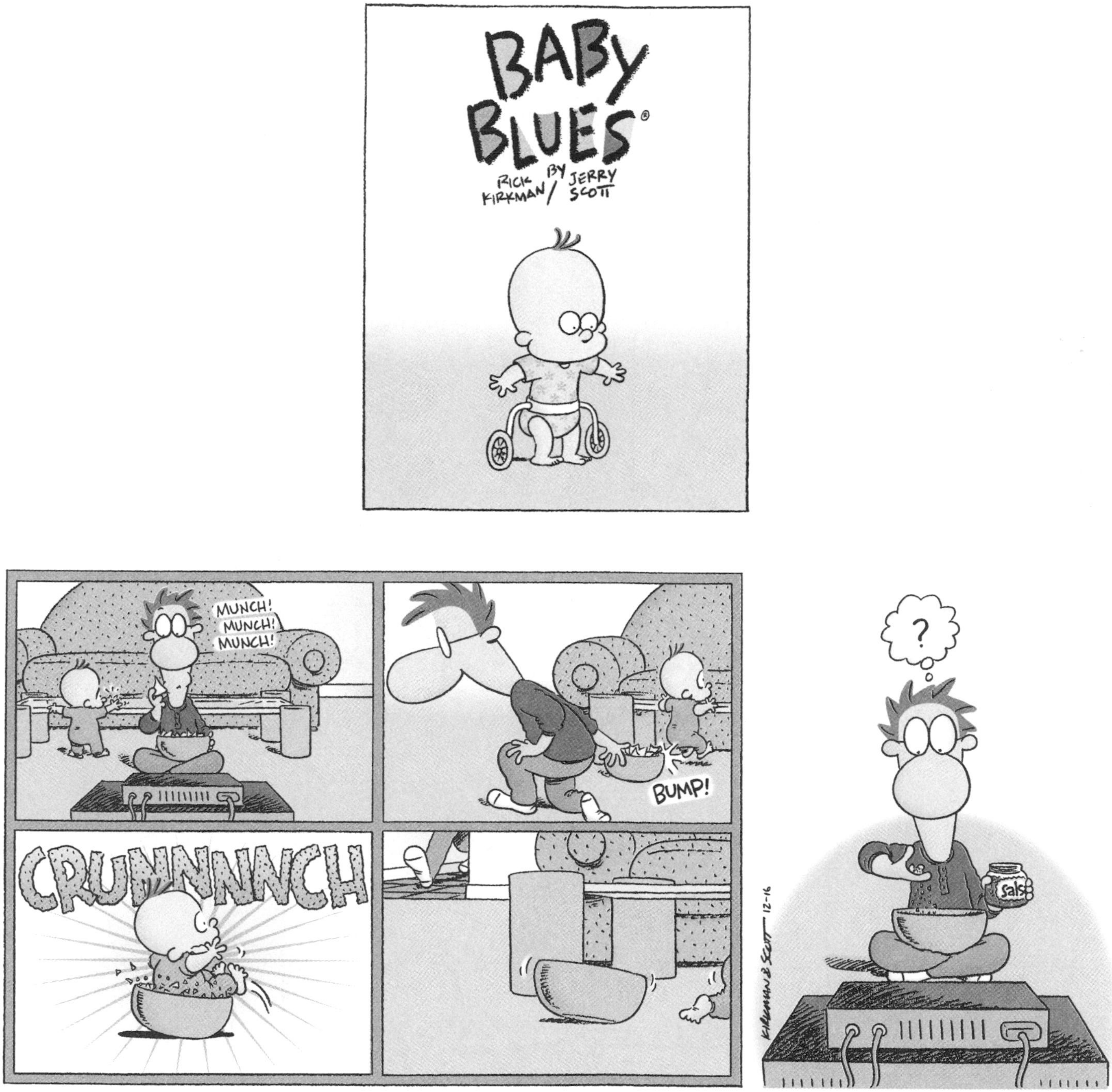
BABY BLUES®
RICK KIRKMAN / BY JERRY SCOTT
MUNCH! MUNCH! MUNCH!
BUMP!
CRUNNNNCH
?
12-16
KIRKMAN & SCOTT

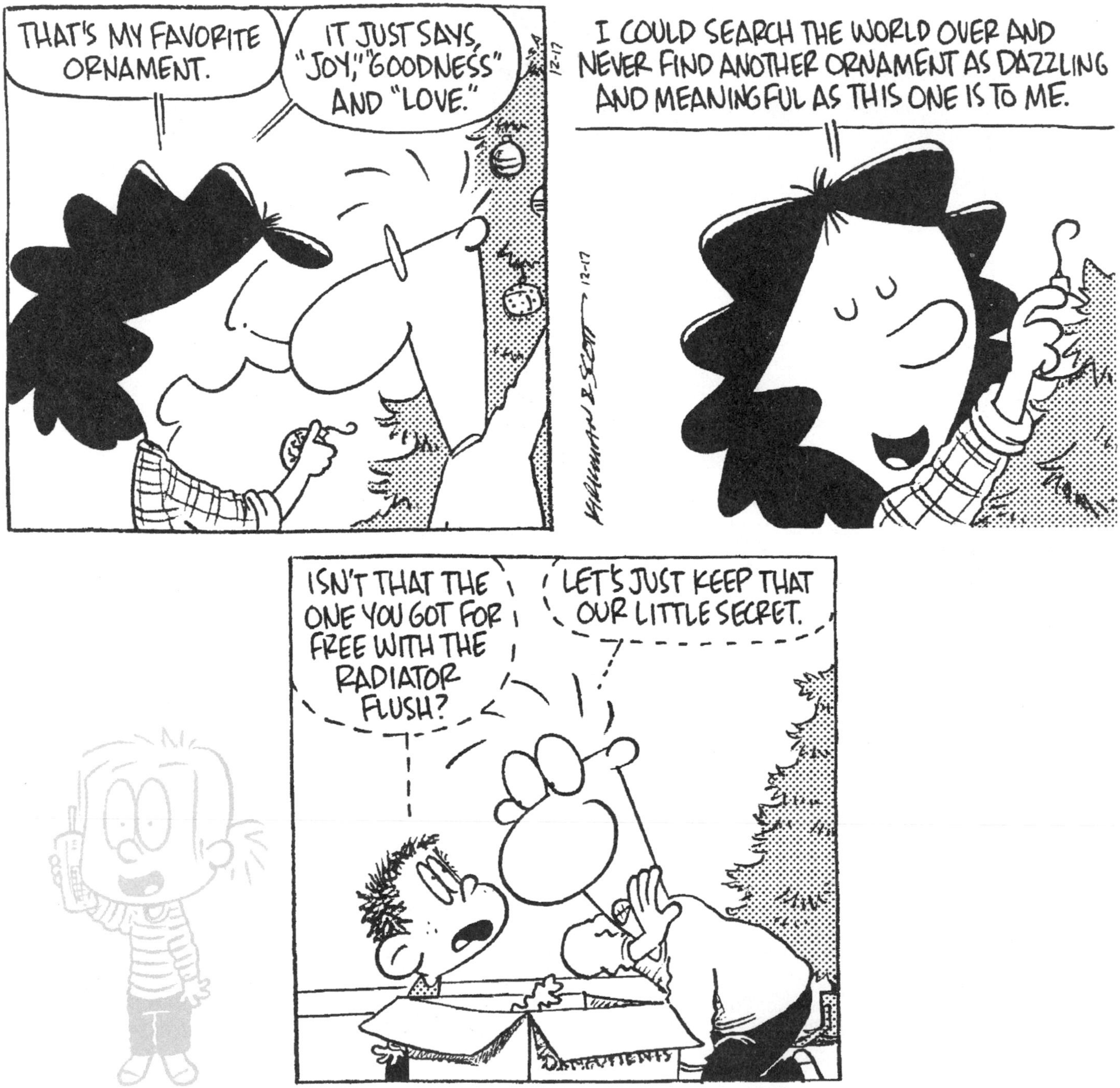

THAT'S MY FAVORITE ORNAMENT.
IT JUST SAYS, "JOY," "GOODNESS" AND "LOVE."
I COULD SEARCH THE WORLD OVER AND NEVER FIND ANOTHER ORNAMENT AS DAZZLING AND MEANINGFUL AS THIS ONE IS TO ME.
ISN'T THAT THE ONE YOU GOT FOR FREE WITH THE RADIATOR FLUSH?
LET'S JUST KEEP THAT OUR LITTLE SECRET.

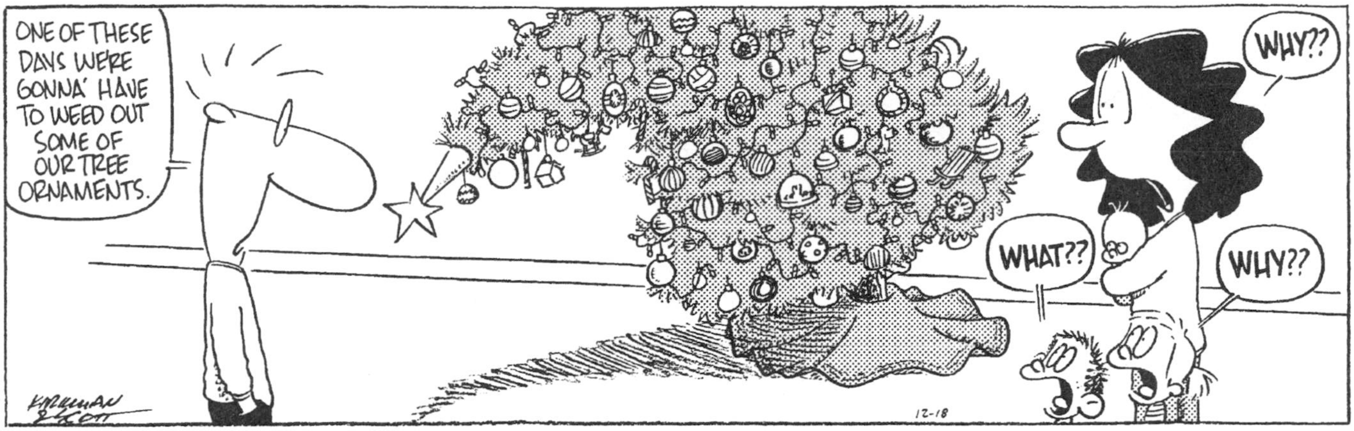
ONE OF THESE DAYS WE'RE GONNA' HAVE TO WEED OUT SOME OF OUR TREE ORNAMENTS.
WHY??
WHAT??
WHY??

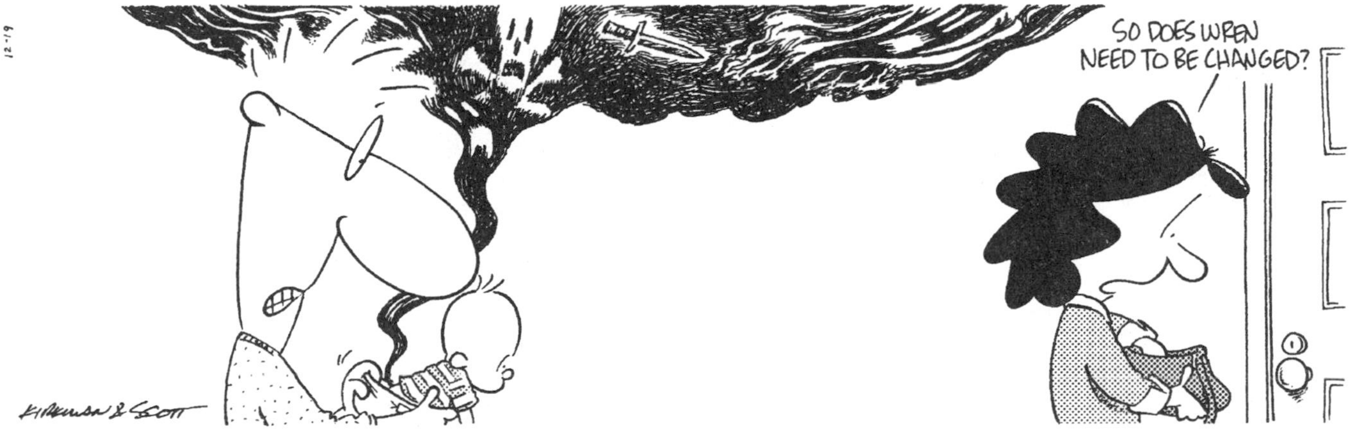
SO DOES WREN NEED TO BE CHANGED?

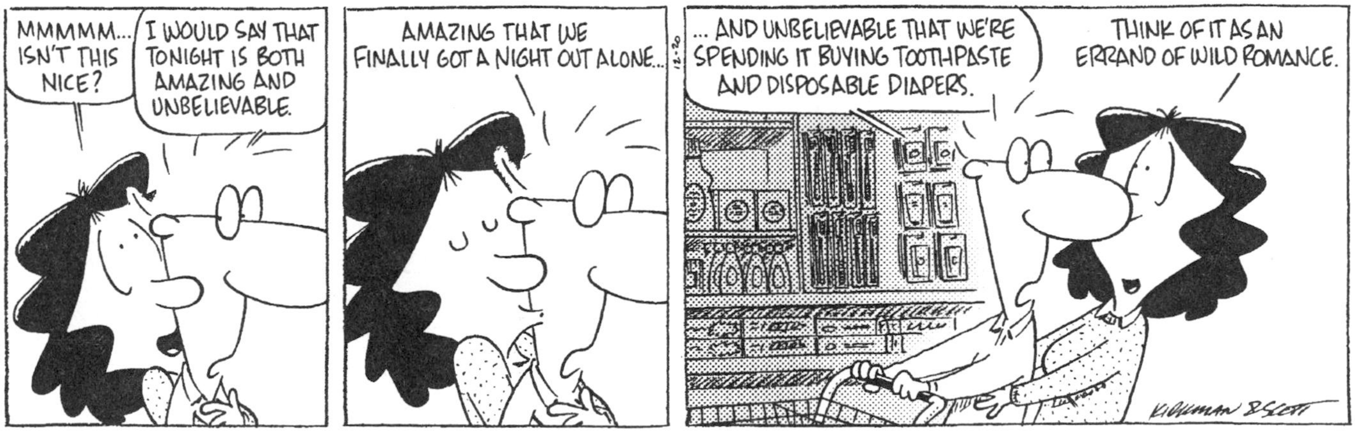
MMMMM... ISN'T THIS NICE?
I WOULD SAY THAT TONIGHT IS BOTH AMAZING AND UNBELIEVABLE.
AMAZING THAT WE FINALLY GOT A NIGHT OUT ALONE...
... AND UNBELIEVABLE THAT WE'RE SPENDING IT BUYING TOOTHPASTE AND DISPOSABLE DIAPERS.
THINK OF IT AS AN ERRAND OF WILD ROMANCE.

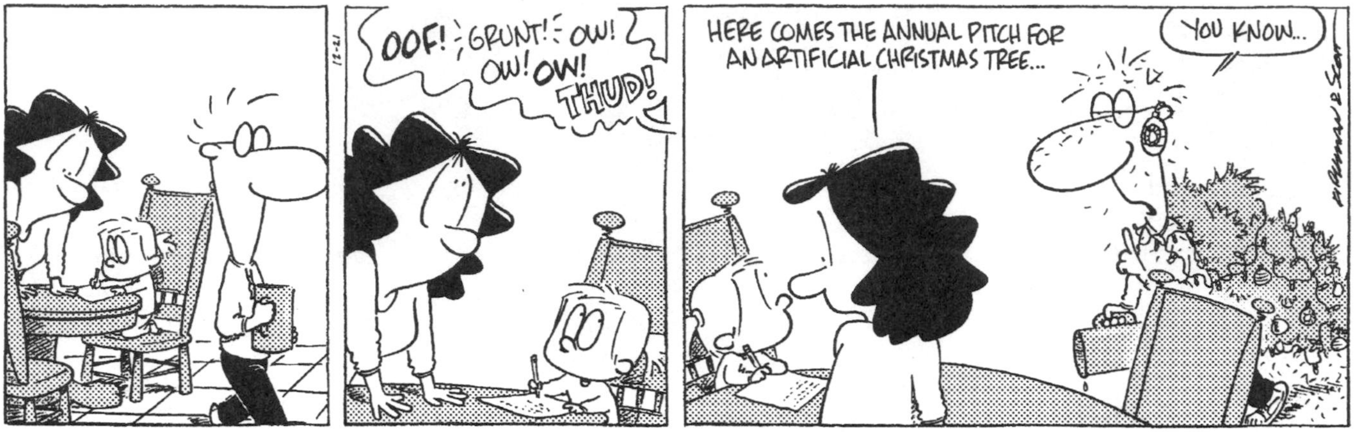
OOF! GRUNT! OW!
OW! OW!
THUD!
HERE COMES THE ANNUAL PITCH FOR AN ARTIFICIAL CHRISTMAS TREE...
YOU KNOW...

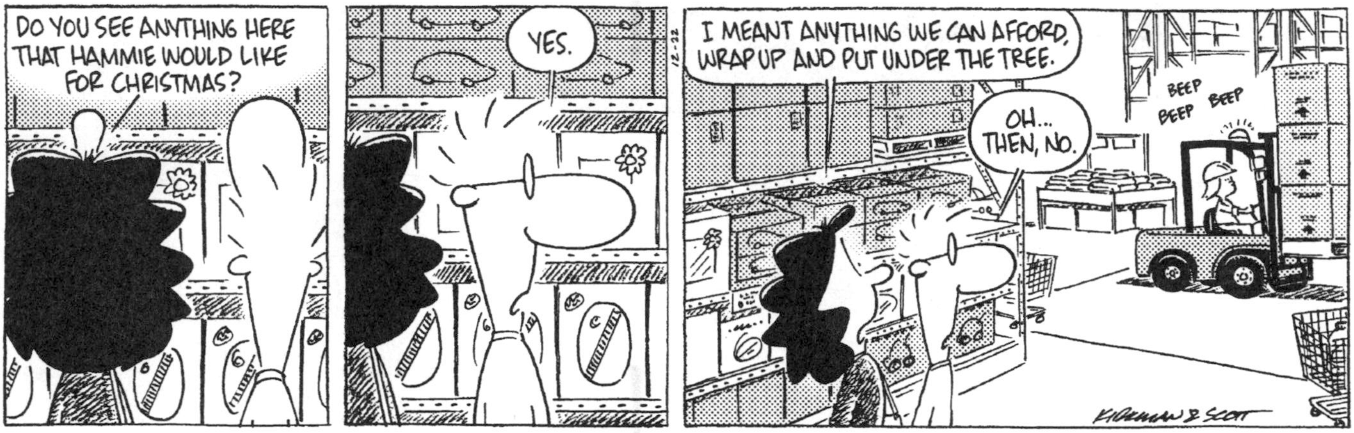
DO YOU SEE ANYTHING HERE THAT HAMMIE WOULD LIKE FOR CHRISTMAS?
YES.
I MEANT ANYTHING WE CAN AFFORD, WRAP UP AND PUT UNDER THE TREE.
OH... THEN, NO.
BEEP BEEP BEEP
KIRKMAN & SCOTT

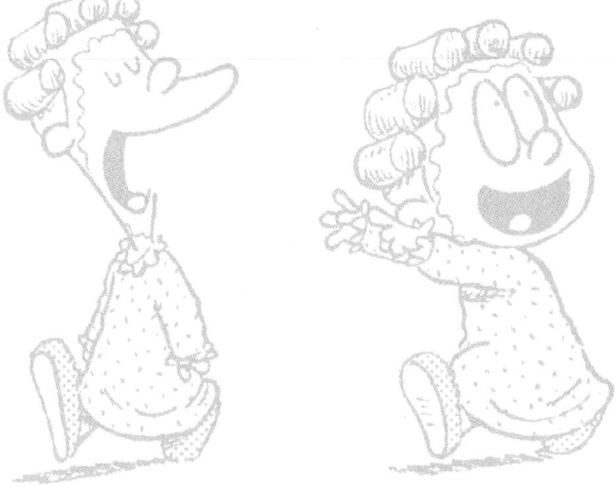

BABY BLUES®
BY RICK KIRKMAN / JERRY SCOTT

HEY DAD! IS THAT FRUIT PUNCH? CAN I HAVE SOME?
ME, TOO!
I ASKED FIRST, SO IF THERE ISN'T ENOUGH FOR TWO, TOO BAD!
HOW IS THAT FAIR?
WHO SAYS IT HAS TO BE FAIR? FIRST COME, FIRST SERVED!
STOP SHOVING! DAD! TELL HER THAT SHE HAS TO SHARE THE FRUIT PUNCH!
YOU WANT PUNCH! HERE'S ONE!
HA! I GOT IT! YOU LOSE!
IT WASN'T FRUIT PUNCH. IT WAS WATER FOR THE CHRISTMAS TREE.
THAT'S ONE I HOPE SANTA DIDN'T SEE.

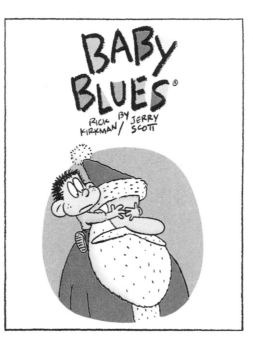

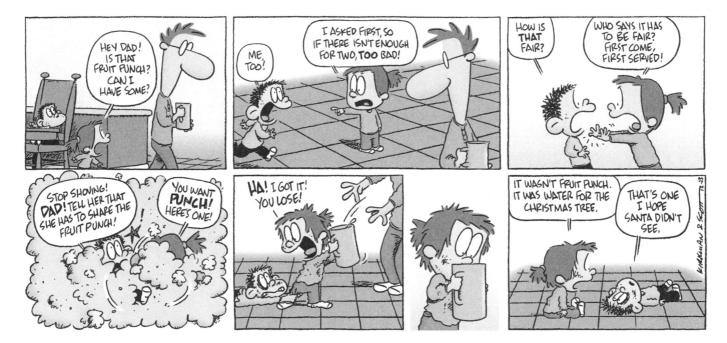

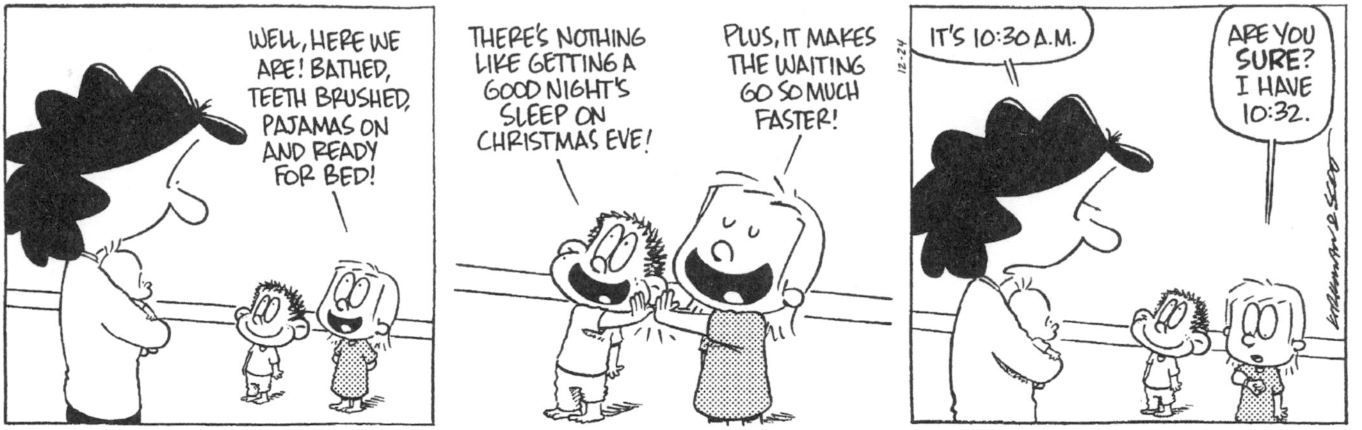

WELL, HERE WE ARE! BATHED, TEETH BRUSHED, PAJAMAS ON AND READY FOR BED!
THERE'S NOTHING LIKE GETTING A GOOD NIGHT'S SLEEP ON CHRISTMAS EVE!
PLUS, IT MAKES THE WAITING GO SO MUCH FASTER!
IT'S 10:30 A.M.
ARE YOU **SURE**? I HAVE 10:32.

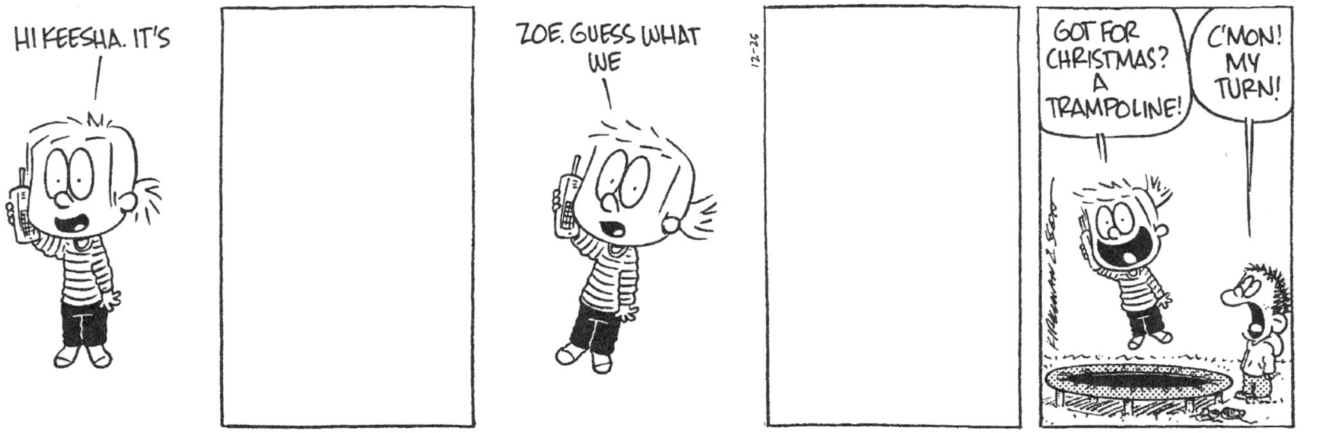

HI KEESHA. IT'S
ZOE. GUESS WHAT WE
GOT FOR CHRISTMAS? A TRAMPOLINE!
C'MON! MY TURN!

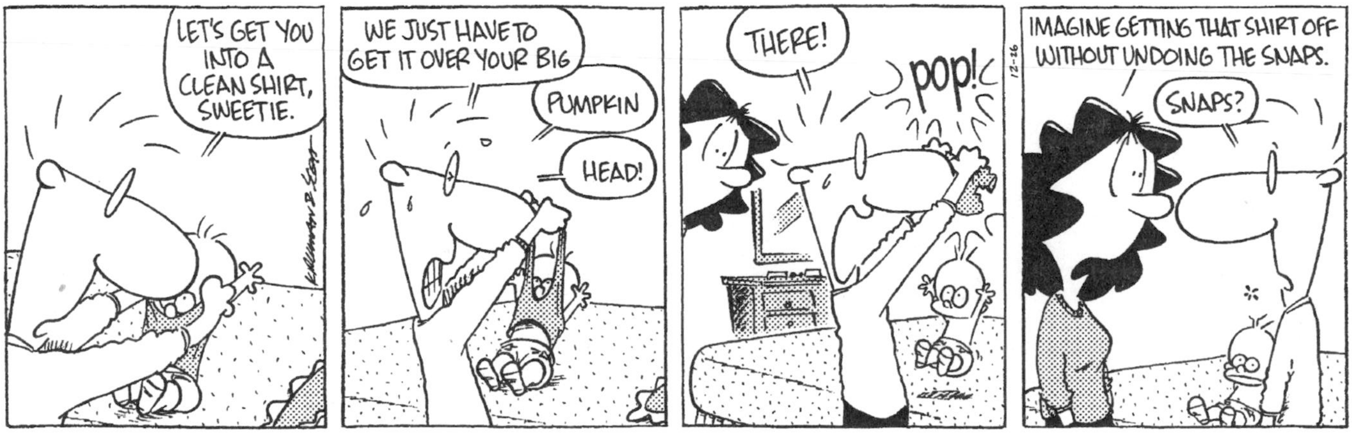

LET'S GET YOU INTO A CLEAN SHIRT, SWEETIE.
WE JUST HAVE TO GET IT OVER YOUR BIG
PUMPKIN
HEAD!
THERE!
pop!
IMAGINE GETTING THAT SHIRT OFF WITHOUT UNDOING THE SNAPS.
SNAPS?

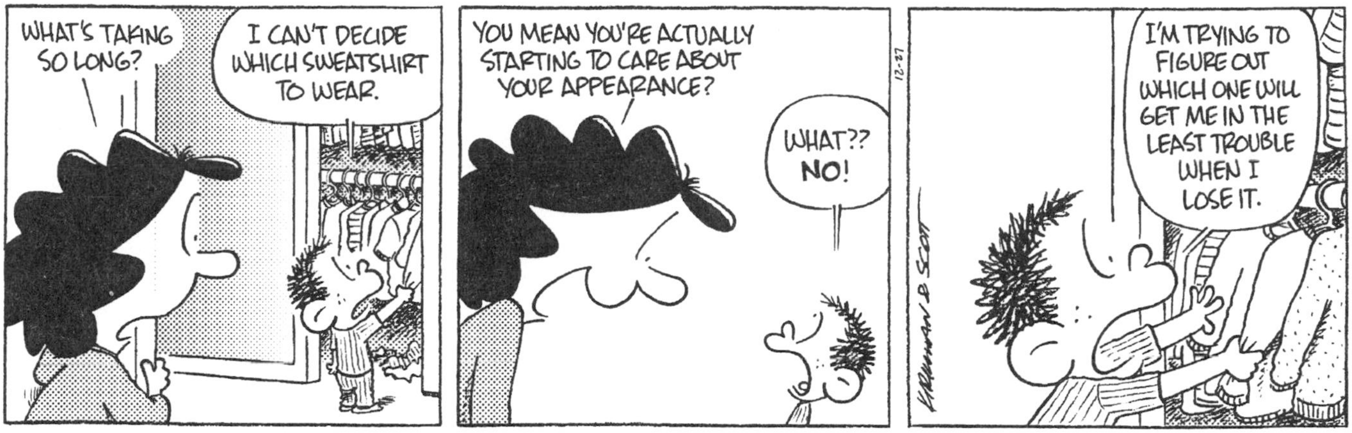
WHAT'S TAKING SO LONG?
I CAN'T DECIDE WHICH SWEATSHIRT TO WEAR.
YOU MEAN YOU'RE ACTUALLY STARTING TO CARE ABOUT YOUR APPEARANCE?
WHAT?? NO!
12-27
KIRKMAN & SCOTT
I'M TRYING TO FIGURE OUT WHICH ONE WILL GET ME IN THE LEAST TROUBLE WHEN I LOSE IT.

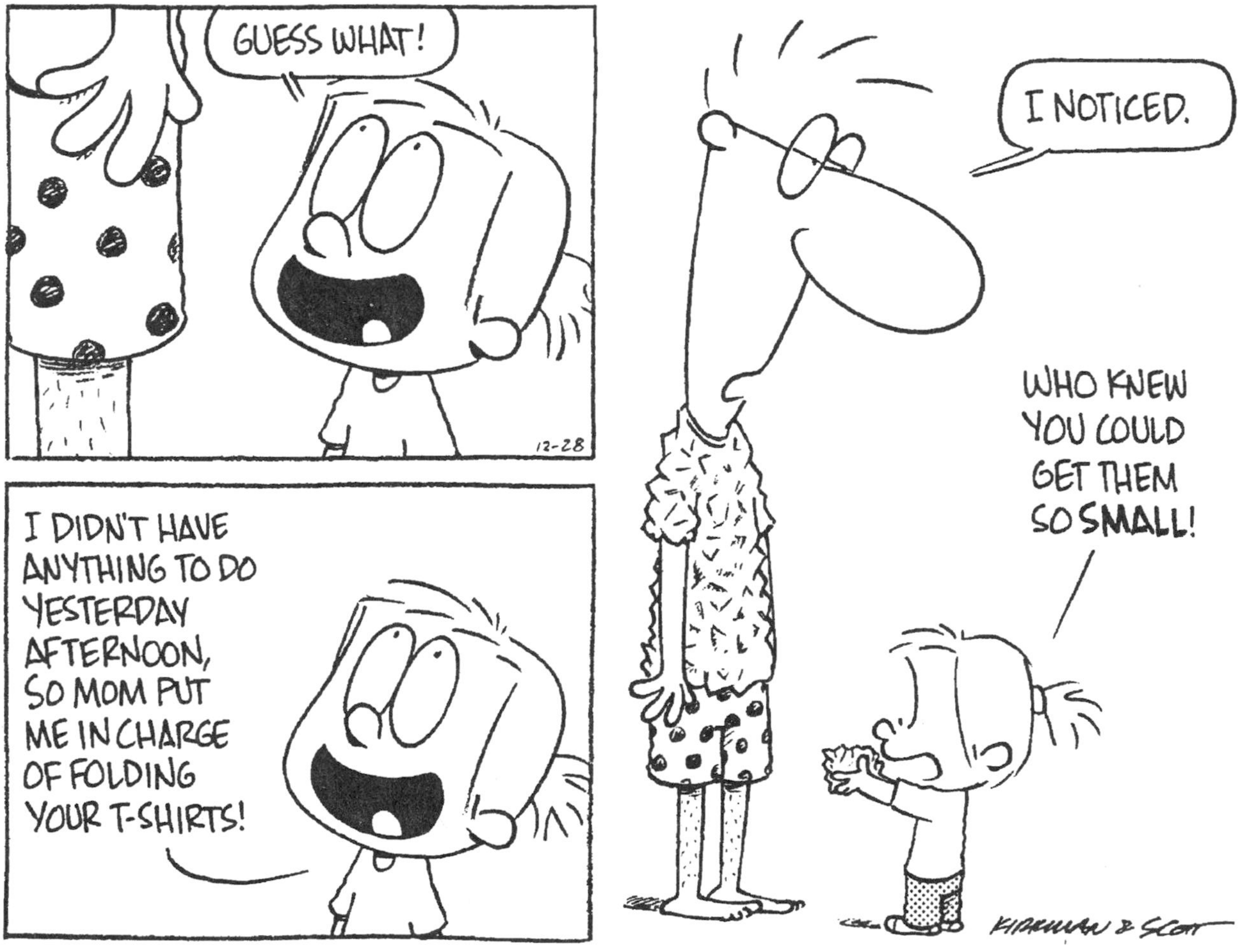
GUESS WHAT!
12-28
I DIDN'T HAVE ANYTHING TO DO YESTERDAY AFTERNOON, SO MOM PUT ME IN CHARGE OF FOLDING YOUR T-SHIRTS!
I NOTICED.
WHO KNEW YOU COULD GET THEM SO SMALL!
KIRKMAN & SCOTT

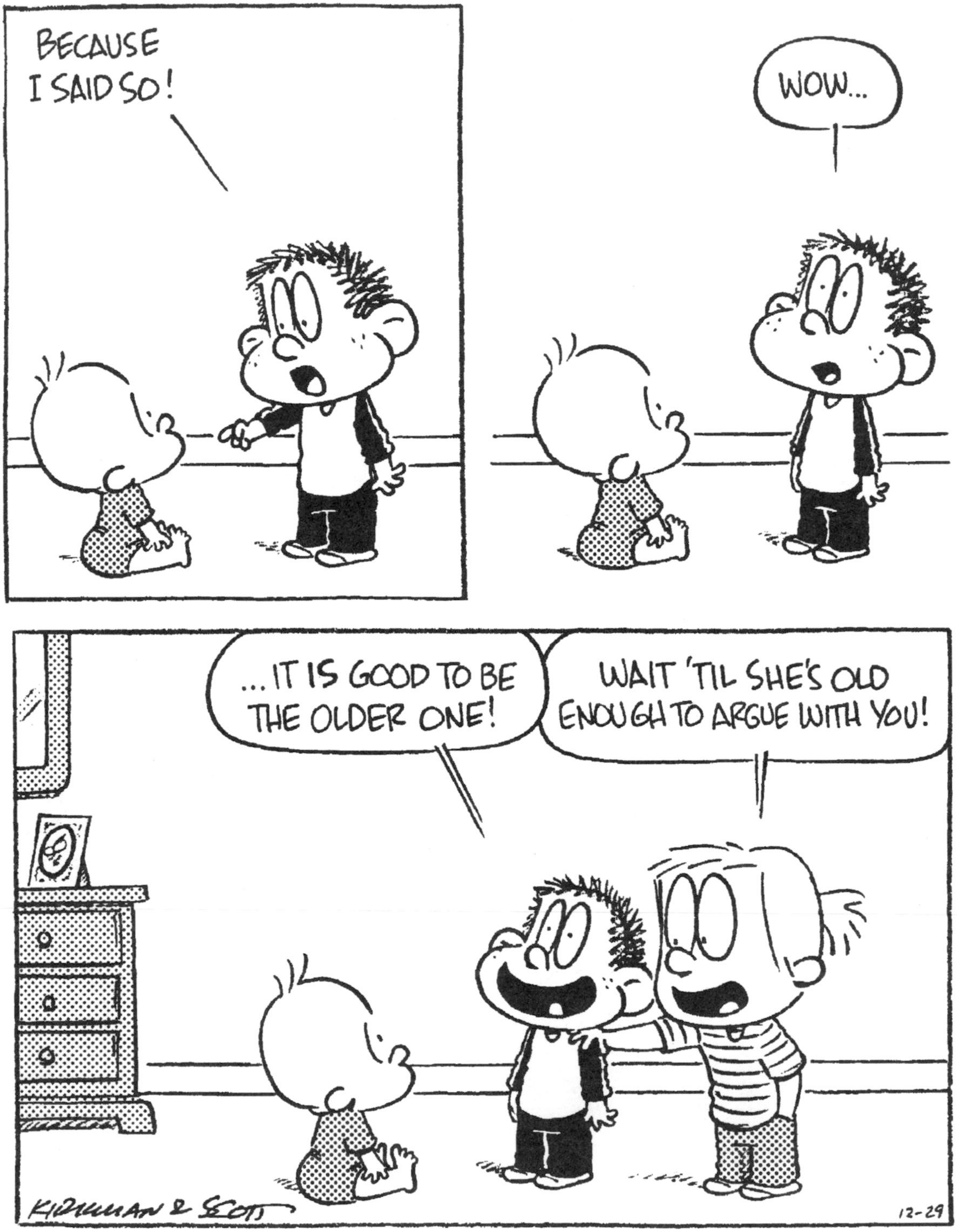
BECAUSE I SAID SO!
WOW...
...IT IS GOOD TO BE THE OLDER ONE!
WAIT 'TIL SHE'S OLD ENOUGH TO ARGUE WITH YOU!
KIRKMAN & SCOTT
12-29

BABY BLUES®
BY RICK KIRKMAN/ JERRY SCOTT

DO YOU WANT TO DO SOMETHING FOR NEW YEAR'S EVE?
ARE YOU SERIOUS?
DARRYL, IT'S TOMORROW NIGHT!
RESTAURANTS ARE FULL! CONCERTS ARE SOLD OUT!
IF YOU DON'T PLAN MONTHS IN ADVANCE, YOU'RE GOING TO END UP STAYING HOME ON NEW YEAR'S EVE!
THEN MY STRATEGY IS WORKING PERFECTLY.
KIRKMAN & SCOTT
12-30

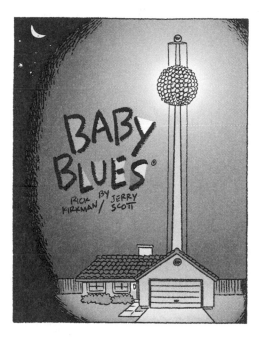

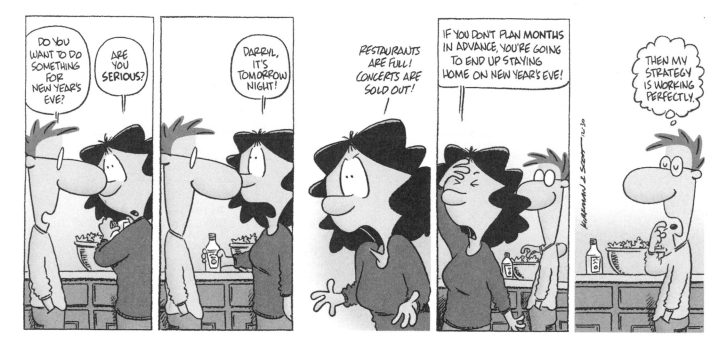

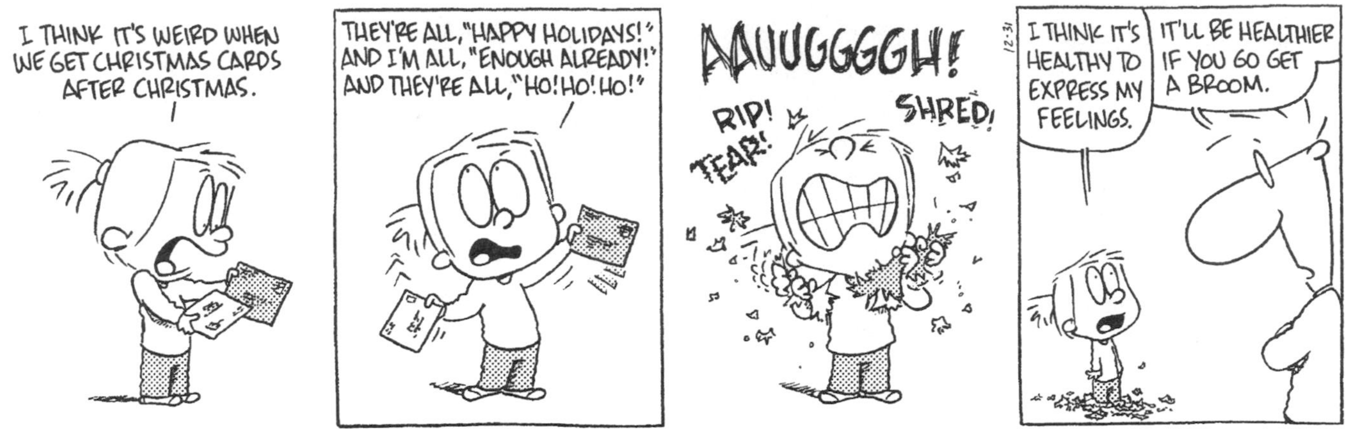
I THINK IT'S WEIRD WHEN WE GET CHRISTMAS CARDS AFTER CHRISTMAS.
THEY'RE ALL, "HAPPY HOLIDAYS!" AND I'M ALL, "ENOUGH ALREADY!" AND THEY'RE ALL, "HO! HO! HO!"
AAUUGGGGH!
RIP! TEAR!
SHRED!
I THINK IT'S HEALTHY TO EXPRESS MY FEELINGS.
IT'LL BE HEALTHIER IF YOU GO GET A BROOM.

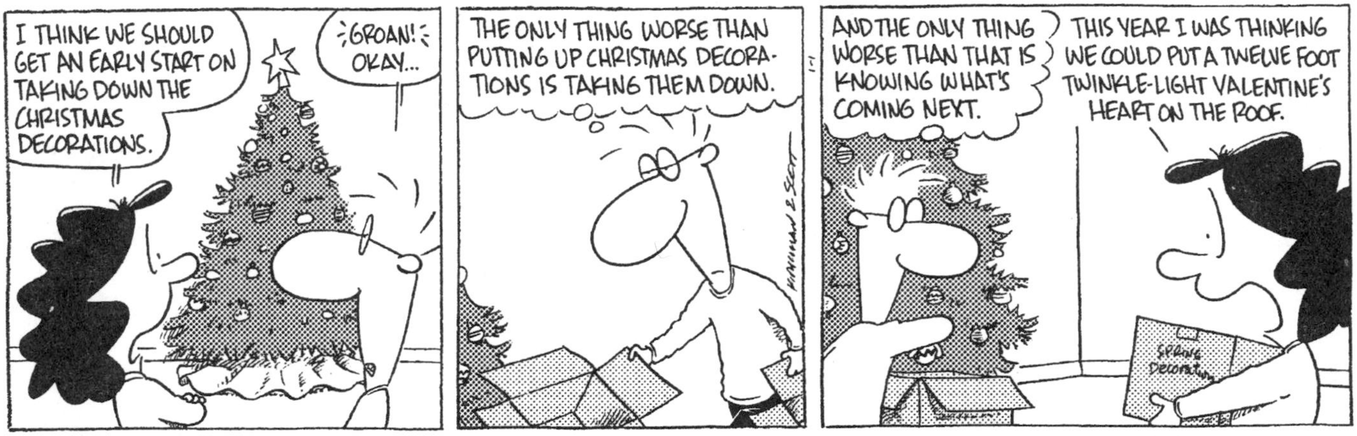
I THINK WE SHOULD GET AN EARLY START ON TAKING DOWN THE CHRISTMAS DECORATIONS.
GROAN! OKAY...
THE ONLY THING WORSE THAN PUTTING UP CHRISTMAS DECORATIONS IS TAKING THEM DOWN.
AND THE ONLY THING WORSE THAN THAT IS KNOWING WHAT'S COMING NEXT.
THIS YEAR I WAS THINKING WE COULD PUT A TWELVE FOOT TWINKLE-LIGHT VALENTINE'S HEART ON THE ROOF.

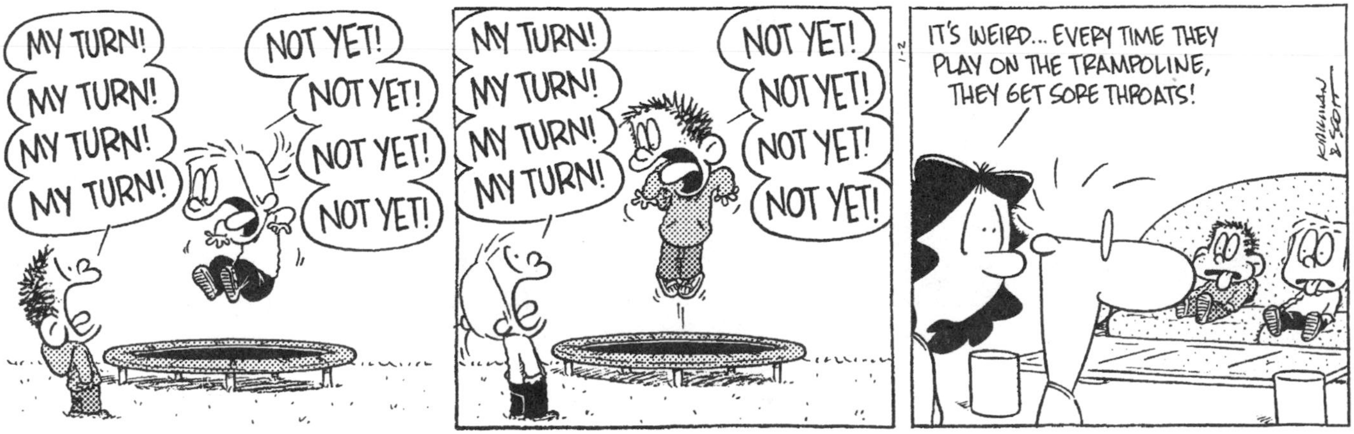
MY TURN! MY TURN! MY TURN! MY TURN!
NOT YET! NOT YET! NOT YET! NOT YET!
MY TURN! MY TURN! MY TURN! MY TURN!
NOT YET! NOT YET! NOT YET! NOT YET!
IT'S WEIRD... EVERY TIME THEY PLAY ON THE TRAMPOLINE, THEY GET SORE THROATS!

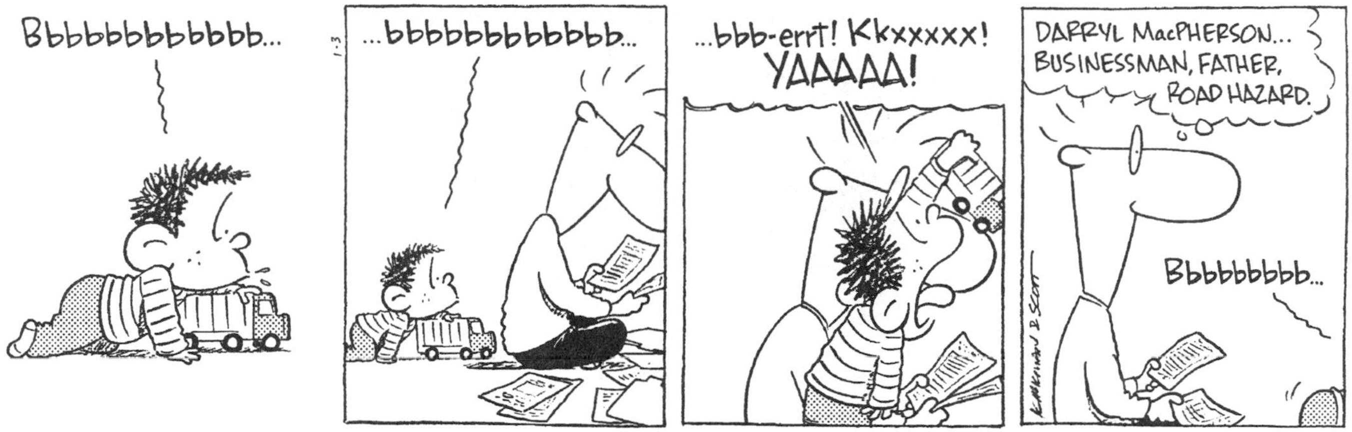
Bbbbbbbbbbbb...
...bbbbbbbbbbbb...
...bbb-errt! Kkxxxxx!
YAAAAA!
DARRYL MacPHERSON... BUSINESSMAN, FATHER, ROAD HAZARD.
Bbbbbbbbb...

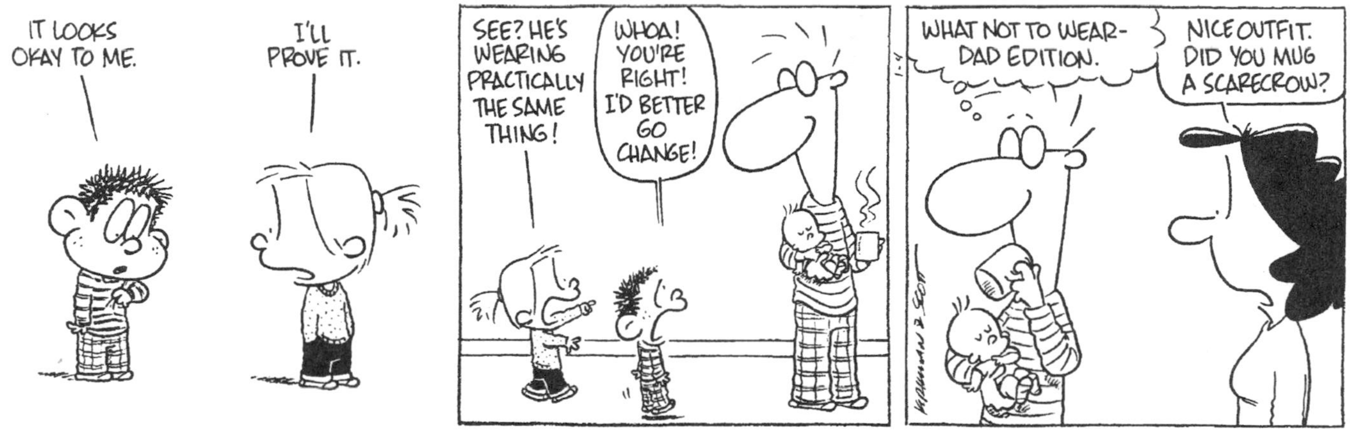
IT LOOKS OKAY TO ME.
I'LL PROVE IT.
SEE? HE'S WEARING PRACTICALLY THE SAME THING!
WHOA! YOU'RE RIGHT! I'D BETTER GO CHANGE!
WHAT NOT TO WEAR- DAD EDITION.
NICE OUTFIT. DID YOU MUG A SCARECROW?

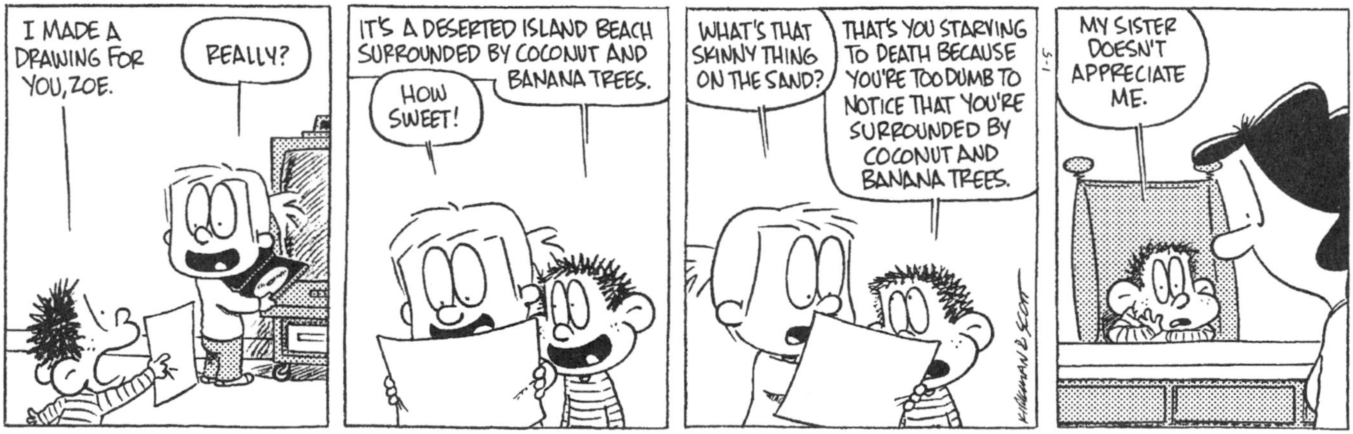
I MADE A DRAWING FOR YOU, ZOE.
REALLY?
IT'S A DESERTED ISLAND BEACH SURROUNDED BY COCONUT AND BANANA TREES.
HOW SWEET!
WHAT'S THAT SKINNY THING ON THE SAND?
THAT'S YOU STARVING TO DEATH BECAUSE YOU'RE TOO DUMB TO NOTICE THAT YOU'RE SURROUNDED BY COCONUT AND BANANA TREES.
MY SISTER DOESN'T APPRECIATE ME.

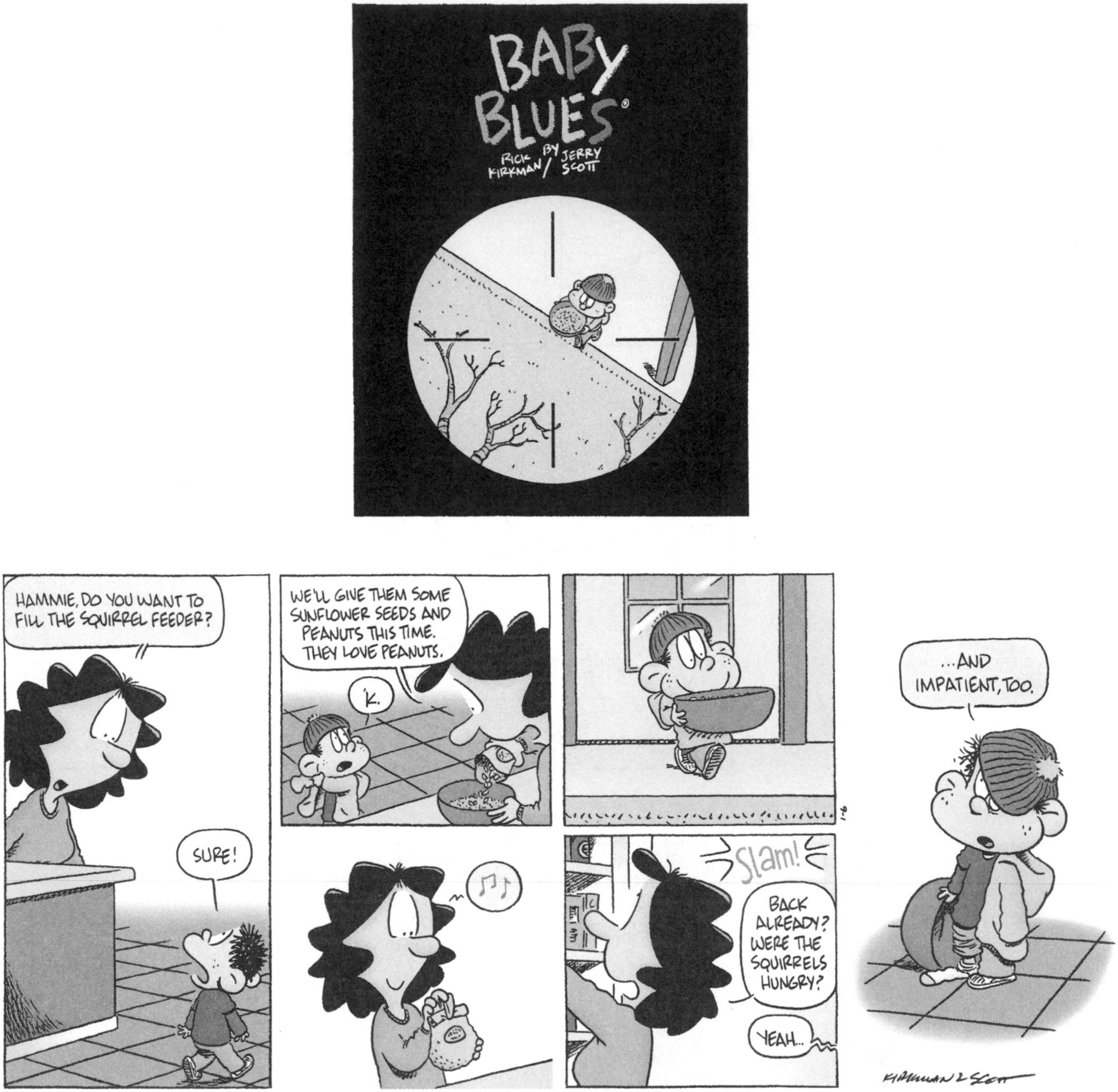
BABY BLUES®
BY RICK KIRKMAN / JERRY SCOTT
HAMMIE, DO YOU WANT TO FILL THE SQUIRREL FEEDER?
SURE!
WE'LL GIVE THEM SOME SUNFLOWER SEEDS AND PEANUTS THIS TIME. THEY LOVE PEANUTS.
'K.
SLAM!
BACK ALREADY? WERE THE SQUIRRELS HUNGRY?
YEAH...
...AND IMPATIENT, TOO.
KIRKMAN & SCOTT

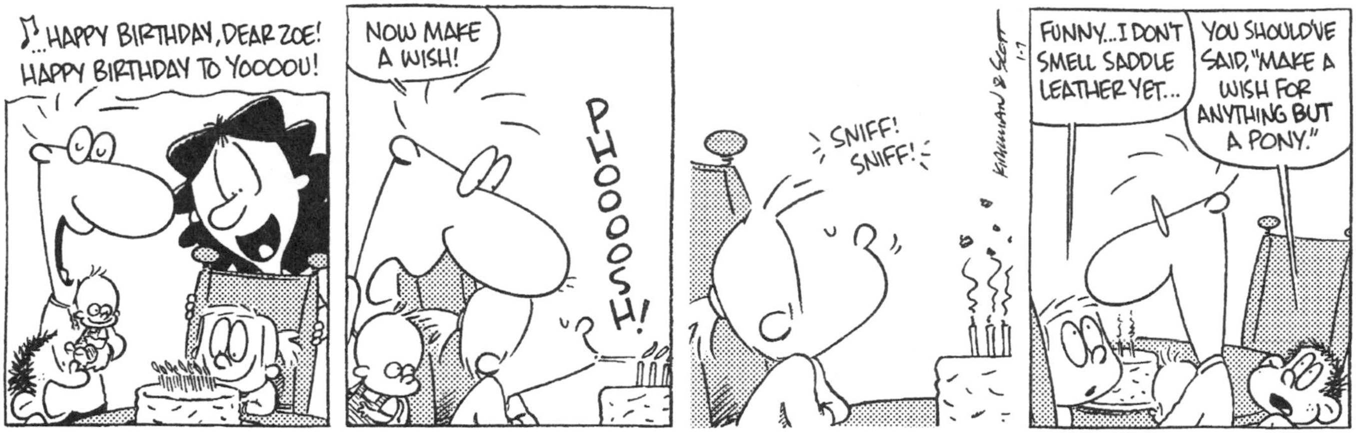
♪...HAPPY BIRTHDAY, DEAR ZOE! HAPPY BIRTHDAY TO YOOOOU!
NOW MAKE A WISH!
PHOOOOOSH!
SNIFF! SNIFF!
FUNNY...I DON'T SMELL SADDLE LEATHER YET...
YOU SHOULD'VE SAID, "MAKE A WISH FOR ANYTHING BUT A PONY."

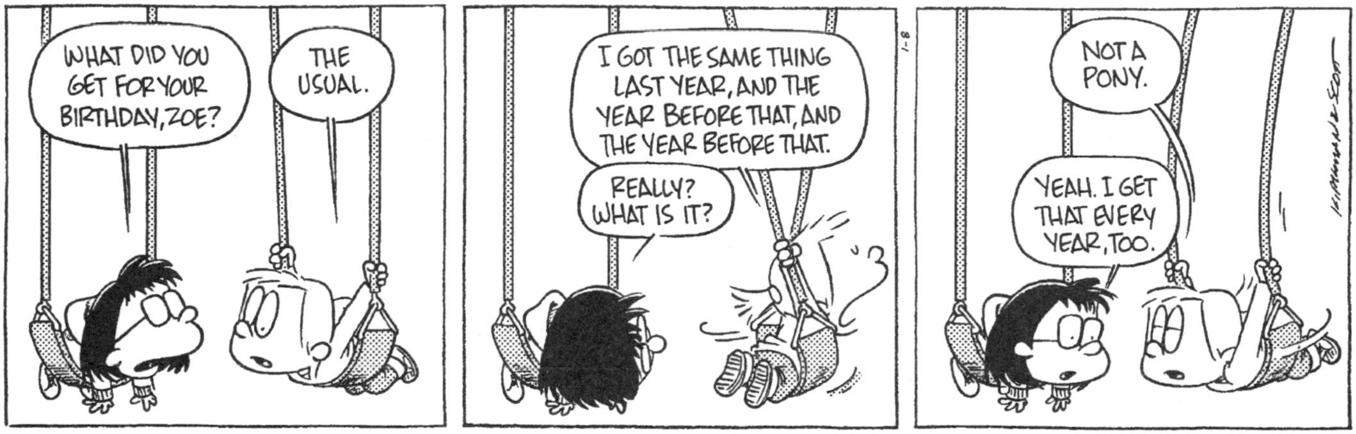
WHAT DID YOU GET FOR YOUR BIRTHDAY, ZOE?
THE USUAL.
I GOT THE SAME THING LAST YEAR, AND THE YEAR BEFORE THAT, AND THE YEAR BEFORE THAT.
REALLY? WHAT IS IT?
NOT A PONY.
YEAH. I GET THAT EVERY YEAR, TOO.

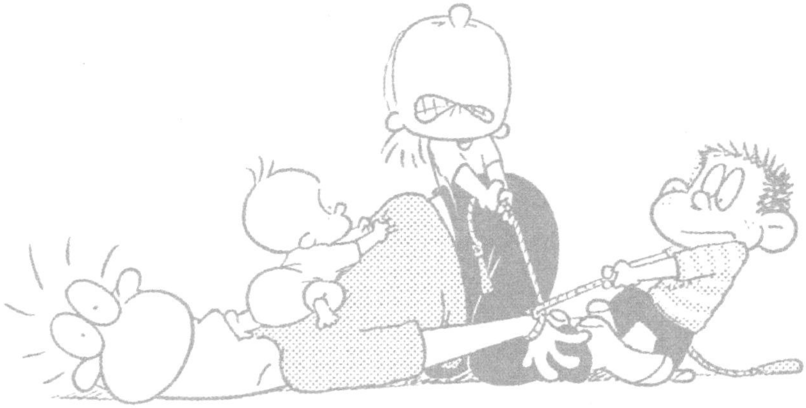

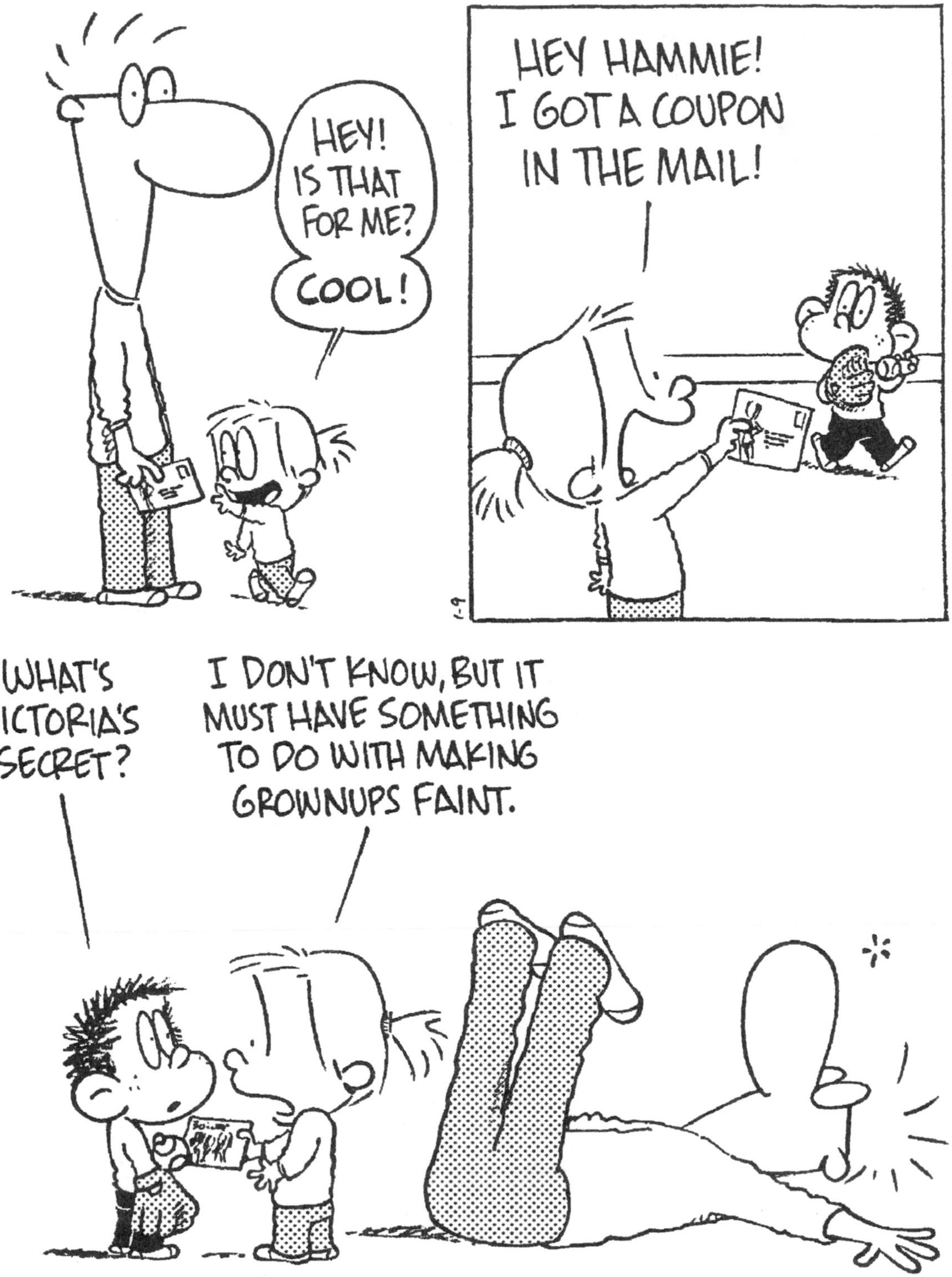
HEY! IS THAT FOR ME?
COOL!
HEY HAMMIE! I GOT A COUPON IN THE MAIL!
WHAT'S VICTORIA'S SECRET?
I DON'T KNOW, BUT IT MUST HAVE SOMETHING TO DO WITH MAKING GROWNUPS FAINT.

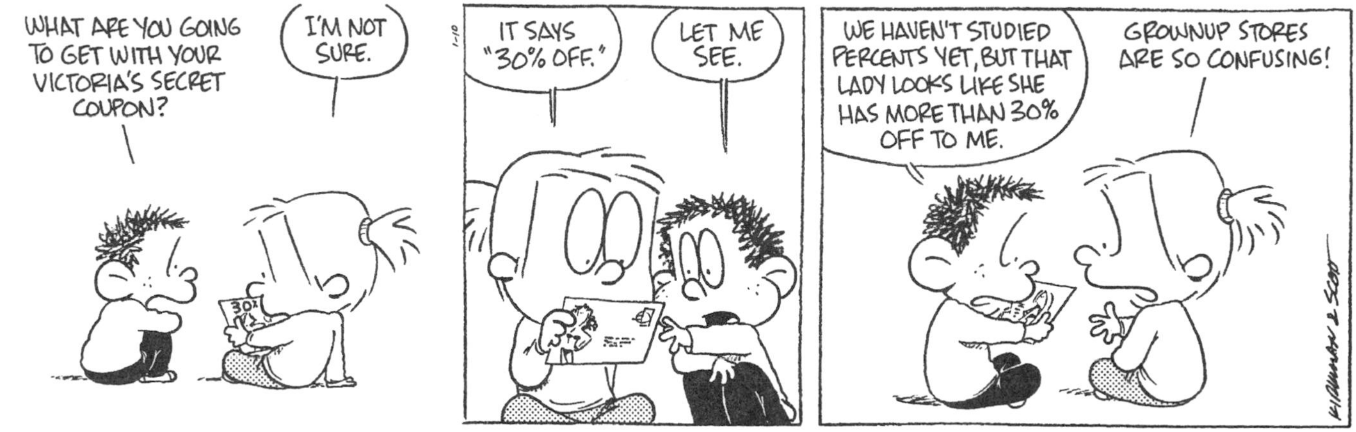
WHAT ARE YOU GOING TO GET WITH YOUR VICTORIA'S SECRET COUPON?
I'M NOT SURE.
IT SAYS "30% OFF."
LET ME SEE.
WE HAVEN'T STUDIED PERCENTS YET, BUT THAT LADY LOOKS LIKE SHE HAS MORE THAN 30% OFF TO ME.
GROWNUP STORES ARE SO CONFUSING!

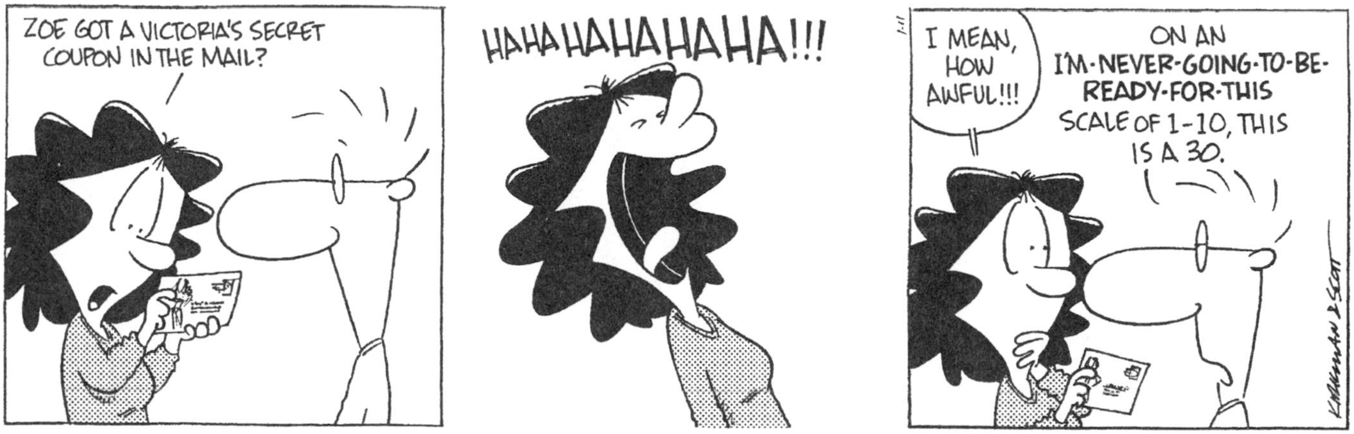
ZOE GOT A VICTORIA'S SECRET COUPON IN THE MAIL?
HAHAHAHAHAHAHA!!!
I MEAN, HOW AWFUL!!!
ON AN I'M-NEVER-GOING-TO-BE-READY-FOR-THIS SCALE OF 1-10, THIS IS A 30.

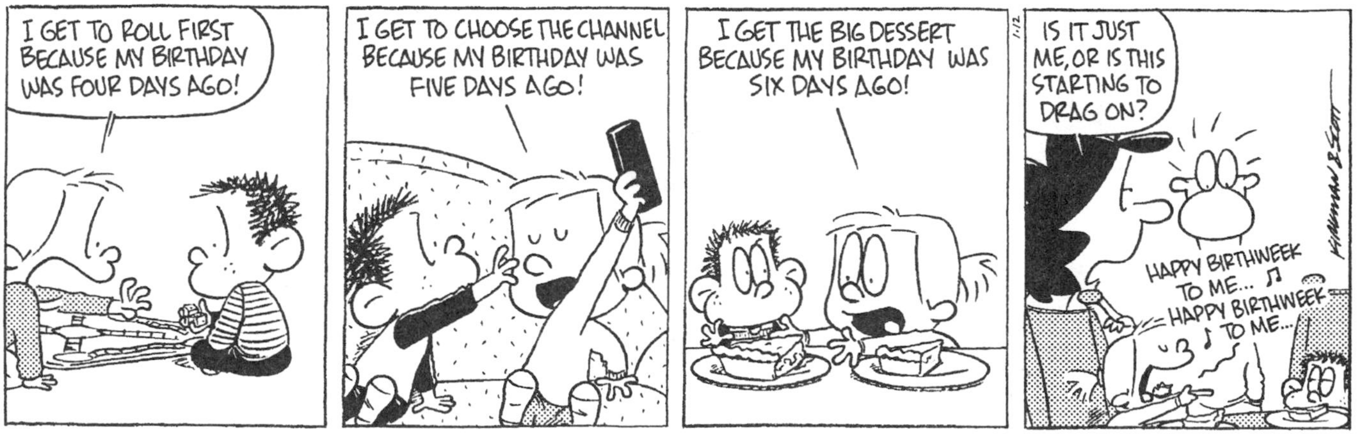
I GET TO ROLL FIRST BECAUSE MY BIRTHDAY WAS FOUR DAYS AGO!
I GET TO CHOOSE THE CHANNEL BECAUSE MY BIRTHDAY WAS FIVE DAYS AGO!
I GET THE BIG DESSERT BECAUSE MY BIRTHDAY WAS SIX DAYS AGO!
IS IT JUST ME, OR IS THIS STARTING TO DRAG ON?
HAPPY BIRTHWEEK TO ME... ♫ HAPPY BIRTHWEEK ♪ TO ME...

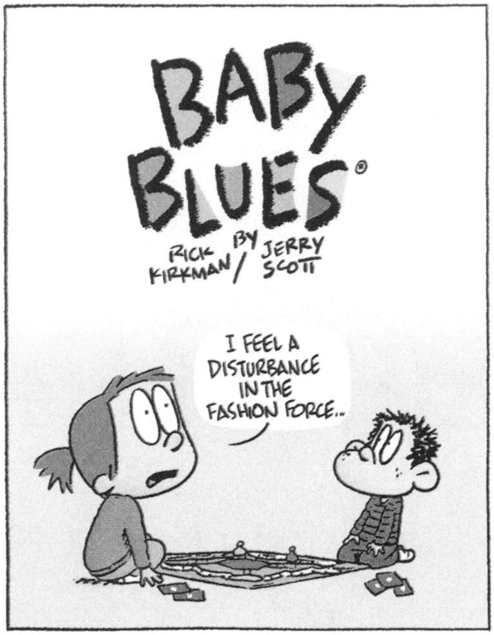
BABY BLUES®
BY RICK KIRKMAN / JERRY SCOTT
I FEEL A DISTURBANCE IN THE FASHION FORCE...

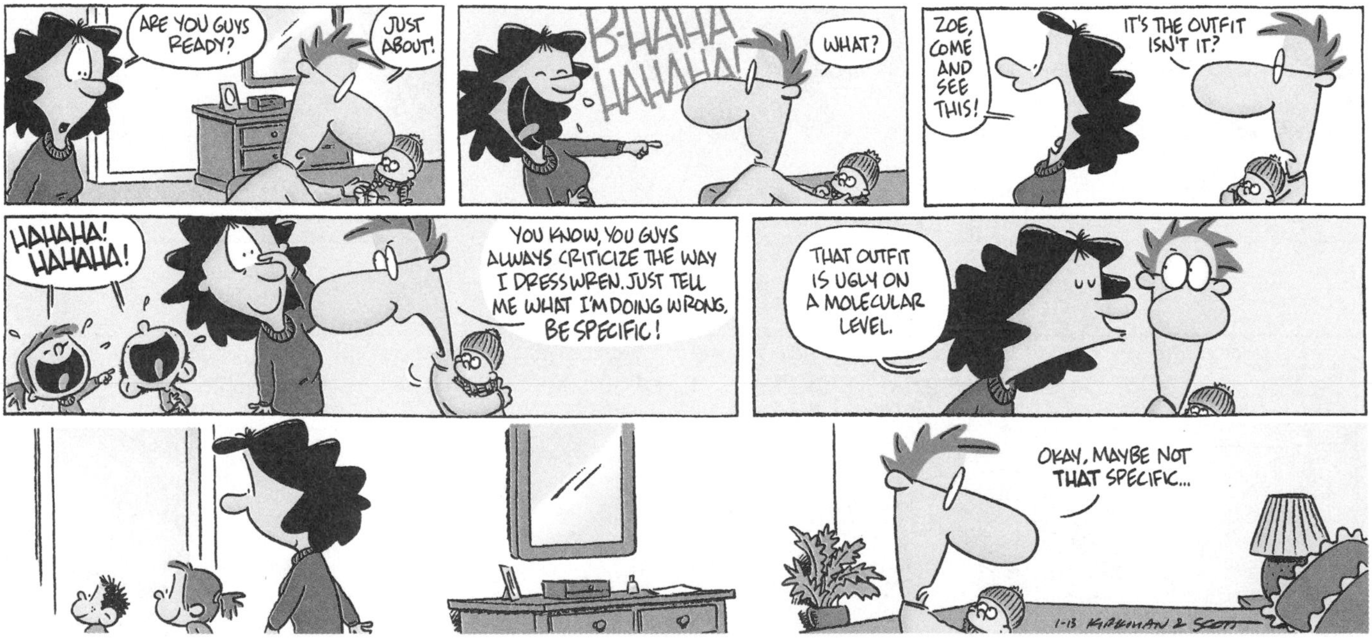
ARE YOU GUYS READY?
JUST ABOUT!
B-HAHA HAHAHA!
WHAT?
ZOE, COME AND SEE THIS!
IT'S THE OUTFIT ISN'T IT?
HAHAHA! HAHAHA!
YOU KNOW, YOU GUYS ALWAYS CRITICIZE THE WAY I DRESS WREN. JUST TELL ME WHAT I'M DOING WRONG. BE SPECIFIC!
THAT OUTFIT IS UGLY ON A MOLECULAR LEVEL.
OKAY, MAYBE NOT THAT SPECIFIC...
1-13 KIRKMAN & SCOTT

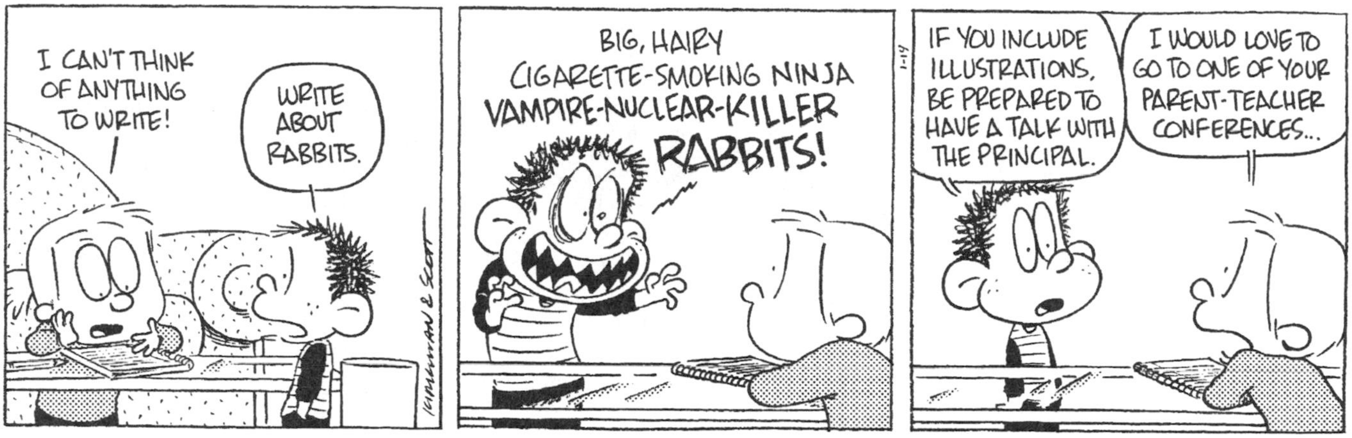
I CAN'T THINK OF ANYTHING TO WRITE!
WRITE ABOUT RABBITS.
BIG, HAIRY CIGARETTE-SMOKING NINJA VAMPIRE-NUCLEAR-KILLER RABBITS!
IF YOU INCLUDE ILLUSTRATIONS, BE PREPARED TO HAVE A TALK WITH THE PRINCIPAL.
I WOULD LOVE TO GO TO ONE OF YOUR PARENT-TEACHER CONFERENCES...

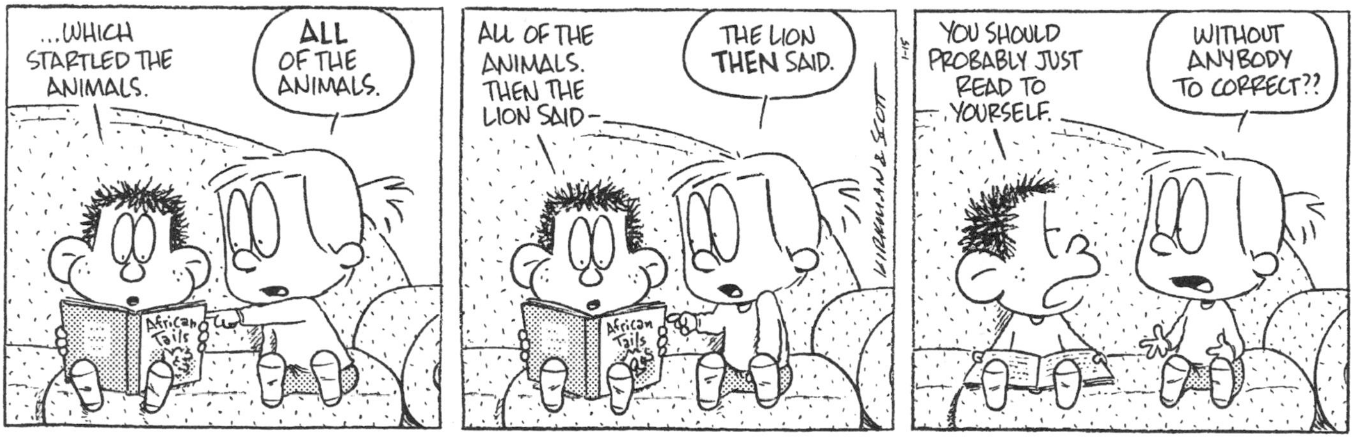
...WHICH STARTLED THE ANIMALS.
ALL OF THE ANIMALS.
African Tails
ALL OF THE ANIMALS. THEN THE LION SAID—
THE LION THEN SAID.
YOU SHOULD PROBABLY JUST READ TO YOURSELF.
WITHOUT ANYBODY TO CORRECT??

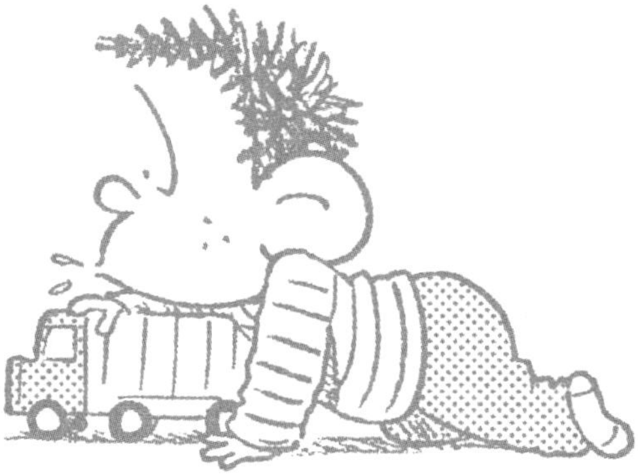

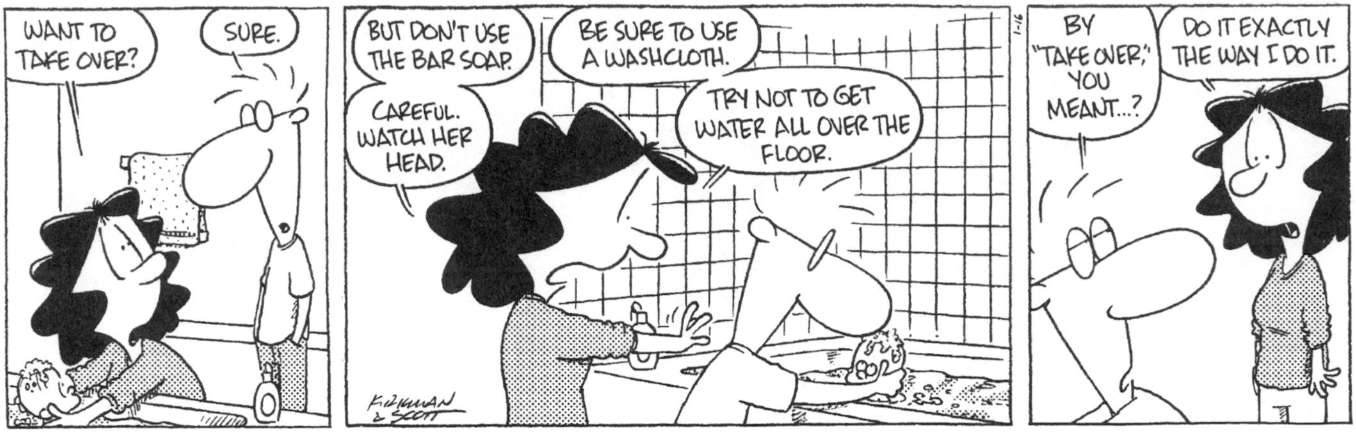
WANT TO TAKE OVER?
SURE.
BUT DON'T USE THE BAR SOAP.
BE SURE TO USE A WASHCLOTH.
CAREFUL. WATCH HER HEAD.
TRY NOT TO GET WATER ALL OVER THE FLOOR.
BY "TAKE OVER," YOU MEANT...?
DO IT EXACTLY THE WAY I DO IT.
KIRKMAN & SCOTT
1-16

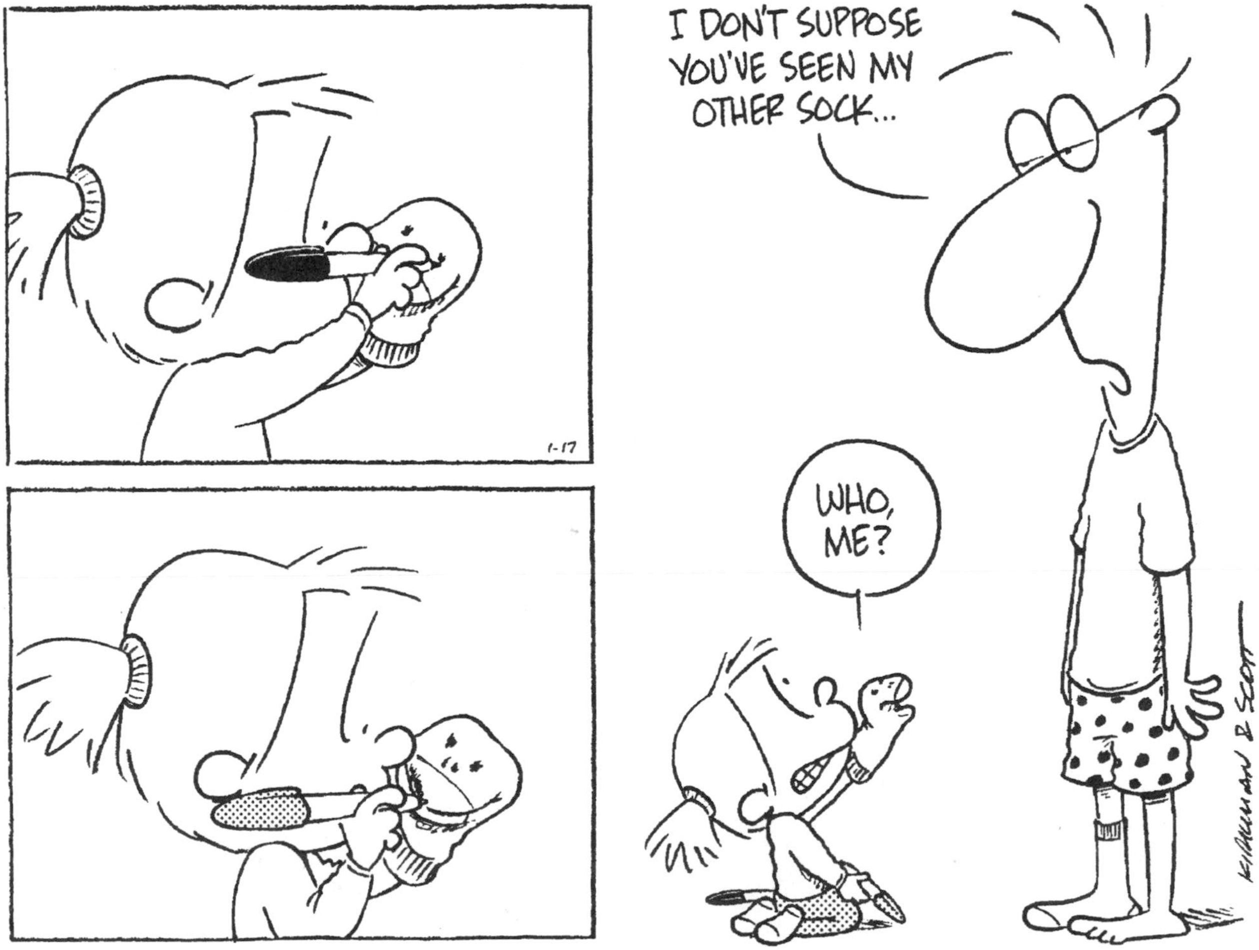
1-17
I DON'T SUPPOSE YOU'VE SEEN MY OTHER SOCK...
WHO, ME?
KIRKMAN & SCOTT

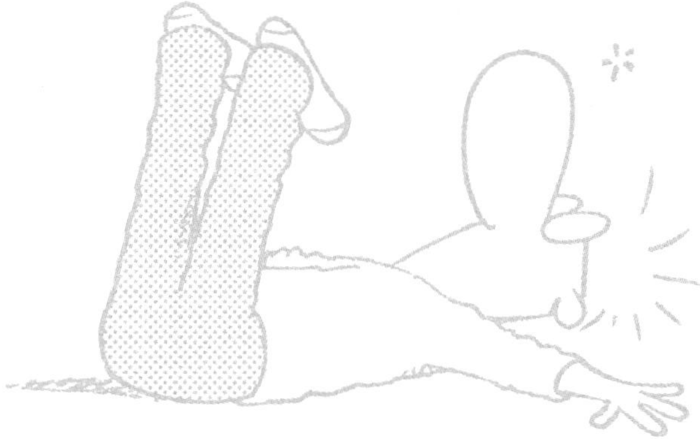

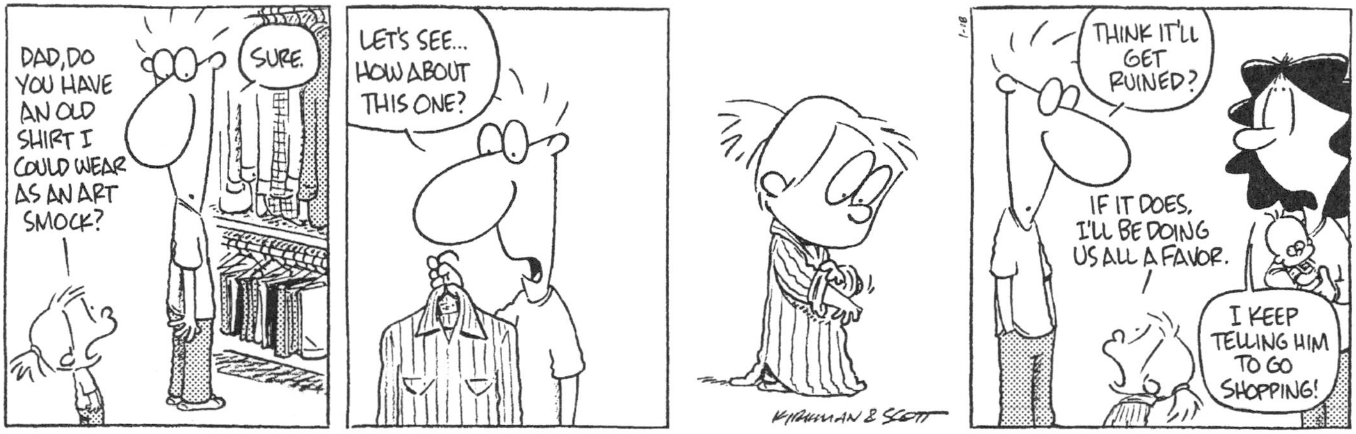
DAD, DO YOU HAVE AN OLD SHIRT I COULD WEAR AS AN ART SMOCK?
SURE.
LET'S SEE... HOW ABOUT THIS ONE?
KIRKMAN & SCOTT
THINK IT'LL GET RUINED?
IF IT DOES, I'LL BE DOING US ALL A FAVOR.
I KEEP TELLING HIM TO GO SHOPPING!

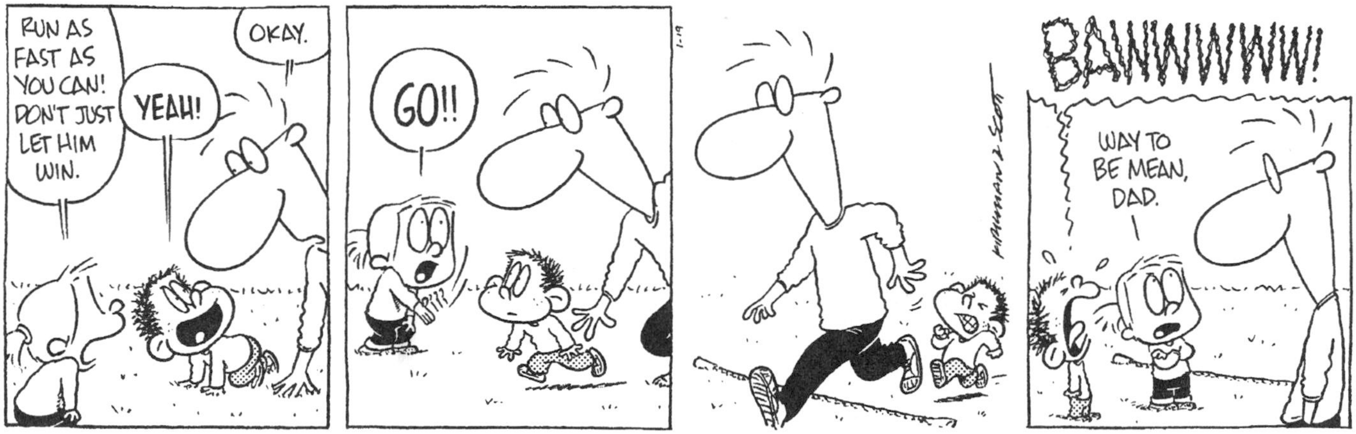
RUN AS FAST AS YOU CAN! DON'T JUST LET HIM WIN.
YEAH!
OKAY.
GO!!
BAWWWWW!
WAY TO BE MEAN, DAD.

BABY BLUES®
BY RICK KIRKMAN / JERRY SCOTT

COULD YOU GET THE MILK, HAMMIE?
SURE.
MILK
HEY, I THOUGHT YOU WANTED SOME MILK.
NAW, I JUST WANTED TO WATCH MOM'S FACE WHILE YOU CARRIED IT.
KIRKMAN & SCOTT

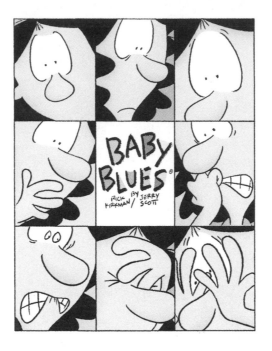

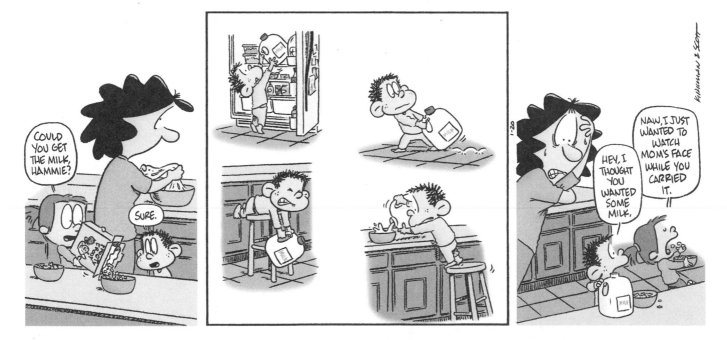

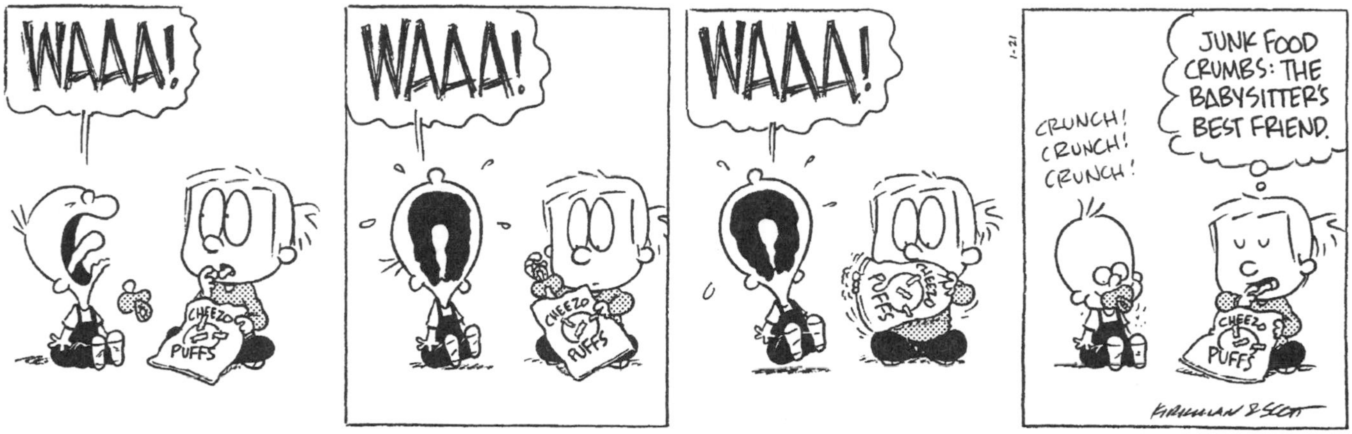
WAAA!
CHEEZO PUFFS
WAAA!
CHEEZO PUFFS
WAAA!
CHEEZO PUFFS
1-21
CRUNCH! CRUNCH! CRUNCH!
JUNK FOOD CRUMBS: THE BABYSITTER'S BEST FRIEND.
CHEEZO PUFFS
KIRKMAN & SCOTT

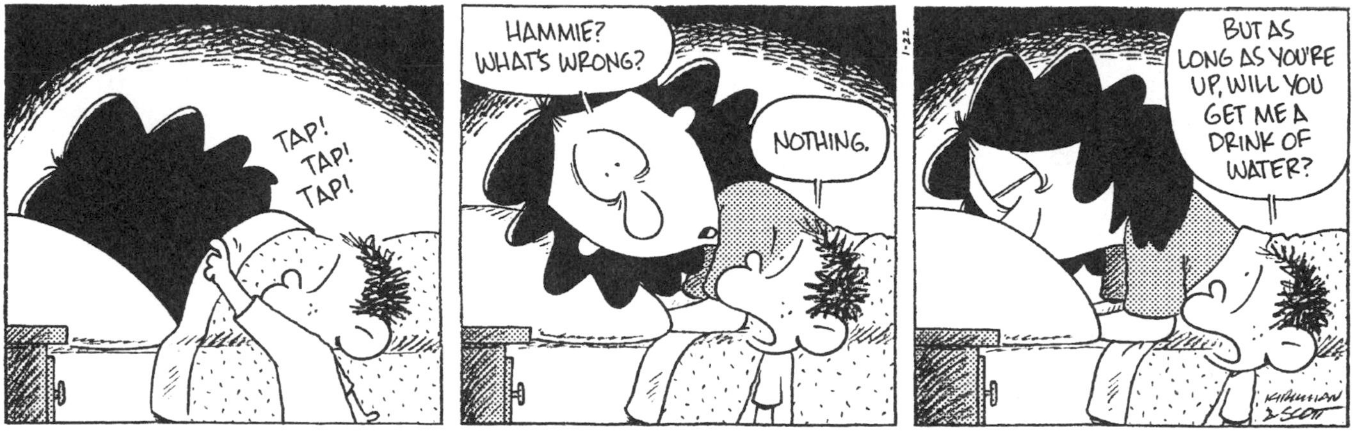
TAP! TAP! TAP!
HAMMIE? WHAT'S WRONG?
1-22
NOTHING.
BUT AS LONG AS YOU'RE UP, WILL YOU GET ME A DRINK OF WATER?
KIRKMAN & SCOTT

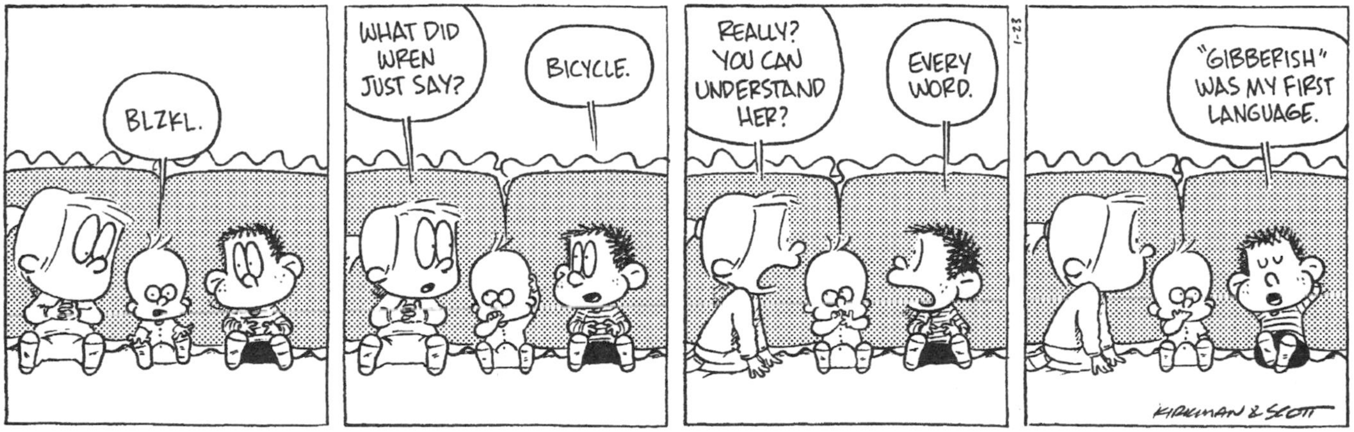
BLZKL.
WHAT DID WREN JUST SAY?
BICYCLE.
REALLY? YOU CAN UNDERSTAND HER?
EVERY WORD.
1-23
"GIBBERISH" WAS MY FIRST LANGUAGE.
KIRKMAN & SCOTT

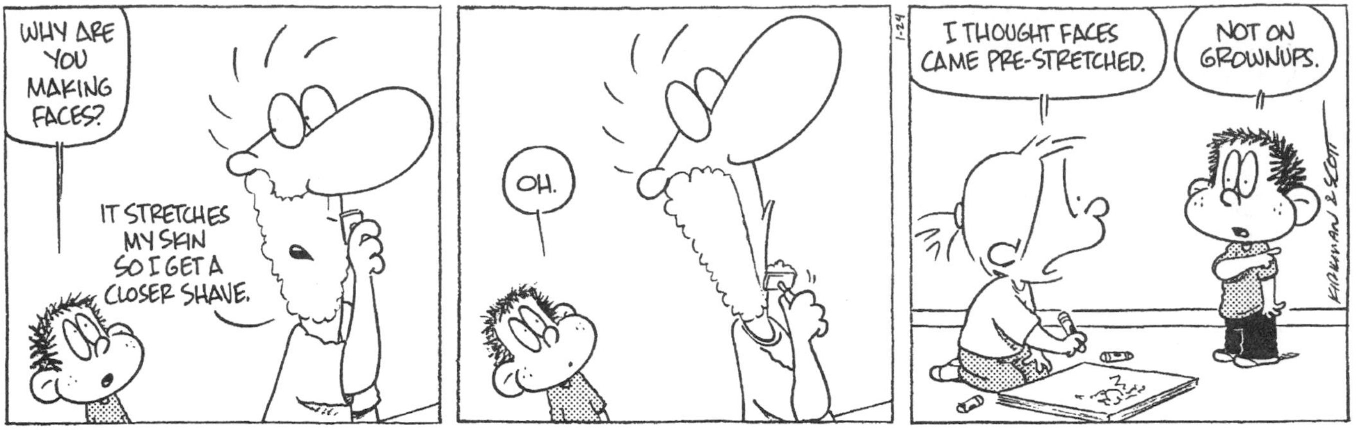
WHY ARE YOU MAKING FACES?
IT STRETCHES MY SKIN SO I GET A CLOSER SHAVE.
OH.
1-24
I THOUGHT FACES CAME PRE-STRETCHED.
NOT ON GROWNUPS.
KIRKMAN & SCOTT

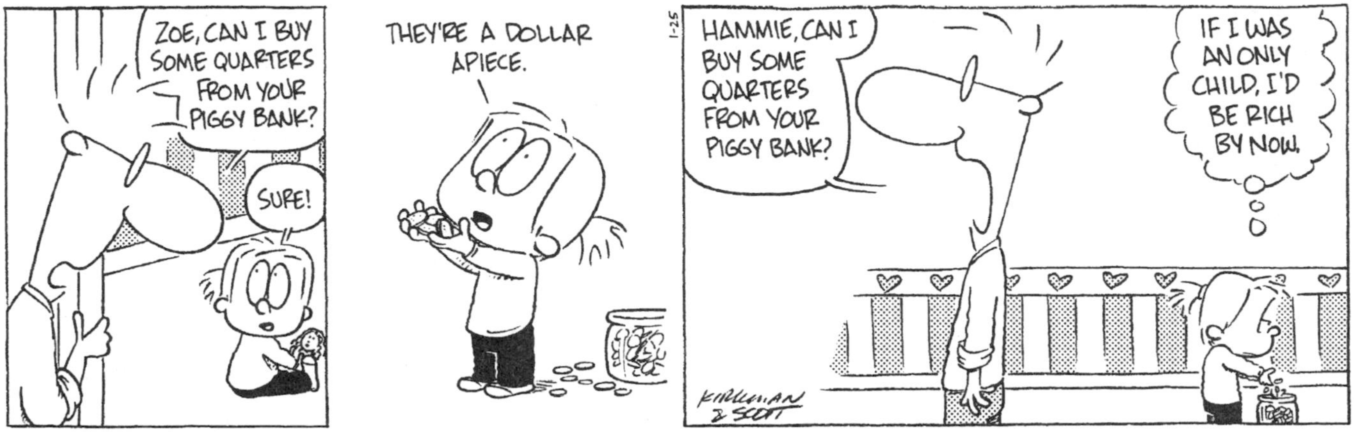
ZOE, CAN I BUY SOME QUARTERS FROM YOUR PIGGY BANK?
SURE!
THEY'RE A DOLLAR APIECE.
1-25
HAMMIE, CAN I BUY SOME QUARTERS FROM YOUR PIGGY BANK?
IF I WAS AN ONLY CHILD, I'D BE RICH BY NOW.
KIRKMAN & SCOTT

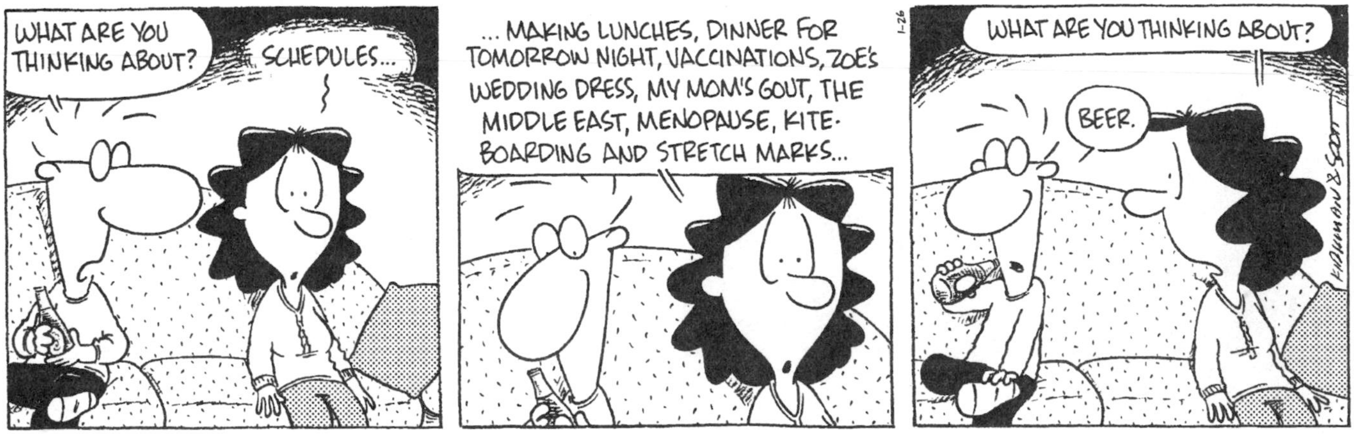
WHAT ARE YOU THINKING ABOUT?
SCHEDULES...
... MAKING LUNCHES, DINNER FOR TOMORROW NIGHT, VACCINATIONS, ZOE'S WEDDING DRESS, MY MOM'S GOUT, THE MIDDLE EAST, MENOPAUSE, KITE-BOARDING AND STRETCH MARKS...
1-26
WHAT ARE YOU THINKING ABOUT?
BEER.
KIRKMAN & SCOTT

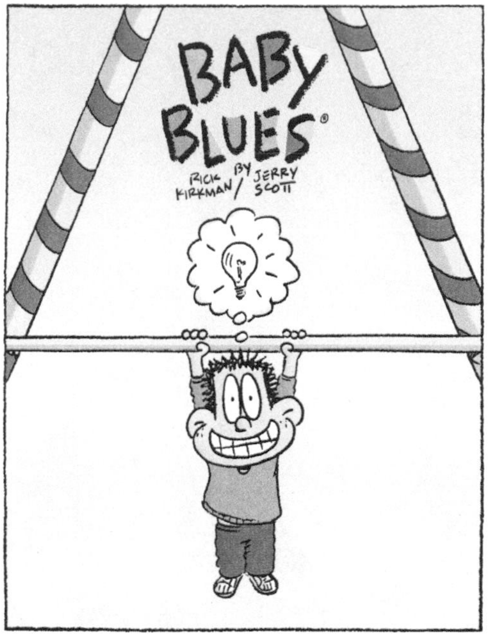
BABY BLUES®
BY RICK KIRKMAN / JERRY SCOTT

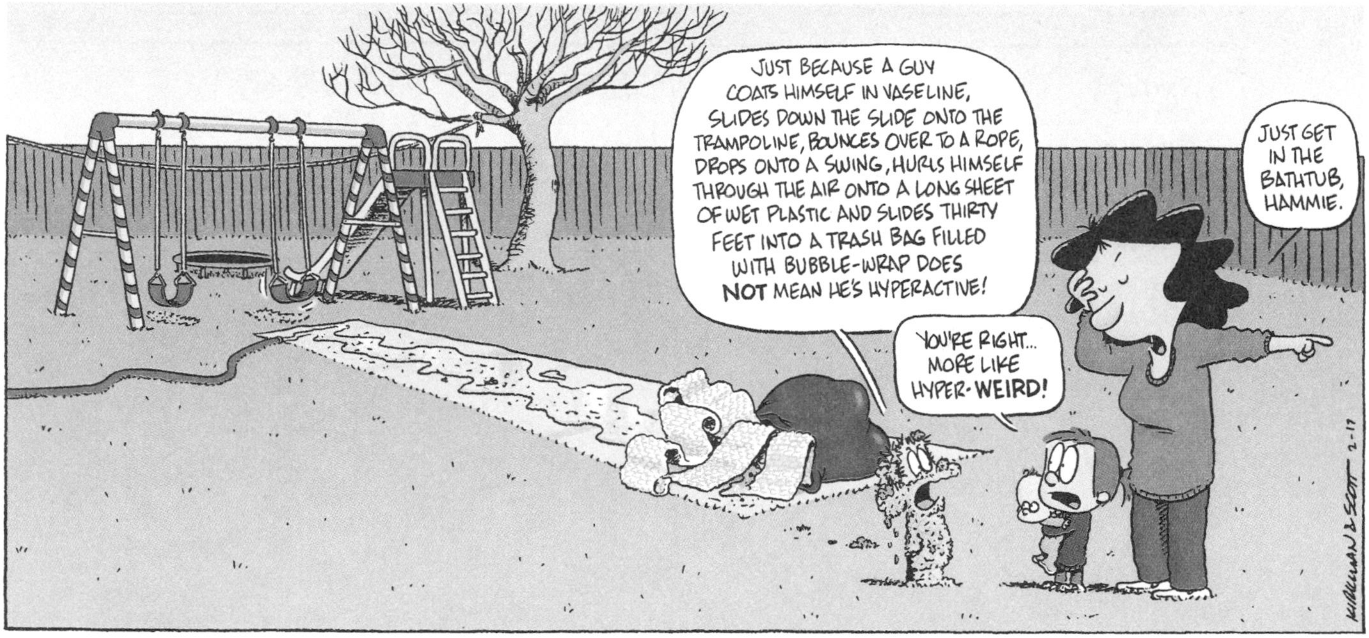
JUST BECAUSE A GUY COATS HIMSELF IN VASELINE, SLIDES DOWN THE SLIDE ONTO THE TRAMPOLINE, BOUNCES OVER TO A ROPE, DROPS ONTO A SWING, HURLS HIMSELF THROUGH THE AIR ONTO A LONG SHEET OF WET PLASTIC AND SLIDES THIRTY FEET INTO A TRASH BAG FILLED WITH BUBBLE-WRAP DOES NOT MEAN HE'S HYPERACTIVE!
YOU'RE RIGHT... MORE LIKE HYPER-WEIRD!
JUST GET IN THE BATHTUB, HAMMIE.
KIRKMAN & SCOTT 2-17

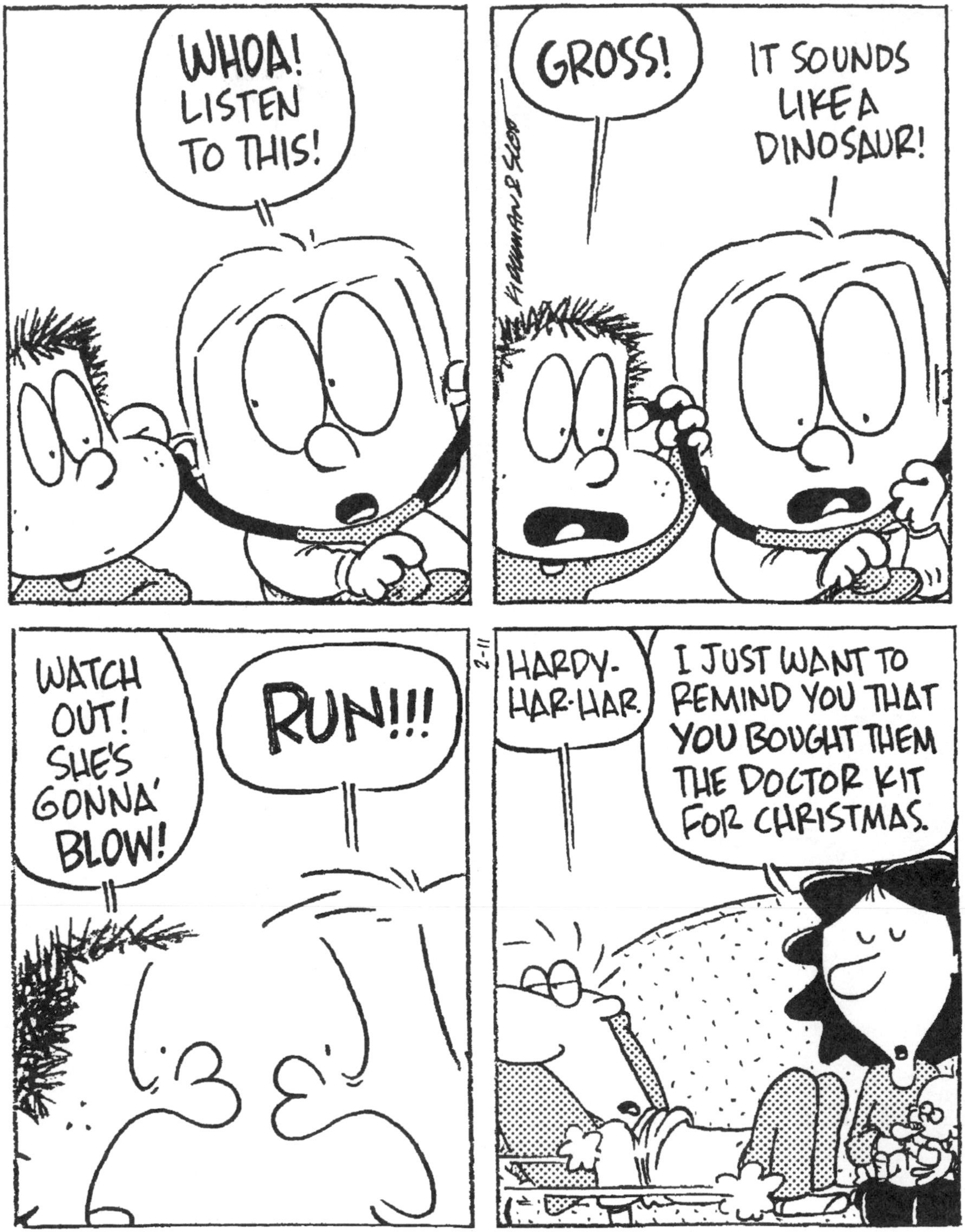
WHOA! LISTEN TO THIS!
GROSS!
IT SOUNDS LIKE A DINOSAUR!
WATCH OUT! SHE'S GONNA' BLOW!
RUN!!!
HARDY-HAR-HAR.
I JUST WANT TO REMIND YOU THAT YOU BOUGHT THEM THE DOCTOR KIT FOR CHRISTMAS.

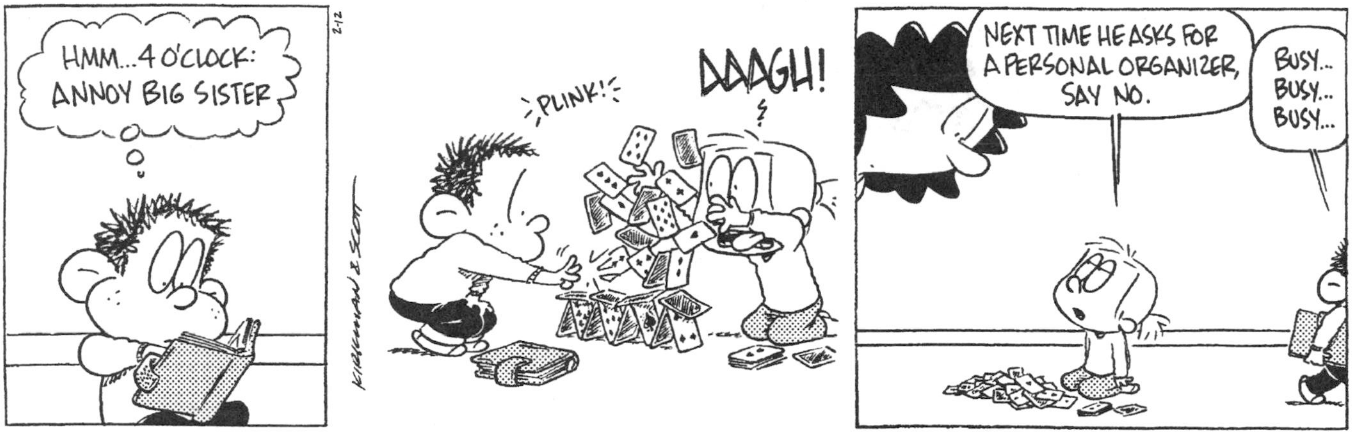
2-12
HMM...4 O'CLOCK: ANNOY BIG SISTER
PLINK!
DAAGH!
KIRKMAN & SCOTT
NEXT TIME HE ASKS FOR A PERSONAL ORGANIZER, SAY NO.
BUSY... BUSY... BUSY...

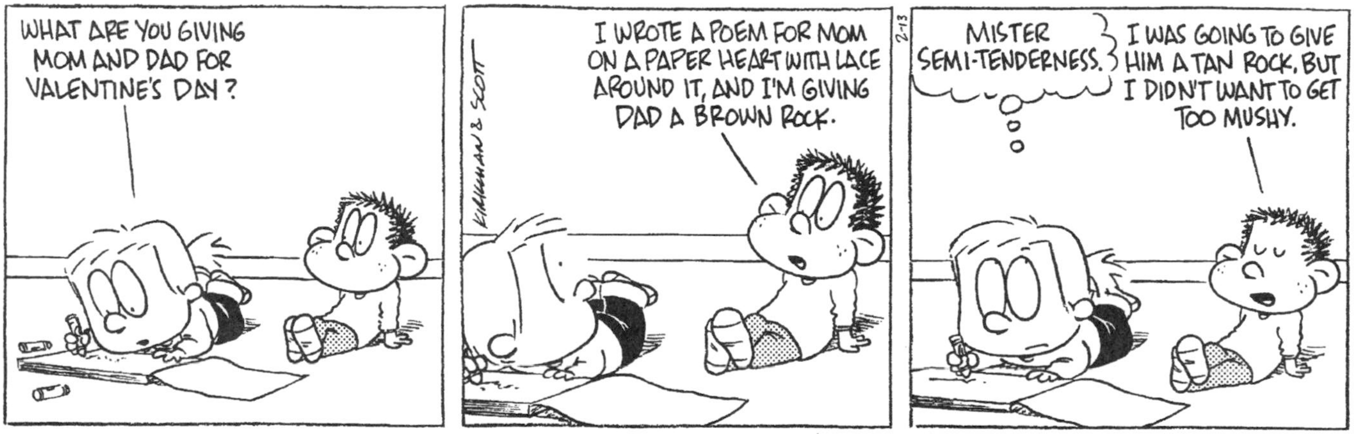
WHAT ARE YOU GIVING MOM AND DAD FOR VALENTINE'S DAY?
KIRKMAN & SCOTT
I WROTE A POEM FOR MOM ON A PAPER HEART WITH LACE AROUND IT, AND I'M GIVING DAD A BROWN ROCK.
2-13
MISTER SEMI-TENDERNESS.
I WAS GOING TO GIVE HIM A TAN ROCK, BUT I DIDN'T WANT TO GET TOO MUSHY.

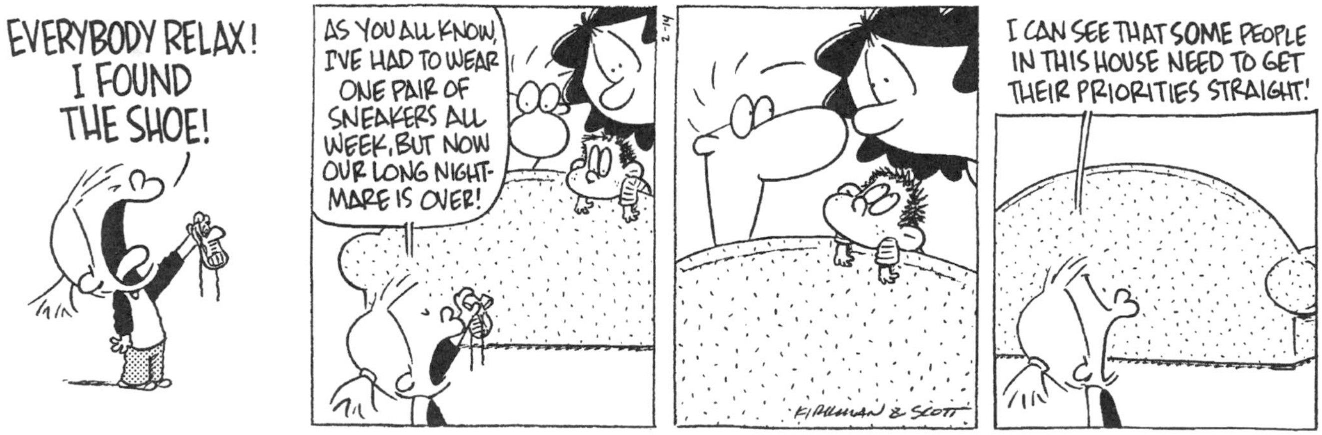
EVERYBODY RELAX! I FOUND THE SHOE!
AS YOU ALL KNOW, I'VE HAD TO WEAR ONE PAIR OF SNEAKERS ALL WEEK, BUT NOW OUR LONG NIGHTMARE IS OVER!
2-14
KIRKMAN & SCOTT
I CAN SEE THAT SOME PEOPLE IN THIS HOUSE NEED TO GET THEIR PRIORITIES STRAIGHT!

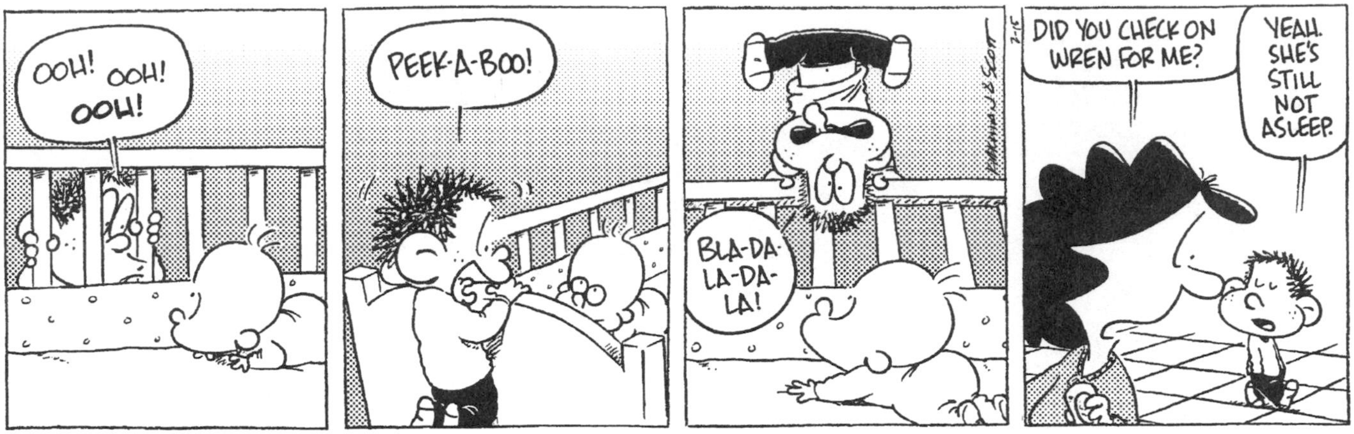
OOH! OOH! OOH!
PEEK-A-BOO!
BLA-DA-LA-DA-LA!
2-15
KIRKMAN & SCOTT
DID YOU CHECK ON WREN FOR ME?
YEAH. SHE'S STILL NOT ASLEEP.

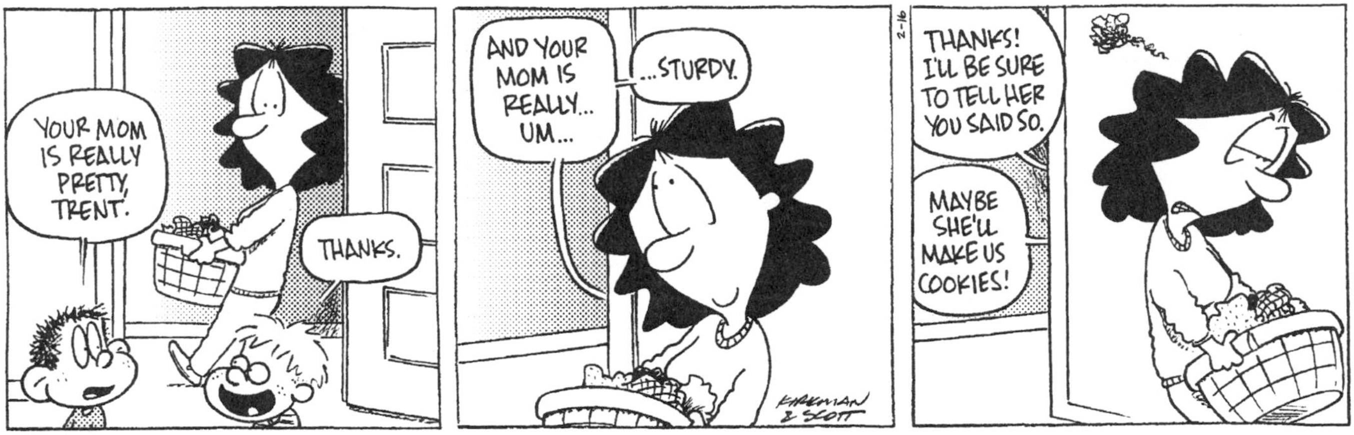
YOUR MOM IS REALLY PRETTY, TRENT.
THANKS.
AND YOUR MOM IS REALLY... UM...
...STURDY.
KIRKMAN & SCOTT
2-16
THANKS! I'LL BE SURE TO TELL HER YOU SAID SO.
MAYBE SHE'LL MAKE US COOKIES!

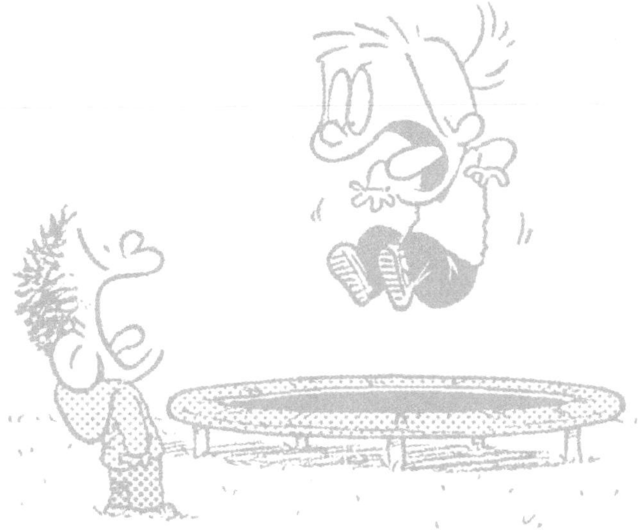

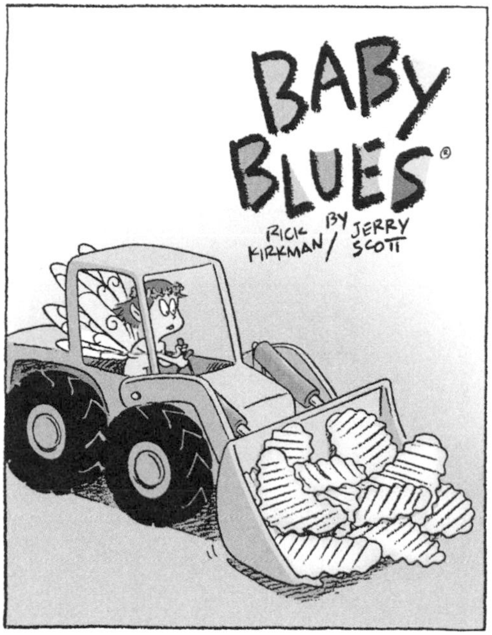
BABY BLUES®
BY RICK KIRKMAN / JERRY SCOTT

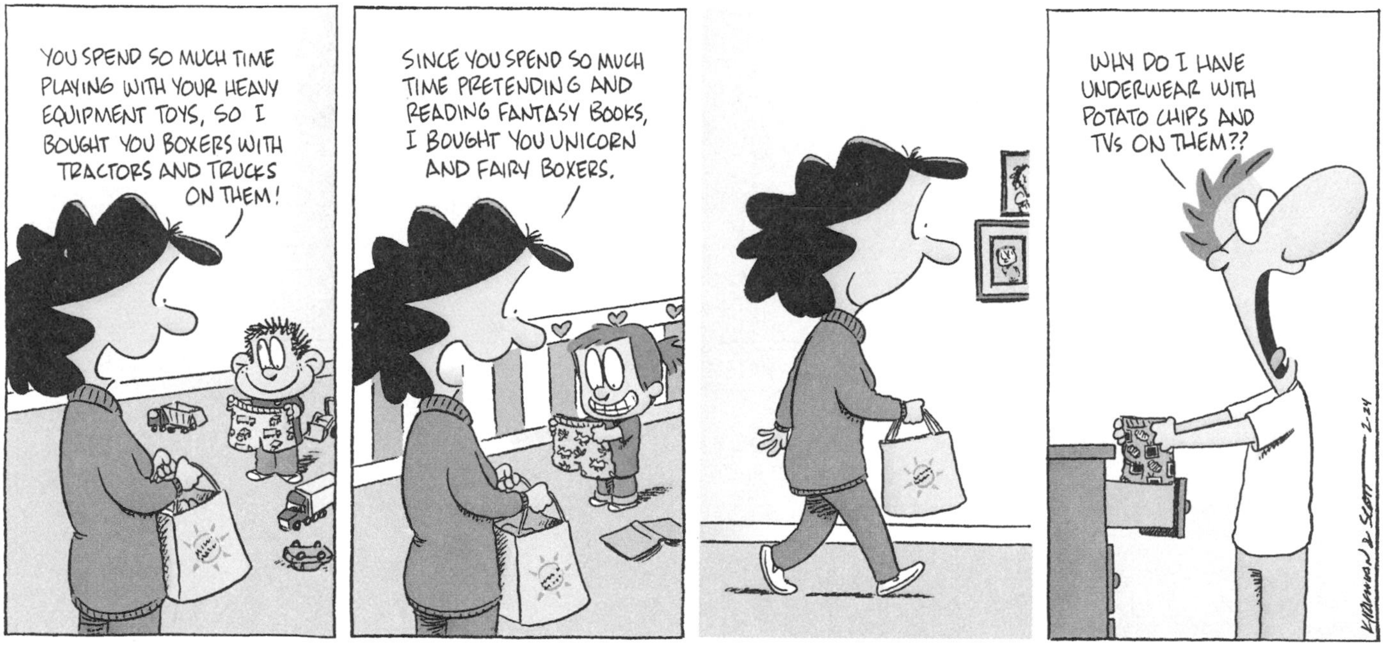
YOU SPEND SO MUCH TIME PLAYING WITH YOUR HEAVY EQUIPMENT TOYS, SO I BOUGHT YOU BOXERS WITH TRACTORS AND TRUCKS ON THEM!
SINCE YOU SPEND SO MUCH TIME PRETENDING AND READING FANTASY BOOKS, I BOUGHT YOU UNICORN AND FAIRY BOXERS.
WHY DO I HAVE UNDERWEAR WITH POTATO CHIPS AND TVs ON THEM??

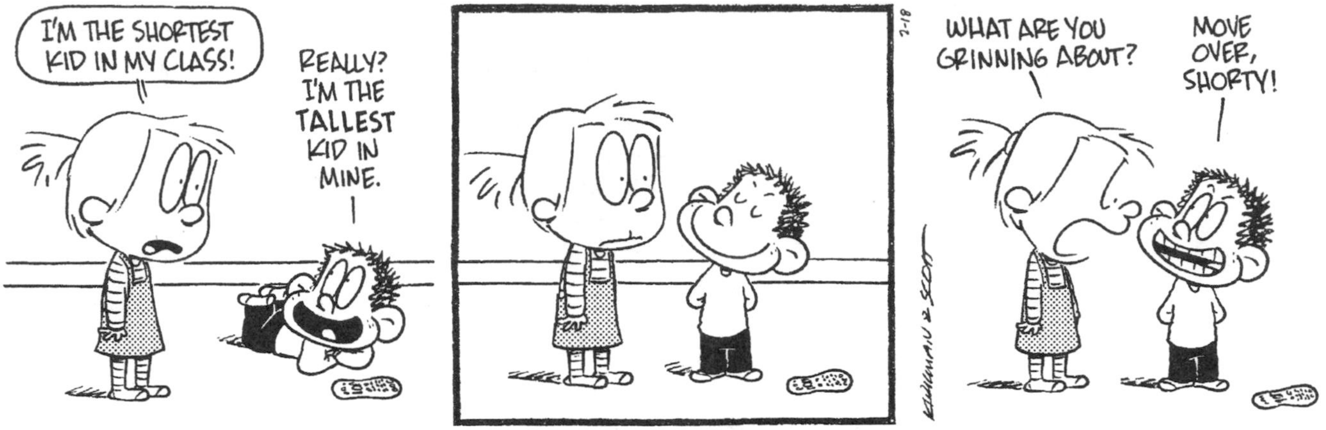
I'M THE SHORTEST KID IN MY CLASS!
REALLY? I'M THE TALLEST KID IN MINE.
2-18
WHAT ARE YOU GRINNING ABOUT?
MOVE OVER, SHORTY!
KIRKMAN & SCOTT

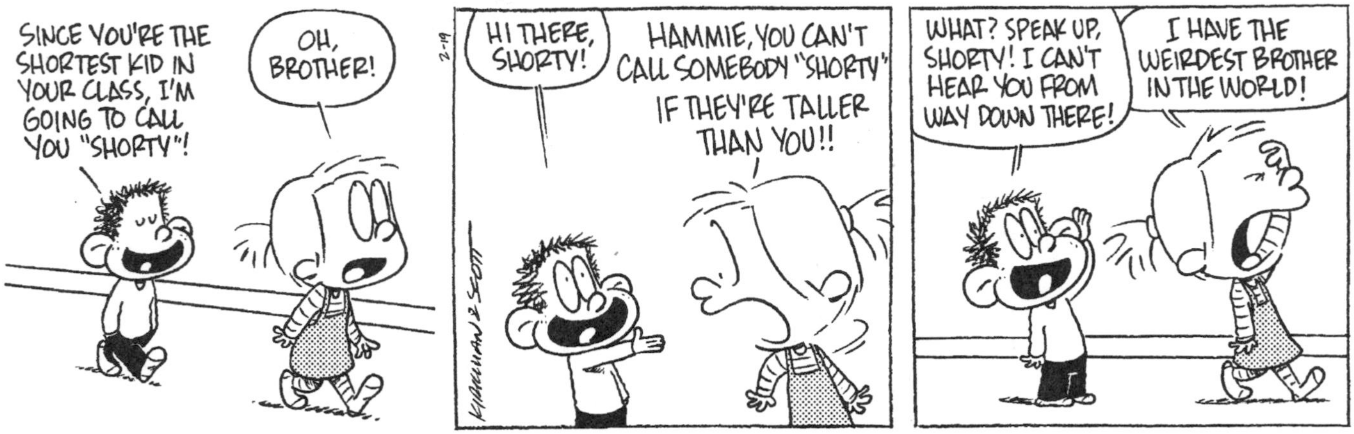
SINCE YOU'RE THE SHORTEST KID IN YOUR CLASS, I'M GOING TO CALL YOU "SHORTY"!
OH, BROTHER!
2-19
HI THERE, SHORTY!
HAMMIE, YOU CAN'T CALL SOMEBODY "SHORTY" IF THEY'RE TALLER THAN YOU!!
KIRKMAN & SCOTT
WHAT? SPEAK UP, SHORTY! I CAN'T HEAR YOU FROM WAY DOWN THERE!
I HAVE THE WEIRDEST BROTHER IN THE WORLD!

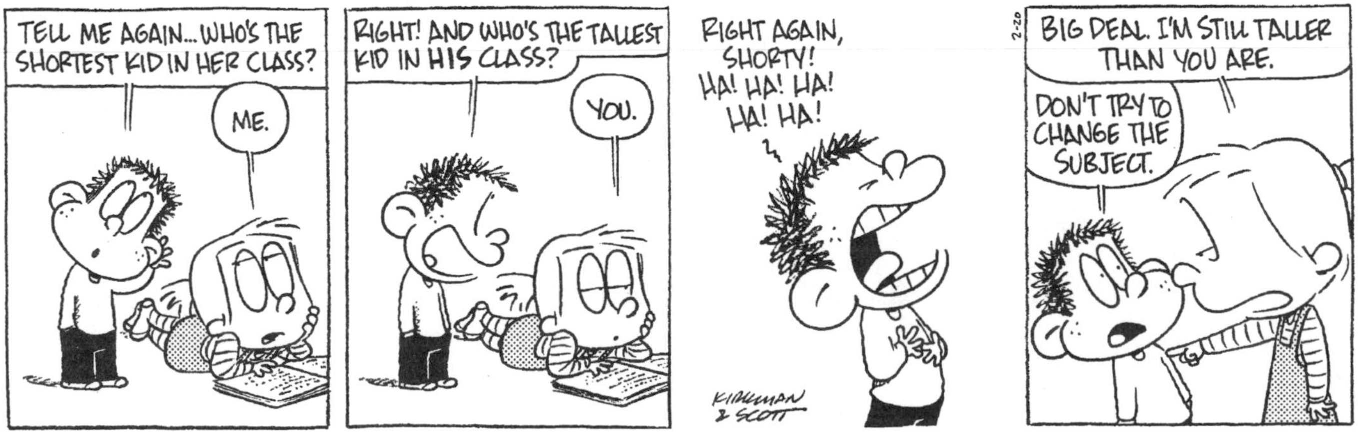
TELL ME AGAIN... WHO'S THE SHORTEST KID IN HER CLASS?
ME.
RIGHT! AND WHO'S THE TALLEST KID IN HIS CLASS?
YOU.
RIGHT AGAIN, SHORTY! HA! HA! HA! HA! HA!
KIRKMAN & SCOTT
2-20
BIG DEAL. I'M STILL TALLER THAN YOU ARE.
DON'T TRY TO CHANGE THE SUBJECT.

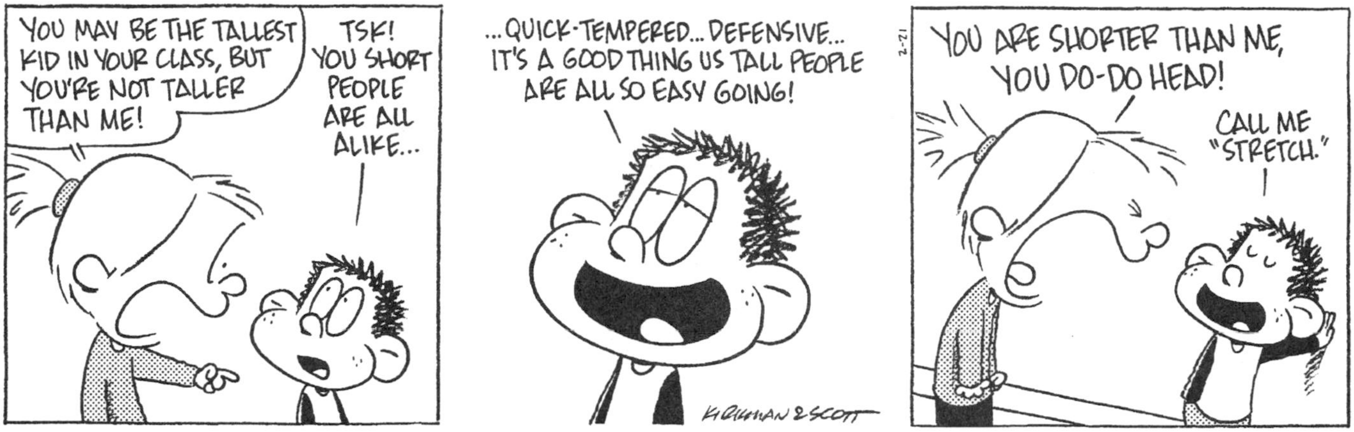
YOU MAY BE THE TALLEST KID IN YOUR CLASS, BUT YOU'RE NOT TALLER THAN ME!
TSK! YOU SHORT PEOPLE ARE ALL ALIKE...
...QUICK-TEMPERED... DEFENSIVE... IT'S A GOOD THING US TALL PEOPLE ARE ALL SO EASY GOING!
KIRKMAN & SCOTT
2-21
YOU ARE SHORTER THAN ME, YOU DO-DO HEAD!
CALL ME "STRETCH."

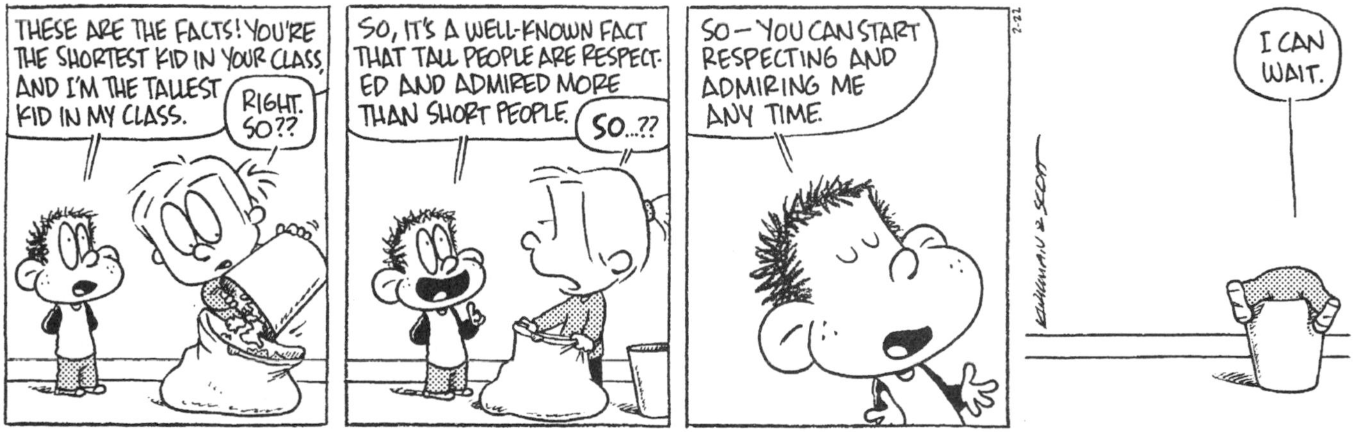
THESE ARE THE FACTS! YOU'RE THE SHORTEST KID IN YOUR CLASS, AND I'M THE TALLEST KID IN MY CLASS.
RIGHT. SO??
SO, IT'S A WELL-KNOWN FACT THAT TALL PEOPLE ARE RESPECTED AND ADMIRED MORE THAN SHORT PEOPLE.
SO...??
2-22
SO— YOU CAN START RESPECTING AND ADMIRING ME ANY TIME.
KIRKMAN & SCOTT
I CAN WAIT.

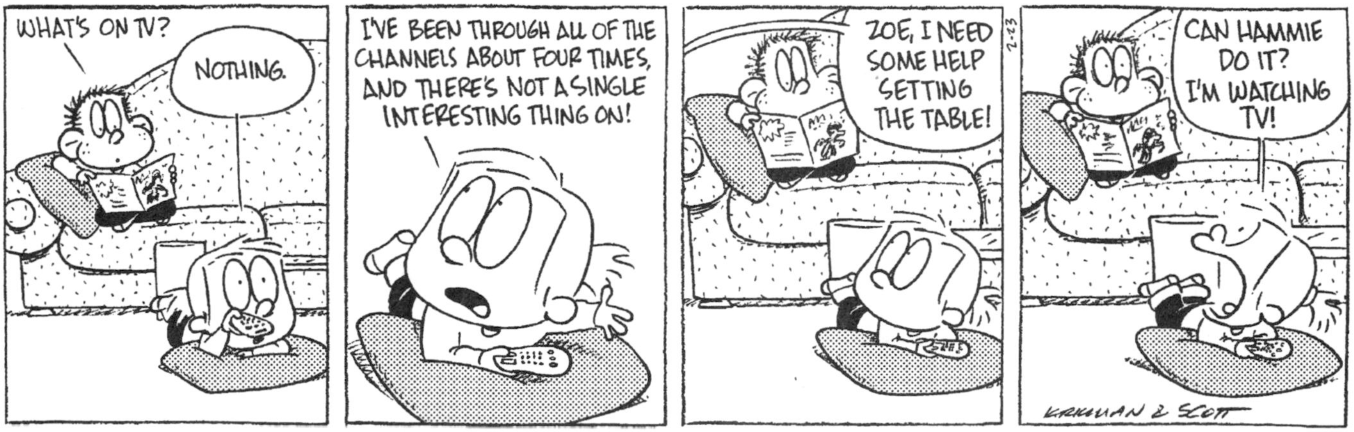
WHAT'S ON TV?
NOTHING.
I'VE BEEN THROUGH ALL OF THE CHANNELS ABOUT FOUR TIMES, AND THERE'S NOT A SINGLE INTERESTING THING ON!
2-23
ZOE, I NEED SOME HELP SETTING THE TABLE!
CAN HAMMIE DO IT? I'M WATCHING TV!
KIRKMAN & SCOTT

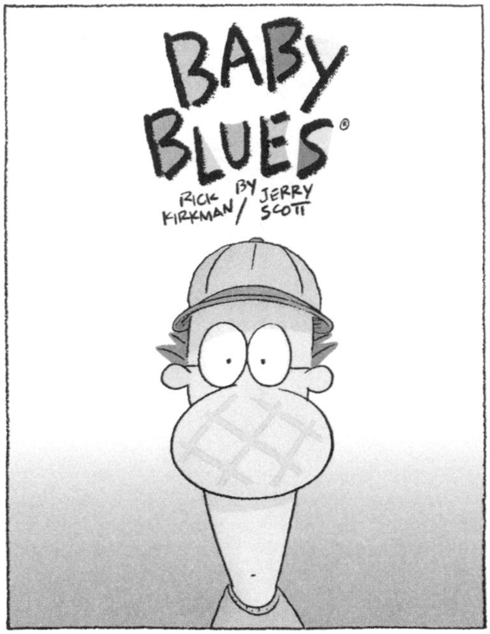
BABY BLUES®
RICK KIRKMAN / BY JERRY SCOTT

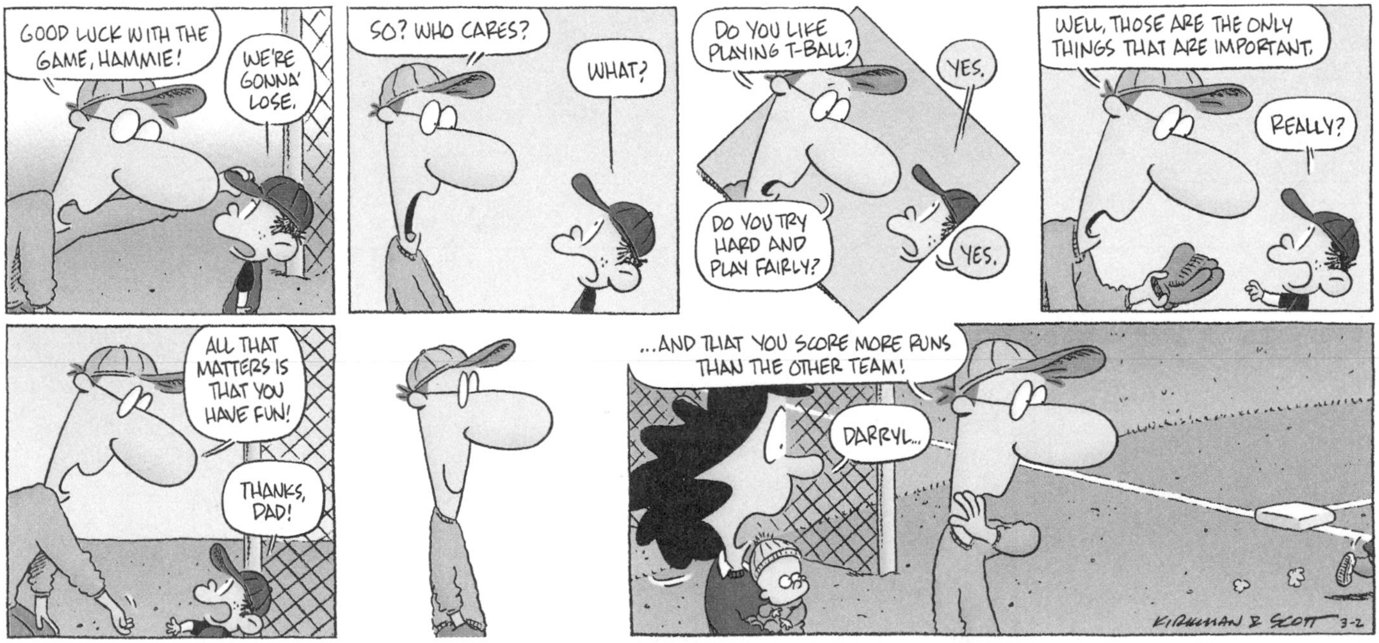
GOOD LUCK WITH THE GAME, HAMMIE!
WE'RE GONNA' LOSE.
SO? WHO CARES?
WHAT?
DO YOU LIKE PLAYING T-BALL?
YES.
DO YOU TRY HARD AND PLAY FAIRLY?
YES.
WELL, THOSE ARE THE ONLY THINGS THAT ARE IMPORTANT.
REALLY?
ALL THAT MATTERS IS THAT YOU HAVE FUN!
THANKS, DAD!
...AND THAT YOU SCORE MORE RUNS THAN THE OTHER TEAM!
DARRYL...
KIRKMAN & SCOTT 3-2

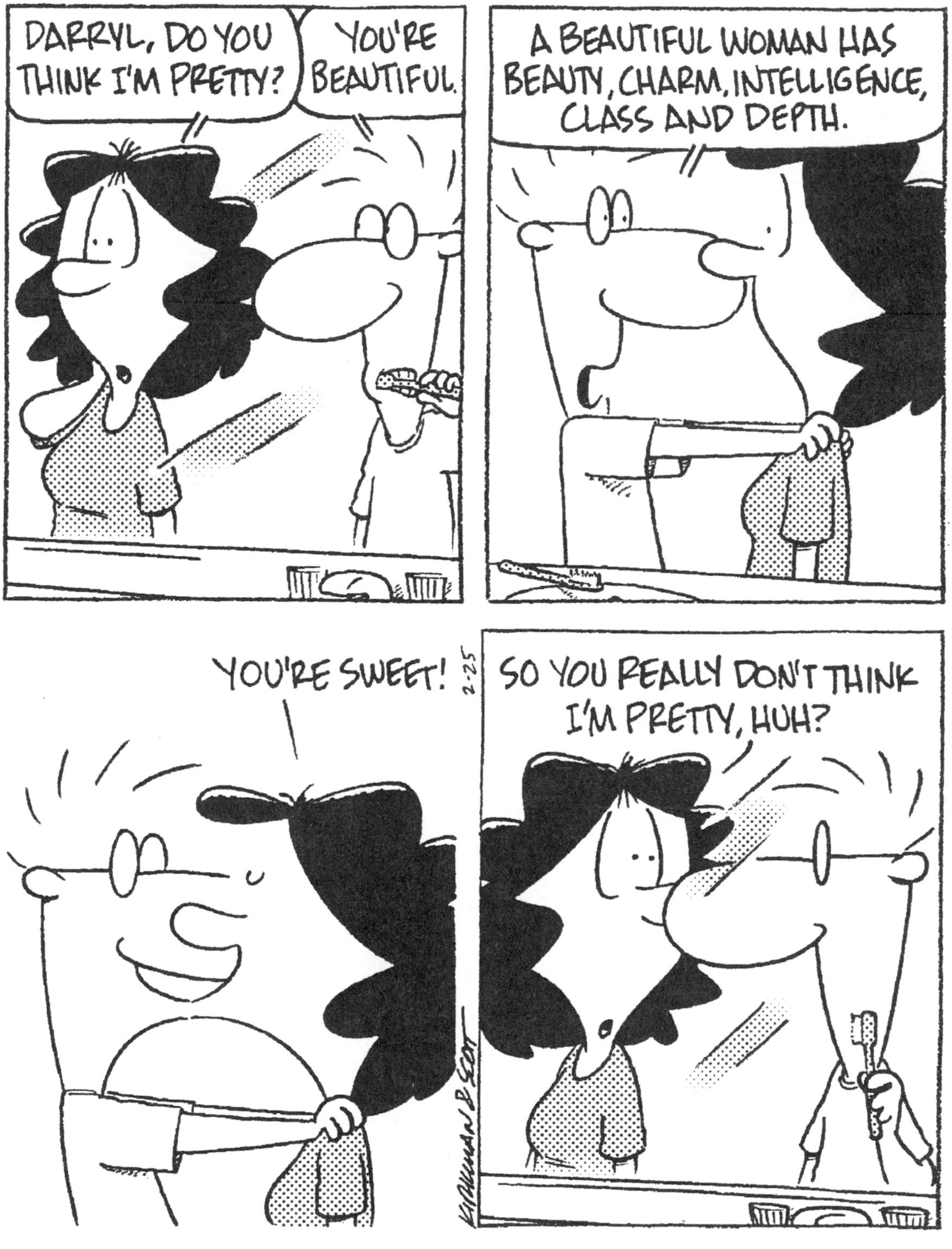
DARRYL, DO YOU THINK I'M PRETTY?
YOU'RE BEAUTIFUL.
A BEAUTIFUL WOMAN HAS BEAUTY, CHARM, INTELLIGENCE, CLASS AND DEPTH.
YOU'RE SWEET!
2·25
KIRKMAN & SCOTT
SO YOU REALLY DON'T THINK I'M PRETTY, HUH?

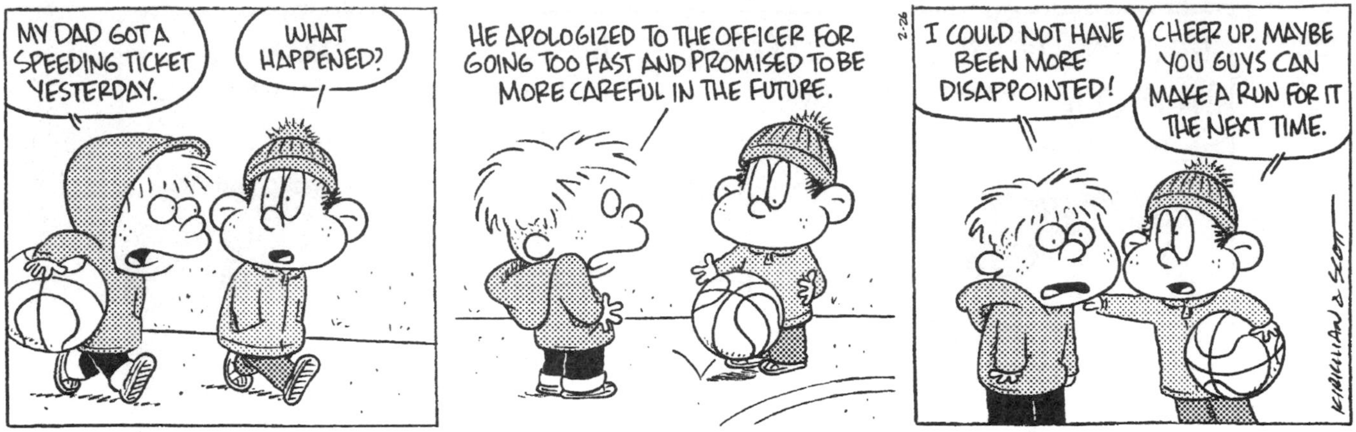
MY DAD GOT A SPEEDING TICKET YESTERDAY.
WHAT HAPPENED?
HE APOLOGIZED TO THE OFFICER FOR GOING TOO FAST AND PROMISED TO BE MORE CAREFUL IN THE FUTURE.
I COULD NOT HAVE BEEN MORE DISAPPOINTED!
CHEER UP. MAYBE YOU GUYS CAN MAKE A RUN FOR IT THE NEXT TIME.

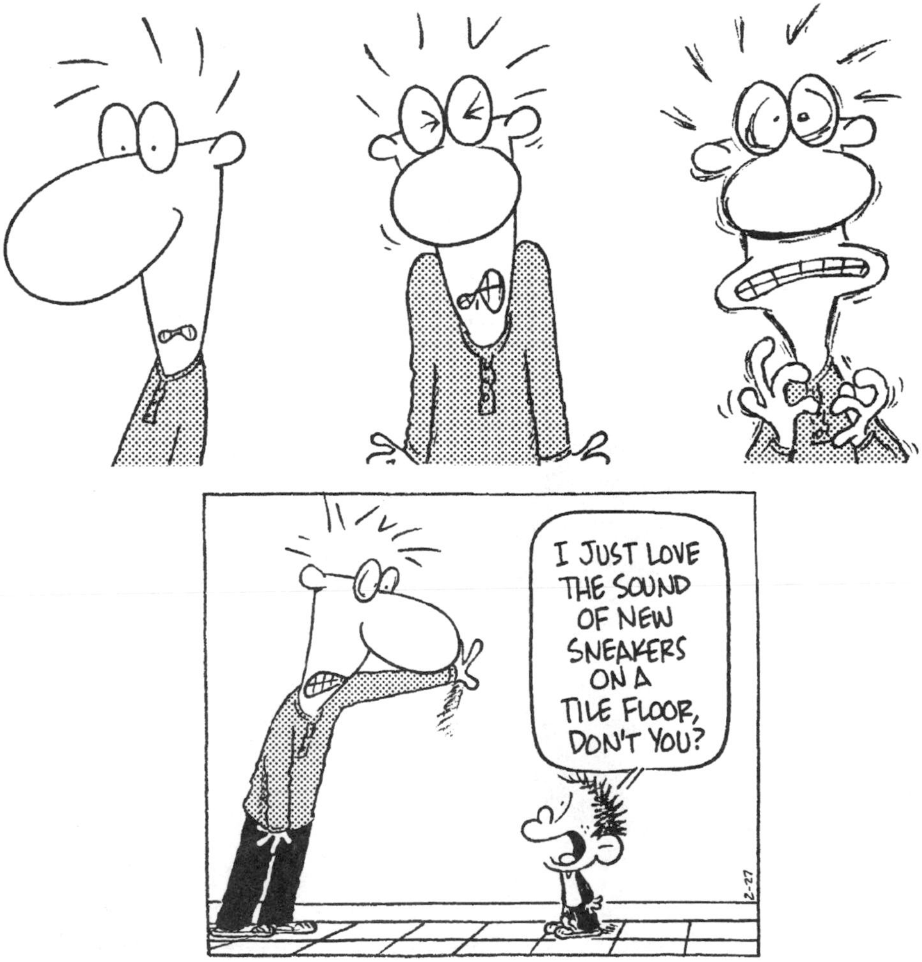
I JUST LOVE THE SOUND OF NEW SNEAKERS ON A TILE FLOOR, DON'T YOU?

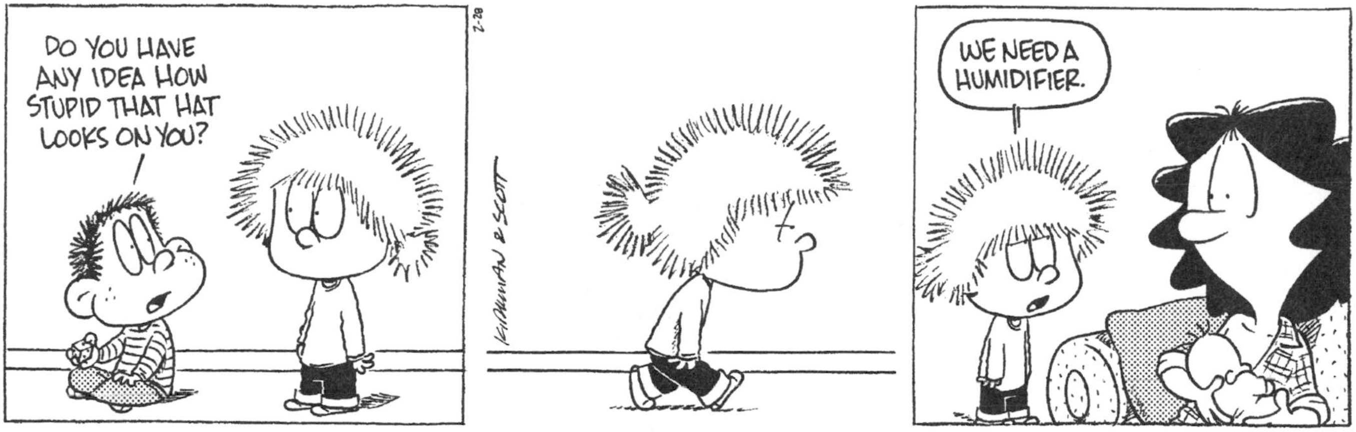
2-28
DO YOU HAVE ANY IDEA HOW STUPID THAT HAT LOOKS ON YOU?
KIRKMAN & SCOTT
WE NEED A HUMIDIFIER.

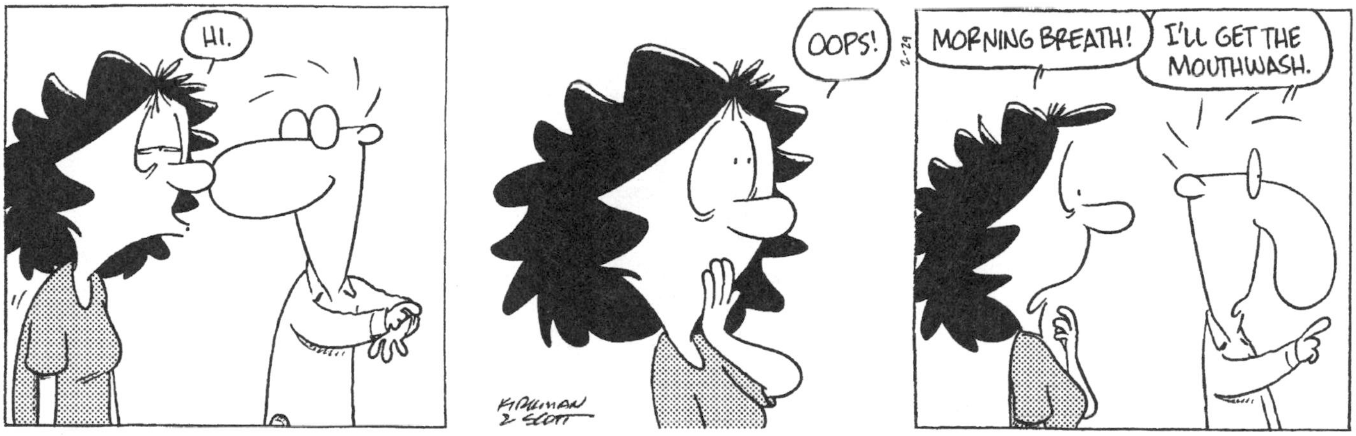
HI.
OOPS!
KIRKMAN & SCOTT
2-29
MORNING BREATH!
I'LL GET THE MOUTHWASH.

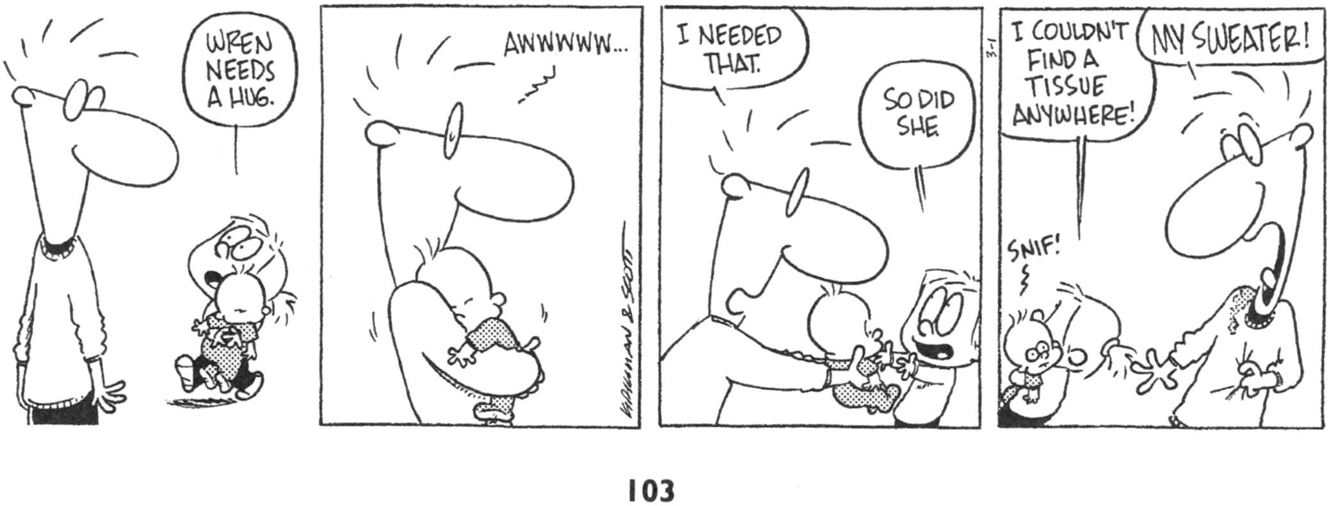
WREN NEEDS A HUG.
AWWWWW...
KIRKMAN & SCOTT
I NEEDED THAT.
SO DID SHE.
3-1
I COULDN'T FIND A TISSUE ANYWHERE!
MY SWEATER!
SNIF!

BABY BLUES®

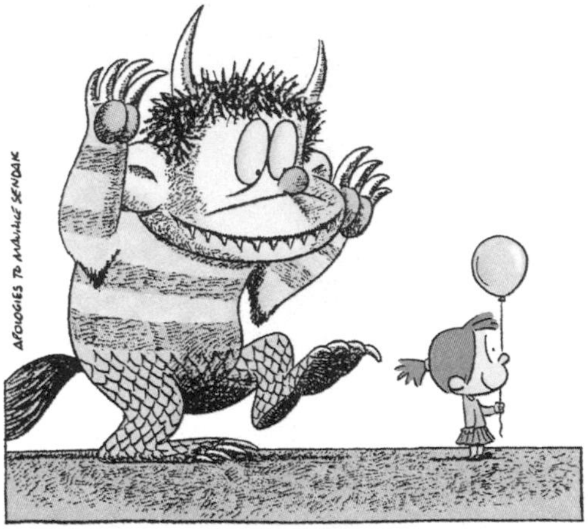
APOLOGIES TO MAURICE SENDAK

BY RICK KIRKMAN AND JERRY SCOTT

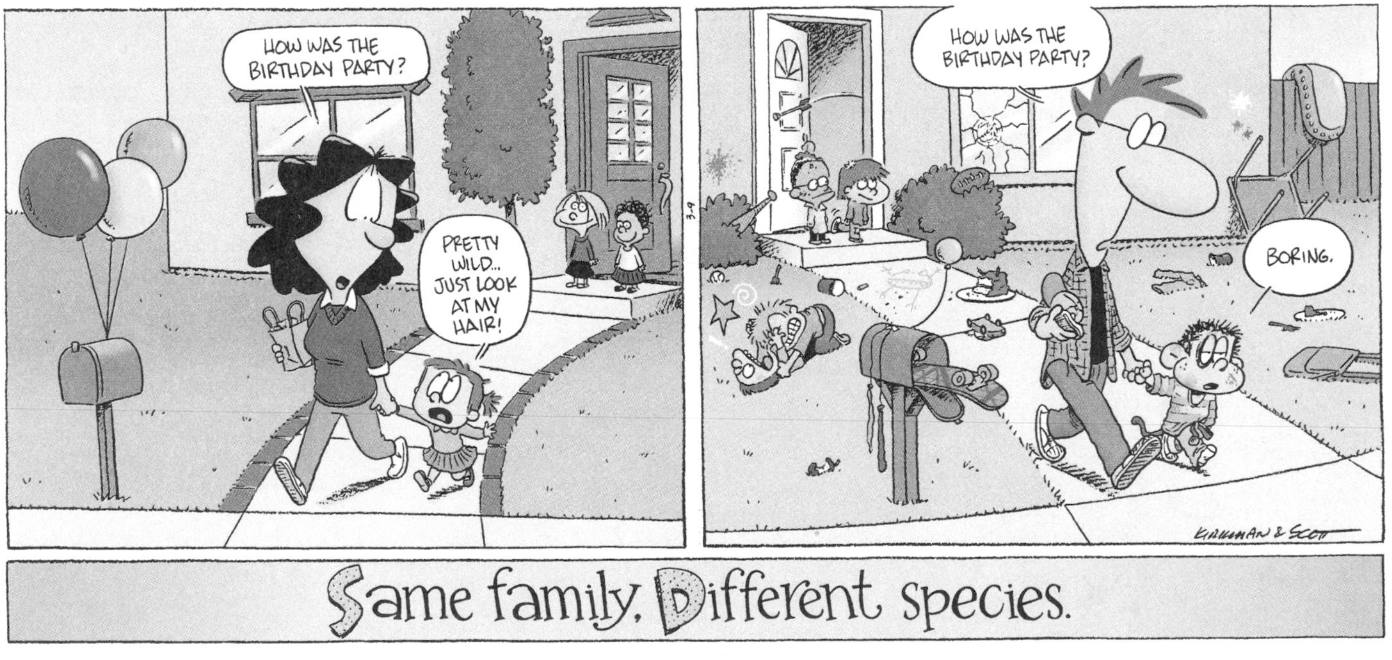
HOW WAS THE BIRTHDAY PARTY?
PRETTY WILD... JUST LOOK AT MY HAIR!
3-9
HOW WAS THE BIRTHDAY PARTY?
BORING.
KIRKMAN & SCOTT

Same family. Different species.

HI GUYS.
DAD'S HOME!!
WHAT DID YOU BRING US?
CAN I HAVE THIS GUM?
DIBS ON THE PAPERCLIP!
IS THIS CANDY OR AN ANTACID?
I SEE YOU'VE ALREADY BEEN GREETED BY THE KIDS.
YUP. HUGGED AND MUGGED.

LOOK AT THE TRASH!
YEAH. THE PLAY-GROUND IS LIKE THIS EVERY DAY.
THAT'S RIDICULOUS! FROM NOW ON, I'M GOING TO PACK YOU GUYS ZERO-WASTE LUNCHES IN REUSABLE CONTAINERS!
TRANSLATION: LEFTOVERS.
AAAGGHHH!

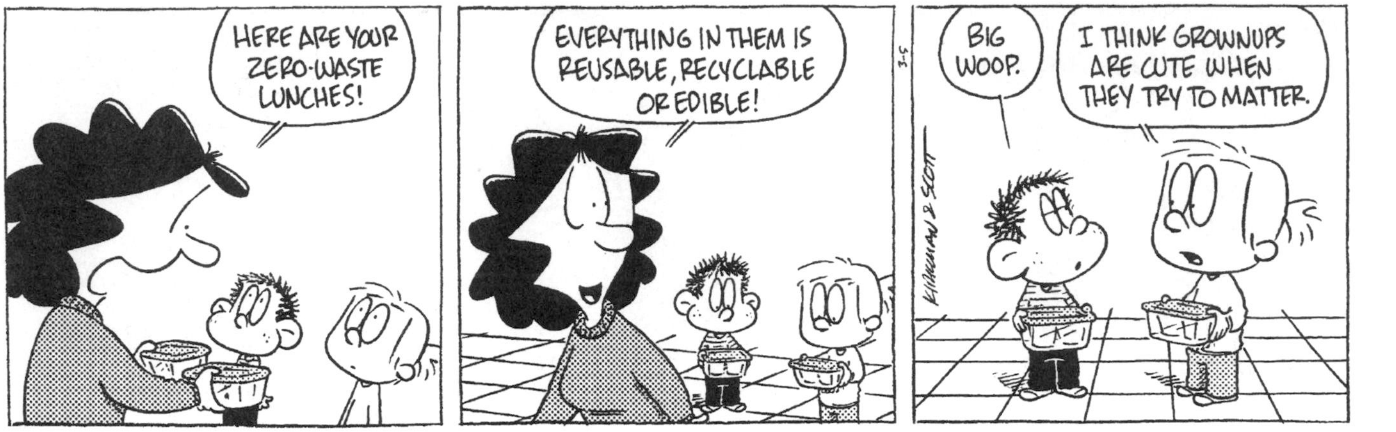
HERE ARE YOUR ZERO-WASTE LUNCHES!
EVERYTHING IN THEM IS REUSABLE, RECYCLABLE OR EDIBLE!
3-5
KIRKMAN & SCOTT
BIG WOOP.
I THINK GROWNUPS ARE CUTE WHEN THEY TRY TO MATTER.

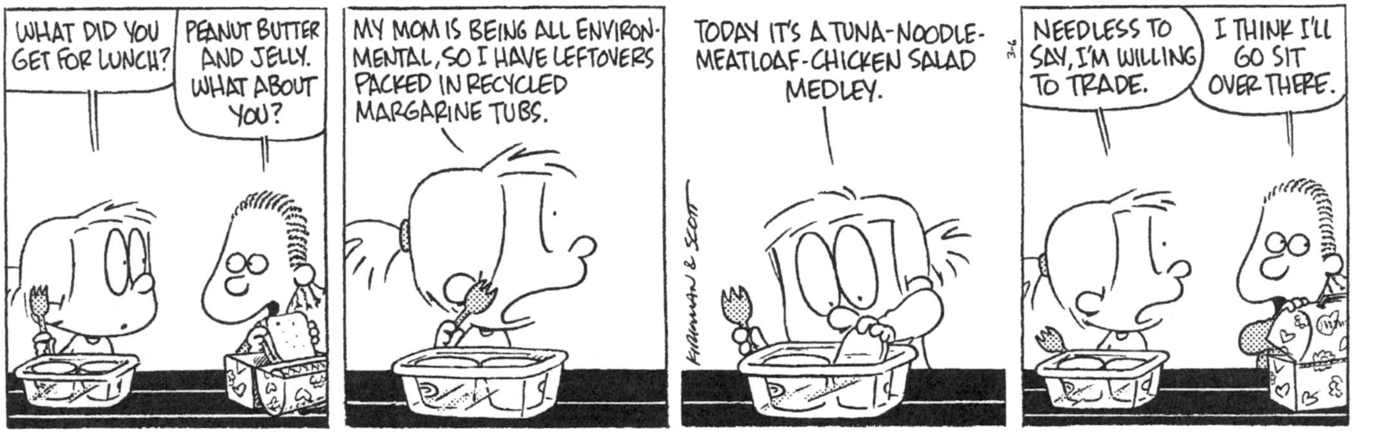
WHAT DID YOU GET FOR LUNCH?
PEANUT BUTTER AND JELLY. WHAT ABOUT YOU?
MY MOM IS BEING ALL ENVIRON-MENTAL, SO I HAVE LEFTOVERS PACKED IN RECYCLED MARGARINE TUBS.
KIRKMAN & SCOTT
TODAY IT'S A TUNA-NOODLE-MEATLOAF-CHICKEN SALAD MEDLEY.
3-6
NEEDLESS TO SAY, I'M WILLING TO TRADE.
I THINK I'LL GO SIT OVER THERE.

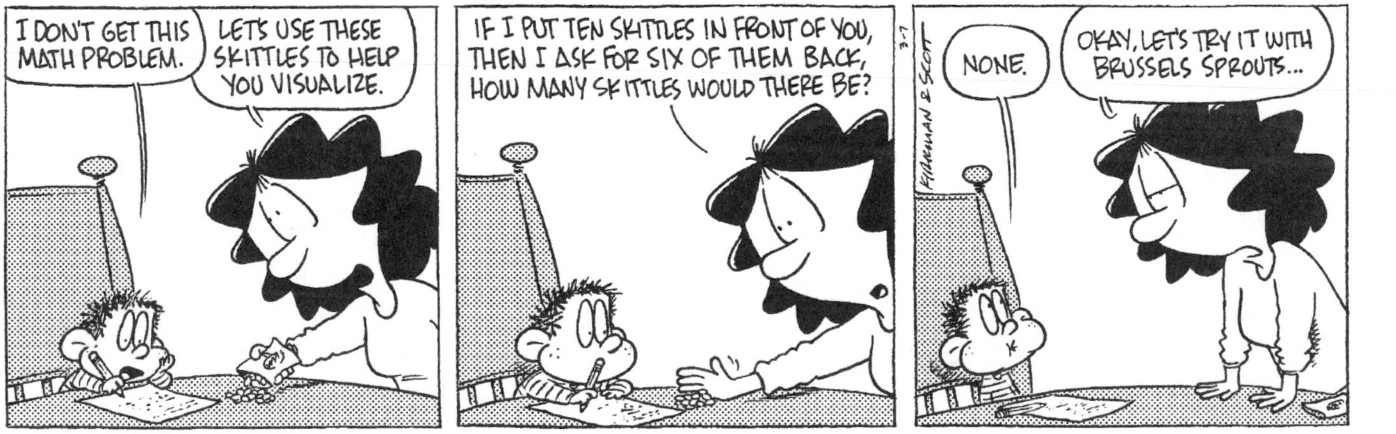
I DON'T GET THIS MATH PROBLEM.
LET'S USE THESE SKITTLES TO HELP YOU VISUALIZE.
IF I PUT TEN SKITTLES IN FRONT OF YOU, THEN I ASK FOR SIX OF THEM BACK, HOW MANY SKITTLES WOULD THERE BE?
3-7
KIRKMAN & SCOTT
NONE.
OKAY, LET'S TRY IT WITH BRUSSELS SPROUTS...

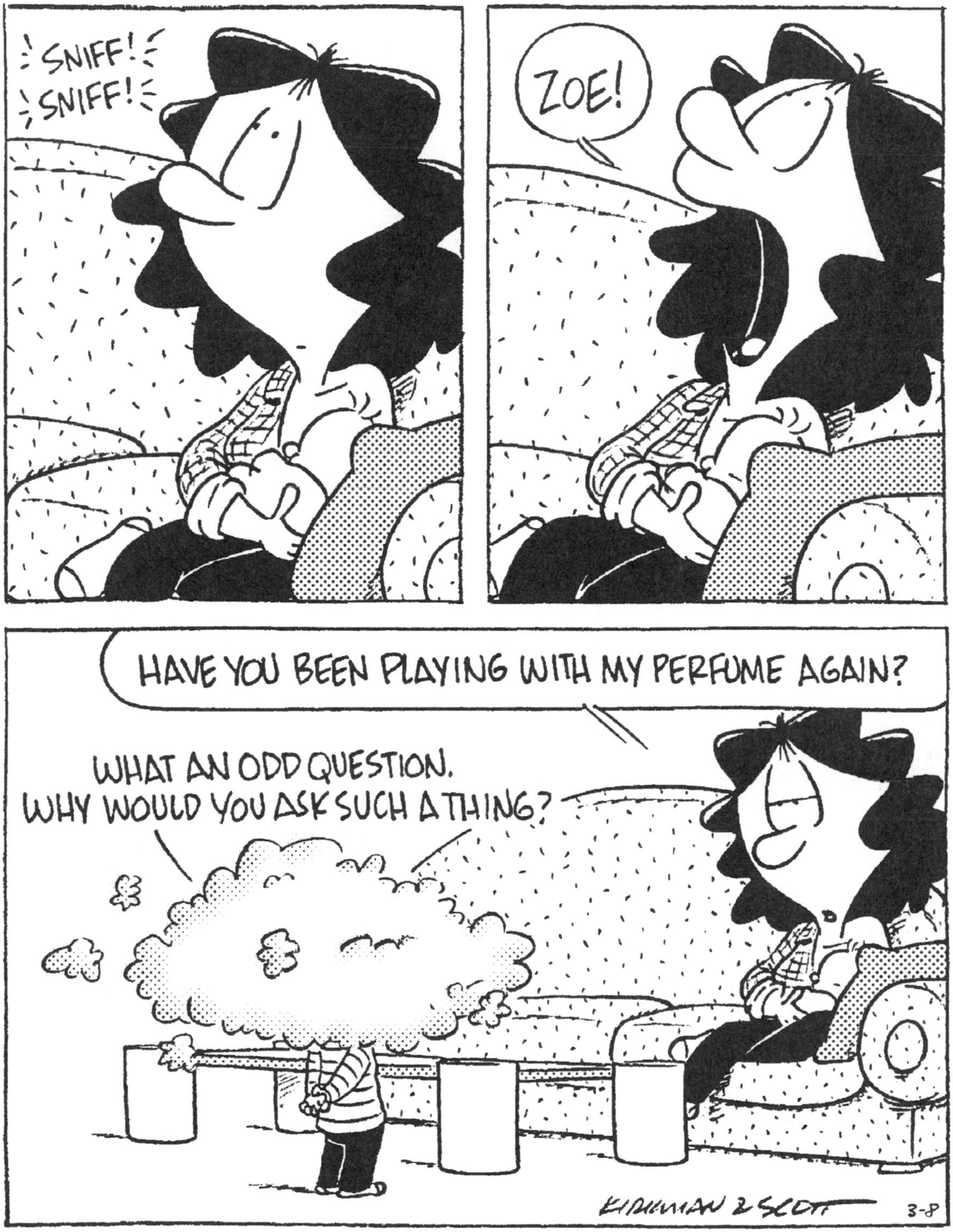
SNIFF!
SNIFF!
ZOE!
HAVE YOU BEEN PLAYING WITH MY PERFUME AGAIN?
WHAT AN ODD QUESTION.
WHY WOULD YOU ASK SUCH A THING?
KIRKMAN & SCOTT
3-8

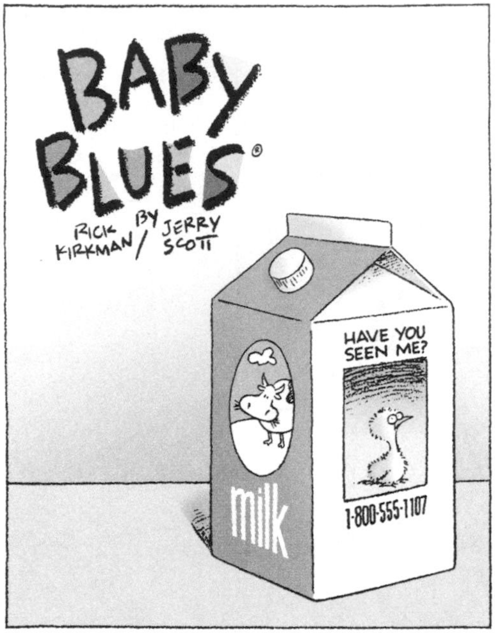
BABY BLUES®
BY RICK KIRKMAN / JERRY SCOTT
HAVE YOU SEEN ME?
1-800-555-1107
milk

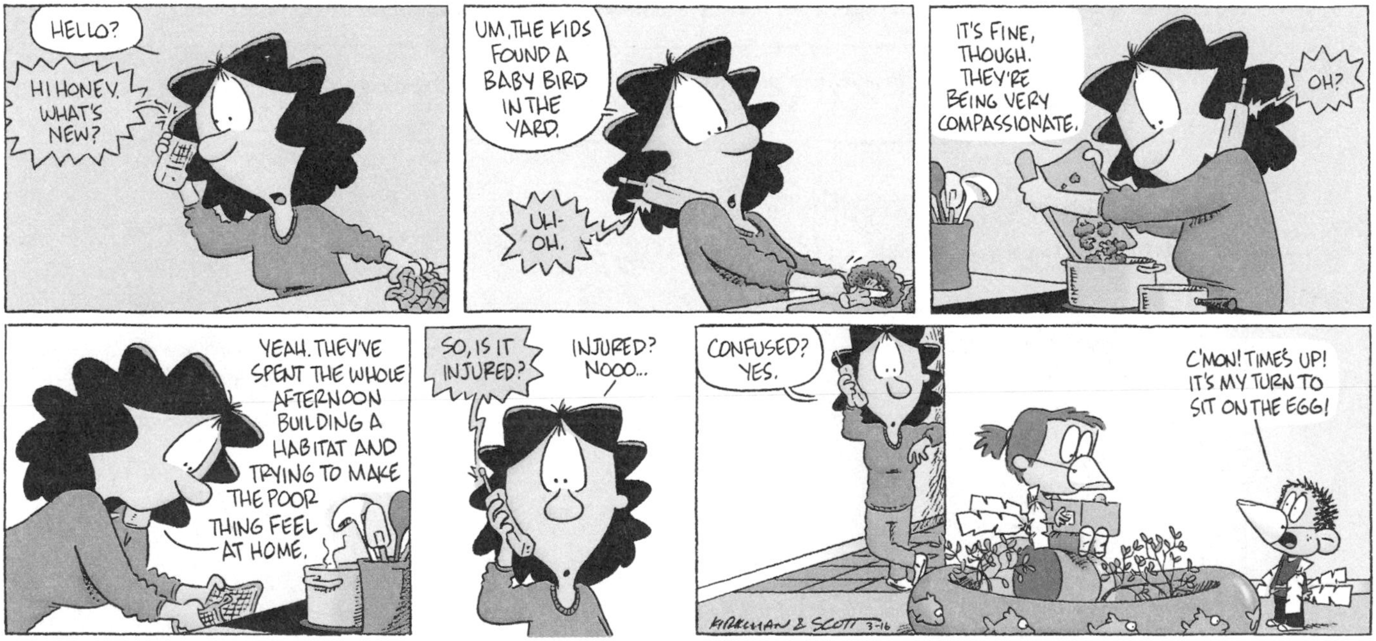
HELLO?
HI HONEY. WHAT'S NEW?
UM, THE KIDS FOUND A BABY BIRD IN THE YARD.
UH-OH.
IT'S FINE, THOUGH. THEY'RE BEING VERY COMPASSIONATE.
OH?
YEAH. THEY'VE SPENT THE WHOLE AFTERNOON BUILDING A HABITAT AND TRYING TO MAKE THE POOR THING FEEL AT HOME.
SO, IS IT INJURED?
INJURED? NOOO...
CONFUSED? YES.
C'MON! TIME'S UP! IT'S MY TURN TO SIT ON THE EGG!
KIRKMAN & SCOTT 3-16

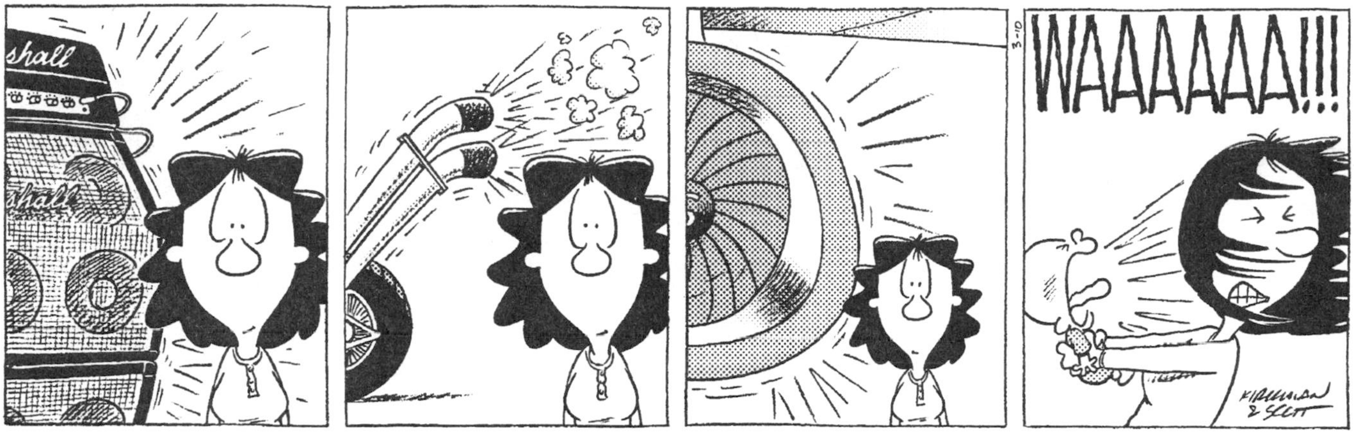
WAAAAAA!!!
KIRKMAN & SCOTT

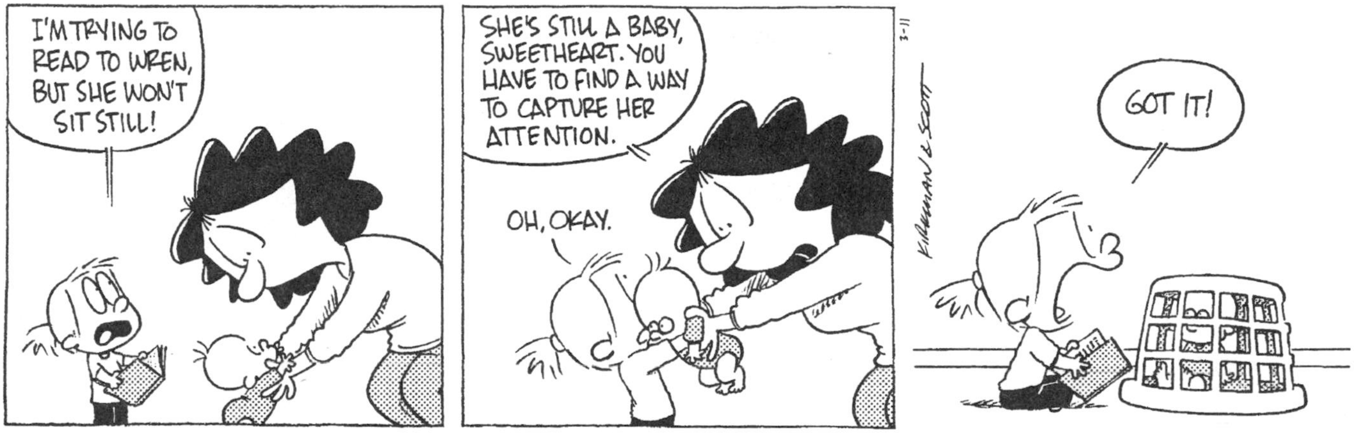
I'M TRYING TO READ TO WREN, BUT SHE WON'T SIT STILL!
SHE'S STILL A BABY, SWEETHEART. YOU HAVE TO FIND A WAY TO CAPTURE HER ATTENTION.
OH, OKAY.
KIRKMAN & SCOTT
GOT IT!

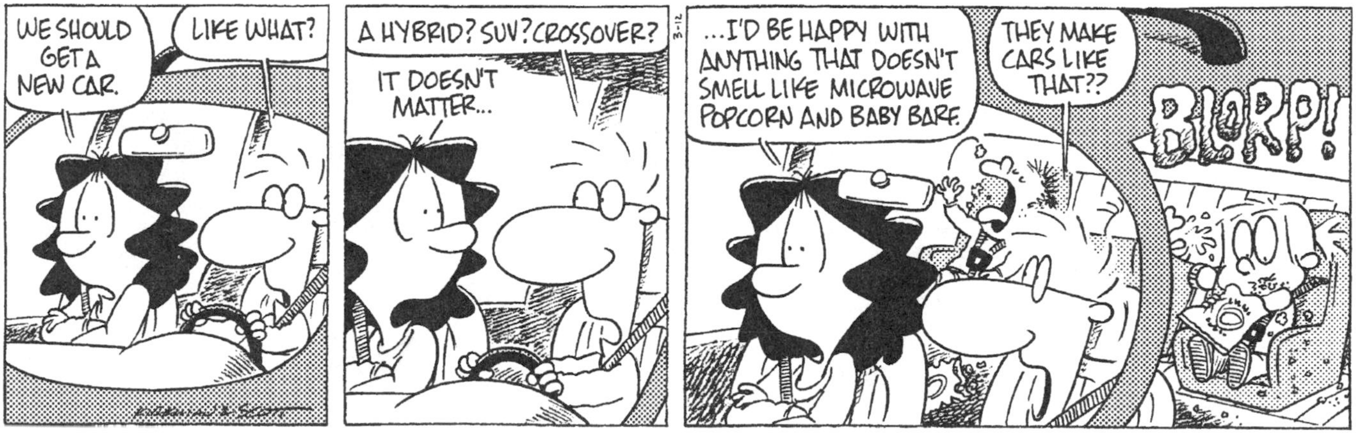
WE SHOULD GET A NEW CAR.
LIKE WHAT?
KIRKMAN & SCOTT
A HYBRID? SUV? CROSSOVER?
IT DOESN'T MATTER...
...I'D BE HAPPY WITH ANYTHING THAT DOESN'T SMELL LIKE MICROWAVE POPCORN AND BABY BARF.
THEY MAKE CARS LIKE THAT??
BLORP!

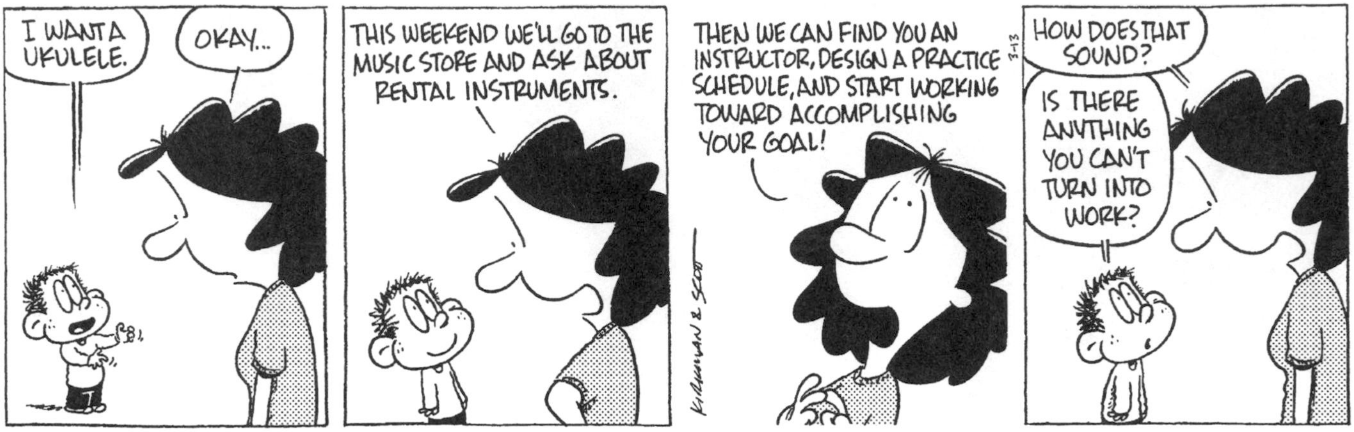
I WANT A UKULELE.
OKAY...
THIS WEEKEND WE'LL GO TO THE MUSIC STORE AND ASK ABOUT RENTAL INSTRUMENTS.
THEN WE CAN FIND YOU AN INSTRUCTOR, DESIGN A PRACTICE SCHEDULE, AND START WORKING TOWARD ACCOMPLISHING YOUR GOAL!
HOW DOES THAT SOUND?
IS THERE ANYTHING YOU CAN'T TURN INTO WORK?

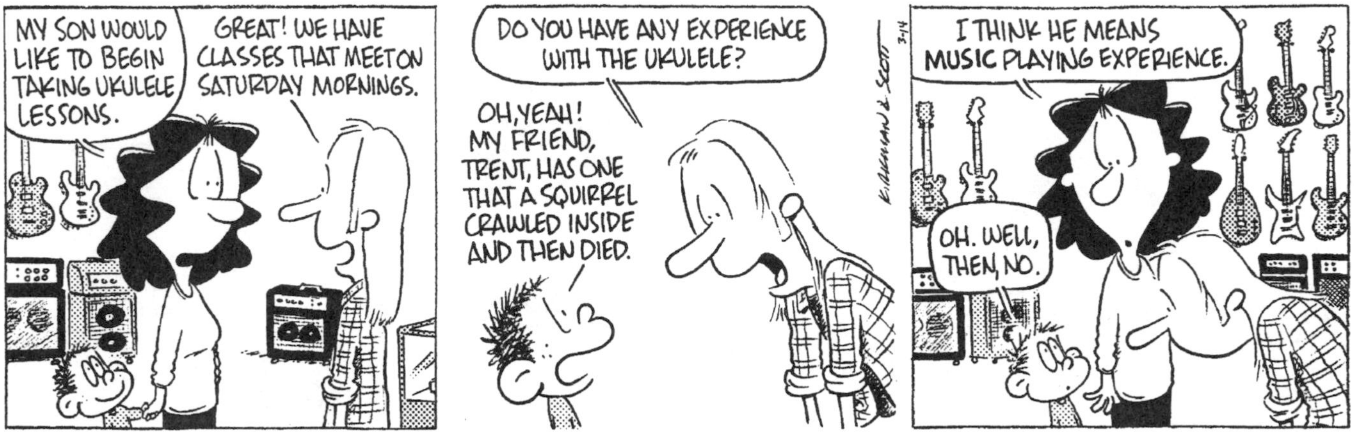
MY SON WOULD LIKE TO BEGIN TAKING UKULELE LESSONS.
GREAT! WE HAVE CLASSES THAT MEET ON SATURDAY MORNINGS.
DO YOU HAVE ANY EXPERIENCE WITH THE UKULELE?
OH, YEAH! MY FRIEND, TRENT, HAS ONE THAT A SQUIRREL CRAWLED INSIDE AND THEN DIED.
I THINK HE MEANS MUSIC PLAYING EXPERIENCE.
OH. WELL, THEN, NO.

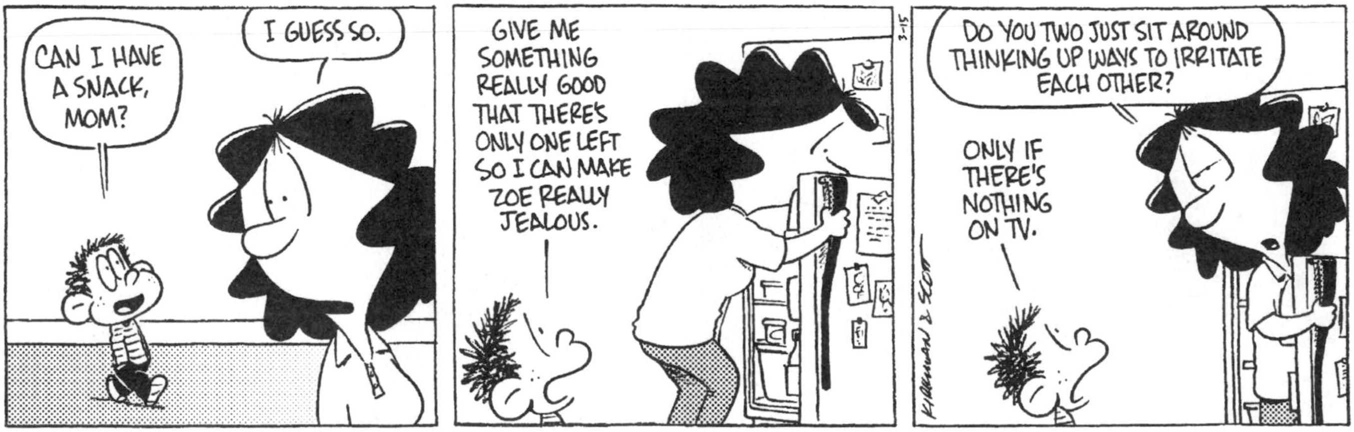
CAN I HAVE A SNACK, MOM?
I GUESS SO.
GIVE ME SOMETHING REALLY GOOD THAT THERE'S ONLY ONE LEFT SO I CAN MAKE ZOE REALLY JEALOUS.
DO YOU TWO JUST SIT AROUND THINKING UP WAYS TO IRRITATE EACH OTHER?
ONLY IF THERE'S NOTHING ON TV.

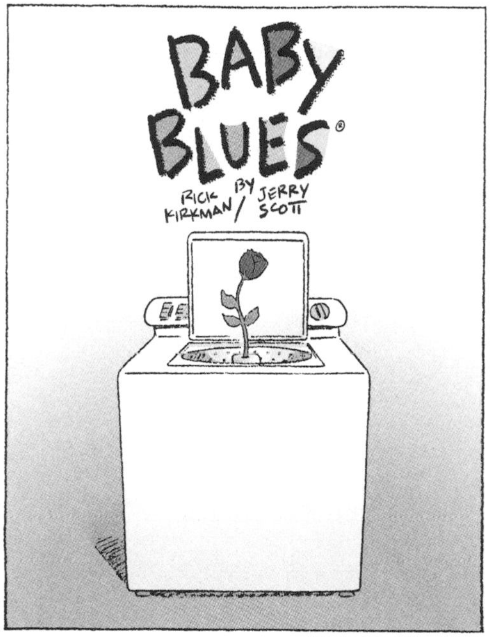
BABY BLUES®
BY RICK KIRKMAN / JERRY SCOTT

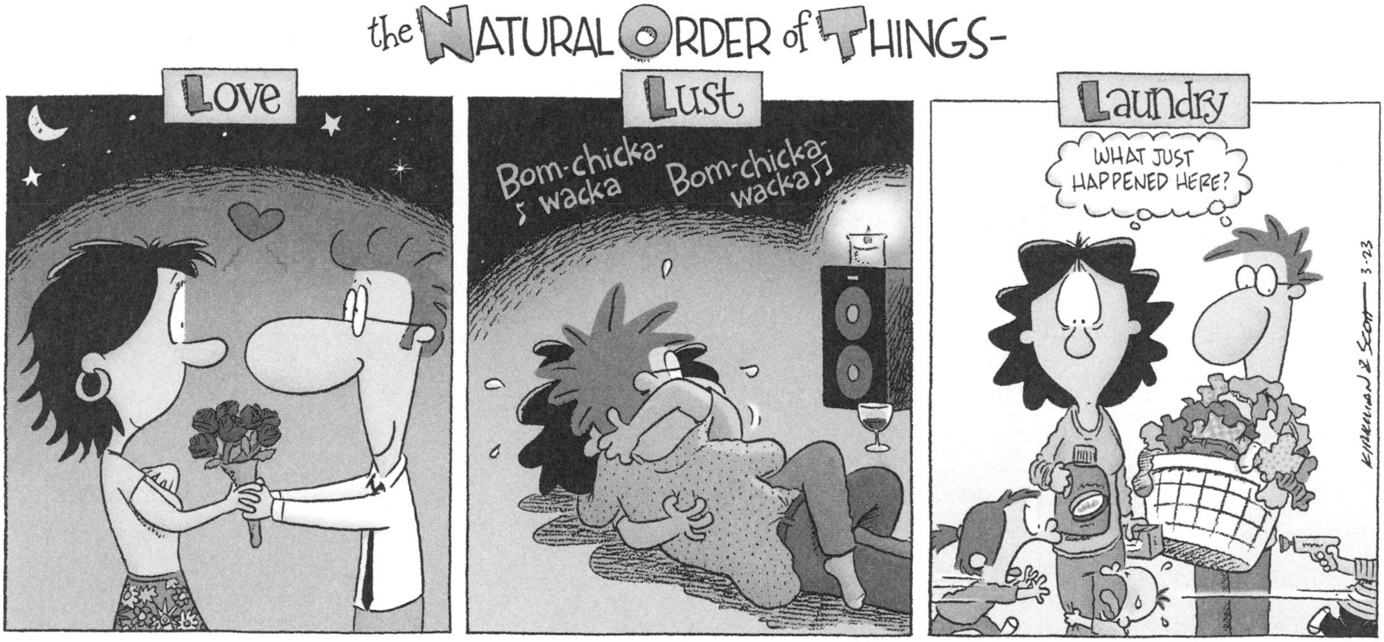
the NATURAL ORDER of THINGS-
Love
Lust
Bom-chicka-wacka
Bom-chicka-wacka
Laundry
WHAT JUST HAPPENED HERE?
KIRKMAN & SCOTT
3-23

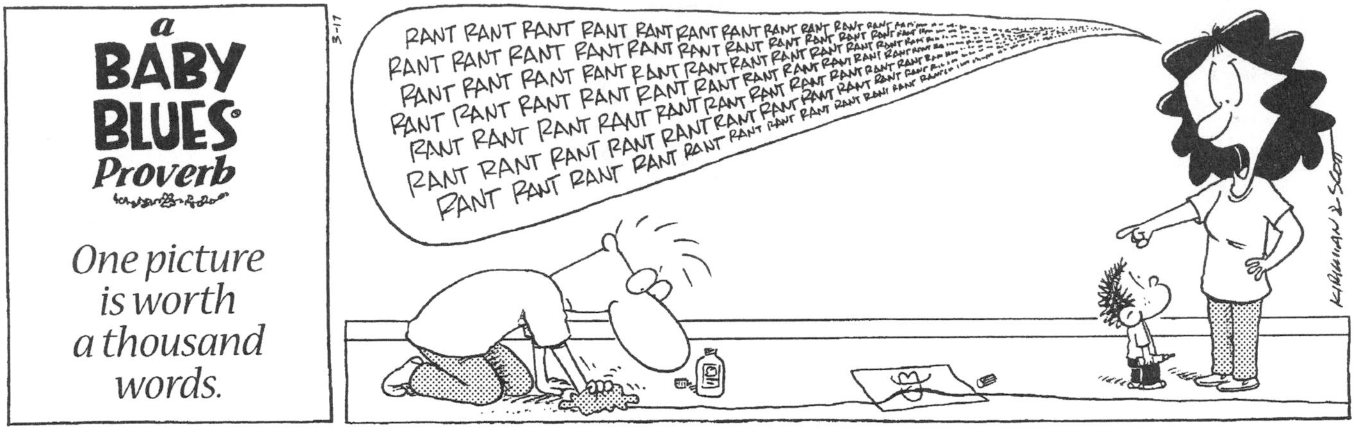
a BABY BLUES® Proverb
One picture is worth a thousand words.
3-17
RANT RANT RANT RANT RANT RANT RANT RANT RANT RANT
RANT RANT RANT RANT RANT RANT RANT RANT RANT RANT
RANT RANT RANT RANT RANT RANT RANT RANT RANT RANT
RANT RANT RANT RANT RANT RANT RANT RANT RANT RANT
RANT RANT RANT RANT RANT RANT RANT RANT RANT
RANT RANT RANT RANT RANT RANT
RANT RANT RANT
KIRKMAN & SCOTT

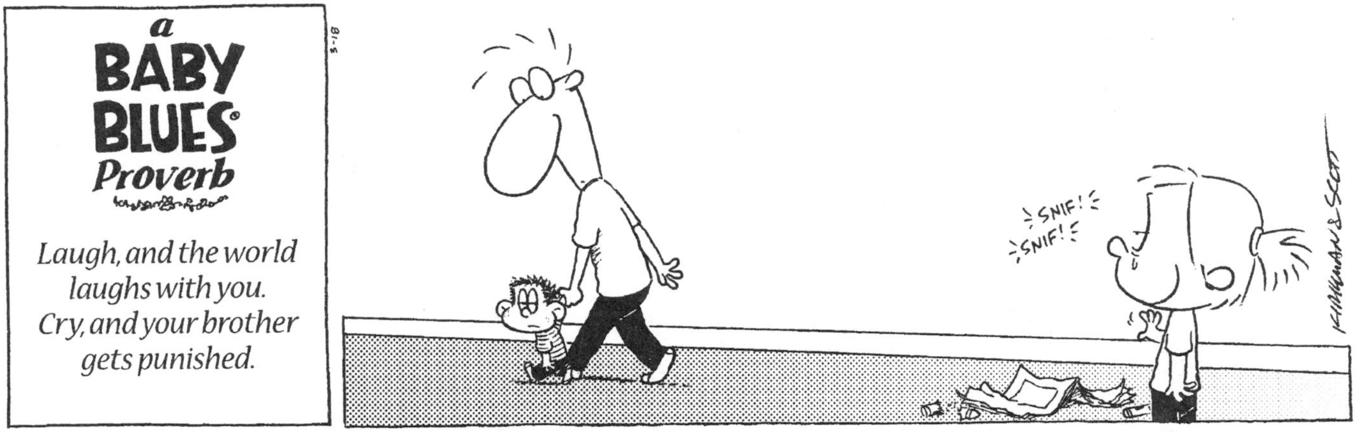
a BABY BLUES® Proverb
Laugh, and the world laughs with you. Cry, and your brother gets punished.
3-18
SNIF!
SNIF!
KIRKMAN & SCOTT

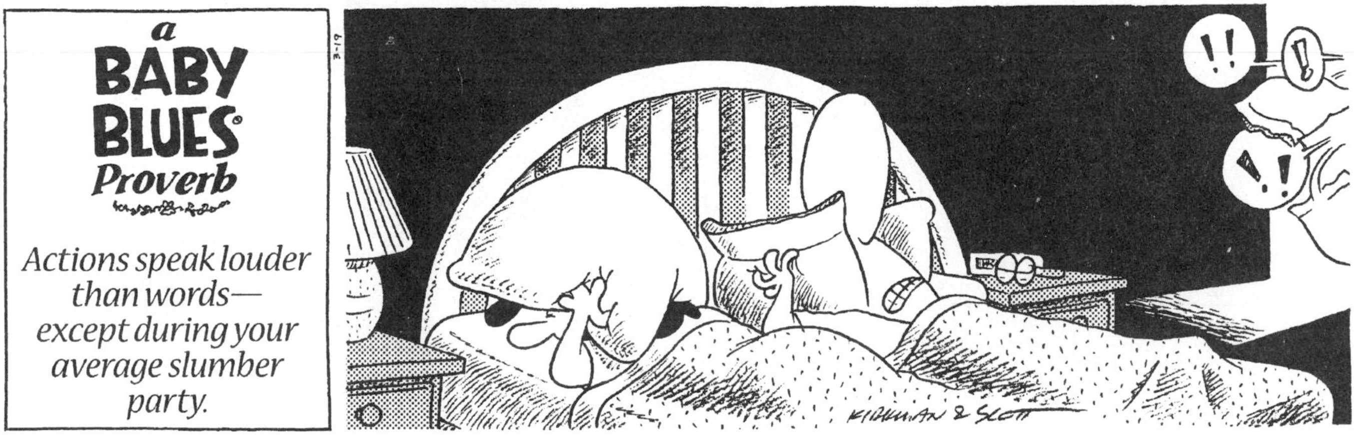
a BABY BLUES® Proverb
Actions speak louder than words—except during your average slumber party.
3-19
!!
!
!!
KIRKMAN & SCOTT

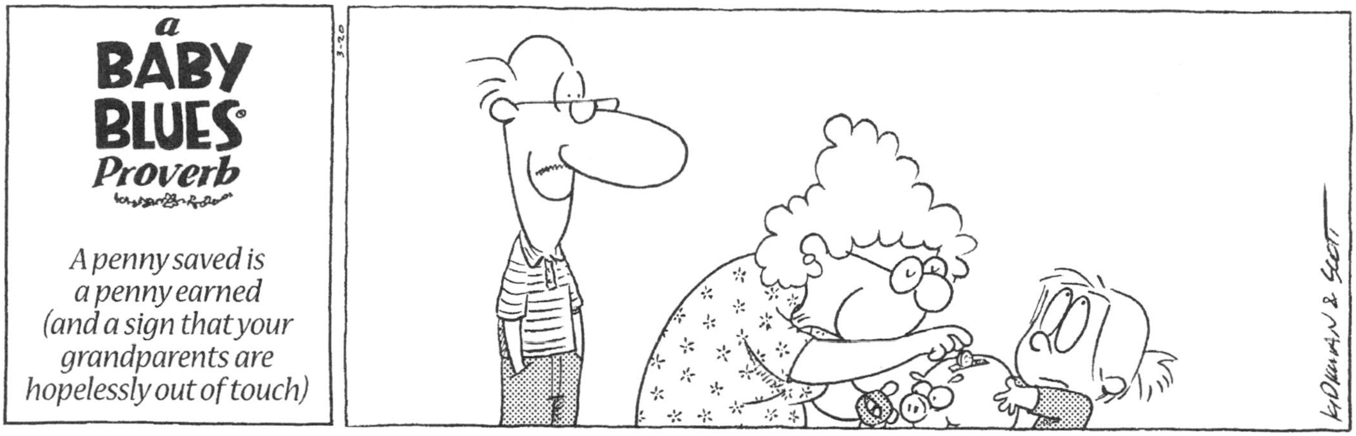
a BABY BLUES Proverb
A penny saved is a penny earned (and a sign that your grandparents are hopelessly out of touch)
KIRKMAN & SCOTT

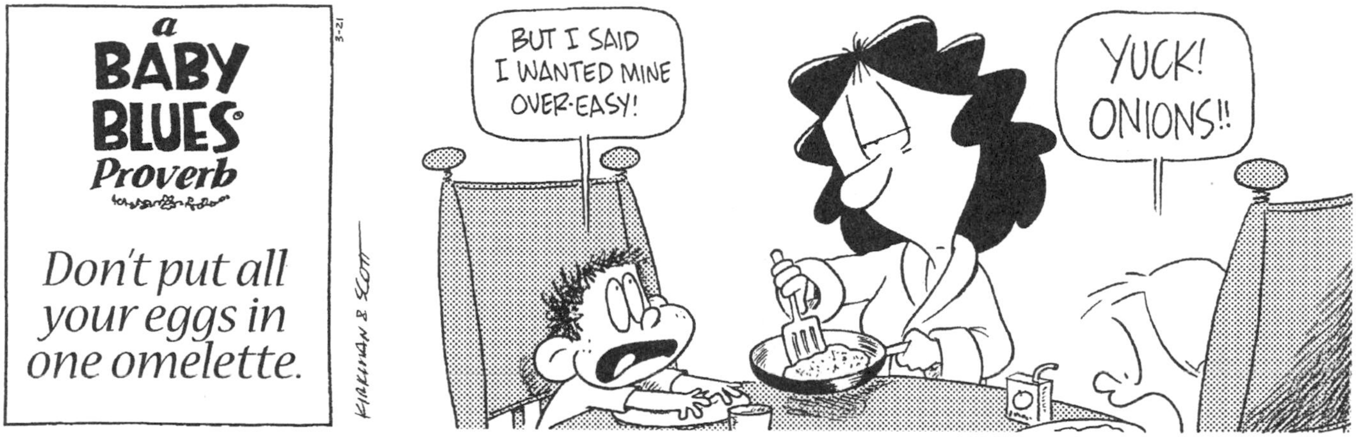
a BABY BLUES Proverb
Don't put all your eggs in one omelette.
BUT I SAID I WANTED MINE OVER-EASY!
YUCK! ONIONS!!
KIRKMAN & SCOTT

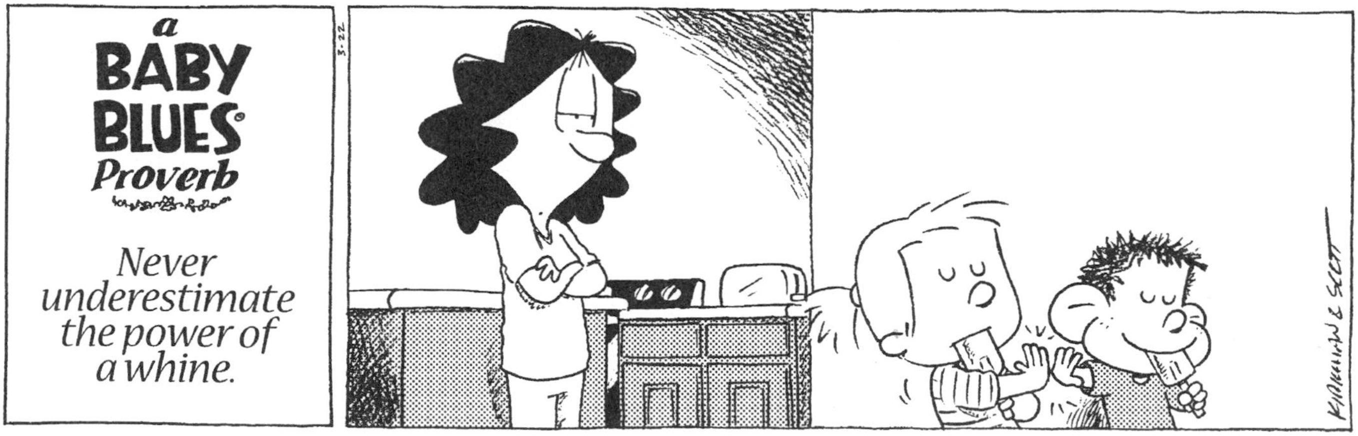
a BABY BLUES Proverb
Never underestimate the power of a whine.
KIRKMAN & SCOTT

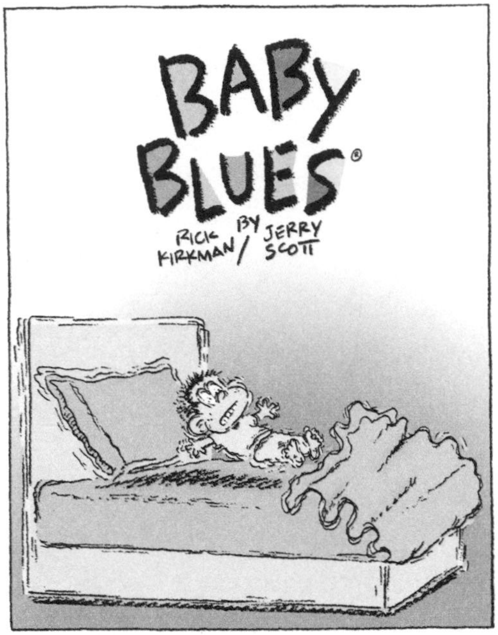
BABY BLUES®
BY RICK KIRKMAN / JERRY SCOTT

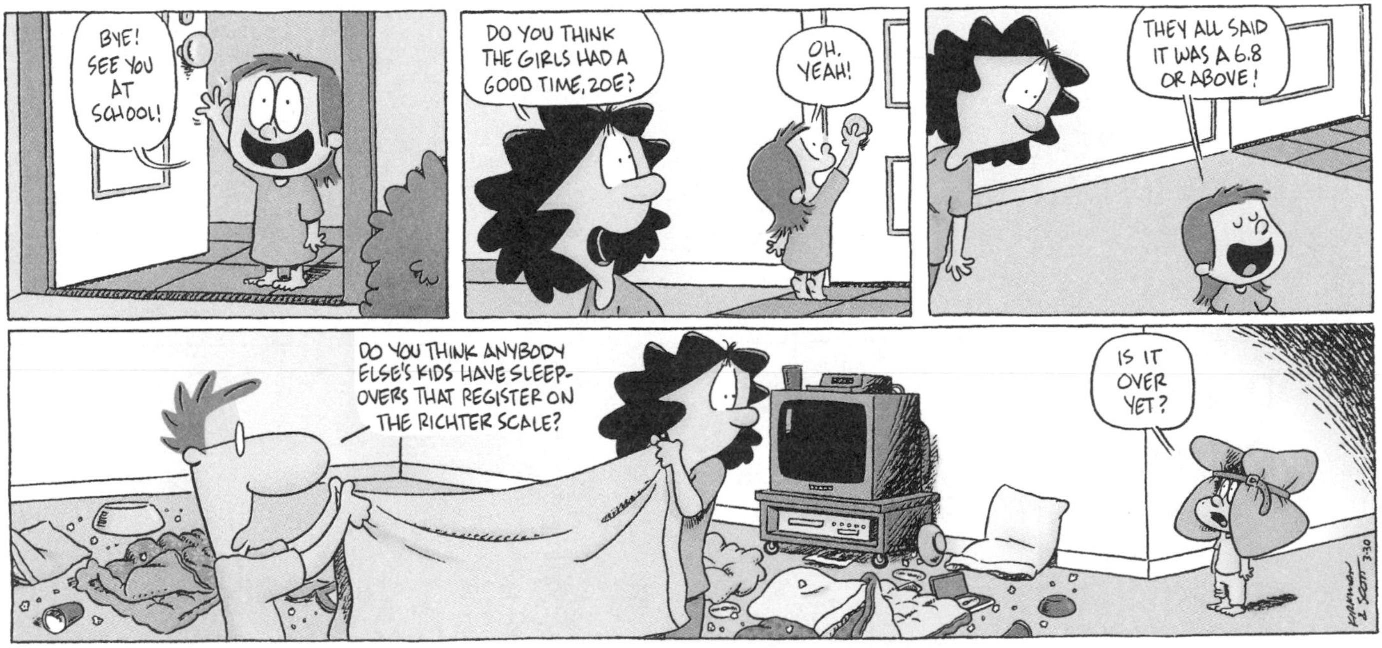
BYE! SEE YOU AT SCHOOL!
DO YOU THINK THE GIRLS HAD A GOOD TIME, ZOE?
OH, YEAH!
THEY ALL SAID IT WAS A 6.8 OR ABOVE!
DO YOU THINK ANYBODY ELSE'S KIDS HAVE SLEEP-OVERS THAT REGISTER ON THE RICHTER SCALE?
IS IT OVER YET?

The Days Are Long...

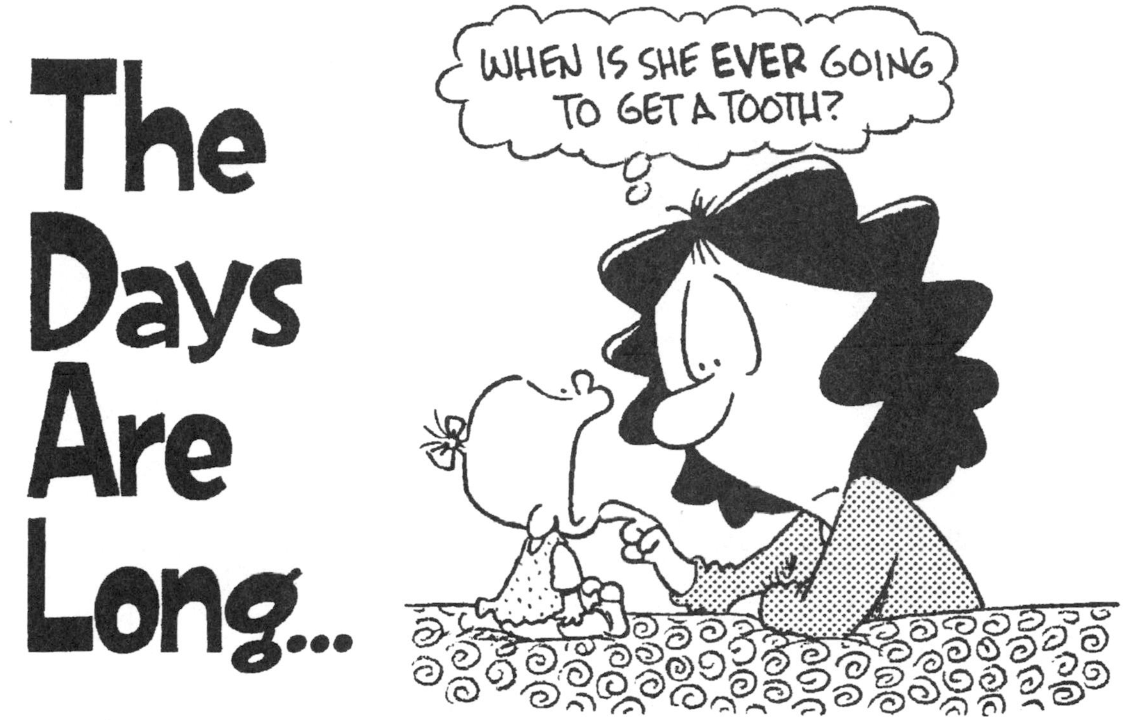
WHEN IS SHE EVER GOING TO GET A TOOTH?

But The Years Are Short

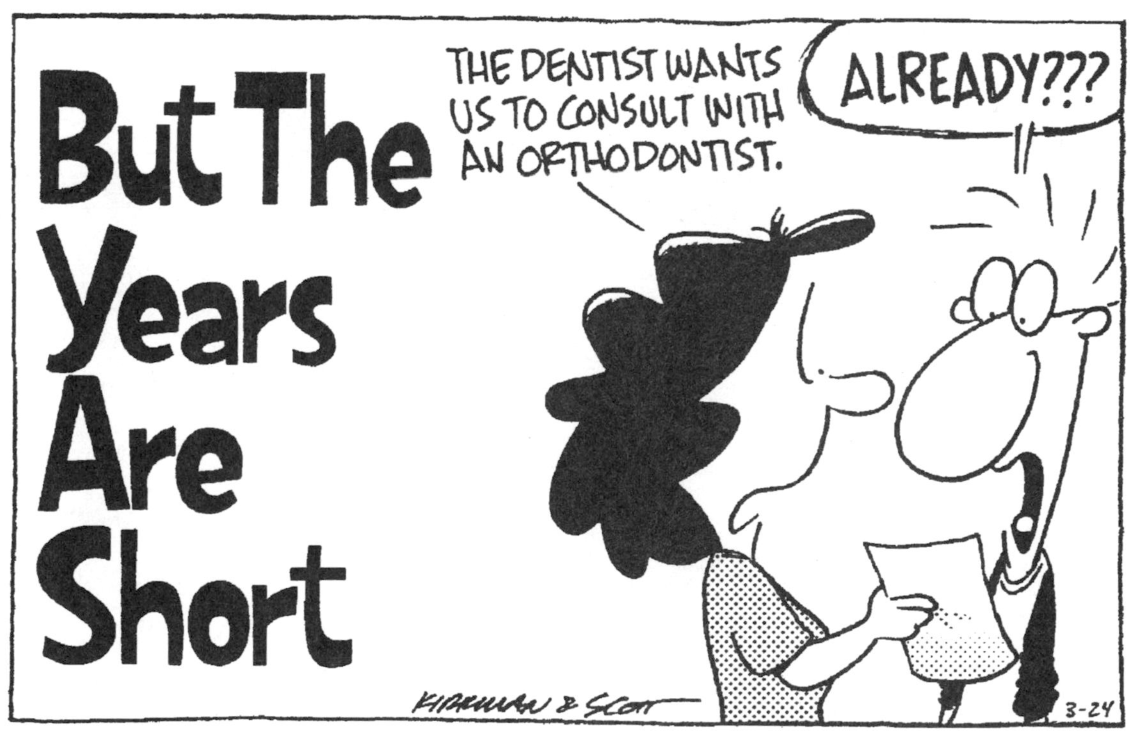
THE DENTIST WANTS US TO CONSULT WITH AN ORTHODONTIST.
ALREADY???
3-24

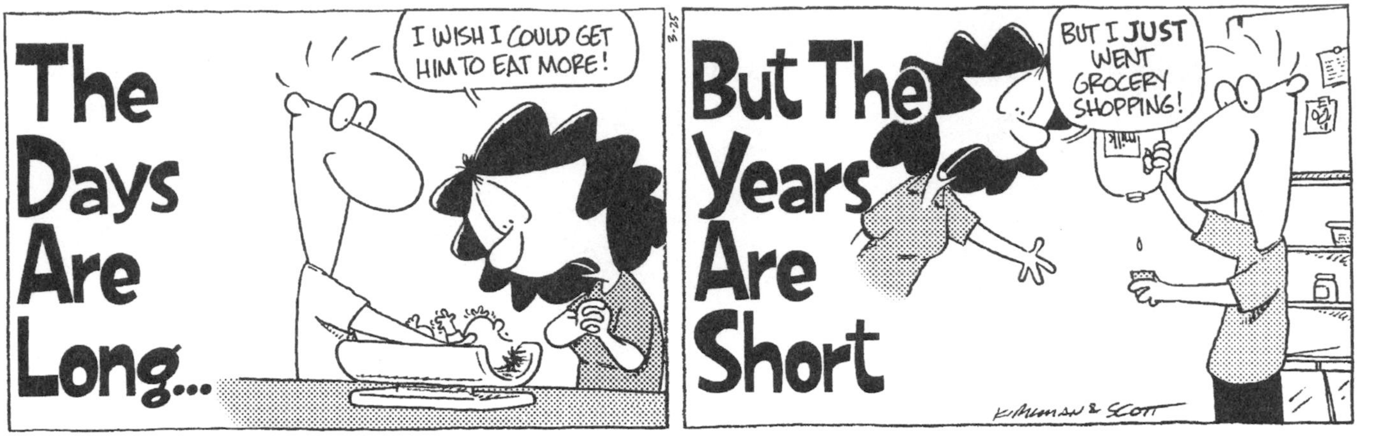
The Days Are Long...
I WISH I COULD GET HIM TO EAT MORE!
3-25
But The Years Are Short
BUT I JUST WENT GROCERY SHOPPING!
KIRKMAN & SCOTT

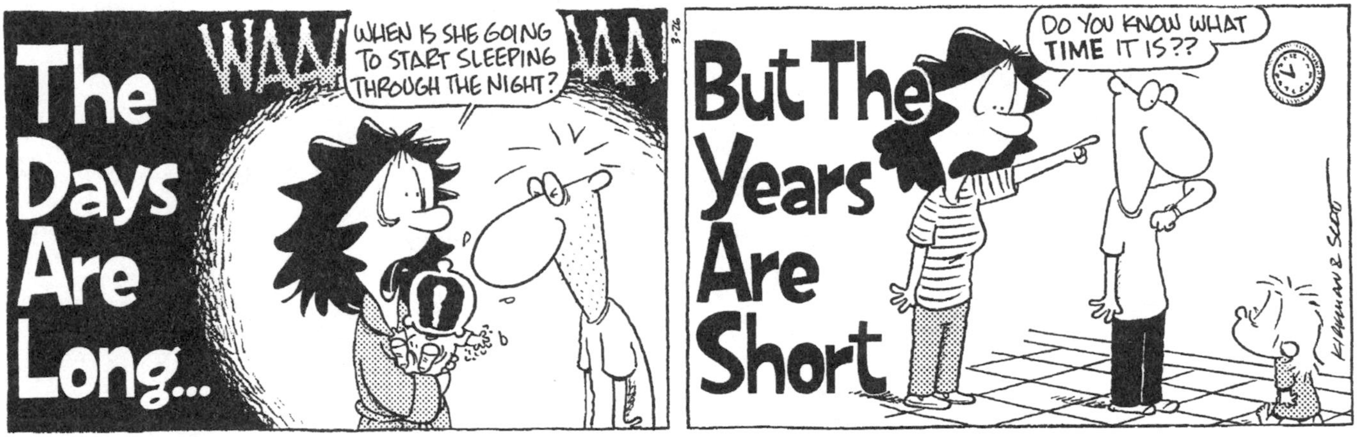
The Days Are Long...
WHEN IS SHE GOING TO START SLEEPING THROUGH THE NIGHT?
3-26
But The Years Are Short
DO YOU KNOW WHAT TIME IT IS??
KIRKMAN & SCOTT

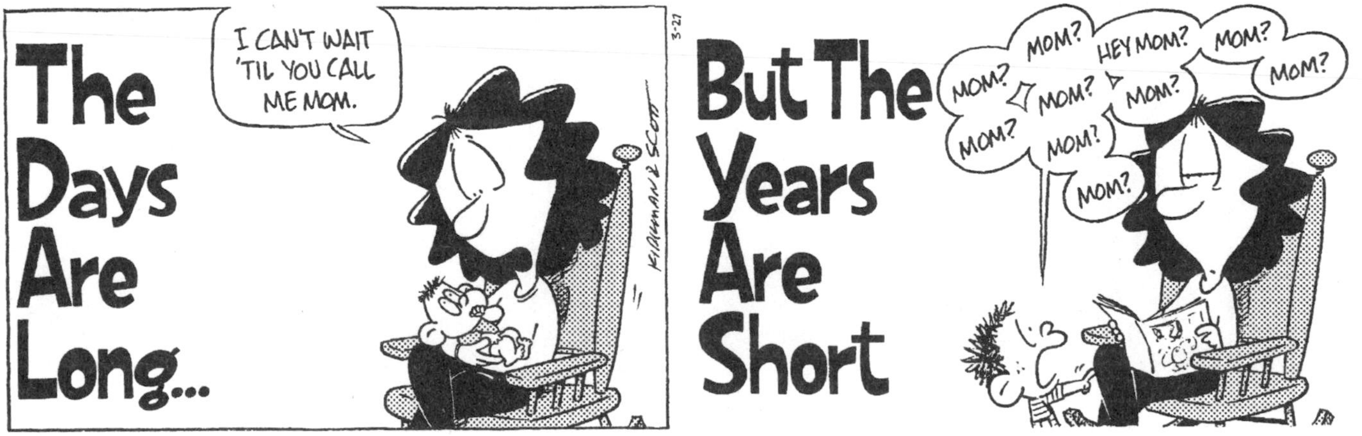
The Days Are Long...
I CAN'T WAIT 'TIL YOU CALL ME MOM.
3-27
KIRKMAN & SCOTT
But The Years Are Short
MOM?
MOM?
HEY MOM?
MOM?
MOM?
MOM?
MOM?
MOM?
MOM?
MOM?
MOM?

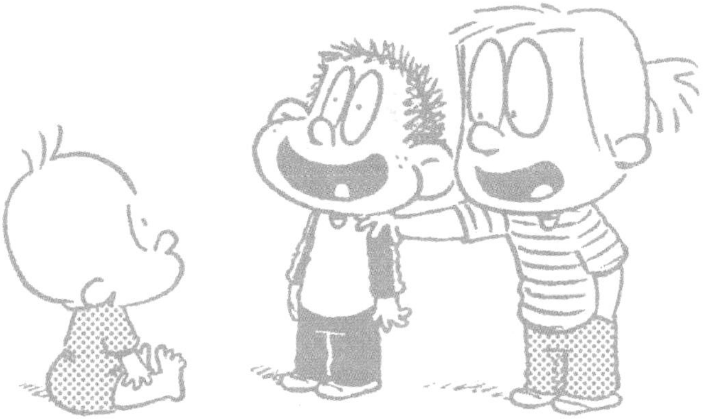

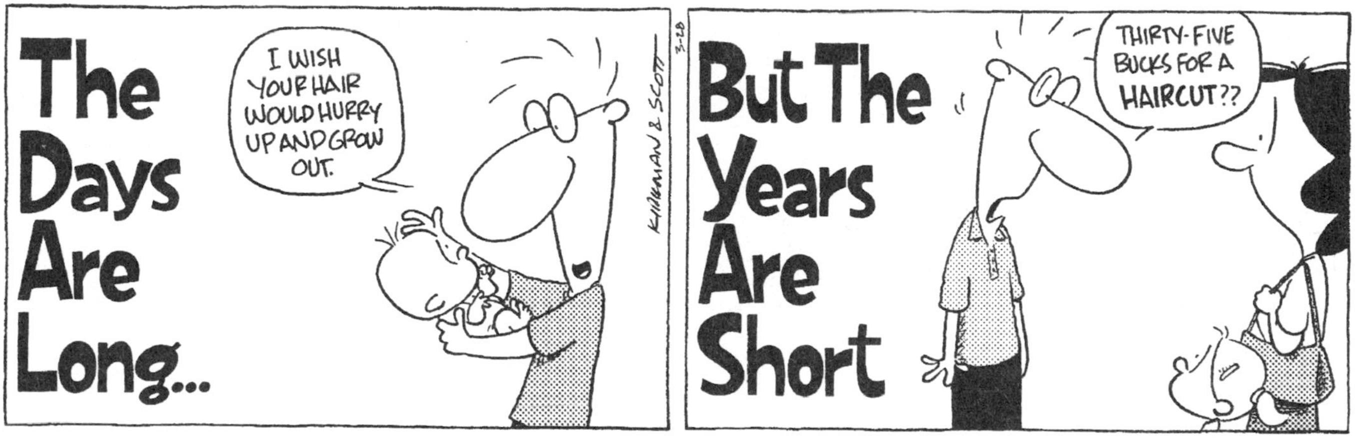
The Days Are Long...
I WISH YOUR HAIR WOULD HURRY UP AND GROW OUT.
KIRKMAN & SCOTT
3-28
But The Years Are Short
THIRTY-FIVE BUCKS FOR A HAIRCUT??

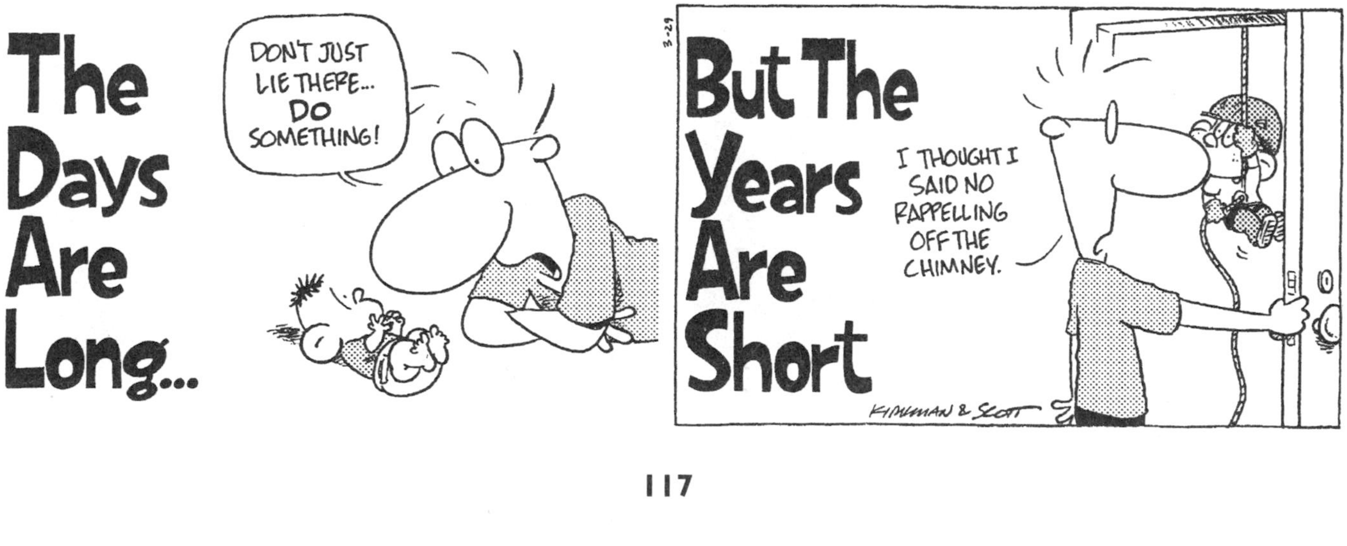
The Days Are Long...
DON'T JUST LIE THERE... DO SOMETHING!
3-29
But The Years Are Short
I THOUGHT I SAID NO RAPPELLING OFF THE CHIMNEY.
KIRKMAN & SCOTT

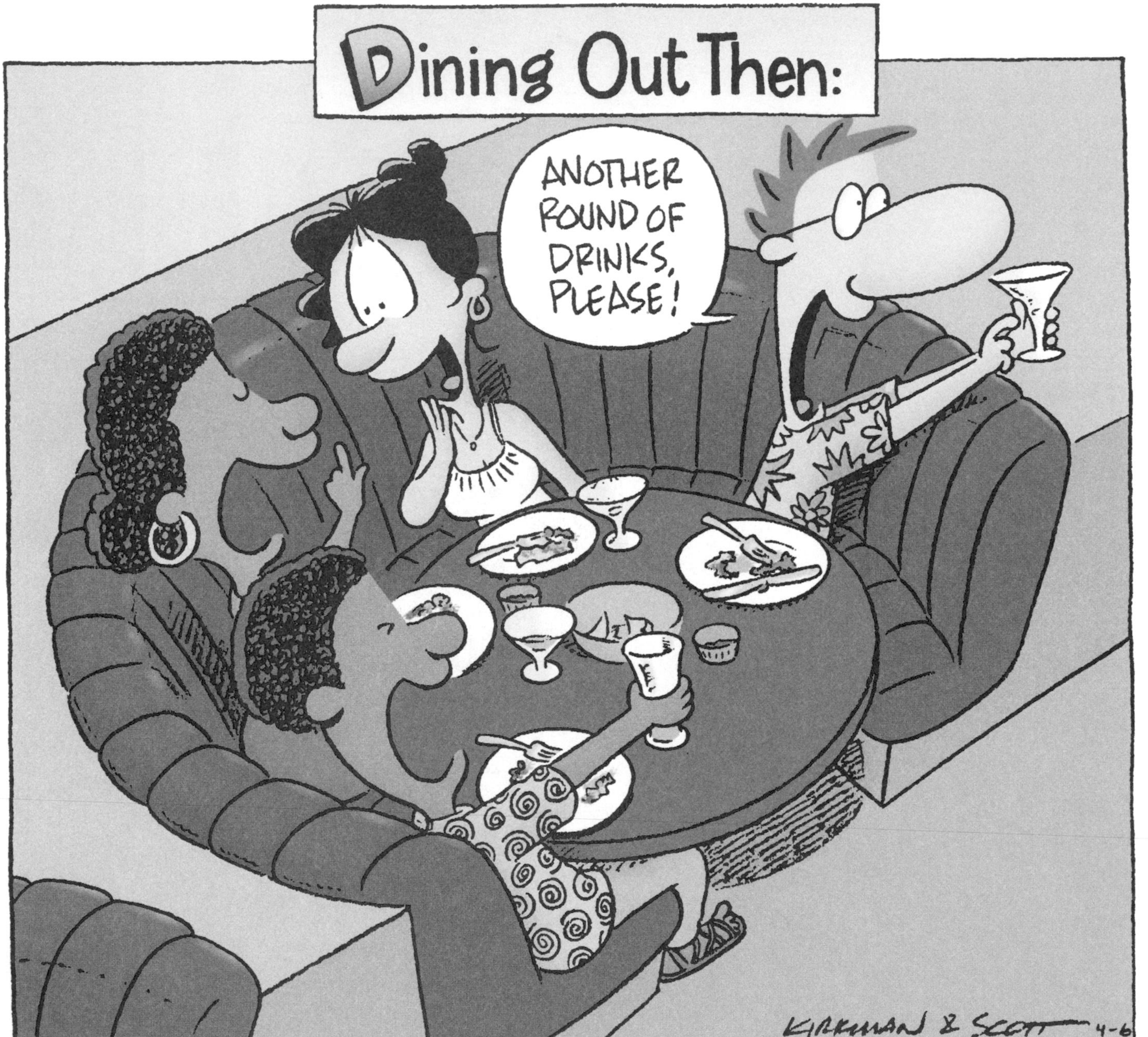
Dining Out Then:
ANOTHER ROUND OF DRINKS, PLEASE!
KIRKMAN & SCOTT 4-6

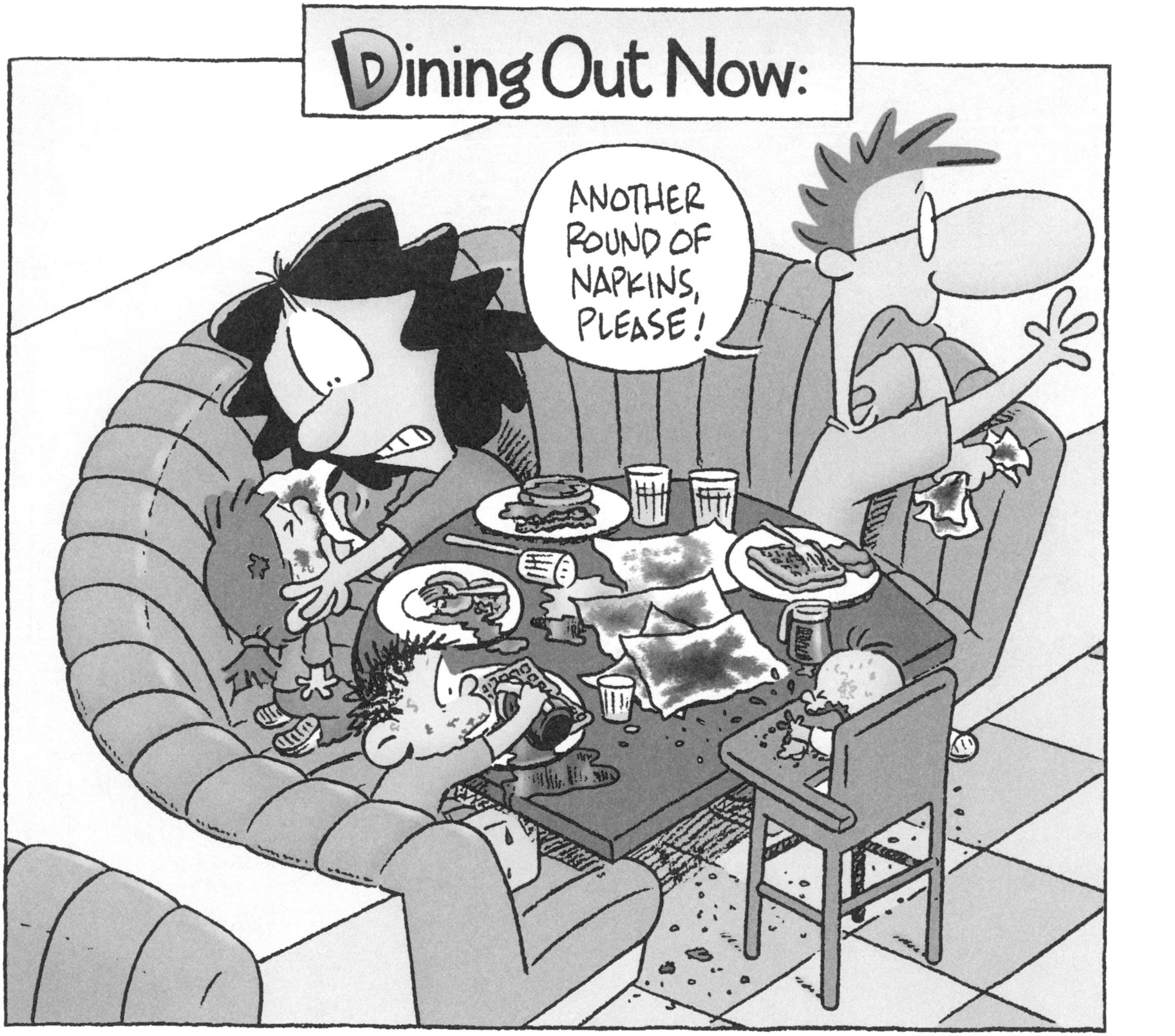
Dining Out Now:
ANOTHER ROUND OF NAPKINS, PLEASE!

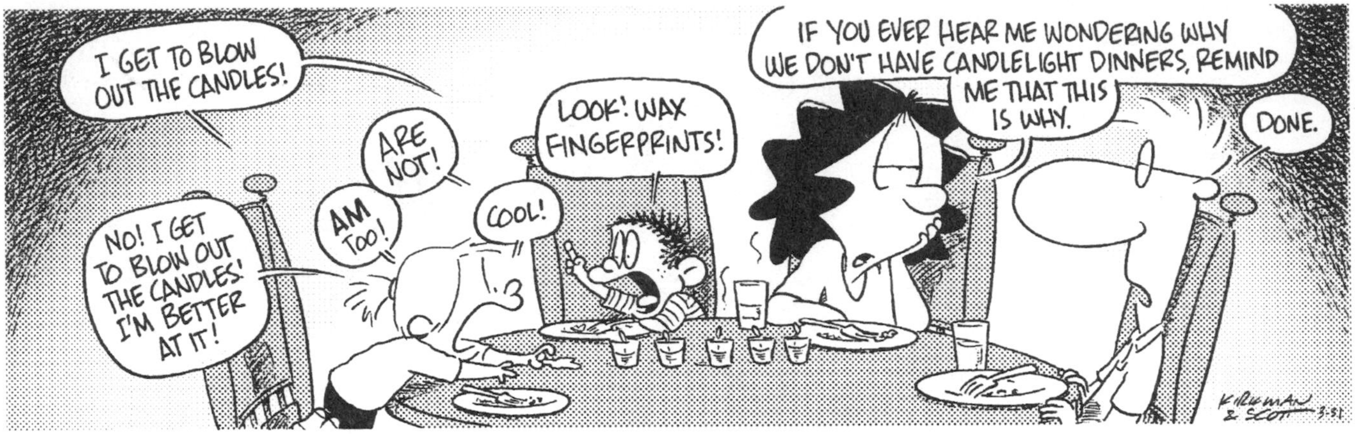
I GET TO BLOW OUT THE CANDLES!
NO! I GET TO BLOW OUT THE CANDLES! I'M BETTER AT IT!
AM TOO!
ARE NOT!
COOL!
LOOK! WAX FINGERPRINTS!
IF YOU EVER HEAR ME WONDERING WHY WE DON'T HAVE CANDLELIGHT DINNERS, REMIND ME THAT THIS IS WHY.
DONE.
KIRKMAN & SCOTT 3-31

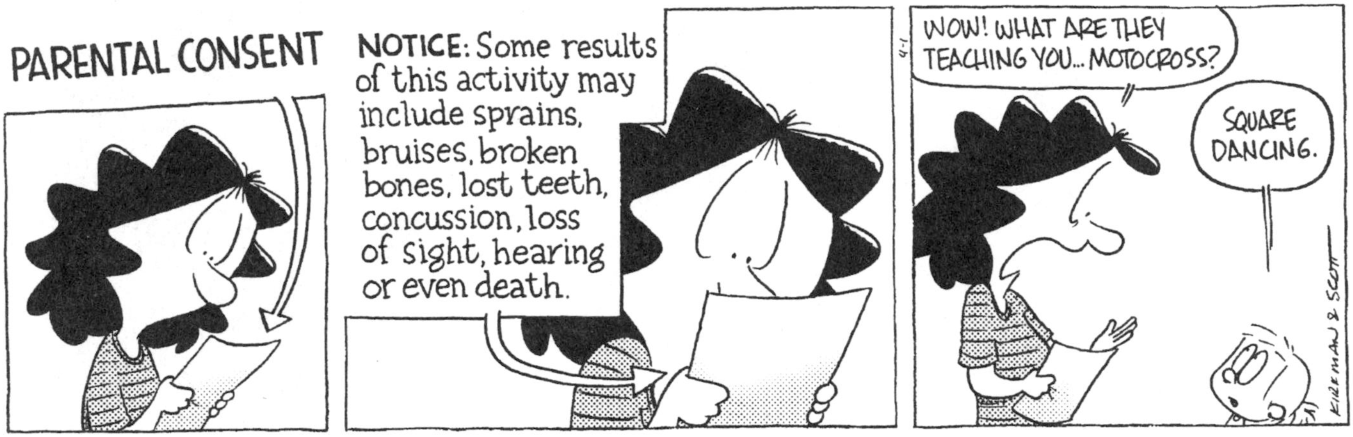
PARENTAL CONSENT
NOTICE: Some results of this activity may include sprains, bruises, broken bones, lost teeth, concussion, loss of sight, hearing or even death.
4-1
WOW! WHAT ARE THEY TEACHING YOU... MOTOCROSS?
SQUARE DANCING.
KIRKMAN & SCOTT

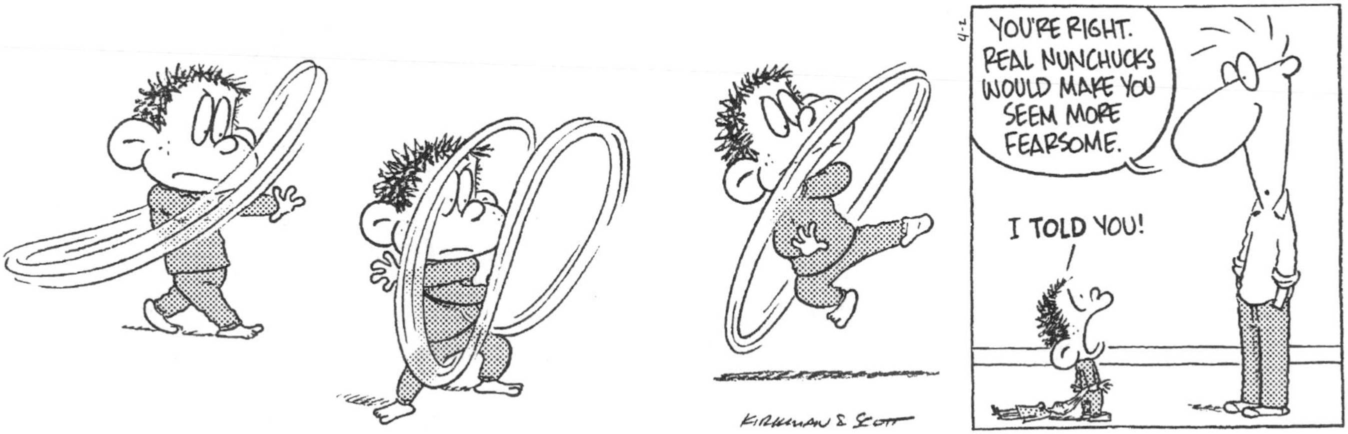
KIRKMAN & SCOTT
4-2
YOU'RE RIGHT. REAL NUNCHUCKS WOULD MAKE YOU SEEM MORE FEARSOME.
I TOLD YOU!

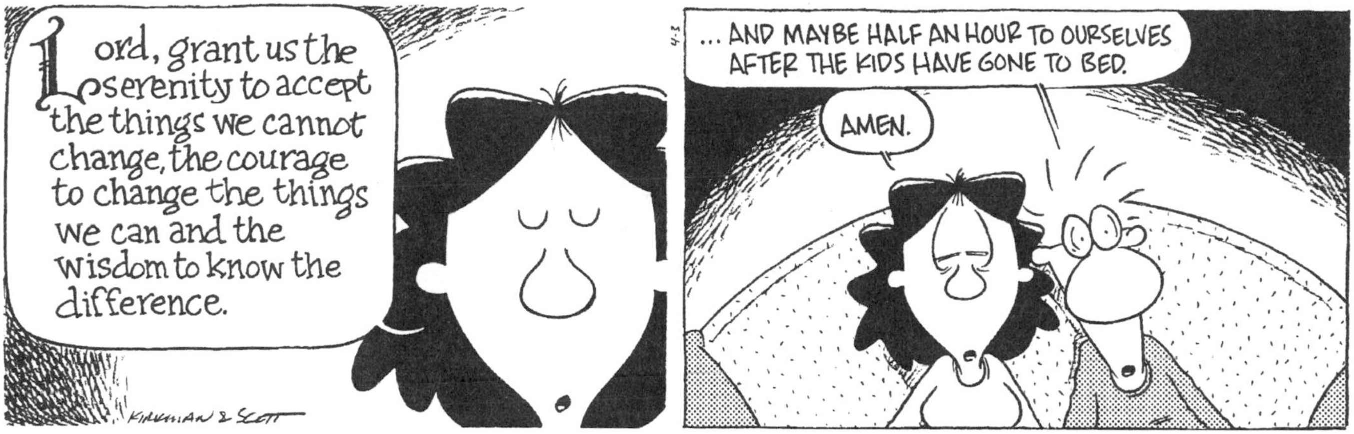

Lord, grant us the serenity to accept the things we cannot change, the courage to change the things we can and the wisdom to know the difference.
... AND MAYBE HALF AN HOUR TO OURSELVES AFTER THE KIDS HAVE GONE TO BED.
AMEN.

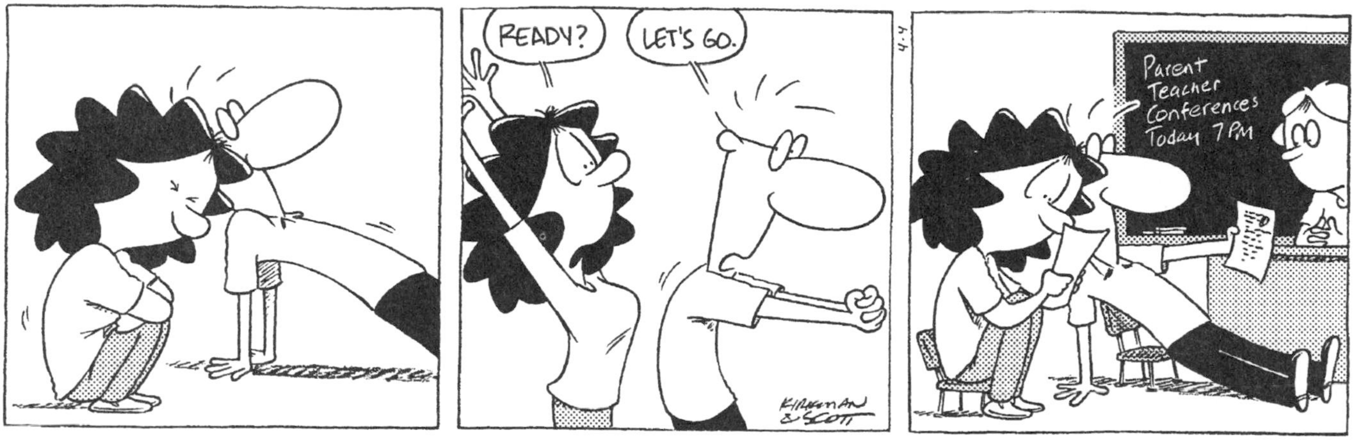

READY?
LET'S GO.
Parent Teacher Conferences Today 7PM

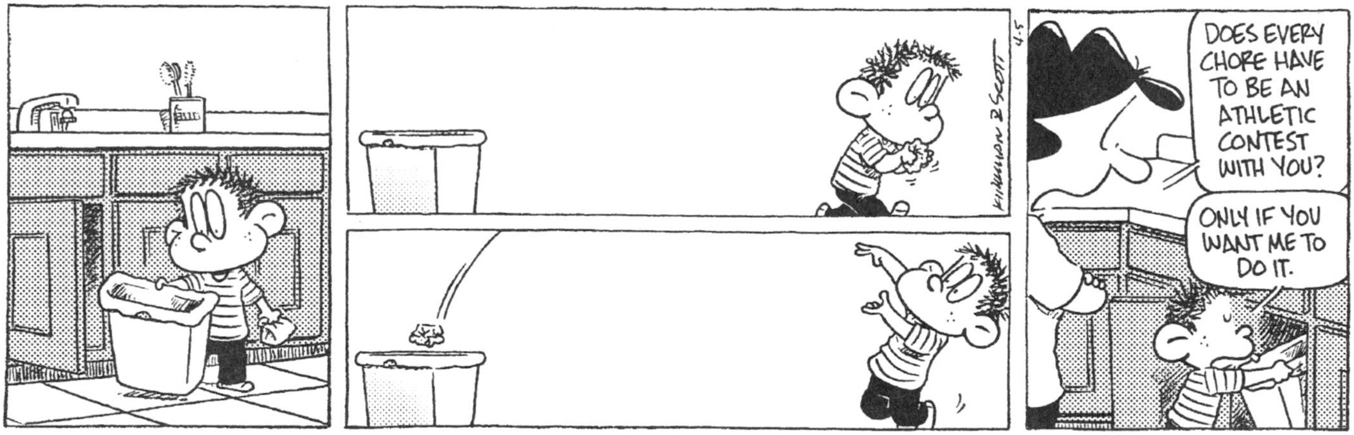

DOES EVERY CHORE HAVE TO BE AN ATHLETIC CONTEST WITH YOU?
ONLY IF YOU WANT ME TO DO IT.

BABY BLUES®
RICK KIRKMAN / BY JERRY SCOTT

I HAVE A TON OF HOMEWORK TONIGHT!
SO? I HAVE **SIX** TONS OF HOMEWORK TONIGHT!
WELL, IF YOU HAVE SIX TONS, THEN I HAVE **ELEVEN** TONS!
I HAVE **20** TONS!
THEN I HAVE A HUNDRED TONS!
I HAVE A MILLION-BILLION-TO-**INFINITY** TONS!
FINE. YOU WIN. YOU HAVE MORE HOMEWORK THAN ME.
HA!
IF YOU HAVE SO MUCH HOMEWORK, WHY AREN'T YOU DOING IT?
I FINISHED IT WHILE WE WERE ARGUING.
KIRKMAN & SCOTT 4-13

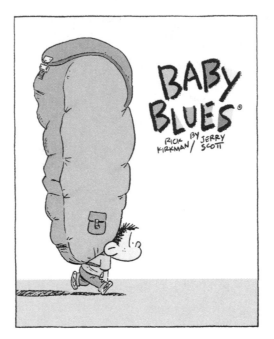

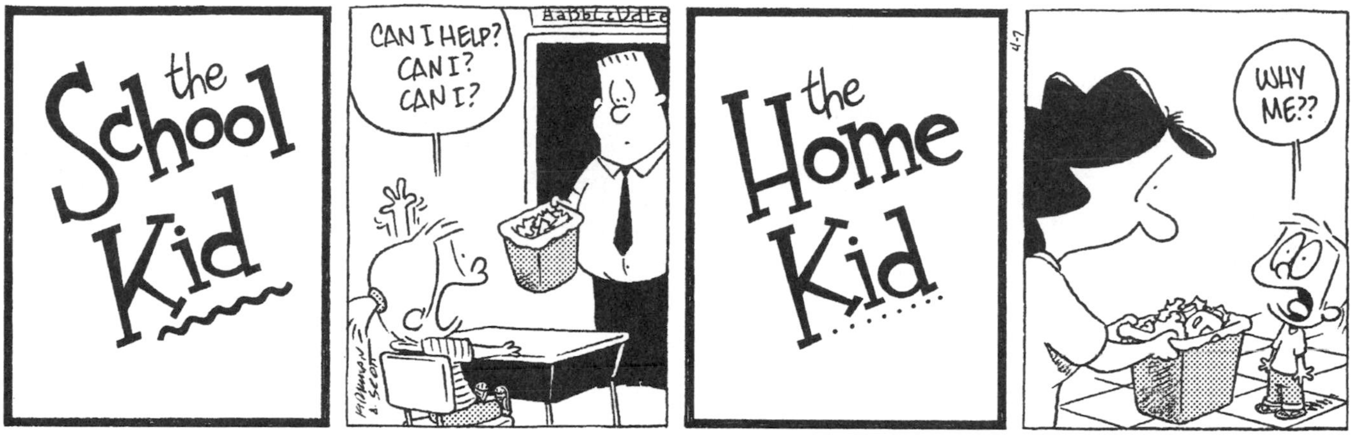
the School Kid
CAN I HELP? CAN I? CAN I?
the Home Kid
4-7
WHY ME??

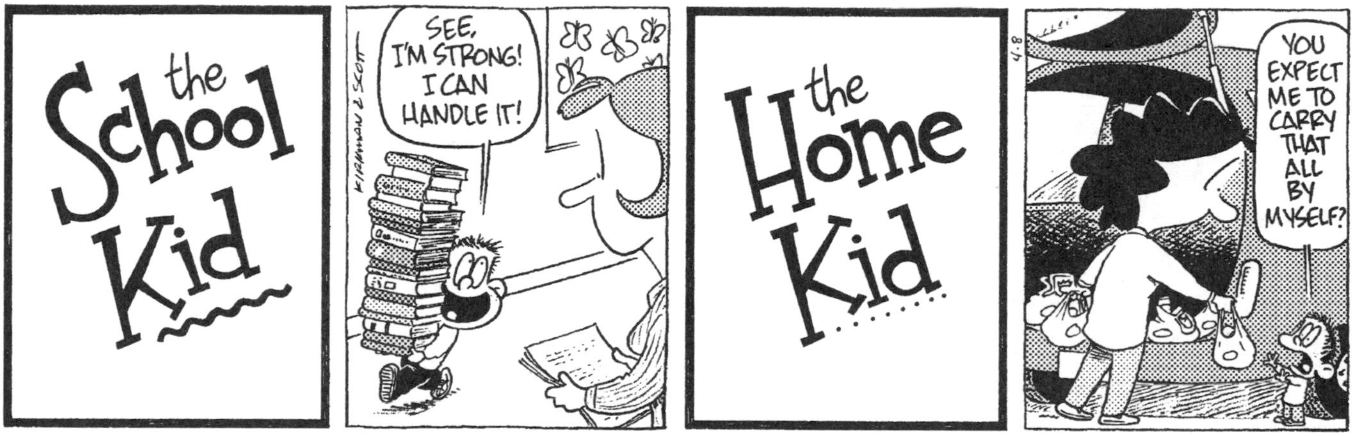
the School Kid
SEE, I'M STRONG! I CAN HANDLE IT!
the Home Kid
4-8
YOU EXPECT ME TO CARRY THAT ALL BY MYSELF?

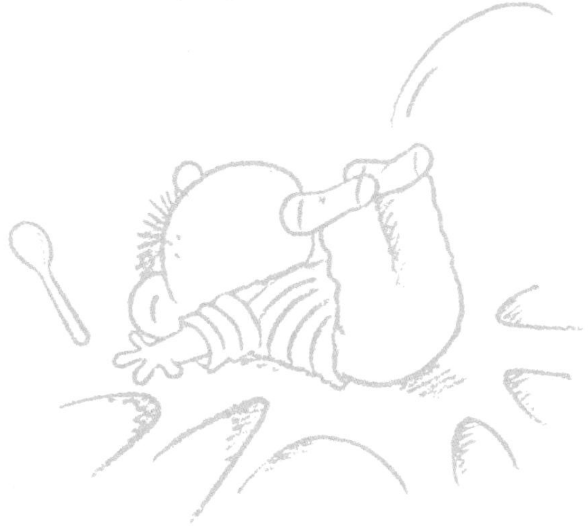

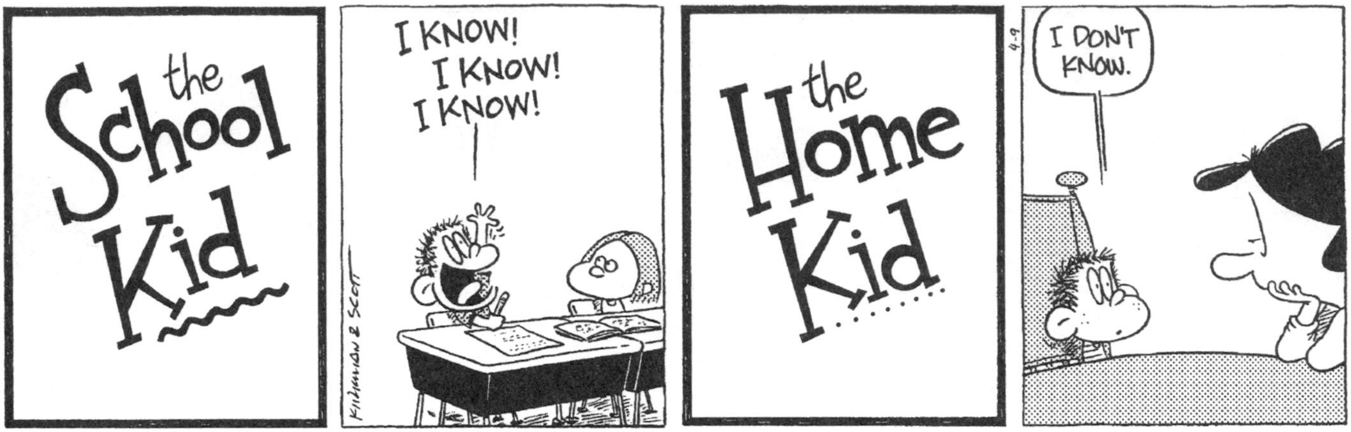
the School Kid
I KNOW! I KNOW! I KNOW!
KIRKMAN & SCOTT
the Home Kid
4-9
I DON'T KNOW.

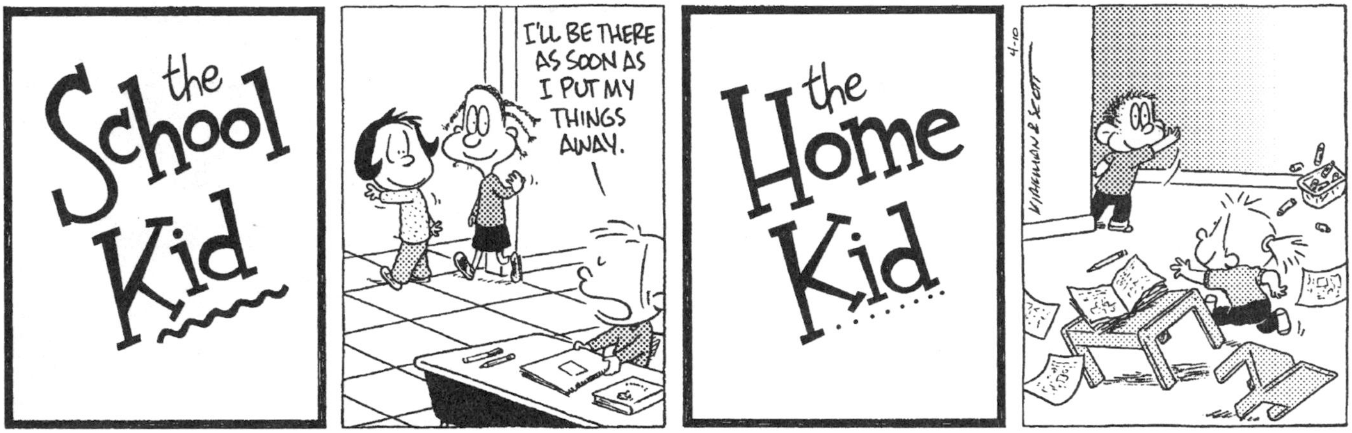
the School Kid
I'LL BE THERE AS SOON AS I PUT MY THINGS AWAY.
the Home Kid
4-10
KIRKMAN & SCOTT

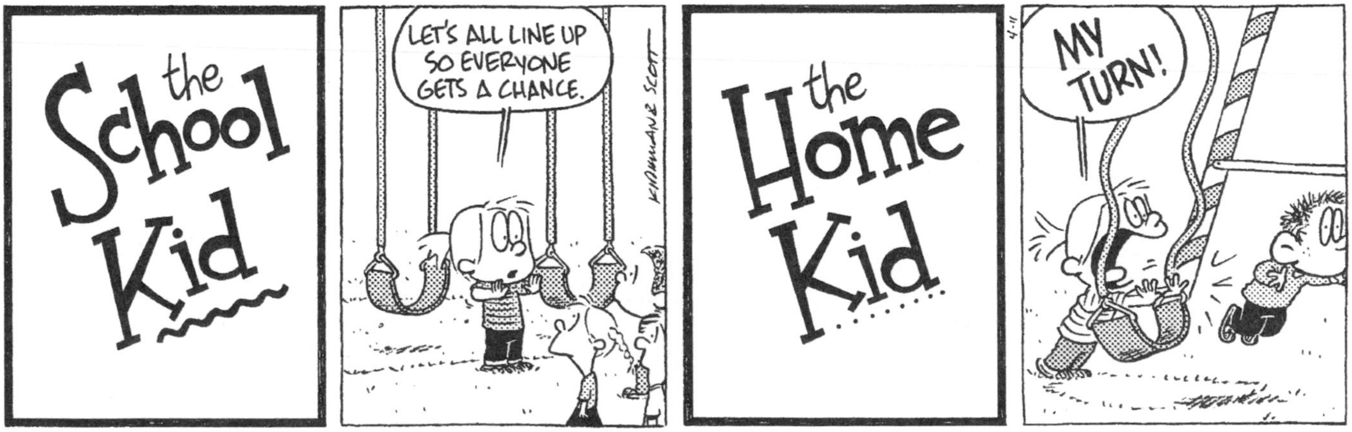
the School Kid
LET'S ALL LINE UP SO EVERYONE GETS A CHANCE.
KIRKMAN & SCOTT
the Home Kid
4-11
MY TURN!

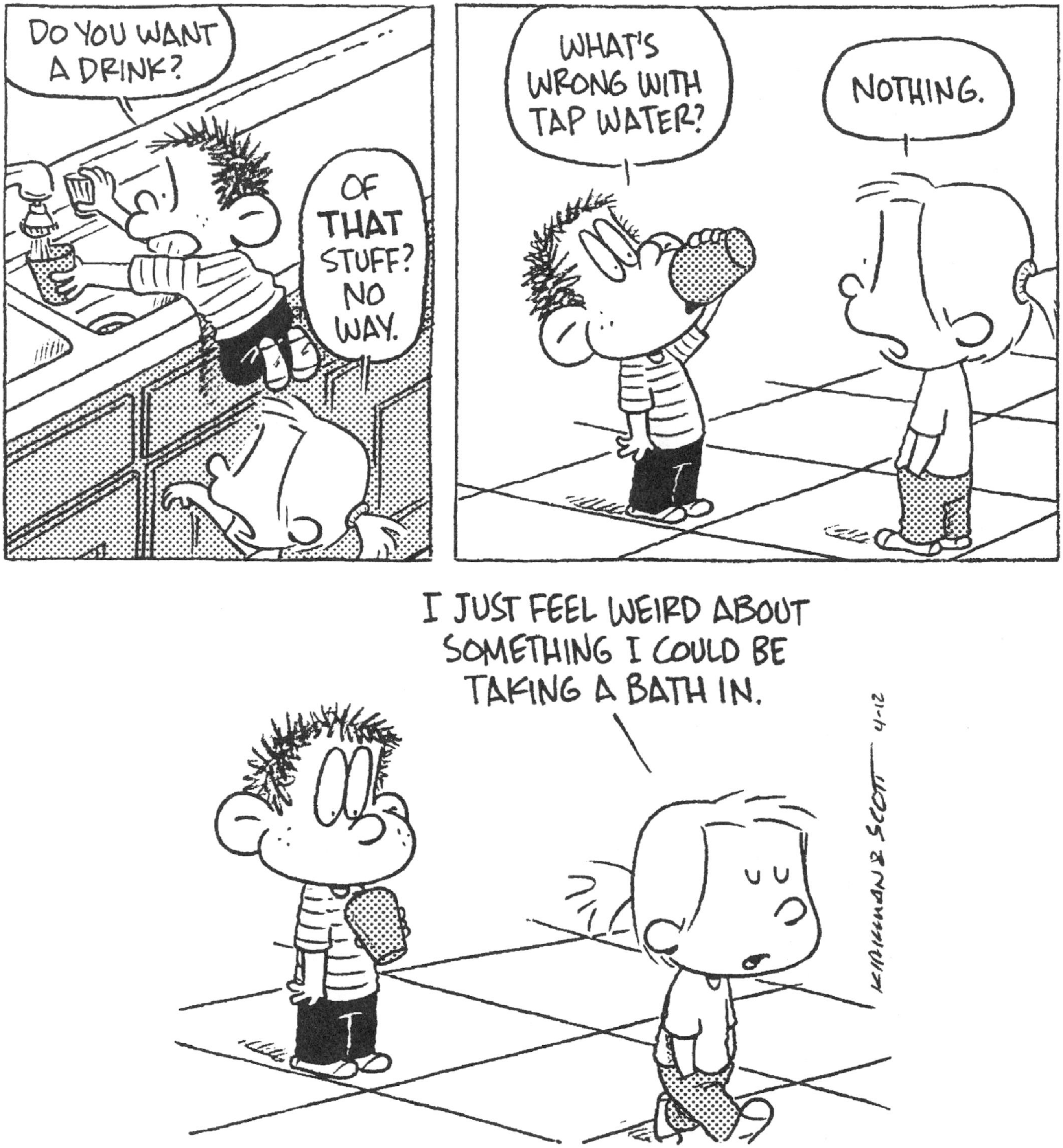
DO YOU WANT A DRINK?
OF THAT STUFF? NO WAY.
WHAT'S WRONG WITH TAP WATER?
NOTHING.
I JUST FEEL WEIRD ABOUT SOMETHING I COULD BE TAKING A BATH IN.
KIRKMAN & SCOTT
4-12

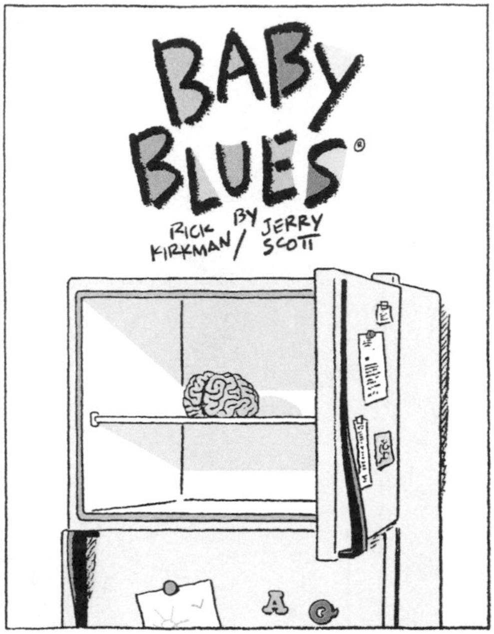
BABY BLUES®
BY
RICK KIRKMAN / JERRY SCOTT

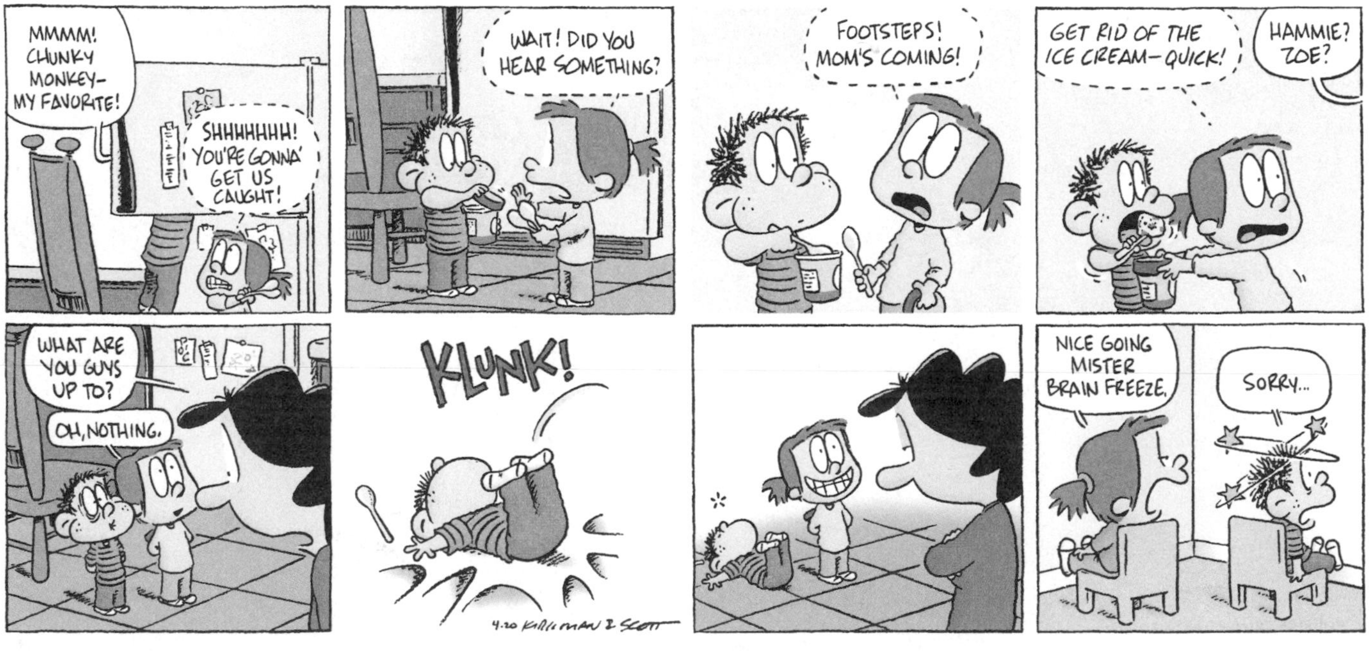
MMMM! CHUNKY MONKEY- MY FAVORITE!
SHHHHHHH! YOU'RE GONNA' GET US CAUGHT!
WAIT! DID YOU HEAR SOMETHING?
FOOTSTEPS! MOM'S COMING!
GET RID OF THE ICE CREAM—QUICK!
HAMMIE? ZOE?
WHAT ARE YOU GUYS UP TO?
OH, NOTHING.
KLUNK!
NICE GOING MISTER BRAIN FREEZE.
SORRY...
4.20 KIRKMAN & SCOTT

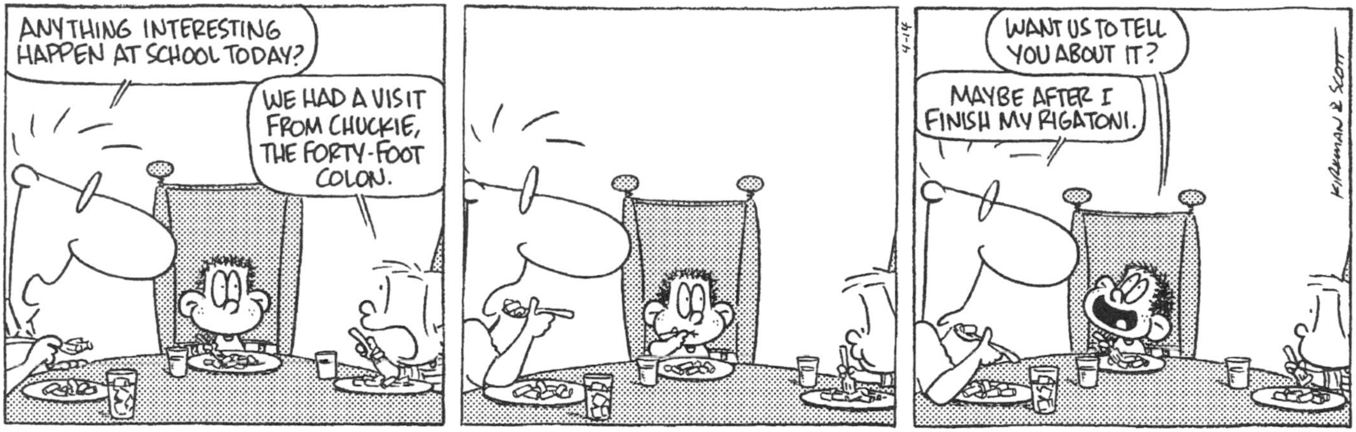
ANYTHING INTERESTING HAPPEN AT SCHOOL TODAY?
WE HAD A VISIT FROM CHUCKIE, THE FORTY-FOOT COLON.
4-14
WANT US TO TELL YOU ABOUT IT?
MAYBE AFTER I FINISH MY RIGATONI.
KIRKMAN & SCOTT

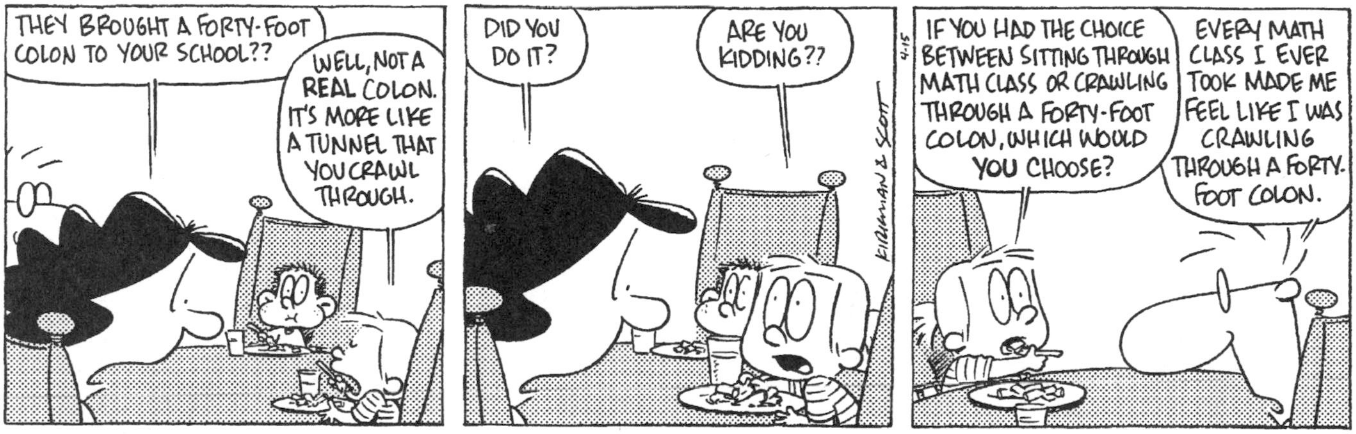
THEY BROUGHT A FORTY-FOOT COLON TO YOUR SCHOOL??
WELL, NOT A REAL COLON. IT'S MORE LIKE A TUNNEL THAT YOU CRAWL THROUGH.
DID YOU DO IT?
ARE YOU KIDDING??
KIRKMAN & SCOTT
4-15
IF YOU HAD THE CHOICE BETWEEN SITTING THROUGH MATH CLASS OR CRAWLING THROUGH A FORTY-FOOT COLON, WHICH WOULD YOU CHOOSE?
EVERY MATH CLASS I EVER TOOK MADE ME FEEL LIKE I WAS CRAWLING THROUGH A FORTY-FOOT COLON.

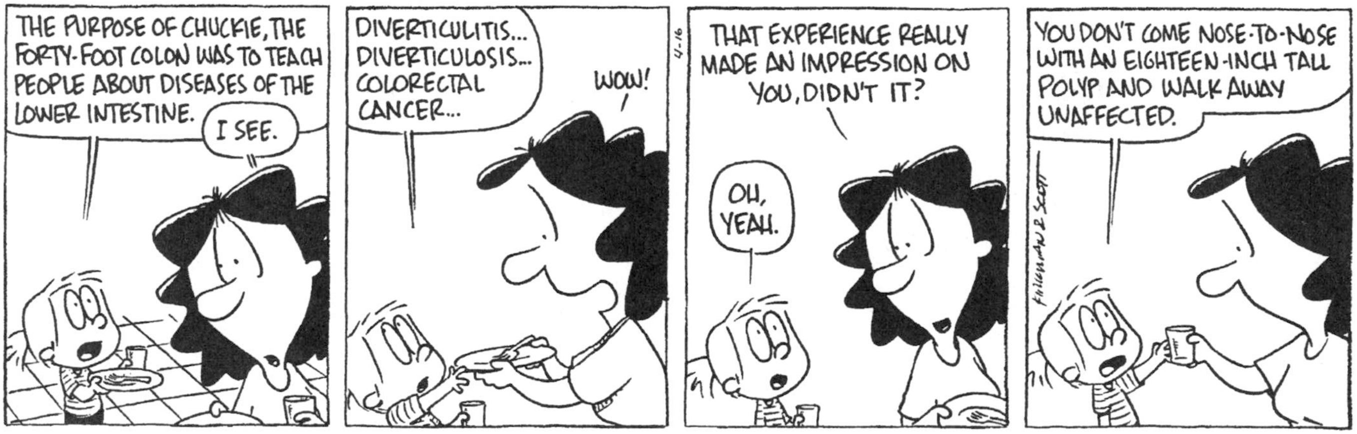
THE PURPOSE OF CHUCKIE, THE FORTY-FOOT COLON WAS TO TEACH PEOPLE ABOUT DISEASES OF THE LOWER INTESTINE.
I SEE.
4-16
DIVERTICULITIS... DIVERTICULOSIS... COLORECTAL CANCER...
WOW!
THAT EXPERIENCE REALLY MADE AN IMPRESSION ON YOU, DIDN'T IT?
OH, YEAH.
KIRKMAN & SCOTT
YOU DON'T COME NOSE-TO-NOSE WITH AN EIGHTEEN-INCH TALL POLYP AND WALK AWAY UNAFFECTED.

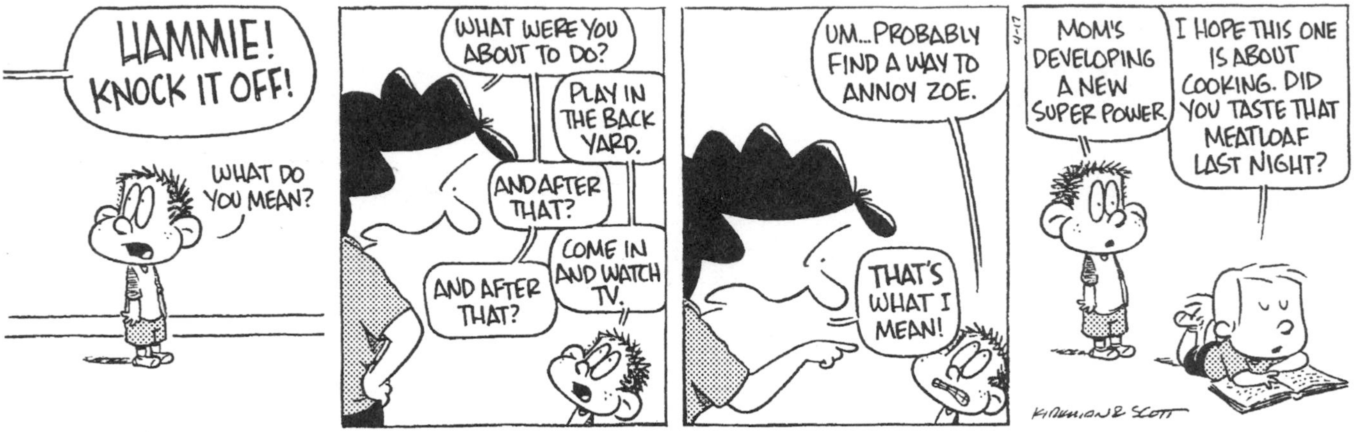
HAMMIE! KNOCK IT OFF!
WHAT DO YOU MEAN?
WHAT WERE YOU ABOUT TO DO?
PLAY IN THE BACK YARD.
AND AFTER THAT?
COME IN AND WATCH TV.
AND AFTER THAT?
UM...PROBABLY FIND A WAY TO ANNOY ZOE.
THAT'S WHAT I MEAN!
4-17
MOM'S DEVELOPING A NEW SUPER POWER.
I HOPE THIS ONE IS ABOUT COOKING. DID YOU TASTE THAT MEATLOAF LAST NIGHT?
KIRKMAN & SCOTT

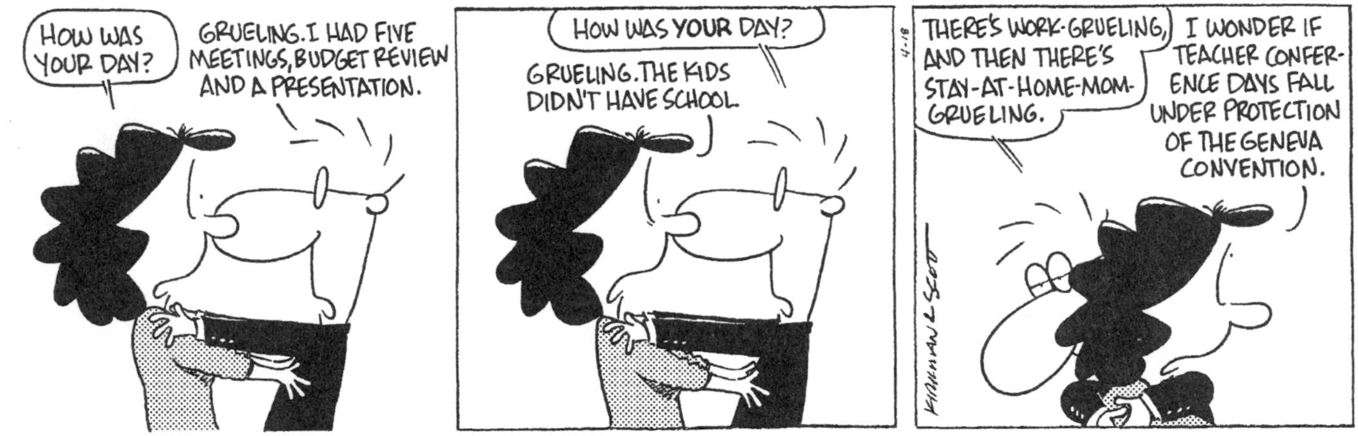
HOW WAS YOUR DAY?
GRUELING. I HAD FIVE MEETINGS, BUDGET REVIEW AND A PRESENTATION.
HOW WAS YOUR DAY?
GRUELING. THE KIDS DIDN'T HAVE SCHOOL.
4-18
THERE'S WORK-GRUELING, AND THEN THERE'S STAY-AT-HOME-MOM-GRUELING.
I WONDER IF TEACHER CONFERENCE DAYS FALL UNDER PROTECTION OF THE GENEVA CONVENTION.
KIRKMAN & SCOTT

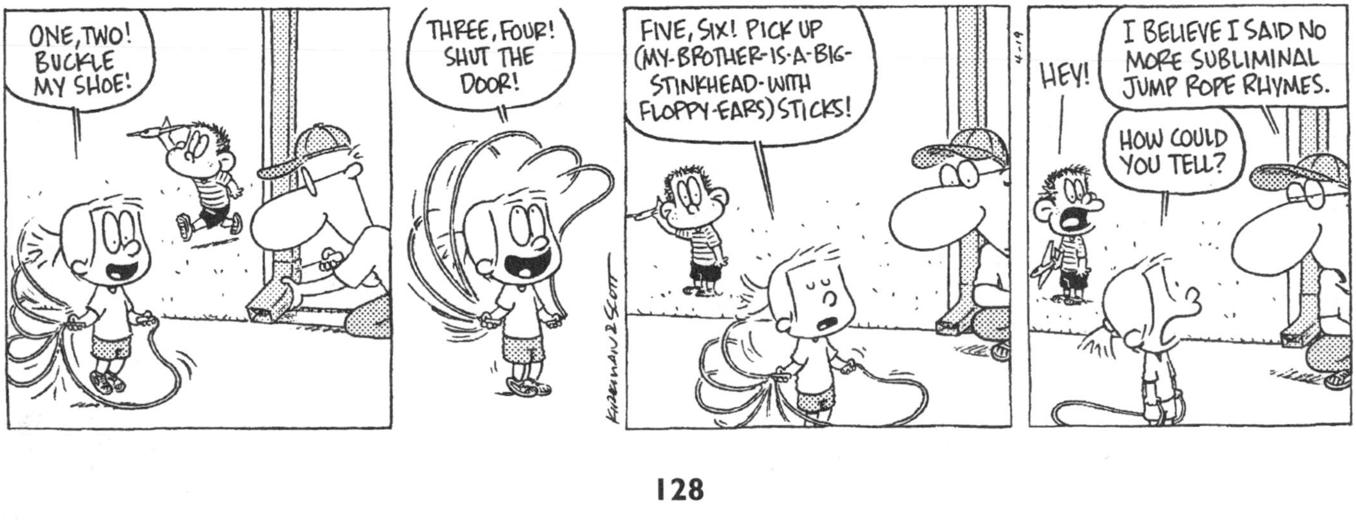
ONE, TWO! BUCKLE MY SHOE!
THREE, FOUR! SHUT THE DOOR!
KIRKMAN & SCOTT
FIVE, SIX! PICK UP (MY-BROTHER-IS-A-BIG-STINKHEAD-WITH FLOPPY-EARS) STICKS!
4-19
HEY!
I BELIEVE I SAID NO MORE SUBLIMINAL JUMP ROPE RHYMES.
HOW COULD YOU TELL?